Casebook of

Sexual Abuse Treatment

Also by William N. Friedrich
Psychotherapy of Sexually Abused Children and Their Families

A NORTON PROFESSIONAL BOOK

Casebook of
Sexual Abuse Treatment

edited by

WILLIAM N. FRIEDRICH, Ph.D.

Associate Professor of Psychology
Mayo Medical School
Rochester, Minnesota

W. W. NORTON & COMPANY
New York · London

First Edition.

Library of Congress Cataloging-in-Publication Data

Casebook of sexual abuse treatment / edited by William N. Friedrich.
       p.   cm.
    Includes bibliographical references and index.
    ISBN 0-393-70113-1
    1. Sexually abused children — Mental health — Case studies.
  2. Child psychotherapy — Case studies.   I. Friedrich, William N.
  RJ507.S49C37   1991
  618.92'8583 — dc20   91-2548

W. W. Norton & Company, Inc., 500 Fifth Avenue, New York, N.Y. 10110
W. W. Norton & Company, Ltd., 10 Coptic Street, London WC1A 1PU

1 2 3 4 5 6 7 8 9 0

To my children, Hannah and Karl

Contents

Acknowledgments

THIS BOOK COULD not have been done without the help of many people. I initially broached the idea for the book with Sue White and Marge Steward in an Italian restaurant in Washington, D.C., and was heartened by their enthusiastic support. I received encouragement from Sandra Hewitt and her colleagues at Midwest Children's Resource Center. Excellent editing was provided by Susan Barrows, who probably read more sordid stories in one sitting than anyone should. In addition, those authors whose work was not used provided me with even more opportunities to witness some wonderful therapy.

My secretary, Gloria Mensink, has been a lifesaver. She routinely met my precipitous deadlines in a professional and competent manner. My family, again, has been remarkable. I have learned a great deal about attachment from my wife, Wanda, and my two children, Hannah and Karl. When I have gotten caught up in the rush of writing and publishing, they have taught me a great deal about emotional self-regulation.

Introduction

WORKING WITH SEXUALLY abused children can be terribly isolating. Other therapists with similar interests may not be easily available. The stories we hear are difficult or impossible to share with family members, even in the most general way. The conscientious therapist asks, "Am I doing good therapy?" We can attend conferences, and most of us do. But most of us want pragmatic, "how to do it" information. This book was designed to do just that—to allow the reader to sit in on the therapy of sexually abused children facilitated by experienced therapists in this field.

This is a casebook concerning the treatment of primarily younger victims. Therapists were asked to write about each child in a standard format to allow for ease of comparison. Identifying characteristics have been altered in each case. Each author was instructed to be as detailed as possible within the page limitations. The cases included are preschoolers, latency-age children, teenagers, and sexually aggressive children. Individual, group, and family therapies are represented. Three cases describe very sadistic, even ritualistic abuse.

The process of writing this book began by soliciting a number of expert therapists to write about tough cases. In each case, these children and families had taught and stretched the therapist. Clinicians I either knew personally or had heard had reputations for quality therapy were invited to participate. While many fine therapists are included as authors, many more were excluded. The end result leaves me very proud to be in the community of sexual abuse therapists.

Several themes are evident. The first is that there is no one treatment program for sexually abused children. These are highly eclectic and pragmatic treatment approaches.

A second theme is that these therapists exemplify an integral blend of tough and tender, asking for maturity from these children in the context of unconditional regard and compassion for them and their families.

The third theme pertains to the active and interested involvement by each of these therapists. They extend themselves routinely to advocate on the child's behalf. Therapy was rarely over after the treatment session.

These cases usually involve long-term treatment. As I outlined in a recent paper (Friedrich, Luecke, Beilke, & Place, in press), positive outcome for sexually abused children is directly related to length of treatment. Some of the children discussed here have been seen as long as five years, and their therapy is still ongoing. While this length of treatment is not available for many children, these cases illustrate the enormity of the corrective emotional experiences needed by many victimized children in order to return to, or reach for the first time, adequate functioning.

Active and frequent interaction with social services is an absolute must; this is the fifth theme. Despite the fact that, in some cases, the therapists found themselves at odds with social services, social services is a primary advocate for the child and must be involved in the treatment process.

Finally, psychological evaluations were used to direct treatment and monitor outcome. Additionally, they provided a valuable contribution to case formulation and treatment. I would like to see, as a product of this book, an increased reliance on objective assessment of our treatment efficacy.

These children and families have a way of working the same therapeutic ground over and over again. To borrow a phrase from Barbara Boat's case, issues have a way of "spiraling" around and around. Children keep coming back to the same issues, two of which I have distilled from my reading of these cases. They are 1. attachment and 2. emotional regulation.

Regarding the first issue, attachment, these children's relationships with caregivers have been betrayed by the abuse. Multigenerational abuse, which is often present, further compounds their attachment failure with their current caregiver. Parent-child attachment is routinely derailed. These betrayed children act out their failed attachment with therapists, social services, workers, and parent figures. Repair of these attachments takes considerable time, as evidenced by the length of these children's therapy.

A second treatment issue pertains to the concept of emotional regulation. Trauma leads to initial and sometimes persisting difficulties with the regulation of affect, thinking, and behavior. This is evidenced by the frequent diagnosis of post-traumatic stress disorder among sexually abused children.

Treatment can be too arousing to these children and interfere with their ability to regulate their emotions. It is important as you read this book to watch how both planfully and intuitively these therapists help to make the treatment situations tolerable and in so doing allow essential and important work to be done. I have provided brief commentary on each case, designed to identify specific techniques, flag pertinent issues, and/or raise questions to facilitate the reader's understanding of the material.

Contributors

Pamela C. Alexander, Ph.D., is an associate professor in the Department of Psychology at the University of Maryland, College Park. She was formerly on the faculty of Memphis State University.

Arnon Bentovim, M.D., is a child psychiatrist at the Hospital for Sick Children, London, England, and on the faculty of the Institute of Family Therapy in London.

Lucy Berliner, MSW, is a clinical assistant professor in the School of Social Work at the University of Washington and a social worker at the Sexual Assault Center, Harborview Medical Center, Seattle, WA.

Barbara W. Boat, Ph.D., is an assistant professor of psychology in the Division of Child Psychiatry, School of Medicine, at the University of North Carolina at Chapel Hill. She is affiliated with Childhood Trauma and Maltreatment Program.

Judith A. Cohen, M.D., is an Assistant Professor in the Department of Psychiatry, Western Psychiatric Institute and Clinic, University of Pittsburgh, Pittsburgh, PA.

Linda Damon, Ph.D., is the clinical director of Child Abuse Services and head of the Family Stress Center at the San Fernando Valley Child Guidance Clinic, Van Nuys, CA.

Alison J. Einbender, Ph.D., is in private practice in child psychology in Madison, Wisconsin.

William N. Friedrich, Ph.D., is an associate professor, Department of Psychiatry and Psychology, and Consultant, Mayo Clinic, Rochester, MN.

Susan E. Hall-Marley, Ph.D., is on the staff of the San Fernando Valley Child Guidance Clinic, Van Nuys, CA.

Sandra K. Hewitt, Ph.D., is in private practice in St. Paul and formerly Chief Psychologist at the Midwest Children's Resource Center, St. Paul Children's Hospital, St. Paul, Minnesota.

Toni Cavanaugh Johnson, Ph.D., is in private practice in South Pasadena, California. She is formerly the assistant director/clinical supervisor, Child Sexual Abuse Center, Children's Institute International, Los Angeles, CA.

Marilyn J. Krieger, Ph.D., is in private practice in San Francisco, California, and an assistant professor at the University of California, San Francisco, Medical School. In addition, she is the clinical consultant for the Child and Adolescent Sexual Abuse Resource Center in San Francisco.

Anthony P. Mannarino, Ph.D., is an associate professor of Child Psychiatry and Psychology at the Western Psychiatric Institute and Clinic, University of Pittsburgh, Pittsburgh, PA.

Harvey Ratner is a senior social worker, Marlborough Family Service, London. In addition, he is a lecturer at the Institute of Family Therapy, London.

Ann. M. Uherek, Psy.D., is in private practice in Manhattan Beach, California.

J. Robert Wheeler, Ph.D., is a psychologist in private practice in Lynwood, Washington, and formerly the clinical director at Luther Child Center, Everett, Washington.

Casebook of
Sexual Abuse Treatment

1

Caregivers as Surrogate Therapists in Treatment of a Ritualistically Abused Child

BARBARA W. BOAT

Dr. Boat is impressive in the advocacy role that she took for this child. In high risk families, early intervention, even before documentation of abuse, is absolutely critical. This case is also important because it documents the reaction of parents — in this case, future adoptive parents — to ritualistic abuse. The reader is urged to contrast this case with the cases of Anonymous and Uherek, given the sadistic and ritualistic nature of the abuse.

The distinctly different behavior patterns seen in Lauren by her foster mother may represent the beginnings of multiple personality disorder. Lauren's dissociative style adds further credence to this possibility. A more parsimonious explanation is that children of this age do rapidly shift from one behavioral mode to the other, although maybe not as extremely as seen in Lauren.

It is interesting that, despite a supportive adoptive home environment, Lauren's periods of confusion and forgetfulness increased over time. I believe she could relax her hypervigilant stance and regress in the service of the ego.

Lauren, along with Dr. Hewitt's child, demonstrates that with increasing language the child is better able to articulate what abuses have been perpetrated against her. Only after one year of therapy did the recovery of ritualistic abuse memories begin to occur. This argues for time and also for the need to have verbal sophistication and safety in order to talk about such matters.

It is also important to see that, despite good therapy, Lauren continues at risk. Even at age 6, after successful treatment and a move to a safe environment, she was engaged in sex play by two older kids in the neighborhood. — Editor

LAUREN'S SURROGATE TREATMENT began the day she was enrolled at the day-care center where Miss Karen taught. Lauren was three and a half years old. Miss Karen, who would become her future foster and adoptive mother, watched the petite girl in pink, whose large blue eyes were smudged by dark circles, move hesitantly toward her from across the room. Lauren locked her thumb in her mouth as she clutched the hand of the day-care director. "Miss Karen," said the director, "This is Lauren and she's yours." In Miss Karen's words, "Lauren reached up and took my hand and never let go."

AUTHOR'S THEORETICAL ORIENTATION

The perspectives that guide my work with sexually traumatized young children are eclectic, with caregiver interactions as a focal point. Conditioned learning and cognitive theories explain how negative feelings (fear, anxiety), thoughts (guilt, shame), and behaviors (avoidance) become associated with the child's perceptions of the abuse (Berliner & Wheeler, 1987). A vast range of stimuli can elicit stress responses in the child, which may be manifested as intrusive thoughts, nightmares, flashbacks, hypervigilance, exaggerated startle response and fears. Because abused children may develop coping mechanisms such as repression and dissociation, at times the stimuli that trigger stress responses can only be known over time and through exposure to a variety of settings. The child often appears as startled and unprepared for the recovery of a traumatic memory as do the therapist and primary caregivers.

Maltreated young children frequently respond to triggers located in their daily home environments: tastes, smells, sounds, and items found in bedrooms, kitchens, bathrooms, cars, and stores. Fear reactions may be expressed as the child begins to feel secure in the new environment and better supported to deal with repressed or dissociated memories. It is difficult for a therapist to be consistently proactive in coaching a caregiver to anticipate the child's reactions. A more realistic goal is to support caregivers in being appropriately reactive to the abused child, as well as to their own needs and those of other family members.

In the course of living in an abusive environment, the young child also may learn to behave in sexual or aggressive ways because such behaviors were modeled or reinforced. These behaviors are usually "up front" and easier for caregivers and therapists to manage through behavioral techniques than the unpredictable expression of powerful memories of the trauma.

One therapeutic task in working with traumatized young children and their caregivers is to enable the child to return to the pain (James, 1989).

This work involves supporting the recall of traumatic memories. Children tend to minimize the impact of the abuse. This tendency is supported by well meaning caregivers and therapists who would "normalize" the child, reinforcing the child for adjusting promptly to a new caregiving environment. If the child and caregivers collude to deny the abuse, the traumatic memories are stored to emerge in other ways and on other days, hidden from the child, caregivers, and therapist. Therapy for sexually abused children is unique because of the potential impact of abuse in areas of sexuality and stigmatization (Finkelhor & Browne, 1985), which must be dealt with by the child, caregiver, and therapist. Treatment of the child using caregivers as surrogate therapists must address the comprehensive issues of the child's sense of safety, mastery of fears, and distorted beliefs as manifested in the child's functioning at home and school or day-care. In addition, therapist and caregivers must deal with the impact of other influential systems, especially the school, social services, and the courts, on the progress of the child.

Therapists often must base initial treatment decisions on partial information about the case. In Lauren's case, her ongoing disclosures, new information provided by the *guardian ad litem* and the inability of her birth mother to participate in her care shifted the focus from temporary to permanent out-of-home care. Decisions about how treatment should progress often are not under therapists' control, nor can therapists or caregivers necessarily prevent further traumatization. As Lauren worked through memories of past traumatic events, she was simultaneously coping with demands of daily routines, day-care, school-based learning tasks, and peer relationships, as well as the unique stressors of adjusting to living in alternative care, managing visits with her birth mother and termination of parental rights, court hearings, adoption, and finally moving to a new state. No small order for a young child.

The concept of using caregivers as primary and surrogate therapists is not new in the child treatment literature. One approach to training caregivers to be therapeutic agents with foster/adoptive children is filial therapy (Ginsberg, 1989; Gurney, 1983). The caregiver is systematically trained to respond to the child using client-centered play therapy techniques. Caregiver and child have a play therapy session at home for 30 minutes per week. By comparison, the surrogate therapist caregiver has an expanded role in providing therapeutic interventions tailored to the traumatized child's specific behaviors and disclosures. Faller (1988) discusses several reasons for using this approach with young children. First, the children need persons in their natural environment who will respond therapeutically to their needs on a long-term basis. In addition, young children confide their fears to people whom they know and trust and often recover memories for abusive episodes at times that do not coincide with therapy appointments (e.g., bathtime, bedtime). Finally, caregivers, too, are traumatized by sexual abuse. They need coaching in how to respond to their own reactions as well as their child's. As the usually soft-spoken Miss Karen said on the phone one day, "If Lauren tells me about one more totally gross and disgusting incident, I think I will explode!" Then she added, "But I tell myself that, if Lauren has survived living and remembering those horrors, I can survive hearing about them and reassuring her that she is safe."

DESCRIPTION OF THE CASE

It is not uncommon for abuse to occur for years before a child is afforded protection, and Lauren's case was no exception. Child Protective Services (CPS) first became involved when she was two. At that time, staff at a day-care center reported that Lauren had multiple bruises on her body. A medical exam revealed findings consistent with physical and sexual abuse, including severe bruising of her soft palate. Lauren's stepfather was arrested as the suspected offender, released on bail and ordered out of the home for six months. Charges were later dropped due to insufficient evidence and monitoring was discontinued by CPS.

One year later an abuse report was made from another day-care center. Notes written by staff at the center indicated that Lauren was "extremely afraid" to go alone to the bathroom. Lauren had said that Daddy (step-father) had put "nail polish" as well as "soap, baby powder, Desitin and pee" on her bottom. Lauren would plead to go home with her teacher and reportedly said her Daddy would "pull out my teeth and my tongue and my hair if I talk." Lauren was very fearful in day-care. She told her teacher that her parents were "mean" and "put spiders in my neck." Her stepfather frequently brought her to school and the staff noted that he would caress Lauren as one would caress a lover—stroking her hair as he combed it, slowly smoothing down her clothing and kissing her goodbye on the lips.

The Birth Mother

The family history is incomplete because during the evaluation Lauren was removed from the home and we were unable to obtain additional data. However, the mother did state that she, at 32, was the oldest of six siblings and that her father, whom she claimed was abusive to her, was a physician who had died three months earlier of a heart attack. She stated that her mother currently was hospitalized with psychiatric problems and she herself had been hospitalized twice for depression and alcohol abuse. She could not keep a job. She said she had not seen her two children (ages eight and ten) from her first marriage since they were preschoolers. They were living with their father in another state. Lauren's father was described as a drug addict who died in a car accident when Lauren was an infant. The mother's current marriage was her third.

Four months later, additional facts emerged, which revealed serious problems with the mother's credibility as a reporter and raised concerns that she may have had an undiagnosed multiple personality disorder. The mother's medical and psychiatric reports were obtained by Lauren's *guardian ad litem* and documented several other hospitalizations and a long psychiatric history of affective disturbances and personality disorders. Lauren had also been placed in temporary foster care at six months due to maternal neglect. The maternal grandparents were alive and well, living in another state, and had adopted their grandchildren several years ago. The mother was prohibited by restraining order from ever seeing the children again. The maternal grandmother believed her daughter was a very "sick, destructive, frightening and evil" woman and denied any maltreatment of her daughter. Although the maternal grandparents knew of Lauren's existence, they could not raise another child.

The Stepfather

Little information was obtained from the stepfather before Lauren was removed. He reportedly lost his job following the publicity of his first arrest. He had participated in group treatment for men who batter. Both he and his wife described Lauren as "loving" him, and said they "broke the rules" concerning the court-ordered restriction on visitation because Lauren missed him so much. The mother also believed that Lauren's behaviors of "being in fantasy" and "having screaming tantrums" were caused by the stepfather's working two jobs and being gone so much.

The Team

I am on the faculty of the department of psychiatry in a large medical school setting, involved in the training of psychiatry child fellows and residents, psychology interns, and practicum students and social work interns. In addition, I am consultant to and evaluator for the Child Mental Health Evaluation Program. Over 200 child psychiatrists and psychologists are rostered statewide in this unique program, which provides consultation to CPS during their investigations of difficult abuse and neglect cases. The role of the Child Mental Health Evaluator is to respond to CPS questions about the impact of the alleged abuse and make recommendations for future interventions. When I received the referral on Lauren, I decided to bring the case to my diagnostic training team for evaluation. Although this team later became the "childhood maltreatment team," we claimed no such expertise at that time. The evaluation was obtained using trainees in critical interviewing roles. In retrospect, this role was too demanding for novices, and today we acknowledge that interviewing the abused child requires specialized skills. Thus, our trainees observe, take notes, and participate on a preceptor basis rather than conduct independent interviews.

PSYCHOLOGICAL ASSESSMENT

Our initial assessment of Lauren was conducted over a two-month period, with direct interviews and observations of Lauren in play and day-care and with her parents. Collateral information was obtained from her parents, day-care personnel, and review of CPS and medical records. As consultants to CPS we were in close communication with the worker; implementation of a protection plan for Lauren was greatly facilitated by this relationship. No formal tests or structured questionnaires were filled out as part of the assessment.

Lauren separated readily from her mother during the initial interview. Despite her advanced ability at age three and a half to converse about day-care and other experiences, she was inarticulate about the alleged abuse. Hesitant statements such as "Daddy put cream on" or "Daddy does wrong things," remained unelaborated. She put a plastic bucket over her head when the anatomical dolls' genitals were exposed. When asked where her mother was when Lauren came home from day-care, Lauren replied, "In her cage." During interaction time with her parents, Lauren showed toys to her stepfather, who responded and asked questions while her mother looked on, smiling. No overt fear of either parent was noted.

The turning point in the case came when our team went to observe Lauren in her day-care setting. In contrast to the other children, Lauren appeared listless, withdrawn and sad, frequently sucking her thumb. She was easily frustrated, demanding Miss Karen's attention and crying. She wandered aimlessly during transition times and appeared weary. Before snack Lauren called Miss Karen into the bathroom where she had urinated and wiped her perineal area with a paper towel. There was a small amount of blood on the towel but no stool in the toilet. I asked Lauren what happened and she said "Daddy did it. He put on Desitin." Again, she could not elaborate.

Professionals are frequently faced with the dilemma of defining their various roles: investigator, evaluator, therapist, child advocate. Such confusion can be compounded when we work as consultants during an investigation. In this case, team members agreed that Lauren was highly stressed and that collateral reports and observed behaviors were consistent with sexual abuse. But was there enough "evidence" to protect this child? We chose to strongly recommend that CPS take Lauren into protective custody and we would admit her to inpatient pediatrics for further evaluation.

The hospitalization offered further opportunity to observe Lauren and her parents. We visited Lauren on the pediatric ward before any decisions about placement had been made. She looked at us calmly and said, "My Mommy's not coming to see me and my Daddy's not coming to see me and I don't ever want to go home." The mother came to the hospital intoxicated, furious at Lauren for telling lies about her stepfather. She also admitted that alcohol was the only way she could "survive" in her marriage.

Based on past abuse reports and Lauren's current statements, Lauren's dysphoric and regressed behaviors in day-care, Lauren's reported fear of her home and desire to live elsewhere, and most powerfully, the perceived inability of the mother to protect this child, we recommended that Lauren be placed in foster care. There was no physical evidence of sexual abuse, nor did we know that the mother's initial reporting of her family history was inaccurate.

We went a step further in our advocacy role during the child mental health evaluation. We believed that Lauren required a foster care setting with parents who were knowledgeable about early child development, who could make careful observations about her adjustment and skills, and who would work closely with a therapist. We recommended to the *guardian ad litem* (GAL) attorney that Miss Karen, Lauren's day-care teacher, be licensed to provide temporary specialized foster care. CPS disagreed. In court CPS argued they had adequate homes already licensed to care for this child. However, the GAL attorney prevailed, and Lauren was placed with Miss Karen. This decision, forged in an adversarial setting, had unforeseen negative ramifications for my future interactions with professionals in the Department of Social Services (DSS). They had lost a bid for control. The close, collaborative relationship we had enjoyed with the CPS worker was not continued with the foster care worker.

COURSE OF THERAPY

Treatment of Lauren was court-ordered and I was asked to continue working on the case. Lauren's mother was mandated into her own therapy and allowed to see Lauren twice a month for one-hour supervised visits. The stepfather was arrested and released on $20,000 unsecured bond.

As Lauren had experienced many changes, I wanted her to settle in with the foster family before beginning to come to the hospital setting where she had last seen her parents. Rushing this phase could create negative associations to me and illustrates one of the potential problems when the evaluator becomes the treating therapist.

The foster family consisted of Karen's husband, Don, and 15-year-old daughter, Sue. The family was to be in the area for 18 months while Don completed a graduate degree, at which time he would leave the state. Initial expectations that Lauren would be returned to her mother changed as the mother's pathology became more evident during the first two months of placement. Then the foster family was faced with the decision of whether to keep Lauren in longer-term care.

Karen kept copious notes. Initially I had frequent phone conferences and read her notes about Lauren's adjustment to foster care. It soon became apparent that the triggers for Lauren's memories, which precipitated further disclosures, were items such as smells, colors, lights, vans, and dogs. These items did not exist in my office, nor did Lauren respond to talking about the triggers in their absence. I decided that I would need to engage the caregivers as surrogate therapists. I labeled my role as primary therapist and their coach. Both Karen and Don were amenable to this arrangement. Karen was a former nurse and a childcare teacher. She felt prepared both by training and experience to take on the role. Later I learned she had prayed for a child who needed her care and believed that Lauren's arrival was part of God's plan. I had been viewed by the foster parents throughout the evaluation phase as Lauren's advocate and had solicited their observations and feedback early in the process. Thus, a working alliance was established by the time treatment began and I was viewed favorably by the foster family as a support person for them and Lauren.

Impact on Foster Family

New caregivers have little knowledge of the consequences of volunteering to care for a sexually traumatized child like Lauren. That fact may be fortunate for the child, because Lauren's foster family remarked that, if they had known what was coming, they probably would not have agreed to the temporary placement.

Professionals must not minimize the life-wrenching aspects of giving daily care to a child who has been abused. First of all, the myth of parents as protectors of their children is shattered. As Lauren disclosed abusive events and reenacted her traumas daily, the foster family's fear and loathing of the birth mother and stepfather escalated. How could those people do such things to this beautiful, innocent child? Initially, the birth mother frequently called the sympathetic foster mother. However, one day she told them that her husband had anally raped her at knife point and had threatened to shoot her and the foster family. The birth mother called me to

report that the stepfather had been in Lauren's room several times, masturbating into her pillow. She sounded drunk and queried, "What will happen
now that he does not have the child to relieve himself on?"

Events like these are powerful stressors for caregivers and require immediate intervention from the coach. I instructed the foster parents to change
their phone number and to report the threat to the police, and I insisted
that the CPS worker serve as liaison for all subsequent communications
between the mother and the caregivers. I told the caregivers that under no
circumstances were they to attempt to meet the needs of the mother. Their
job now was to help Lauren.

A second life-wrenching event for the caregivers is that they must confront facts of brutality that most of us spend our lives dodging and denying.
They *must* acknowledge the abuse to permit the child further disclosure.
Frequent attempts to not hear, divert, redirect, excuse and minimize occur
daily. Coaches must continually counteract the tendency of caregivers to
normalize the child prematurely and short-circuit disclosures and related
difficult behaviors. In the beginning, the task was to expose, not eliminate,
behaviors. This meant tolerating unpredictable disclosures from the child
and, once the issues were revealed, developing predictable adult responses.
Thus, I warned the foster parents that we did not know what they would
encounter. My telephone line was open 24 hours a day and we had frequent
appointments. Their words would tumble out like a waterfall when a dam
is opened, as I was their only contact for sharing feelings, frustrations, and
horror. Lauren's behaviors were not an appropriate topic for general social
conversation and we guarded her right to not be publicly labeled as "sexually abused."

A third difficult aspect of doing surrogate therapy with sexually abused
children is that caregivers must behave in ways that run counter to their
nurturing instincts. Lauren had a nine-month phase when she was dissociat-
ing frequently. One evening Karen was playing hide and seek with Lauren
and Lauren crept under the bed covers. Karen approached the bed playfully
and said, "Now I'm going to get you!" turning back the covers. Lauren
leaped up with a contorted, enraged expression on her face, extended her
hands like animal claws and sprang at Karen, leaving bloody scratches on
the foster mother's face. When Lauren saw the blood, she could not recall
hurting Karen and seemed terrified, crying "I didn't do it! I didn't do
it!" Karen said she wanted desperately to say "Forget it. That's all right."
However, she had been coached to bypass those instincts so she said firmly,
"Lauren, you scratched me and you hurt me. You must go in time-out."

Finally, new foster families tend to believe they really have "room for
one more" and only good will accrue to everyone from their generosity.
This simply is not true. In Lauren's foster family the teenage daughter,

Sue, confided how hurt she felt that she was no longer her Daddy's only girl. She voiced fear and hatred of Lauren, who was so physically intrusive, unpredictable, and embarrassing. Sue would lock her door at night to keep Lauren out and had her share of scratches, too. This verbal adolescent struggled with options of prematurely separating from her family or competing for attention by increasing her risk-taking behaviors.

Other areas of family interaction suffered when Lauren arrived. The foster family had recently moved to our town and had few close friends. The foster father's research required long library hours and reduced the amount of time the family could spend together. Added to this were the pressures and constraints of caring for Lauren. During her first three weeks in foster care she awakened six or seven times a night and both parents' coping skills suffered when they were physically tired and emotionally drained. The extended family network was stressed as well. The sudden appearance of a four-year-old traumatized "grandchild" who was indifferent to the attentions of well-meaning grandparents led to subtle and overt admonitions to the foster parents to rethink their commitment to the "poor thing."

Karen increasingly focused her energies on "saving" Lauren. She continued to be her day-care teacher and was with her 24 hours a day. At one point, the foster father initiated correspondence with an old female friend and eventually the marriage appeared threatened. The focus of treatment expanded as I met with the foster parents. Gradually they acknowledged that Lauren could not be the center of their lives. I told them that Lauren had enough to manage without becoming responsible for the breakup of their marriage. I also told them, with utmost sincerity, that they did not have to keep Lauren and must never feel trapped because they once had volunteered to care for her.

Initially the treatment task was to provide a protective, therapeutic environment for this child. That was the role of the foster parents. My role was to guide their interactions with the child and supervise a third-year child psychiatry fellow who saw Lauren for individual work on a bimonthly basis. I planned to be in close contact with the DSS worker who supervised visits between the mother and child. The goals were enhancement of Lauren's sense of safety, improvement in her ability to interact in day-care activities, and reduction of the symptoms of dysphoria and fear that had been observed. We were expected to make recommendations at the end of six months about returning Lauren to her parental home. We had only vague details of what had happened sexually to Lauren but suspected at least vaginal fondling and fellatio. We did not discount her reports of threats by her stepfather but neither did we understand the nature of the threats and what they portended for Lauren's recovery.

The treatment of Lauren was "disclosure based," in that Lauren would reveal the issues and I would assist the foster parents in maximizing predictability and a sense of safety. A retrospective look at this case reveals a course of therapy that can best be described as a spiral, an image which I frequently use in parent work. Symptoms and fears initially appeared, abated, then reappeared in a slightly different context requiring a new level of mastery. The image of a spiral captures the changing of levels rather than simply cycling through old fears.

An old adage was true in this case: "Things tend to get worse before they get better." Lauren's course of therapy had no neat beginning, middle, and end points, but can be described in four phases. Lauren's early reactions to her traumatic past were triggered by overt stimuli, e.g., a bathtub, a van. Later in her treatment, the triggers incorporated more internalized memories. This progression paralleled the development of her cognitive and language abilities from age three and a half to six and a half years and her increased tolerance of threatening memories.

Phase 1. Fostering Expression of Initial Memories, Encouraging Mastery Through Play, and Dealing With the Foster Family's Response to Lauren's Behaviors (Three Months)

Lauren arrived at her new home, hollow-eyed, with her thumb in her mouth. She was afraid of going down the bathtub drain, electricity, putting on a nightgown, being licked by the dog, and going to the bathroom. We assumed she was associating her fears to previously traumatic events and operated on the premise that she could not realistically avoid these feared objects or the associations they triggered. With consistent reassurance of her safety and no harmful consequences, her hypervigilance gradually decreased over the next several months.

Family routines and time were immediately compromised and within two weeks exhaustion and tensions were evident. Lauren woke several times per night to check on Karen. She drank orange juice with such fervor that they had to cut it with water. Gradually, her little pot belly began to shrink and her dark-circled eyes lightened.

Sexualized and aggressive play first emerged at bathtime 10 days after her arrival. Initially a toy horse was her main symbol of expression and she would poke it into her vagina, anus and mouth. Several weeks later, small dolls replaced the horse as mean characters and were identified by Lauren as her birth mother and stepfather. This was the first time she reenacted sexual abuse using her stepfather's name. The bathtub depictions of oral, anal, and vaginal sex were very disturbing to Karen, Don, and Sue. They were appalled to see a young child demonstrate such explicit knowledge and their anger at the stepfather increased with each reenactment. Don took over kitchen duties to enable Karen to spend time with Lauren. As evenings were focused more on Lauren, the older daughter, Sue, began to feel threatened and jealous.

During the next two months, the sexualized violence in bathtub play gradually diminished. Lauren eventually asked to throw the dolls away. However, the horses were "nice" and, for the next 20 months, her main symbol of expression in play at home and in my office.

Phase 2. *Elaboration of Fears and Maintaining Caregiver Investment (10 Months)*

During this phase, Lauren became less lovable. She bared her teeth and held her hands like claws and would kick and bite. Lauren had strong self-protective needs and requested a She-Ra doll, sleeping with the small plastic dagger in her hand. She was easily outraged and violent with little provocation. Her behavior following the bimonthly visits with her mother was anxious and demanding. She made unprovoked attacks on the dog and family members. Stress was compounded for the family when the CPS worker was replaced by a less supportive foster care worker. Karen and Don struggled with their commitment and ability to help this child.

Three months into foster care an increase in dissociative episodes was noted. The foster parents were very troubled by Lauren's behaviors. Symptoms included the forgetting of recent past events—seeing a movie yesterday, eating at McDonald's, and the name of her pet hermit crab. Lauren was very concerned that she would be kidnapped whenever she saw a white van. Karen labeled Lauren's behavior as "distinctly different patterns of personality or behavior which seem to appear and disappear instantaneously":

1. Cooperative, cheerful, easy to reason with—by far the most common pattern.
2. Angry, uncontrolled, capable of violence and extremely defensive.
3. Withdrawn, fearful, eyes often staring, sucking thumb, extremely quiet.
4. "Cute" acting, grinning and moving in a seductive manner, rubbing hands over body, often seen at bathtime.
5. Very babyish behavior, talking baby talk, walking like a toddler, pretending to drink a bottle.
6. Indignant, shaking a finger when talking and often prefacing lectures with "I have something very important to tell you."
7. Loud frightened crying, usually seen after a violent act such as scratching someone and often accompanied by saying, "I'm sorry!"

Abrupt changes in patterns of behavior were accompanied by Lauren's blinking her eyes distinctly and giving a little shudder or moving her head sharply in a different direction. Karen noted: "In a split second her behavior, attitude, tone of voice, and even her appearance seemed to change."

Throughout the next four months, periods of confusion and forgetfulness increased. She continued to be abusive toward the dog but always gentle with the cats. She exhibited incontinence and soiling for the first time. She would ask, "Did we go to school today? Did we go to church today?" She stopped flushing the toilet, refused to go alone to the bathroom, and expressed extreme fear of having her hair washed. At times she would appear to be talking to family members, but when they responded, she would angrily say, "I wasn't talking to you!" She told her foster parents that her stepfather "cut off my cat's head with a knife."

Her play in home and office therapy had the consistent theme of being saved. She would be the baby kitty, pony, or horse and ask the adult to save her. Often she would take the dog's leash, attach the clasp to her shirt collar and the other end to the door knob and call, "Mommy, mommy. Help me! I'm all tied up!" Sometimes she would ask Karen to tie her up. Ordinary words and phrases triggered unpredictable responses. "You have such soft hair, Lauren," said her foster sister, and Lauren scratched and tried to bite the bewildered adolescent. Another time Karen said, "I love you, Lauren." Lauren responded sassily, "[Stepfather] said that to me when he kissed my bottom—'I love you, Lauren.'"

Lauren was also gaining greater verbal mastery of her fears and her abuse disclosures were spoken as often as demonstrated through play. Instead of reacting to traumatic memories behaviorally (screaming, scratching, dissociation), she was learning to verbally mediate her fearful feelings. "That happened at my old house, not here." "A screwdriver is for fixing things. My new daddy will not put that in my bottom." Gradually she was learning that thinking and talking about traumatic memories were not the same as experiencing them. She crafted elaborate but realistic plans for how people could save her if her stepfather would appear. She forced others to help her control her behavior and tested if she would be returned to her mother if she were bad.

Initially, each disclosure was accompanied by an increase in fearful, anxious behaviors. For example, she said that her stepfather "put a collar around my neck—really tight—a dog collar just like Lady's. He put chains on my arms and my legs so I couldn't get away. He put that little gray part that hooks on the collar—he put that part on my nose and I couldn't breathe." Very early the next morning she awakened disoriented and hid behind the couch screaming, "Stay away from me!"

However, 10 months into foster care she said calmly one day after bath, "My [stepfather] made me eat his bottom. I didn't want to but he made me.

He put a knife against my throat. He peepeed in my mouth and it tasted like blood. It choked me and I spit it out, but he made me swallow some." Karen responded, "I'm sorry that happened to you, but I'm really glad he can't do that to you anymore." "I know," said Lauren. "We would call the police." That night she ate and slept well.

Continued mastery was also noted as Lauren began to work on the difference between real and unreal, a difficult concept for a four-year-old. She was having frequent nightmares, which included a bear cutting off her head, a unicorn breathing fire on her so that she died, and Karen's being dead. She asked many questions about dreams and nightmares and was told, "A dream is something you are thinking when you are asleep, but it's not really happening. Even if it's about something that happened before, it's not really happening in the dream. It's only what you are thinking about."

During this time Don, the foster father, was able to establish a closer relationship with Lauren. Initially she was wary of him and he was respectful of her fear. Now she sought him to pick her up and tease and tickle her and asked him to read her stories. Don was a fun-loving man whose loud voice contrasted with Karen's soft-spoken style. Lauren gradually became very comfortable in his presence. She also had moved from Karen's class in day-care and adjusted well.

In this phase there was a resurgence of anger and lashing out physically at others, which was managed by use of time-out techniques and the pillow person (see p. 21). By the time Lauren had been in surrogate therapy with the foster family for 11 months, she was basically cheerful and cooperative. There had been no violence toward the pillow person for several weeks and bathtub and other play was not sexualized or violent. She rarely pretended to be an animal or play "danger." She was focused on her dollhouse, dishes, toy ponies, and magic markers. She drew rainbows and appeared happy and self-confident. When I saw the foster parents, they held out their scarred hands and grinned. "Look! No new scratches!"

Phase 3. Recovery of Ritualistic Abuse Memories and Managing the Traumatic Impact on Lauren and the Foster Family (12 Months)

This phase, which spanned a year, was the most difficult to manage, and perhaps more traumatic for the caregivers than for Lauren. Lauren was approaching age five when parental rights were terminated. Court and adoption issues were stressful to the family and difficult for Lauren to comprehend. There were interminable system delays. Although the foster family wanted to adopt Lauren, they were told that other families were eligible and they would need to "get in line" and not expect special consideration. I immediately contacted the adoption worker to inform her that because of Lauren's special needs I would be strongly recommending that Karen and Don be the adoptive parents. Eventually, I received reassurance that this was social services' plan as well. Lauren's play themes with me concerned little animals who must leave and live elsewhere. Lauren had nightmares that she returned to live with her birth mother and was hyper-vigilant, fearful that if Karen talked on the phone that she was calling someone else to adopt her.

During this period, the foster parents had an opportunity to go away for five days, the first sustained separation from Lauren. The foster maternal grandmother arrived to care for Lauren. We could not arrange for me to see Lauren in her foster parents' absence, but I kept in phone contact. Sue was also at home. The separation clearly was stressful for Lauren. She was described as "sassy" the entire time, she would not allow her hair to be washed, her art work regressed, and she forgot familiar songs. When the foster parents returned, she was more assertive, provocative, and sexy. For the first time she made sexualized approaches to the foster father, asking to see his bottom. At bathtime, Lauren would cup her vaginal area as if holding a penis and say in a deep voice, "Hey Lauren! Look at this!" She was again wakening at night and wetting the bed.

The separation triggered a new wave of memories and fears. Lauren's descriptions of abuse escalated and became more specific. Her talk was dominated by "eating stinky" and "drinking peepee." She talked about "drinking blood" and "praying to God for mean things to happen." She said her mother and stepfather said there was a black hand with claws that comes out of the bathtub faucet. She said that her stepfather was going to kill Karen with a knife. Her face had several self-administered scratches.

One day Lauren began to talk about a movie camera and another man named Kevin. Her stepfather would take pictures of Lauren "eating Kevin's bottom—so he would remember." She said, "I made my mouth like this," and closed it tightly, but her stepfather held her nose, forcing her to open her mouth.

A kitten named Missy figured prominently. In a relatively rare disclosure during a session with me, she said that her stepfather "cut Missy's tail off and she bleeded in my bedroom. He didn't want cats in the house. Only blood in the house. They ate the blood and made me drink it too." Then she said, "That's all I want to talk."

It was difficult to anticipate where and what might trigger associations of ritualistic abuse. Several memories were related to food. Eating several muffins, she asked, "Are there dead people in there?" Observing her foster mother shred lettuce, she said, "I thought you were cutting up skin." As Karen was removing a roast from the oven, Lauren queried, "Is that people meat or cow meat?" Lauren had difficulty eating food with tomato bits or noodles which reminded her of blood and vessels. She displayed intimate knowledge of the location of intestines, hearts and stomachs in humans and animals. She questioned why people died when all their blood ran out.

One day she asked her foster mother why babies were all gray and sticky when they were born. She went on to graphically reenact the delivery of her birth mother's baby, saying "pretend it takes a long time to slide out." She then stated that her stepfather cut out the baby's heart and fed it to the dog. One day she took a round dog dish, held a table knife as if the hilt end were inserted in the side of the dish with the blade pointed outward. She then described her stepfather staking a man to the ground, attaching a knife to the car tire and her mother driving the car over the man until the knife pierced his chest. This event was matter-of-factly reenacted on the kitchen floor. She also described how the skin fell off people her stepfather burned in a fire.

She fell and broke a tooth and the trip to the dentist triggered a new wave of memories, especially about an old man whose eye was taken out by her stepfather. Frequently she would spontaneously draw the event, although she did not dwell exclusively on morbid recollections.

These disclosures came in bits and pieces. Lauren appeared calmer as she described these events, seeking corrective information. Perhaps the most difficult material for the foster parents was her description of the killing of children. Initially she described her stepfather shooting two of her "sisters," Aorphia and Clorsin. Karen was badly shaken by this disclosure because she believed Lauren could have been killed and there were no relatives to question Lauren's disappearance. Over time, Lauren disclosed more details and said her stepfather made her "kill a baby for Satan" by holding her wrist as she stabbed it. Heather, who was her best friend, was the most difficult death for Lauren. Initially she said her stepfather killed Heather. Much later Lauren said that she had been made to kill Heather.

The basis of her negative reaction toward the family dog became clear when she described a dog licking her bottom and having to suck its penis. She described the loss of several pets, but most significantly a horse named Cupcake and her kitten, Missy. At times she would fall asleep in Lady's dog cage. She also would pull at Karen's face and ask if she were wearing a mask. She said her birth mother had said that Karen was really her birth mother wearing a mask.

As memories continued to be divulged, pressure on the foster family increased. At one point, the now 16-year-old Sue said, "Do I really have to deal with this? I hate it!" At the same time, she was growing more fond of Lauren. Sue was quite stressed at home and school and in her social life. She was a dramatic, labile adolescent, a talented actress and singer, and a bright but distractible student, who had moved several times. Her parents had promised she would not need to move away during her senior year. As her parents' focus on Lauren enabled her to have more freedom, her risk-taking behaviors increased. She had a serious car accident but emerged unhurt. She became obsessed with a boyfriend and during the next two years clung to this relationship with an intense neediness that ultimately insured she would be rejected. She also was approached sexually by her drama teacher and decided that she would need to change schools for her senior year. During this time, Sue's needs were as often a focus of the intervention as Lauren's. Both parents felt guilty about neglecting Sue and angry that she would not "grow up." They had been overwhelmed at times by Sue's behavior since she was a young child, and the mounting household tensions did not enhance anyone's ability to cope.

It is not uncommon for caregivers who are dealing with ritualistic and satanic abuse issues to cope by immersing themselves in the literature. Karen began to read many books, met a colleague who also believed children in our area were exposed to cult activities, determined from Lauren's fragmented descriptions where the site of satanic activities may have been in our county, continually sought evidence to convict the stepfather, and believed she had a God-given mission to do all of this for Lauren. Karen was fearful for her own safety and that of her family and began to interpret several incidents (e.g., phone calls to Sue) as possibly cult-related.

This phase of treatment involved other major stressors. The adoption was finalized and was a happy event for the family. However, two years after the arrest of the stepfather, there was no court date set for his trial. The adoptive family wanted to see him and Lauren's birth mother punished for the atrocities they believed were committed against their child and other children. Two months before the family left the state, the assistant district attorney interviewed Lauren, her adoptive parents, and me about the case. We were concerned that Lauren's dissociative behaviors and talk of ritualistic abuse would discredit her testimony. During the first interview, Lauren was clear in describing the sexual abuse in the bathtub. However, in the ensuing two weeks, she had several memories of animal sacrifice; when questioned again by the attorney, she stated that she had sucked a goat penis and named a location in a different county. The DA said, "I cannot put this child on the stand," and she did not believe that the disclosures obtained in treatment would withstand the scrutiny of a jury trial. Thus, the stepfather accepted a plea bargain of three years probation for indecent liberties. Several months later, he inherited some land and moved to a farm community in another state. He said that Lauren's mother, with whom he still lived, had told him that Lauren died of illness and that the mother had signed to have Lauren's organs donated; thus, he was surprised to know she was still alive.

Another stressor for the family was the termination visit between Lauren and her birth mother. Following the visit, Lauren's fears increased with puzzling intensity. She checked the locks on the windows and doors each night and her concerns about being kidnapped increased. She was more comfortable at day-care than at home. Hesitantly she divulged the details of her final visit. She said her birth mother had whispered, "I know where Miss Karen lives and I am going to kill her with a knife. You must kill her too." The adoptive family was furious at the DSS worker for not adequately supervising the visit and enabling the threats to continue.

Phase 4. Family Adjustment to the Move and Resurgence of Dissociative Symptoms (Nine Months)

The decision to move was very difficult because Sue decided to stay behind and complete her senior year. Despite offers of places to live for the year, Sue sought a setting with minimal restrictions in order to pursue her boyfriend. My contacts with the family post-move focused on caring for Sue. She was frequently ill with respiratory viruses, missed a great deal of school, and phoned her parents constantly for advice and to share her misery and indecisiveness about all aspects of her life. She would come by infrequently to talk but could not contract for ongoing sessions, much as she was unable to commit to any path. She missed her family, especially Lauren, and was angry that they had left her. She also expressed relief that Lauren was away from threats of harm. She worried about her own safety, but that diminished when Lauren's stepfather moved away. She exhibited symptoms of depression and was placed briefly on an antidepressant. At the same time, she participated in a youth theater program, playing demanding lead parts in several productions, and maintained several close friendships with peers. Ultimately, Sue was hospitalized overnight on an adolescent unit. Following this episode, she vacillated between being with her family and pursuing her boyfriend. In the spring, she decided to move home, get a job, and repeat her senior year in the new city. By her report and her parents, she is doing well. She has not contacted her former boyfriend and is physically healthy.

The move for the family was financially stressful, and the living quarters were very small. I repeatedly urged the family to find a therapist. However, with the demands made by Sue, the adoptive mother's need to work part-time, and lack of money and time, establishing a new treatment relationship was not a high priority. Although Lauren was six, the initial plan was to place her in kindergarten since she had not attended formal school. The school system tested her for readiness and strongly recommended, based on her skill level, that she be in first grade. Academically, she did quite well. Her birthday, Halloween, and Christmas triggered difficult memories.

In late fall, her dissociative and aggressive behaviors increased with puzzling intensity. Ultimately, it was discovered that two older neighborhood children were engaging her in sex play. With the cessation of this stressor, her behavior improved.

SPECIFIC TECHNIQUES USED IN THERAPY

Lauren's treatment with me spanned over two years of intermittent work and follow-up phone contacts when the family moved to another state. Initially the treatment was disclosure-based. Lauren revealed her fears and concerns in her home setting, and I coached her foster parents to maximize predictability and her sense of safety in her new setting. As part of this process, Lauren clung to "rituals," i.e., standard ways of doing bathtime and bedtime, and insisted on consistency of responses from her caregivers. Part of our work was to provide the consistency when it was feasible and extend her flexibility.

I suggested and demonstrated specific intervention techniques for the caregivers to use with Lauren. I collaborated with them, soliciting their opinions and feedback. Many times my ideas were modified and often they were improved upon. In addition, I learned several creative approaches from the caregivers.

Phase 1 Techniques

1. *Teaching caregivers a conceptual model for understanding Lauren's fearful responses.* Exposure to feared stimuli could not be prevented, but the caregivers struggled with wanting her to have *no* adverse experiences. We discussed mastery by facing feared stimuli in a safe setting. They were encouraged to name the feared item and stress that such an item was safe in *this* house. For example, one day Karen was folding Lauren's blanket that she used at naptime at day-care. Suddenly Lauren screamed fearfully, "I can't breathe if you do that!" "If I do what?" asked Karen. "If you put that blanket on my face and hold it on me!" Then Lauren said her birth mother put a blanket on her face so she would not scream. Karen offered reassurance, "I'm sorry that happened. I will not put a blanket on your face. If you see me with a blanket you won't have to worry about that." On another day Lauren sobbed, "The mean horsie put black fur on my face and I couldn't breathe."

2. *Log notes and phone contacts.* Karen liked to write and was encouraged to keep copious notes. These notes served to track Lauren's

treatment and provided Karen with an effective way to share the burden of seeing and hearing Lauren deal with her abusive past. Don later took on the role of transcribing the notes and would add his own observations. Karen said that my availability by phone was very important and supportive.

3. *Therapy appointments.* Initially, I was seeing the foster family every other week, and Lauren was seen for 30 minutes by the child psychiatry fellow. Lauren's play in therapy was a narrated monologue with occasional violent themes. No sexualized material was noted. The main focus was on her adjustment to the foster setting, and this time was used to reintroduce her gradually to the hospital setting.

4. *Bathtub therapy.* Bathtub therapy enabled the caregiver to provide therapeutic interventions in the setting where the behaviors occurred. Lauren's initial reenactment of sexual abuse was limited to the bathtub. Early in the "horse" play I added a mastery intervention. Karen was to tell the horse that Lauren's bottom belonged to her and that if Lauren said the horse could not kiss her bottom, the horse must stop. This statement precipitated a series of attempts by the horse to kiss Lauren's genital area with Karen saying, "No!" Then Lauren would proceed to punish the horse in a violent manner, drowning it and calling it names. The lucidity of her recollections increased. She would say, "The horse is peepeeing in my mouth. I'm getting ready to throw up!" and then pretend to gag and spit into the tub. She would hold the horse over her tummy and chest and say "Look! He's doo-dooing and pooping on me!" Then she would forcefully yell, "No!" and scrub at her chest and tummy. Karen would reinforce that the horse was to mind Lauren.

Bathtub therapy and other on-site incident-related interventions required structuring endpoints and transitions. In the therapist's office, closure was enhanced by leaving the setting, but bathtub therapy became a time- and energy-consuming process and Lauren would emerge looking like a prune. In response, I limited bathtime to 30 minutes, monitored by a timer, and stories were initiated as transition to bedtime. Also, if Karen felt tired she could structure short bath with no toys. Karen said having permission *not* to be a therapist was very important. This approach also ensured more time for the foster parents and their daughter in the evenings without Lauren present.

Phase 2 Techniques

These were difficult months and it was important to employ several strategies to help the caregivers manage Lauren's behavior and their own relationship.

1. *Management of physical aggression.* A time-out program which included labeling the unacceptable behavior and making Lauren sit in a chair was instituted at home and day-care. Karen was familiar with time-out techniques and this approach helped the foster parents be in charge when Lauren was aggressive.

2. *Limiting adult roles in therapy.* In both office and home therapy we continued to participate in "rescuing" Lauren when she was in distress. However, no adult was to act as perpetrator of abuse (e.g., when Lauren requested to be tied up). I did not want her perception of us as safe adults to be altered when she was already exhibiting confusion and forgetfulness.

3. *Management of dissociative episodes.* When Lauren did not seem to know her surroundings, the foster parents were encouraged to be soothing, reassure her of her safety, call her by name, and be patient. The foster parents were urged to take frequent pictures so if Lauren forgot an outing they could show her the pictures.

4. *Using concrete problem-solving approaches to experience mastery.* When Lauren asked Karen what she would do if the stepfather came to the house to kidnap her, the adult reassurance was "That will never happen." I instructed Karen to be very specific and to carefully describe how they would "escape," e.g., go out the back door, get in the car and drive away. Subsequently, Lauren carefully instructed the baby-sitter what she was to do if the stepfather should appear while her foster parents were gone.

5. *Managing the issue of the fragility of the child.* Caregivers wonder "Will she ever be normal?" I teach that the reactions of abused children are normal responses to an abnormal range of stressors and experiences. Furthermore, Lauren was a survivor with definite strengths. It is essential that caregivers, day-care personnel, and others who interact with abused children assume that the child is robust. Lauren's appearance was one of fragility—bluish-white skin, a tiny frame, and enormous eyes. As she was consistently held responsible for her actions, Lauren eventually came to feel less fragile and developed the aura and reality of robustness.

6. *The pillow person.* During this phase Lauren needed to learn that her foster parents would not let her hurt anyone or herself. However, her anger was very physical and needed an outlet. I instructed the foster parents to construct a pillow person (an old pillow or pillow case stuffed with whatever was handy) that Lauren could attack. She immediately named the pillow person her stepfather and, even as it was being constructed, stuck pins in its head saying, "I'm really hurting him." For two days she punished the pillow person, stomping on it, instructing the dog to walk on it, and piling on toys and blankets so it

"couldn't breathe." Eventually, the pillow person was destroyed and replace by another to be used intermittently at Lauren's discretion or the caregiver's suggestion.

7. *Containment of talk and play related to traumatic memories.* Toys which triggered sexualized play were not brought to day-care or used when interacting with peers, nor was conversation about the abuse allowed at the dinner table. Throughout treatment, Lauren was guided in limiting her disclosures to her foster family, her day-care teacher, and me.

Phase 3 Techniques

1. *Therapist self-care.* My most intense interactions with the caregivers and Lauren occurred during this phase. It was essential that the ritual-istic abuse disclosures be relayed to me so that the family did not have to carry the burden alone. My priority was to take care of myself so I could better treat this traumatized family and child. I read books on satanism to desensitize myself to the spectrum of ritualistic abuse. Nothing in my training had prepared me for this aspect of human cruelty and I resisted finding out more about it. My consistent advice to the foster parents was to let the new information in slowly. There was no need to process it all at one time. Karen said this advice was most helpful, as was my warning her not to think, "The worst is over — now I can relax." In attempting to monitor my professional role as therapist, I called a former State Bureau of Investigation agent for advice. He was clear: "Unplug from the drama and treat the trauma." Adults were tempted to use Lauren to satisfy their own needs to know more about cults, but such curiosity was destructive for Lauren. I set firm limits on pumping Lauren for details.

2. *Containing Karen's intense interest in cult behaviors.* I stressed the importance of her not asking Lauren questions and informed her that Lauren's credibility as a witness could be compromised if it were believed that the foster mother had "Put these notions in Lauren's mind." It was important to balance the needs of the foster mother and Lauren and to stay informed of the foster mother activities. I met weekly with Lauren to provide greater support. Lauren's memo-ries, *not* the realities of her experience, were the focus of treatment.

3. *Active liaison role with community professionals.* I notified the juve-nile authorities and the county attorney about Lauren's disclosures. I checked and rechecked impending trial dates of the stepfather. These actions reinforced my advocacy role for the child and family. I also called in a State Bureau of Investigation agent for a series of inter-

views with the caregivers shortly before they left the state. This use of the legal and law enforcement systems was an opportunity to disseminate knowledge and responsibility for the case. My goal was for the caregivers to leave the state with all the information they believed important on file. They reported that this action was particularly helpful.

4. *Reinforcement of caregiver creativity.* Lauren and Karen devised games that were healing and reeducative. One was the Baby Game. Following the enactment of her mother giving birth and the baby being killed, Lauren wanted to pretend she was having a baby. She took a doll, put it under her dress and pulled it out and gave it to Karen. Karen cuddled the infant, told her how special she was, and rocked and sang to her. At first Lauren played the role of a dog, watching the interaction intently. The game was requested over and over. Eventually Lauren climbed into Karen's lap to be the infant and slowly "grew" to be child who initiated games instead of needing to be cuddled.

5. *Office therapy.* Lauren liked to come and see me. At times my office was a haven from intense flashbacks and work at home and Lauren insisted on her time alone with me. We first talked with her foster parents about the past week. Lauren could choose to share in what was being described and at times she would correct her parents. We dealt with many issues, including her name change, adoption and the stepfather's trial. After I spent time alone with Lauren, she would join her foster father to get a treat and I would meet with Karen. Additional sessions were scheduled as needed.

Phase 4 Techniques

1. *Engaging a new therapist.* Finding a therapist whom they felt they could trust was very difficult for the caregivers. Their distrust was reinforced by accounts of cult survivors who reported that cult members have infiltrated every aspect of society. I was very firm and said they were hurting Lauren and themselves by not getting on-site professional help. I said I could not provide effective phone therapy, that Lauren's symptoms had escalated and they must find a therapist. I gave them a list of professionals in their area who worked with dissociative disorders and harangued them until they contacted one.

2. *Support for the adolescent daughter.* I worked intermittently with Sue, who remained behind, during several crises. Much of my contact with the caregivers focused on Sue's adjustment, which provided a link but did not replicate my former "coach" role around Lauren's adjustment.

OUTCOME OF TREATMENT

Improvement was measured by a decrease in the ability of objects to trigger Lauren's fears, her tolerance for separation from her parents, her ability to learn school-based skills, and continued enhancement of her secure relationship with her caregivers. Lauren was functioning better in all aspects of her development.

OBSTACLES TO TREATMENT

One obstacle to treatment was the strategy employed by the Department of Social Services. The foster care system is mandated to preserve families and a series of steps are delineated to protect parental and child rights. Specific goals must be met before the child can be returned home. These goals (e.g., pay child support, get a job, be in treatment, visit the child on schedule) are reviewed in court after six months. In Lauren's case, setting goals for returning Lauren to her birth mother was difficult because Lauren had disclosed such gross neglect and possible abuse. Thus, we were working to terminate parental rights while DSS focused on preserving them.

In addition, the cheerful and supportive CPS worker was replaced by a foster care worker who appeared judgmental and powerful to the foster family. The caregivers felt scrutinized and criticized. Next to the difficulties in managing the traumatized child, interacting with a worker whom we did not perceive as supportive was a tremendous challenge. At the end of six months of treatment, I elaborately justified why visitation should be reduced, as I foresaw no possibility of Lauren returning to her mother. The worker informed me that she was going to recommend *increased* visits because the mother had fulfilled the initial set of goals. As Lauren's disclosures became more graphic and frightening, we often perceived anyone not on the team (i.e., thinking the way we did) as contributing to Lauren's pain. Since we could not vent our feelings directly on Lauren's mother and stepfather, the DSS worker was the recipient of our anger and this interfered with our working relationship.

The coach/therapist must be forceful in obtaining a new caseworker if the match is flawed. I informed DSS that I believed the presence of the worker was inducing stress in Lauren because she associated seeing the worker with seeing her mother and continued visits between the worker and Lauren were not advisable. I also requested a meeting where misunderstandings were aired. The worker was convinced that the foster mother had attempted to break up Lauren's family and that Karen had exaggerated, embellished, and indeed, implanted many of Lauren's fears. I countered that this foster family was the major reason that Lauren was recovering and that, instead of being grateful and supportive, DSS had taken on an adversarial role. The worker's future contact with the family was minimized because the case moved into adoptions. Lauren's termination visit with her mother, in which the mother threatened to kill Karen, has already been discussed. When children's disclosures are not taken seriously, then the effort required to keep them safe during parental visits will not be made and children will continue to be victimized by threats and emotional abuse.

A second treatment obstacle was the foster family's move. This disruption was significant for all family members. Although initially they were relieved to have the security of anonymity, all support systems were disrupted, with a substantial increase in stress for the entire family.

A third treatment obstacle was the constant threat of the presence of the stepfather in the community and the delay in adjudicating of the case. The knowledge that this dangerous person was not going to be punished and could be harming other children underscored the lack of protection of children and fueled the caregivers' anger and desire to "find the bastards" and prove the stepfather's guilt. I believe the intensity of the foster parents' interest in cults would have been less pervasive had the legal system removed some of this burden of proof from their shoulders.

OTHER SYSTEMS INVOLVED

The roles of DSS, law enforcement, and the court system have been described.

MISTAKES

My mistakes were grounded in my lack of knowledge. I knew little about dissociative disorders in children or ritualistic abuse and did not pick up the early cues Lauren was presenting (e.g., spiders on her neck). Being more knowledgeable might have enabled me to forewarn the caregivers of possible associated behaviors and decrease some of the impact of the memories on both Lauren and the caregiver.

In retrospect, during the Phase 3 recovery of ritualistic memories, I would have taken a more active role in teaching Lauren to contain her fears using such techniques as boxing up memories and leaving them at my office (Friedrich, 1990) or putting memories in a trash bag (James, 1989). This approach may have diverted the intensity of her reactions away from the home setting. Maintaining a balance between being parent and therapist requires constant fine tuning and Karen, in particular, needed more frequent breaks from her surrogate therapist role.

Karen said she made a mistake by initially assuming that Lauren had done nothing bad to others. She would attempt to support Lauren by saying, "Only mean people would hurt a child or animals," not realizing she was labeling Lauren as "mean." After Lauren's disclosures of her own involvement in the rituals, Karen changed her approach saying, "Only mean people would force a child to do that."

THERAPISTS' REACTION TO THE CASE

This case has been an invaluable teaching aid for my own growth and with trainees, colleagues, and families. Ritualistic abuse is not a subject about which I voluntarily became informed. I questioned every disclosure and sought alternative explanations for the experiences that Lauren was describing. I even explored the possibility that abuse might be ongoing in the foster home and that I was missing important clues. There were times when I felt personally threatened, vulnerable, and overwhelmed, and I turned to my colleagues for guidance and support. Despite my incredulity at what was being revealed, I gained increased confidence that, in order to treat the symptoms, I did not have to (and could not) know what really happened to Lauren.

A foster family is a gift to a child like Lauren and her hope for a future. The daily healing of a severely traumatized child occurs not in my office but in the ministerings of her caregivers. I have learned to celebrate the tenacity of the human spirit and the awesome power of the mind to deal with trauma.

2

Parallel Treatment of a Sexually Abused Five-Year-Old Girl and Her Mother

SUSAN E. HALL-MARLEY   LINDA DAMON

This case illustrates that court-ordered treatment can work but it must be rewarding to the family if it is not initially palatable. The high likelihood of co-victimization in the mothers of these sexually abused children makes the parallel group treatment demonstrated here a logical approach.

Although psychological assessment was not used in this case, it would have helped in identifying Carrie's academic difficulties earlier. The shock of school failure could have been prevented, with the result that school would have been a more rewarding and successful experience.

Again, the key issue of attachment is evident when the family reacts to the first therapist's departure by perceiving it as betrayal. We often fail as therapists to remember how important connection is. The more ambivalent the family, the more critical the attachment issues.

Several instances regarding the regulation of emotional intensity present themselves in this case. When the intensity of work with a male therapist is balanced by involvement in a parallel group, the therapist gender difference has less effect. A second example is the use of time-out during group. This helps to teach emotional and behavioral regulation to overly aroused children. Carrie initially needed this to tolerate the intensity of her group work.

Family treatment was used with Joanna and her mother to correct extended family relationships. A result was that Joanna became a better parent for Carrie. It was obvious that this needed to be done in stages to keep the relationship from blowing apart, but in the end it was quite helpful.

I would like to react to the comments about organic contributors to ADHD that were raised with Carrie. Developmental research by Sroufe and his colleagues at the University of Minnesota indicate that ADHD in young children is not related to pre- or postnatal variables or physiological measurements taken at the time of birth (Jacobvitz & Sroufe, 1987). The most important predictor of ADHD in young children is chaotic and inconsistent parenting, certainly the case with Carrie.

Finally, rather than simply using parallel group treatment, the therapists adapted their program by shifting to a conjoint therapy focus for Carrie and Joanna at the end of therapy. This demonstrates that successful therapists are adaptable. — Editor

AUTHORS' THEORETICAL ORIENTATION

The theoretical perspective underlying the treatment presented in this chapter is generally psychodynamic in orientation, utilizing systems theory and behavioral interventions as well. In our work with young victims of sexual abuse and their nonoffending caretakers, we have found that a combination of group therapy for both child and caretaker and individual/family therapy is most effective. The group treatment program utilized in this case follows the parallel group treatment model proposed by Damon and Waterman (1986). This model addresses in a systematic fashion the common issues, conflicts, and themes shared by the mothers and their young children in the context of two groups—one for the mothers and one for the children—which meet simultaneously in different rooms once a week for 90 minutes.

In describing the usefulness of the parallel group model, Damon and Waterman point out that many mothers of sexually abused children were themselves sexually abused as children, and they tend to deal with their children's abuse in much the same manner as they themselves were handled. The result is that the mothers "are likely to be unable to help the children unless they are assisted to work through their feelings and thoughts about their own sexual trauma" (1986, p. 245). The model provides a structured and directive therapeutic format, which produces immediate results with the children and also facilitates the mothers' ability to explore feelings about their own early sexual abuse while at the same time learning to respond more appropriately to their children.

The children's group is a play therapy group that incorporates a curriculum of structured activities designed to meet the needs of children who have been sexually abused and who are at high risk for re-abuse because of sexualized behavior, inadequate sense of personal or sexual boundaries, and so on. Briefly summarized, the activities in the children's group are oriented toward goals of helping the young victims work through and resolve issues related to their molestation and other traumas subsequent to the disclosure, providing them with assertion and self-protection skills that will, it is hoped, reduce the risk of remolestation, reducing the children's sense of guilt and responsibility, and helping them begin to understand and integrate their ambivalent feelings toward the perpetrators of their abuse.

The curriculum is divided into 13 modules which address issues related to the child's abuse experience. The first modules deal with the child's right to say no to inappropriate requests or demands by peers, older children, and adults, and are designed to reinstate the children's sense of personal boundaries and control in their lives, thus reducing the risk for re-abuse. Subsequent modules involve dealing with anger on the part of both perpetrators and nonoffending adults following disclosure, encouraging the children to view the group as a safe place in which to verbalize their memories and feelings about the abuse, and dealing with conflicted feelings about their experience and the perpetrator. The final module is devoted to providing sex education for the children to dispel any confusing or inaccurate ideas they may have about their own sexuality or about human sexual behavior in general.

We have found such group therapy to be the treatment modality of choice for most young victims of sexual abuse, especially because it reduces the individual child's sense of isolation or "differentness" from other children, enabling her to more quickly and completely express and work through the range of affective experiences related to her various traumas. The children's groups are staffed by a combination of staff therapists, predoctoral interns, master's level trainees, and volunteers, with the goal of maintaining a ratio of at least one adult for every two children in the group. This ratio provides for individualized attention to the children when needed, maintains the focus of the group during structured activities, aids children who are having difficulties processing the material presented, and allows for management of behavior problems and the enforcement of limits.

The mothers' group, which meets at the same time as the children's group, provides a safe environment in which the parents can more or less systematically address the common issues and conflicts they share with their children. The group follows a loosely structured format, which allows for a systematic introduction of topics similar to those in the children's group curriculum. This is designed to facilitate the mothers' working through of their own early sexual traumas. The goals of the mothers' group include aiding them in addressing their own abuse so that they can be more emotionally available to their children, helping them to be more protective of their children in the future, and providing them not only an improved understanding of the reasons for their children's behavior but also concrete suggestions for appropriate limit-setting interventions for sexualized and other problematic behaviors.

Our agency offers several groups for young victims of sexual abuse and their families, with assignment to the various groups depending on criteria such as age and gender of the child/victim, identity of the perpetrator (i.e., family member or someone outside the family), and relationship of the primary caretaker to the child (e.g., parent, grandparent, foster parent, and so on).

In addition to group treatment, many of the families are also involved in individual/family therapy on a weekly basis. Individual or family therapy in these cases is considered to be of great importance, since it allows both for reinforcing gains made in group and for dealing at a more individualized and in-depth level with idiosyncratic issues presented by the various families (e.g., issues related to siblings and extended family responses to the disclosure of abuse, redefinition of roles and rules in families, other longstanding problems in the child and/or the mother, and so on). In order to facilitate close coordination of treatment in both modalities, family therapy, when indicated, is conducted by a member of the group treatment team.

DESCRIPTION OF CASE

Carrie,* a female Caucasian who was five and a half years old when first seen at our agency, is the only child of Joanna, a fairly obese woman in her mid-twenties. Joanna married Carrie's father when she was 18 years old, and she became pregnant almost immediately, against her husband's wishes. The marital relationship was very stormy, and following several separations and reunions they separated permanently when Carrie was one and a half years old, due primarily to the father's substance abuse problems, his general lack of responsibility, and his physically and verbally abusive behavior toward Joanna. Since the divorce, Carrie has had only very sporadic contact with her natural father, and he is usually quite rejecting and negative when he does see her. As a result of the divorce proceedings, Joanna was awarded sole legal and physical custody of Carrie, and after a brief, conflict-ridden stay with Joanna's mother, they moved into their own home. Joanna became very preoccupied with "living her own life and having a good time," so Carrie often spent nights and weekends with her maternal grandmother. Joanna had a series of brief, generally unsatisfying relationships with men, most of whom Carrie referred to as "Daddy." Joanna supported herself, her daughter, and frequently her boyfriends by working as a mid-level office clerk.

---

*The names of all individuals in the following description, except those of the authors, have been changed, and certain identifying characteristics have also been altered in order to protect the privacy of the family being described.

Just before Carrie's fifth birthday, Joanna's live-in boyfriend of about six months, Jim, began sexually molesting Carrie. The abuse lasted several months and included genital fondling and digital penetration, in addition to Jim's forcing Carrie to orally copulate him. Carrie was frightened to disclose because Jim had told her that her mother would hate her and send her away if she ever told. As with many young children, Carrie's fear to disclose was eventually overshadowed by the extreme discomfort she was experiencing, especially with forced oral copulation. Carrie finally told Joanna about the abuse. When Joanna confronted Jim with Carrie's accusations, he vociferously denied them. Joanna readily believed Jim and did nothing further to protect her daughter. When asked later why she had been so willing to believe her boyfriend rather than her own daughter, Joanna said that Carrie had been a highly sexualized child since the age of two, and she felt that Carrie had made the allegation because she was jealous of Joanna's relationship with Jim. Sometime later, Carrie told the school nurse about the "secret games" she and Jim played. The nurse explored this further with her and then filed a suspected child abuse report with the Department of Children's Services who cross-reported to the Police Department Abused Child Unit.

The day the report was made, Carrie was taken into protective custody and then placed in a foster home for three days until the detention hearing in Dependency Court. The police initiated an investigation, which included interviewing Carrie and Joanna at the police station. The investigating officer was very rude to Joanna, threatening her with a second abuse report because she spanked Carrie for acting out while being interviewed. This unfortunate incident set the tone for Joanna's perception of "the system," which she saw as hostile and judgmental toward her. The police were unable to interview Jim, the alleged perpetrator, because, although he maintained his denial to Joanna, he left the state on the day the child abuse report was filed. As is typical with children her age, Carrie's physical examination was negative as far as yielding convincing medical evidence of molestation. Because of Carrie's age, which limited her ability to testify in court especially with regard to dates and times, the unknown whereabouts of the boyfriend, and the absence of clear medical evidence, the District Attorney's office rejected the case for criminal prosecution.

After the initial Dependency Court hearing, Carrie was continued as a ward of the court, and physical custody was given to Joanna under order that she and Carrie reside in the home of Joanna's mother. A Children's Services caseworker was assigned to monitor Joanna's compliance with the orders of the court, to ensure that Carrie was adequately protected from further abuse, and to make periodic progress reports to the court. The caseworker, Mrs. Kennedy, proved to be very diligent and committed throughout the two years that the case remained open in Dependency Court, even though Joanna saw her as intrusive, demanding, and antagonistic until the final phase of court involvement. Both Joanna and Carrie were court-ordered to enter psychotherapy and were referred to our agency to begin treatment.

When they first came to the clinic, Carrie and Joanna were seen by Dr. Damon, the therapist in the mothers' group that Joanna would eventually join. Dr. Damon obtained background and a perspective on Joanna's current problems and issues, and also performed a sexual abuse evaluation and interview with Carrie. During the intake interview, Joanna appeared angry and at times very guarded in responding to questions, particularly with regard to her own history. She angrily described Carrie as extremely active, highly sexualized (e.g., constantly masturbating and talking openly in public about sex), oppositional, defiant, and generally negative in her interpersonal interactions. Throughout the interview, Joanna exhibited extremely low tolerance for Carrie's behavior and practically no insight with regard to its causes. She was also quite verbal in her expressions of anger and dissatisfaction with the court and the Department of Children's Services, and she vehemently protested being "forced" into therapy. She did not believe that she needed therapy at all and was ambivalent about Carrie's need for treatment, especially since she still had difficulty believing that anything had really happened to her. She expressed considerable anger with the court's order that she and Carrie reside in her mother's home, describing her mother as critical, domineering, and rejecting.

Joanna described her relationship with her mother as having been quite strained and conflictual for many years. Problems began when Joanna's parents divorced when she was eight years old; Joanna blamed her mother for driving away a father whom she idolized and who was always more attentive and affectionate than her mother. Her mother then remarried, this time to a man who was physically and verbally abusive to her mother and who sexually molested Joanna on several occasions during her early adolescence. Joanna attempted to tell her mother about the abuse, but her mother did not believe her. Although her mother eventually divorced this man as well, her unwillingness to believe Joanna's statements that she had been molested contributed greatly to ongoing tension and conflict in their relationship. The molestation and her mother's denial of it appear to be the most readily identifiable precipitants for several serious suicide attempts by Joanna during her middle and later adolescence. Joanna admitted to fairly heavy drug and alcohol abuse during her teenage years, but at intake denied any current drug use and said that she now only drank socially.

Before describing the initial evaluation of Carrie and the treatment provided, it may be useful to describe the setting in which we work. Our agency is a nonprofit child guidance clinic. In recent years, we have increasingly concentrated on work with young victims of sexual abuse and their families. Although the focus is on the child, therapy also includes working with issues presented by the parents that affect the parent-child relationship and the potential recovery of the child. This usually includes dealing with the parents' own histories of abuse, relationships, and so on. Intensive group and individual treatment is routinely provided to victims and their nonoffending caretakers. We do not provide treatment for perpetrators of sexual abuse except when indicated in the final reunification phase of treatment; initial treatment for perpetrators is provided by a variety of other agencies to whom we refer. Similarly, when the parents we see present treatment needs that fall beyond the scope of our service, we also refer out (e.g., to drug and alcohol treatment programs, day treatment, or for medication evaluations). The clinic of which our program is a part has an American Psychological Association approved internship program; as such, we use predoctoral interns as therapists in both group and individual therapy, under the supervision of licensed clinic staff.

PSYCHOLOGICAL ASSESSMENT

Formal psychological testing was not used during the initial assessment with Carrie since we have found that such methods do not usually contribute much to an in-depth understanding of the child's perceptions about the sexual abuse and its aftermath. Following a fairly informal developmental assessment, a sexual abuse evaluation was performed. This evaluation is designed to elicit information regarding awareness of body parts and functions, including private parts, the child's perceptions of the molestation and the events which followed disclosure, and the child's ability and readiness to talk about the abuse and its impact. Even when a case has been reported to the authorities before referral to our agency, we feel it is important in this initial phase not only to rule out other possible explanations for a child's behavior or statements, but also to rule out other possible perpetrators. In Carrie's case this was especially important, given Joanna's history of unstable relationships with men throughout Carrie's life and her assertion that Carrie had been highly sexualized and provocative even as a toddler.

When Carrie was interviewed, her anxiety and sense of responsibility and guilt were readily apparent when she asked Dr. Damon on the way from the waiting room to her office: "Are you going to take me to jail now?" Carrie was rather subdued throughout the interview, exhibiting little of the high activity level that would emerge later on in treatment. She appeared anxious and giggled when discussing private parts. She was able to tell what had happened to her in a fairly frank and straightforward manner: "He (Jim) made me suck his peepee. It was icky." When asked if anything else had happened, she pointed to her crotch and said, "He used to touch me here. Sometimes it hurt." She denied that anyone else had ever touched her in this manner or asked her to touch them. She moved about in an agitated, anxious manner as she talked about this, but when asked she was unable to say how she was feeling. Although Carrie's verbal skills were generally consistent with her age level, she was below age level in her ability to verbally identify and distinguish among feelings. Her social skills were also somewhat below age level, as were her gross and fine motor skills. Indications of a possible attachment disorder were evident when, after less than one hour with Dr. Damon, Carrie attempted to hug her and said, "I love you. Do you love me?" She was reassured that, although Dr. Damon liked her very much, they did not know each other well enough to exchange hugs yet. Toward the end of the interview, she anxiously asked if her mother was going to leave her at the clinic.

Following a second interview with Joanna, in which further history was taken and tentative treatment goals were established, she and Carrie were referred to both group and individual therapy.

COURSE OF THERAPY

The group program to which Joanna and Carrie were assigned was one in which all of the children were girls who had been involved in a broadly defined incestuous relationship (i.e., abused by father or father figure) and who had been brought to treatment by mothers who were adult survivors of childhood sexual molestation. When Carrie entered the children's group, there were six other girls already in the group, ranging in age from four and a half to seven years.

Joanna and Carrie were also assigned to individual therapy with Mr. Adams, a predoctoral intern assigned to the children's group under the supervision of Dr. Hall-Marley, who was the supervising therapist in the children's group and who was, in turn, supervised by Dr. Damon, the therapist for the mothers' group. We decided to place Joanna and Carrie in treatment with a male therapist because we felt that if they could be effectively engaged in a therapeutic relationship with a man, this could prove to be a corrective experience for both mother and child, counterbalancing their history of unstable and negative relationships with males. The individual therapy began at the same time as entry into group treatment.

Because treatment with Carrie and her mother spanned a period of nearly two years and addressed a number of issues and problems, we have chosen to divide the description of the course of treatment into three broad phases.

Our use of phases in this description is intended to aid the reader in understanding the major turning points in the multimodal treatment of this multi-problem family. As such, we do not mean to suggest that all families involved in the treatment program follow an identical course of treatment.

Phase 1 (First Four Months)

The initial phase of treatment, covering the first few months, was problematic with both Joanna and Carrie. In the children's group, Carrie was a disruptive influence, often requiring time-out or isolation from the rest of the group because of aggression with peers and therapists. Her negative attention-seeking behaviors, very poor peer interaction skills, frequent initiation of inappropriate physical contact, and generally high activity level caused her to be generally disliked by other group members and raised negative countertransference issues for some of the group staff as well. Because of the staff/client ratio and the clearly defined rules of behavior in the group, Carrie did begin to settle down somewhat after the first several sessions in response to the consistency and acceptance she received from the staff. However, she continued to have occasional outbursts of aggressive behavior, and her physical clumsiness caused ongoing concern for her safety during the free-play portion of the group. In addition, she often became highly anxious and disorganized during structured activities, especially those dealing with sensitive issues relating to sexuality or sexualized behavior, at times necessitating brief periods of time-out from the group so that she could de-escalate and regain control.

Joanna initially presented similar problems for the mothers' group. Her anger and lack of trust interfered greatly with her integration into the group at first. During some sessions, she would try to dominate the group with angry tirades against "the system," her mother, and the men in her life, often disclosing extremely intimate details about herself. In the course of such ventilation, she would also express significant frustration with Carrie, exhibiting a complete absence of tolerance for her daughter's behavior. At times she denied that Carrie's molestation had even occurred, and at other times she blamed Carrie for the molestation and her subsequent breakup with her boyfriend. During other sessions, she would refuse to speak at all and would insist that no one cared about her or her problems. At these times she would also express fear that everything she said in therapy would be directly communicated to Mrs. Kennedy, her caseworker, who would then use the information to have Carrie permanently taken away from her. During such sessions, Dr. Damon explored her resistance to sharing, attempted to reassure her about the confidentiality of treatment sessions, and empathized with her concerns about too much self-disclosure, encouraging her to share only as much about herself as she felt comfortable doing. Because of her emotional lability and apparent lack of interest in issues or problems raised by other group members, it took quite a while for the other mothers in the group to warm up to Joanna.

The same issues that presented early obstacles to treatment in group were evident in the initial phase of individual/family therapy. The individual treatment sessions were structured so that Joanna and Carrie were each seen alone for 45 minutes each week. This format was selected because of the apparent need of both mother and daughter to establish a therapeutic alliance with Mr. Adams and to identify and work through individual issues before family therapy could be effective. The treatment alliance formed slowly, primarily due to the mistrust of others, especially males, shared by both Joanna and Carrie.

The early work with Carrie in this context revolved to a large extent around the establishment of appropriate boundaries in the relationship. At first, Carrie was reluctant to be alone in the office with Mr. Adams and said very little during the first session, except to ask Mr. Adams if he, too, was going to touch her. Mr. Adams reassured her that this was not going to happen; although Carrie appeared to accept this, she spent most of the first two sessions engaged in solitary play, avoiding eye contact or verbal interaction with her therapist. By the third session, Carrie became more interested in involving Mr. Adams in her play and in interacting with him. At this point, a new limit-setting issue surfaced. Because of her abuse experience, Carrie seemed convinced that the best way in which to seek and sustain attention and affection from a male was to sexualize the relationship. As a result, she began to greet Mr. Adams with a hug around his waist, her face against his crotch. When they sat near each other to play or to read a story, she would place her hand on his thigh and move it up and down. Whenever this occurred, Mr. Adams would disengage himself and gently but firmly let her know that she did not need to behave in this way with him. He also used the opportunity to provide her with alternative, more acceptable behaviors (e.g., encouraging use of words to express affection, showing appropriate ways of managing physical contact, and so on). At first, Carrie's response to limits on sexual behavior was to explode in rageful tantrum, during which she would yell angrily at Mr. Adams, throw toys, threaten to leave and never come back, and on occasion attempt to hit and kick her therapist. Her feelings of rejection when Mr. Adams redirected her behavior began to diminish when group activities began to focus on the privacy of private parts and the right of individuals, both children and adults, to define and protect personal boundaries.

A parallel issue surfaced in early therapy sessions with Joanna. Her history of unstable sexualized interactions with men caused her to doubt that

Mr. Adams' interest in her was only therapeutic and supportive. Although she was not as blatantly seductive and provocative as Carrie, she often verbalized these concerns, and sometimes wore seductive clothing and makeup as if to test her therapist's resolve to maintain a completely nonsexual relationship.

Shortly after entering therapy, Carrie retracted her allegation, telling both her mother and her therapists that she had "made it all up." We have seen such retractions frequently in the young victims with whom we work, especially when the response of others in the child's environment (mother, grandparents, the system) is negative, confusing, or frightening. The result of Carrie's retraction was that Joanna became enraged with her and saw this as validation of her view that her daughter was a "bad" child who was responsible for causing all of her current problems. Much of our work at this point focused on supporting Joanna and attempting to help her understand why Carrie might feel compelled to recant, especially in light of Joanna's openly expressed anger. The therapists also attempted to be supportive with Carrie, letting her know that they believed her even though she was experiencing a need to deny that the abuse occurred. Later on in treatment, after Joanna stabilized and after the issue of secrets was raised, Carrie was able to return to her original story and talk much more freely, not only about the abuse itself but also about its attendant feelings.

An early issue presented by Joanna in individual and group therapy was her relationship with her mother. As mentioned earlier, there were factors from Joanna's childhood and adolescence that would understandably make this a very negative and potentially volatile relationship. In addition, part of Joanna's rage at "the system" was due to the order that she and Carrie live in her mother's home. Joanna described her mother as cold, critical, and judgmental, in terms of both Joanna's personal life and her ways of caring for and disciplining Carrie. After a few sessions in which these issues and concerns were more clearly delineated, a series of additional weekly sessions were scheduled for Joanna and her mother. The primary purpose of these sessions was to work on parenting issues with the goal of resolving their conflicts so that Carrie could receive firm and consistent limits, and to re-empower Joanna as primary caretaker and parental figure for her daughter. Although Joanna's mother initially proved herself to be quite critical of Joanna, she was able, over the course of six sessions, to agree that Joanna should be the primary parental figure with Carrie, that she should refrain from expressing her criticisms of Joanna in front of Carrie, and that she and Joanna should attempt to agree on discipline techniques and limits for Carrie. An attempt was made during the last of these sessions to address some of the reasons for the underlying hostility between Joanna and her mother. It was hoped that if Joanna and her mother could begin to deal with the issue of Joanna's abuse by her stepfather, Joanna might be better able to understand her own need to deny Carrie's molestation. Although Mr. Adams attempted to raise the issue in as sensitive and non-threatening a manner as possible, the session rapidly deteriorated into an angry shouting match when Joanna began to express anger at her mother for not protecting her from the stepfather's sexual abuse. Joanna stormed out of the office because her mother attacked her verbally in the session and continued to deny that the abuse could have occurred.

The next day, Joanna called and spoke with Mr. Adams' supervisor, Dr. Hall-Marley, expressing considerable anger with him and with the agency. She said that nothing had changed for the better, some things had gotten worse, and she wanted to leave treatment. We consulted and decided that since the parenting issues had been successfully addressed, further sessions involving Joanna's mother would best be suspended until some point in the future when Joanna was able to live on her own. This was communicated to Mr. Adams who then called Joanna. She was still very angry and reluctant to return to the clinic. She became furious when Mr. Adams reminded her that if she chose to leave treatment he would need to let her caseworker know. She did return, but for the next several sessions of group and individual therapy she was angry and generally silent, except to point out that she was only here because she was forced to be, that she could not trust anyone, and that she did not believe anyone cared about her. Apparently she effectively communicated her feelings to Carrie, who regressed to angry acting out in group and defiance in her individual sessions, frequently yelling at Mr. Adams that she hated him and hated coming to the clinic.

This initial phase of treatment culminated in a major crisis during the fourth month of therapy, which resulted in brief hospitalization of Joanna. After several years of no contact whatsoever, Joanna's stepfather called to let her know he was coming to town and wanted to see her. She decided to meet with him, planning to confront him with her feelings about him and his molestation of her. When she did confront him, he did not even bother to deny that he had done it, but rather said that it was "no big deal," that it wasn't really incest because he wasn't her natural father, and that he had "only given her what she was asking for." Joanna became enraged and left him to go to a bar where she had several drinks. She then went home where her mother attacked her verbally for being drunk again. She called the clinic, asked to speak to Mr. Adams, and told him that she had decided to kill herself. Although she was intoxicated and was not able to articulate a clear plan for suicide, we took this threat very seriously because of her past history of suicide attempts. After brief emergency consultation, Mr. Adams called Joanna back and convinced her to agree to voluntary hospitalization. During her week in the hospital, the suicidal ideation subsided and Joanna was able to accept that she was an alcoholic and had used alcohol as a way of coping with problems since adolescence.

After her hospitalization, Joanna reluctantly and shamefully began to talk in both group and individual therapy about her alcohol abuse. She continued to express concern about what would be communicated to Mrs. Kennedy, her caseworker, about this issue; however, the swift intervention of the clinic staff when she was actively suicidal and the supportive, nonjudgmental acceptance on her return to treatment had a tremendous impact in terms of finally impressing on her that her therapists did care about her and could be trusted to help her. She accepted a referral to an outpatient alcohol abuse program, which included mandatory attendance at AA meetings, and agreed to sign a release allowing us to have contact with her counselor in the program. In order to give Joanna a sense of control, we waited to inform Mrs. Kennedy about her alcohol abuse until she had given her reluctant permission. Mrs. Kennedy then monitored her compliance in the alcohol treatment program and, upon our suggestion, also praised Joanna for admitting she had a substance abuse problem.

Phase 2. Reconstruction (Eight Months)

The middle or reconstructive phase of therapy, covering a period of about eight months, was a time of significant progress for both Joanna and Carrie. Joanna gradually became a more positive participant in her group and began perceiving feedback from Dr. Damon and other group members as supportive rather than judgmental or critical. She also participated much more productively in group discussions about problematic behavior in children and appeared to be gradually increasing her tolerance for and understanding of Carrie's behavior. Carrie also began to be more responsive to group therapy. Although she continued to be quite awkward, both physically and socially, her angry aggressive outbursts decreased considerably, and her ability to maintain focus and attend to activities in the group increased. Her mother also reported improved behavior at home and in public and said that Carrie's provocative and sexualized behaviors around other adults and peers had nearly stopped, a change Joanna attributed to Carrie's group participation.

After nine months in therapy, a major turning point occurred. This was the decision in a judicial review hearing in Dependency Court to give Joanna permission to move out of her mother's home and establish her own residence with Carrie. Because Joanna was beginning to make substantial gains in treatment and because of the acrimonious relationship between Joanna and her mother, we concurred with Mrs. Kennedy that this recommendation be made to the court. However, we also agreed with Mrs. Kennedy that Dependency Court jurisdiction be maintained for at least six more months, until Joanna could prove herself able to care for Carrie appropriately and independently. Although relieved finally to be allowed some control over her life, Joanna was not happy with our recommendation that Mrs. Kennedy's supervision continue, and there was a reprise of her earlier anger with us. However, her anger was less intense and less destructive to the therapeutic process than before.

There were new issues to be addressed in individual therapy, most of them involving issues of secrecy. The fact that Joanna had kept the nature and extent of her alcohol abuse a "secret" for the first few months of treatment provided a concrete example of how secrets can be destructive to relationships. Joanna had often complained that Carrie wouldn't share things with her. When Joanna told Mr. Adams that she had actually instructed Carrie not to tell anyone, including her therapist, about her drinking, he was able to point out that Carrie's secretiveness was probably related to her mother's need for secrecy. This issue was especially important, since many of the activities in the children's group involve or relate in some way to the idea that secrets, especially ones about inappropriate behaviors, are not okay. The conflicting messages about secrecy could predictably be very confusing to a child like Carrie, especially since her molestation was also supposed to be kept secret.

The issue of secrecy became even more central and compelling when Joanna and Carrie moved into their own apartment. The initial relief of being "out from under mother's thumb" was quickly replaced by feelings of loneliness and Joanna's realization that she had never been on her own before. Within a matter of weeks, she had found a new boyfriend who moved in and became Carrie's new "daddy." Because of Joanna's poor judgment with regard to men in the past, Mrs. Kennedy had made sure that the court order included a stipulation that Joanna and Carrie reside together, without any male roommates. We endorsed this condition because Carrie was still at high risk for remolestation. As Joanna understood the court stipulation, she did not tell Mrs. Kennedy or her therapists about her new "roommate," and instructed Carrie to keep it a secret as well. However, Carrie "slipped" and told Mr. Adams about her new daddy during a session. She immediately realized that she had made a mistake and began to cry and beg Mr. Adams not to tell her mother that she had told. This raised a number of therapeutic and ethical issues, since the risk of damaging Carrie's trust in the safety and confidentiality of her therapy needed to be balanced against the inadvisability of Joanna's having a male roommate. Further, there was a risk that Mrs. Kennedy might find out on her own and possibly remove Carrie from her mother's custody, or the even darker risk that Carrie might be remolested.

In this instance, there was no time to address these ethical dilemmas. When Joanna came in after Carrie for her session with Mr. Adams, she angrily related to him that Mrs. Kennedy had come to the apartment earlier that day, discovered the situation, and told Joanna that if the boyfriend did not move out that day she would have Carrie removed from the home. Joanna was furious with Mrs. Kennedy and described her in terms unsuitable for print. Following the session, Mr. Adams called Mrs. Kennedy to follow up. She confirmed that her visit had taken place with the results described by Joanna. She also indicated that she planned to increase the frequency of her unannounced visits to the home to ensure that no further contravention of the rules occurred. She acknowledged that she was taking a fairly hard line with Joanna but felt it necessary not only to protect Carrie from further abuse but also to keep Joanna from regressing back into her old life-style of promiscuity and alcohol abuse.

In subsequent sessions, Joanna made frequent, somewhat angry references to "the fire-breathing bitch," but with time and the pressure of Mrs. Kennedy's close scrutiny she was able to begin to feel more comfortable with living alone with Carrie and began to experience a positive turn in her sense of herself as a worthwhile, competent, and independent person. She was also somewhat grudgingly able to admit that in her secretiveness she had again modeled a pattern of withholding and "not saying anything about anything" for her daughter.

A second turning point in the therapeutic process during this phase was the reintroduction of Carrie's maternal grandmother into sessions with Joanna. As indicated earlier, sessions including Joanna's mother had been suspended after it became clear that confrontation of the mother regarding Joanna's abuse as a child could not be productively managed. One reason for the suspension of these sessions was that at the time Joanna was court-ordered to reside with her mother, and such confrontation would in all likelihood exacerbate the already hostile relationship between the two.

Because addressing the issue was viewed as an important part of Joanna's healing process and therefore essential to fully effective treatment of Carrie, a second attempt was made after Joanna had established a home apart from her mother. Although initially very resistant to the notion of further conjoint sessions, Joanna was able to explore the reasons for her resistance and then agree to the sessions. Since the pressure of Joanna's court-ordered dependence on her mother was alleviated, they were able, sometimes civilly and sometimes not, to address the issue of Joanna's molestation as a child. After two sessions that consisted primarily of Joanna's angrily confronting her mother, her mother was finally able to acknowledge that Joanna had told the truth about her stepfather and to apologize for not having believed her when she was first told about it.

Although the mother-daughter relationship was far from positive following these sessions, Joanna finally felt validated in her anger with her mother and her stepfather. She was then able to begin the process of working toward constructive resolution of that anger. This also had the desired effect of freeing Joanna to be more aware of the impact on Carrie of her own denial. Her improved level of insight around this issue, in turn, increased her understanding of Carrie's oppositional acting out behavior with her, and she became more willing to integrate feedback about how to validate Carrie's underlying feelings while setting limits on inappropriate behavior.

As Joanna's acceptance and understanding of Carrie increased, her anger with her daughter was replaced by anger with Jim, the perpetrator. This created a challenge to her therapists in terms of helping her to direct her anger into constructive rather than destructive channels. We supported Joanna's interest in attending advocacy group meetings and hearing oriented toward changing the system in ways that would be more responsive to young victims and their nonoffending caretakers. We also provided direction and support in her efforts to reopen the case and press criminal charges against Jim. Although the District Attorney's office had already rejected the case for criminal prosecution, we saw this as an important step for Joanna, since it represented her growing commitment to manifest control over the situation in an active and positive manner.

Throughout the course of treatment with any child, we attempt to maintain contact with others who also have ongoing interactions with the child, especially teachers. This was true in Carrie's case as well. Periodic calls to and from her kindergarten teacher took place throughout this first year of treatment. We were not surprised early on in treatment to learn from the teacher that Carrie was defiant, oppositional, aggressive with peers, and unable to keep up with other children academically because of her high activity level and inability to remain focused and on-task. This was consistent with our experience of Carrie, and is fairly common in children who have been molested in the context of a chaotically unstable life-style. Carrie's teacher was receptive to our input regarding ways we had found effective in managing her behavior. As Carrie continued in treatment, there was noticeable improvement in her behavior at school: she became less aggressive and oppositional; her peer interaction skills improved; and there were significant declines in sexualized acting out, masturbatory behavior in the classroom, and crude comments suggestive of inappropriate sexual preoccupations. However, she continued to have considerable difficulty academically, and her short attention span and constant need for refocusing were ongoing sources of frustration to her teacher.

During this middle phase of treatment, the school year came to a close, and Carrie's teacher informed Mr. Adams that she was holding Carrie back for a second year of kindergarten because she was not adequately prepared for first grade. This precipitated a crisis of confidence for Joanna, who believed that Carrie's lack of progress at school was indicative of failure on the part of therapy. The crisis abated as Joanna was able to acknowledge and begin to appreciate the significant progress Carrie had begun to make in other areas. However, it became apparent that an organic component to Carrie's school problems needed to be ruled out. She was referred for a psychiatric evaluation to rule out attention deficit disorder and other possible organicity. The results of the evaluation were that attention deficit disorder was not the apparent problem, but that there were clear indications of anxiety that caused Carrie to stop trying and then become distracted when faced with a task she felt she could not accomplish. The evaluation findings also indicated a need for specific remediation due to deficits in visual-motor perception and coordination. The psychiatrist recommended that Carrie receive more individualized attention at school in order to bring her to the level of her potential. Joanna's therapists actively supported and assisted her in her efforts to convince the school system that Carrie had special needs, and the result was an individualized education program that would provide additional attention from resource specialists when Carrie returned to kindergarten in the fall.

This middle phase of treatment ended, as the first phase had, in crisis. Over the summer months, Joanna had agreed to continue in the group program for another year. Although the curriculum in the children's group can be completed in nine or ten months under optimal circumstances, it is common in this particular group of incest victims for families to remain in treatment for 18 months to two years, and for the children to repeat part or all of the curriculum. Because of the problems and crises that had arisen during the first several months of therapy, Carrie's high levels of anxiety and confusion had prevented her from benefitting as much as she might have from the children's group. There were significant gaps in her understanding of certain issues and concern on the part of both the group staff and her individual therapist that she had not really integrated the assertion and self-protection material, leaving her at a continued high level of risk for re-abuse. We also felt that continuing in the group would have a positive effect on her self-esteem, especially when the activities involved material she did know, since it would provide her with a sense of mastery and a chance to be an appropriate peer model. Joanna also looked forward to continuing in her group, where she now felt accepted and supported.

The crisis that occurred at this point had to do with the need to transfer the family to a new individual therapist. Mr. Adams' internship year was ending and he would be leaving the clinic. His replacement would be, in all likelihood, one of the new interns assigned to the group. Because of the duration of the therapeutic relationship, Mr. Adams began introducing the issue of the transfer more than two months before his actual departure. Although Joanna appeared to accept this and was actually able to cite some benefits of having a new therapist, she began missing group and individual sessions, sometimes calling to cancel and at other times simply not showing. She did come in for her final session with Mr. Adams, but arrived almost half an hour late and was very cold and distant throughout the session.

Because our agency is also a training facility, the beginning of the academic year is a time of major upheaval for both staff and clients. With old student therapists leaving and new ones arriving, there is often a period of weeks when many families are "between therapists." The groups continue to meet during this transition period, and the permanent staff members attempt to see as many of the families as possible to maintain their commitment to treatment, to deal with any crises that arise, and to help them prepare for their new therapists. Although Joanna and Carrie did attend group once or twice after Mr. Adams' departure, Joanna refused to attend individual sessions despite several attempts on the part of the group therapists. When she was in group and the issue of reassignment was raised, Joanna vacillated between wanting one of the permanent group therapists to work with her in individual treatment and wanting another male therapist.

Another male intern was assigned to the group, and Joanna was called to schedule their first individual appointment. Joanna agreed to an appointment, but then called Dr. Hall-Marley and said that she was not sure she wanted to meet the new therapist. Her old issues regarding trust and fears that she would be manipulated and taken advantage of by a male therapist had resurfaced, causing her significant distress. Joanna was encouraged to give the new therapist a try for one month, and then, if things had not worked out, a change might be considered. Although she agreed to this plan at the time, after her first session with the new therapist she began canceling individual appointments and either canceling or arriving very late for group sessions.

Carrie appeared very anxious and confused when present in group during this time and announced during one group that it was time for her "Goodbye Party" (the traditional termination session for a child from the group) because she and her mother were not coming back to the clinic. Although Joanna did not make a similar announcement in her group, she was increasingly withdrawn and nonparticipative, and at one point left group early, commenting that she did not know why she had come. If this were not great enough cause for concern, another member of the mothers' group who had a social relationship with Joanna expressed concern one week in

Joanna's absence that she may have "fallen off the wagon" and lost her hard-won sobriety.

During this time, Mrs. Kennedy called the clinic, asking for a letter from us reporting on the progress of Joanna and Carrie in treatment and stating our recommendations with regard to when court jurisdiction in the case should be terminated. Because of the recent negative turn in Joanna's attendance and commitment to treatment, we submitted a report with the recommendation that jurisdiction be continued until Joanna returned and the current crisis could be dealt with and resolved. Joanna's attendance was so sporadic at this point that it was not possible to go over the letter with her prior to sending it. Joanna called on the day of the review hearing, furious with our "interference" in her life and with our efforts to "coerce" her into returning to therapy. Following an angry tirade which lasted nearly 20 minutes, she was able to calm down somewhat and agreed to come in for an appointment with Dr. Damon and Dr. Hall-Marley to discuss the letter and her resistance to treatment.

Prior to the session, we met and reviewed the issues related to the current crisis. During this meeting, we decided that if Joanna would agree to return to therapy, she and Carrie would be seen in individual treatment by Dr. Hall-Marley rather than with the intern, since the issue of trust at this point presented too great an obstacle to overcome without losing much of what had already been accomplished in the first year of treatment.

Phase 3

Joanna came to the session as arranged and agreed to the new treatment plan. This session marked the beginning of the final phase of therapy. The first several sessions with Dr. Hall-Marley, now her therapist as well as Carrie's group therapist, were devoted to dealing with Joanna's feelings of loss and abandonment when Mr. Adams left the agency. She was able to recognize that much of her bad feelings about his departure revolved around the fact that, even though her relationship with him had been very different from any other interaction she had ever had with a man, it ended in much the same way—he left and she had no control or say in his leaving. By being given the opportunity to finally express her anger and grieve about the loss of Mr. Adams, she was also able to mourn the loss of other men who had been important to her and who had left her.

Joanna admitted that, following Mr. Adams' departure, she had lost her sobriety and had again entertained thoughts of suicide when she realized that her return to alcohol represented yet another aspect of her life that was out of her control. She returned to the alcohol abuse program, although this was very difficult for her, and was able to maintain sobriety throughout the rest of treatment and beyond. With her renewed commitment to remaining sober, Joanna was able to use AA as well as her therapy interactions to begin to fill the emptiness she had previously attempted to escape with alcohol abuse and sexual relationships, and to build a support network for herself in the context of a more appropriate peer group.

Joanna continued to be frustrated by the ongoing presence of Mrs. Kennedy in her life, although at times she could reluctantly agree that perhaps she had needed supervision as she attempted to break out of her old patterns and style of life. She admitted to feeling intimidated by Mrs. Kennedy and wanted very much to ask her what she needed to do to "get her out of my life"; however, she was afraid to do so. Dr. Hall-Marley offered to invite Mrs. Kennedy to a therapy session so that she and Joanna could pose this question together, and after some initial hesitation Joanna agreed. The session with Mrs. Kennedy was very enlightening for Joanna, and the result was a very concrete plan for Joanna to follow, which would lead to Mrs. Kennedy relinquishing jurisdiction at the next hearing. At the end of the session, after Mrs. Kennedy left, Joanna smiled somewhat sheepishly and said, "I guess you were right. The old bitch really does care about me." Two months later, reassured by Joanna's renewed commitment to continue with therapy and her compliance with the plan laid out for her, Mrs. Kennedy closed the Department of Children's Services case, and Carrie was again in the sole custody of her mother.

Following termination of court jurisdiction, Joanna and Carrie remained in both group and individual therapy and continued to participate actively and productively in both modalities. Earlier on, after the crisis surrounding Mr. Adams' departure had abated, Carrie began making major strides in group. Her behavior underwent marked improvement, and she was able to use group to work through issues related to her molestation and to demonstrate her acquisition of assertion skills and respect for the personal boundaries of herself and others. Three months before the end of individual therapy, Carrie completed her second run through the sexual abuse group curriculum, and she and her mother were "graduated" from their respective groups. The group termination sessions were positively received by both mother and daughter and although Joanna expressed sadness at leaving her group, she was able to acknowledge that she had benefitted substantially from being in the group and that it felt like a good time to say goodbye.

The last three months of individual therapy involved a final consolidation of the gains made in group and very focused work on the relationship between Joanna and Carrie. Carrie had at that point gained as much resolution of the issues related to her molestation as a child of her age and developmental level could. However, the more general issue of communication between her and Joanna required further intervention. Sessions were restructured so that a substantial portion of the time each week was spent working with Carrie and Joanna conjointly. Both worked hard during these sessions, with the net result being a positive, well-bonded relationship in which communication was open and there were no more secrets.

It is likely that individual/family therapy could have continued at our agency for several more months. However, Joanna became increasingly interested in "making a really fresh start." After a visit with friends in another state, she began talking about a desire to move to their location. She began in a very planful way to explore housing, schools, and employment in the other community. As her plans began to come together, a good part of her individual therapy time was spent discussing the reasons for her wish to relocate and exploring whether she was running away or moving toward something. Termination of treatment came when she was actually able to make the move to the new location.

SPECIFIC TECHNIQUES USED IN THERAPY

In the opening section of this chapter, the parallel group model is described. In the children's group, the goals of the program are approached with a variety of structured play group activities, including games, stories, role-plays, puppet plays, and so on. Group time is managed so that each week there is also a period for nondirective play to balance the directed structure of the activity and to provide the children with an opportunity to dissipate some of the anxiety raised during the structured activity. Behavior management techniques such as time-out and reinforcement with stars and stickers are used to provide the children with a clear and consistent impression of behavioral limits in the group.

In the parent group, insight-oriented work is supplemented by supportive and behavioral interventions as well. Systems theory is applied in working with the mothers toward goals of establishing appropriate roles and communication in their families.

As one might surmise from the description of the program with regard to the adjunctive individual/family therapy, the techniques used in this modality vary depending on the needs and dynamics of the family being treated. In the case under examination, the individual therapy time, especially during the first year of treatment, was often consumed with various crisis management issues. Techniques drawn from the cognitive-behavioral approach were frequently utilized in attempting to deal with Joanna's resistance and negative self-image. At the same time, in Carrie's individual therapy, use of nondirective play therapy as a means of gaining resolution of the traumas she had endured could not be productive until after several months of work in a fairly strict behavioral management and limit-setting mode.

In summary, while the general underlying theoretical orientation toward treatment was psychodynamic in nature, the actual techniques utilized in this case were drawn from a variety of different treatment perspectives and changed over time as the needs of each of the clients changed.

OUTCOME OF TREATMENT

Although a formal outcome evaluation was not done, the progress achieved by both Joanna and Carrie was assessed and discussed at length during the final treatment sessions. Joanna was able to acknowledge significant changes in her daughter, including complete cessation of inappropriate sexualized behaviors and preoccupations, improved self-esteem and social skills with peers, and a very noticeable decrease in oppositional and defiant behavior at home and at school. By the time of termination, several positive changes were evident in Joanna as well. In addition to having been able to acknowledge and address her alcohol abuse problem and to seek appropriate treatment for that, she also eventually used her therapy to gain some closure on her own experience of sexual abuse as a child. She worked hard toward resolution of her issues with authority and realized positive results. And, over the course of treatment, Joanna became much more tolerant and accepting of her daughter and much more positive, appropriate, and consistent in her communication and limit-setting with Carrie. Although recognizing that their relationship needed further work, Joanna and her therapists agreed that it was significantly improved in comparison to what it had been at the outset.

Follow-up is difficult when a family leaves the area. However, we have been encouraged by occasional contact by letter from Joanna, including a note two months after she moved in which she enclosed a release of information form, indicating that we were to provide a treatment summary to a child guidance clinic in her new home town. The note thanked us for our patience with her and asked that the treatment summary be forwarded as soon as possible so that she and Carrie could enter treatment there and "keep on working."

OBSTACLES TO TREATMENT

Several complicating factors presented themselves as obstacles to treatment in this case. A major problem to be addressed both early on and then periodically throughout therapy was Joanna's significant difficulty in dealing appropriately with authority figures. This was especially problematic during the early phase of treatment, since Joanna, referred into therapy by the Dependency Court system, tended to see the clinic and her therapists as arms of the court. This resulted in her responding to her therapists with the same anger and absence of trust that she expressed toward the "system." In both group and individual therapy, Joanna's therapists expended substantial effort in assisting her to differentiate between the court system, which she perceived as cold, judgmental, and punitive, and the supportive, helping nature of the therapeutic relationship.

A second obstacle to be overcome before being able to address the presenting problem of Carrie's abuse and its sequelae was Joanna's own history of sexual abuse as a child, for which treatment was never sought. In order for her to deal appropriately with her daughter's abuse, Joanna first needed to confront her own abuse and the feelings associated with it. Only by doing this would she be able to respond to her daughter's needs without her own overdetermined, unresolved issues interfering and causing anger and denial.

Another problematic area was Joanna's active alcohol abuse during the early months of treatment. Although she did not appear for sessions in an intoxicated state, her refusal for several months to admit that a problem existed and her efforts to conceal it from her therapists eventually proved to be a significant impediment to treatment. When finally recognized, this obstacle was overcome by her agreement to take a referral to treatment in a program specializing in alcohol abuse.

A final obstacle to treatment, not only in this case but in a great many others seen by the authors is the dilemma presented by the legal mandate that therapists report suspected child abuse or endangerment to the authorities. While this mandate is unarguably necessary, the client's awareness of it can drastically affect the level of trust between client and therapist. It also serves to blur the distinction between the therapist and the "system," a distinction which, as indicated earlier, can be a critical factor in the formation of the therapeutic alliance. Because reporting laws exist, and for good reason, it is imperative that issues related to anger, disappointment, and perceptions of betrayal by the therapist be acknowledged and dealt with openly as part of therapy.

OTHER SYSTEMS INVOLVED

As indicated in the case description section, Joanna and Carrie were referred to us by the County Department of Children's Services following the Dependency Court detention hearing. The role of the Children's Services caseworker and the close working relationship between our agency and the caseworker are documented in detail in other sections of this chapter. As is often the case with court-referred families, close collaboration was essential to the effective treatment of the family. It is extremely doubtful that Joanna and her daughter would have entered therapy when they did or remained in treatment long enough to address any issues of importance without the supervision and insistence of the caseworker.

Following Joanna's acknowledgment of her alcoholism, we also maintained ongoing contact with the treatment program she entered, and this served to reassure us that she was in fact committed to addressing this problem and to developing alternative, positive ways of coping with problems. For Carrie's treatment, periodic contact and consultation with her teachers and the school system were also considered to be of great importance.

MISTAKES

Reviewing this case for mistakes we may have made was a somewhat painful process for us, since errors are always more obvious in hindsight than when we are immersed in day-to-day work with a case. The most glaring mistake was the manner in which we dealt with the transfer to a new therapist midway through treatment when Mr. Adams completed his internship. By reassigning them to a new male therapist without taking into consideration the impact of the loss of the first therapist, we nearly lost the family. Joanna's easy acceptance of Mr. Adams' imminent departure when it was first raised made it easy to overlook her true response to the change, although the combination of her behavior (i.e., her increasing withdrawal from the treatment process leading to the loss of her sobriety) and her history of abandonment, loss, and difficulty in relationships with men should have signaled to us that this would create a crisis of significant proportions for her. Her requests that one of the senior staff (Dr. Damon or Dr. Hall-Marley) take over when Mr. Adams left were not taken seriously enough, probably because they alternated with comments indicating Joanna's wish for another male therapist. In hindsight, we should have transferred the case from Mr. Adams to one of the permanent staff who already had a standing relationship with Joanna and Carrie, rather than relying on the continuity of the group alone to sustain their commitment to therapy. Although this eventually happened when Dr. Hall-Marley took over the case, significant problems may have been avoided had it been done in the first place. In fact, with subsequent similar cases, we have attempted whenever possible to transfer cases after the first year of treatment to permanent staff when the first therapist is an intern with a time-limited tenure at the agency; as a result we have seen fewer significant crises occurring as a consequence of the transfer.

A second action we took that might be construed as a mistake was the letter we sent to Mrs. Kennedy for court without Joanna's awareness. Her poor attendance at the time the letter was sent in fact precluded our reviewing it with her. However, when she did return to treatment and the issue of our report was discussed, she indicated that she was less angry with the actual content of the letter than with the fact that we sent it without her knowledge. Given the difficulties presented by her nonattendance at the time, it is hard to see other ways we could have handled the situation responsibly. Nonetheless, it does reinforce for us the importance of reviewing such documents with clients, not for the purpose of changing the report in any substantive way, but to provide them with a sense of control whenever possible.

THERAPISTS' REACTIONS TO THE CASE

Our reactions to this case initially were in general characterized by feelings of frustration and of being overwhelmed. Although many of the issues presented were similar to those in other cases with which we have dealt, the unpredictable vacillation between excessive expressions of anger and sullen withholding and the extreme emotional lability of both Joanna and Carrie were frustrating for group and individual therapists. The lack of trust, difficulty in forming a therapeutic alliance, and Joanna's generally adolescent oppositional attitude ("Change me if you can . . . ") contributed to both very slow progress and feelings close to hopelessness on the part of the treatment team during the first several months of therapy. Joanna's denial of Carrie's molestation, her lack of tolerance for Carrie's behavior, and her frequent inability to see anything positive in her daughter created an ongoing risk for overidentification with Carrie, perceiving her as a victim not only of sexual abuse but also of a cold, demanding, and unloving mother. The threat of such overidentification to successful treatment, especially with regard to improvement of the mother-child relationship, is obvious.

Carrie also presented problems that inspired negative countertransference in group and individual therapists—her social awkwardness, chronic testing of limits, and constant initiation of inappropriate physical contact with peers and adults made it difficult to generate feelings of acceptance and positive regard for her. The physical contact with therapists was a significant issue in this regard. Even when it was not sexualized, Carrie's ongoing attempts to touch or be touched by staff caused feelings of significant discomfort. Careful assessment and introspection revealed that the primary source of discomfort was a realization that Carrie, in demanding such physical attention, was communicating so much neediness that we felt helpless and inadequate to respond. The response, therefore, was one of wanting to push her away and hold her at arm's length to avoid being engulfed by the overwhelming level of need.

The primary way in which these feelings were managed was in ongoing supervision and consultation. In addition to 90-minute group staff meetings each week, there was also weekly supervision of the intern and weekly meetings between Dr. Damon and Dr. Hall-Marley. These supervision and consultation meetings provided a much needed opportunity to ventilate feelings of frustration and to reframe those aspects of the case that engendered feelings of helplessness and hopelessness, thus enabling us to continue working in productive ways with this problematic family. We often used the time to problem-solve around the many ethical and moral dilemmas presented in the context of this case. The final "pay-off" of this mutual support and built-in opportunity for communication and feedback was a growing sense of satisfaction with a job fairly well-done by the final phase of treatment.

Probably the most significant learning experience of this case, aside from the therapeutic considerations already addressed, was one with which most therapists struggle—the need to accept the fact that we have limits, as people and as clinicians. We cannot make a person change, grow, or become aware faster than he or she is willing, and we cannot by ourselves define or meet all the needs of anyone else. In this case, the realization of our own limits enabled us to use that knowledge to help both Carrie and Joanna get some of their needs met elsewhere, by each other, and in the context of a positive, appropriate support network of their own.

3

Development of Expressive Language and the Treatment of Sexual Abuse

SANDRA K. HEWITT

Dr. Hewitt has written about a child who was abused at an early, preverbal age and who clearly elaborated the nature and extent of the sexual abuse only after a considerable time period had elapsed. This is a phenomenon I have also witnessed, in which a child abused prior to his or her second birthday did not recount the abuse until over two years later. There were two critical elements in both Dr. Hewitt's and my cases: the child's language development matured, and the family context changed to be more supportive and receptive to the child's disclosures.

This example is of extrafamilial abuse but, as is most often the case, premorbid family pathology was present. There were clear signs of the need for appropriate parenting techniques prior to the sexual abuse. Sarah was a constitutionally vulnerable child being raised by parents intermittently overwhelmed by day-to-day parenting; they were hard-pressed to meet the needs of an abused child.

It is essential that we follow Dr. Hewitt's lead and go beyond individual therapy with extrafamilially sexual abused children to examine the larger familial context. This enables us to facilitate changes in parenting that can augment the changes the child makes and reinforce the child's appropriate developmental course.

Sarah's overt sexuality appeared to be the behavior that was most disconcerting to the parents. Their reactivity seemed to negatively reinforce Sarah, with the result being increased sexuality.

Other useful suggestions from this case are derived from the frequent return visits of Sarah to the therapist. Initial resolution occurs, and then two additional times, for relatively brief periods, Sarah and her parents return to therapy for continuing problems related to the sexual abuse. I'm sure that for some children episodes of therapy on an as-needed basis are as helpful as a prolonged initial course. Because of the acute nature of the distress, the family is motivated to work and the content to be addressed is usually more readily available. — Editor

THEORETICAL ORIENTATION

In my almost eighteen-year career as a child psychologist, I have come to realize that my practice reflects a variety of strands of influence and is quite eclectic. Operant and social learning behavioral influences have facilitated a pragmatic approach to a variety of behavior problems in this population. I have also come to appreciate the importance of objective behavioral assessment so that specific problems can be targeted.

At the same time, I am influenced by several developmental theories, appropriately so given the population. These include psychoanalytic, cognitive and social developmental approaches. The first enabled me to appreciate primary process, the regulation of emotion, and the concepts of fixation and internalization. The more objective and data-based cognitive and social development theories have helped me to realize not only that young children think differently from the way I do but also that attachments are primary and that failed attachments can have a critical impact in shaping the course of the child's progression into an adult.

Finally, from my doctoral-level training in school psychology, I learned the role of psychological assessment in determining the broad needs of children. In addition, objective observation and evaluation techniques derived from this training have allowed me to observe children and parent-child interaction more systematically, thus leading to more informed and unbiased treatment decisions.

On a more personal note, my "training" as a parent of three children has made me not only humble about the task of childrearing, but also very practical in my response to child behavior problems. Since parents do not want to see their children hurt, rapid and direct resolution is important to them.

When this case began, I was working in a group private practice with at least four other experienced child psychologists. We regularly and rigorously discussed our cases, so I had good access to other professional opinions.

For me, treatment requires an integration of research on traumagenic factors (Finkelhor & Browne, 1985), with the advice of experienced clinicians (Friedrich, 1990). My treatment plan varies depending on the child's premorbid functioning, the nature and extent of the abuse, the child's current psychosocial status, and performance of normal developmental tasks. My aim is to help restore the child to adequate functioning around the normal developmental tasks.

It is critical to understand what sense the child has made of the experience, how he or she is feeling about the abuse and him/herself, and how that understanding has been incorporated into daily life, e.g., a generalized fear of all adolescent males.

I also assess the impact of the abuse on family members and their resultant coping. Since preschoolers are so dependent on their families, at intake I emphasize that work with the child will require parent/caregiver involvement.

DESCRIPTION OF CASE

Sarah, a three-year, eleven-month-old girl had recently been talking repeatedly about "penises, penises, penises . . . Josh put his penis inside me and it felt good, Mom, it felt good." This talk deeply concerned John and Rosemary, her parents. Rosemary informed me that her daughter had been sexually abused by a 14-year-old male babysitter who sat for Sarah between the ages of 18-35 months. Rosemary believed the abuse had occurred some time between the ages of 24-30 months, but it may have been of greater duration. Sarah had been silent about her abuse experience after her initial disclosure at the age of three years, two months. The parents didn't know how to handle this renewed talking of the abuse and desperately wanted help.

John and Rosemary Smith, a middle-class, dual-career couple, had wanted children for many years but had been unable to conceive. Finally, Rosemary became pregnant, and Sarah was later delivered by ceasarian section. From birth, Sarah was a difficult baby, experiencing colic, food allergies, and multiple ear infections, resulting in eustachian tube placement at two. She was described as very active and difficult to soothe. Although parenting had been more stressful than expected, John and Rosemary were deeply committed to this long awaited child. When Rosemary returned to work, Sarah was cared for in in-home day-care settings until she was almost three; then she was transferred to a group day-care setting.

Sarah was also reported as hard to handle by her day care providers. Because of her ear infections, Sarah did not talk until she was two, and even then her speech was difficult to understand and similar to that of a younger child. Physically, she was of good size and seemed to have at least average ability. John and Rosemary had provided numerous enrichment experiences for their child. Their parenting at the time of our initial contact was inconsistent, and they would often give in to Sarah's demands.

When John and Rosemary needed time out from the difficult and new job of parenting, they used a neighborhood adolescent boy to babysit. Sarah loved Josh and looked forward to his coming to play with her. Rosemary gradually became uncomfortable with Josh's sitting because of some things she noticed in Sarah, e.g., increased attention to penises, attention to her vaginal area. Sexual contact was not clearly indicated until

Sarah was three years, two months, about two months after Josh stopped babysitting.

The day of the initial disclosure had been marked by conflict between Rosemary and Sarah. They were trying to patch things up while Sarah was being put to bed. Rosemary recalls Sarah saying something like "Josh has a big tail, not a little tail, a big tail. He showed it to me, Mom." Rosemary asked where he showed it to her and Sarah, in the concrete manner of most preschoolers, pointed to the other room. Rosemary then asked her what Josh did and Sarah pointed to her vagina. Rosemary asked her if it hurt and Sarah said, "No hurt. Daddy has a tail." Rosemary states that she knew then that Sarah had been sexually abused by Josh because it fit with Sarah's earlier, genitally focused behaviors.

The Smiths reported this information to the authorities and Josh was interviewed. Josh did admit to exposing himself to Sarah on two occasions. Because of Sarah's young age and her poor verbal skills, Josh was never charged with any crime, and he did not receive any treatment. His family moved out of the neighborhood shortly after the investigation.

After reporting to the police, Rosemary took Sarah to a pediatrician who specialized in evaluating children who had been sexually abused. The physician's report indicates that Sarah "clearly states that she was sexually abused by Josh. Her verbal report is almost identical to mother's initial report [with Sarah stating] that Josh touched her 'with his big tail', 'right here' [pointing to her crotch]." The report goes on to state that although "Sarah's verbal abilities are limited for her age (three years, three months) [her] temperament [is] clearly not one to be fooled with. It is entirely impossible for her to be taught or coached into any of her statements as she is contrary, stubborn and unwilling to yield to the wishes of others. The abuse was probably not painful and probably not interpreted by her as abusive." Nothing more was done.

Eight months later Sarah began spontaneously to talk about penises and her sexual activity with Josh. What stimulated this talk is unknown. It could be associated with her increased language ability, as her speech had now progressed to the 34-to-38-month level. Another possibility is that, at almost age four, she was expressing verbally the normal, more overt interest four-year-olds express regarding sex and body functions. Whatever the reason, Sarah was now repetitively talking about the events that had occurred 12 to 24 months earlier with Josh.

PSYCHOLOGICAL ASSESSMENT

During an initial intake session, I asked the parents about their needs from therapy, Sarah's current status, her developmental history, and information about the parents and their current status. I learned that Sarah was still seen as a troublesome child at home and at day-care. Her problems included short attention span, difficulties being soothed, acting out, and difficulties getting to sleep. Research has documented that sleep problems are common behavioral difficulties in sexually abused preschoolers (Hewitt & Friedrich, 1991) and reflect the disruption of the abuse and its effect on self-regulation.

Additional early history revealed that Sarah did not walk until 14 months, and she had two major separations from primary caretakers. Rosemary had reconstructive knee surgery when Sarah was six months of age and was away from her for about a month. When Sarah was two years of age Rosemary had hip surgery and Sarah stayed with relatives for about two months. Rosemary said Sarah had some problems with the second separation but not with the first.

Neither parent had a history of sexual abuse. Each felt very guilty about their daughter's abuse, and subsequently they had all but stopped applying any limits to Sarah's behavior. As she became more out-of-control, they felt increasingly angry but they had no strategy for coping with her behavior or their anger.

The Smiths had two needs from therapy: to learn how to handle their daughter, and to prevent Sarah from being damaged for life by the sexual abuse. John, in particular, was concerned about Sarah's having a future normal sexual relationship.

I agreed to help them learn to manage both Sarah's oppositional and sexualized behaviors. Regarding outcome, I did tell the Smiths it was important to treat the child as close as possible to the time the abuse occurred and that Sarah's long-term prognosis was good. Given that Sarah had not been molested by a family member, no apparent force was involved, her family was supportive, and the abuse was of relatively short duration, the literature would support my statement (Friedrich, 1990).

The picture emerging from this intake interview was that of two clients. Sarah had issues with sexual abuse and control to confront. Her parents had their guilt, anger, and sadness to face as well as their daughter's behavior to manage. Behavioral management did not seem realistic until they had addressed the loss and guilt issues.

No psychological testing was done with the parents, given their history of adequate premorbid functioning, and they were willing and able to participate in therapy. Although I usually do behavioral and developmental assessment on child clients, I erred in not getting this with Sarah.

COURSE OF THERAPY

The course of therapy with Sarah reflected features common to therapy with preschoolers: 1. the quick changes the child goes through during these years, and 2. her embeddedness in her family context such that parental issues trigger therapy issues (Kegan, 1982). As a result, therapy with Sarah occurred in three brief and relatively discrete time blocks over the course of 16 months. I will describe each block separately as a different phase. Each individual session with Sarah lasted approximately 60 minutes, with a portion of each session spent with one or both parents to determine progress, review issues that had emerged in the intervening time period, provide consultation for behavioral management, and talk about personal issues related to guilt, etc.

Phase 1

At my first session, Rosemary reported that the past few days she had observed Sarah with her panties off rubbing her vulva against her swing set pole, an activity that had not been reported at day-care. Rosemary wanted to know how to react to this. I suggested that she tell Sarah that her body was special, that she needed to take good care of it, and that to do that outside on the swing was not the right way to take care of it. Rosemary was also to tell her clearly not to do it again. (Later Rosemary informed me with surprise that Sarah had said "okay" to this directive and the behavior stopped.)

My first meeting with Sarah brought me face to face with a dark-haired girl whose short, blunt-cut hair framed two alert eyes. She was of average height for her age and a little bit chubby. Sarah spoke in short choppy sentences and in a very horse, raspy voice, the kind novelists like to call a "whiskey voice." Although interesting in adults, this was odd in a three-year-old. (Several sessions later I discussed with the Smiths the need to refer Sarah for speech and language evaluation. They did this and learned that Sarah was using her vocal cords the wrong way. Sarah would have to learn to create sounds in a new manner, in addition to striving toward the other speech and language goals. This discovery presented yet another loss issue for these parents to process, as well as another management issue, since Sarah did not like speech therapy.)

Sarah separated from her mother and came alone to my office with no problems. I learned the following: she knew some of her colors; her articulation was poor but understandable; her sentence structure was immature; and she would not comply with my suggestions for activities. She wanted to color and that was all she would do. I set firm limits and clear directives, but even then Sarah refused to do any of the evaluation testing I'd planned for this first session. Nevertheless, after talking about her drawings of circles and rainbows (poorly shaped and constructed), her family and day-care structure, her refusal of testing, and her feelings in general, some level of rapport had been established. I had accepted Sarah's comments and productions, and she had accepted me.

I told Sarah that her Mom had told me about Josh and I asked if Sarah could tell me about what games Josh played with her. Sarah replied, "When I take my pants off and get my diaper, him takes him penis and [unintelligible] me." I asked her how that felt and she replied "a little bit tickles, no hurt." I asked her if she would be willing to show me with some dolls I had (SAC dolls) and she was happy to comply. She could not manage multiple doll interaction, but was able to play with a "Josh" doll and "Sarah" doll.

After reviewing body parts and their functions, Sarah spontaneously said "him taking him pants down! Him putting him penis up, him putting him penis up, [it] points to the ceiling!" She went on to repeat this several times while I watched and listened. Then I turned to the Josh doll and told him, "You can't do that anymore, you couldn't do that with kids, and you can't do that with Sarah. That is not the right game to play." Sarah listened quietly and attentively to this exchange.

Shortly after that we left the dolls and she wanted to color again. Now she drew a large, inverted U shaped object on the page, and colored it bright red with some purple on the top end. Neither of us made an interpretation. She then drew a balloon, and our session ended.

I was now able to conceptualize the case in a new way. I believed that Sarah was not scared by any of Josh's touching, but rather she was greatly stimulated. I wanted to begin to open up the area of what Josh had done, but to keep the expression of sexualized behavior within our sessions and not outside, at day-care, in the neighborhood, etc. I wanted the parents to help set limits, but I knew they couldn't until they had dealt with their own guilt and grief.

My second session was with the parents alone. Not only did we talk briefly about Sarah's adjustment and behavior problems, but we also talked about their anger, sense of loss, grief, and fears regarding Sarah's abuse. Helping parents mourn their loss and deal with their guilt over having possibly contributed to their child's abuse is important. Persisting therapy issues with Rosemary and John reflected their guilt over hiring Josh and not having learned of the abuse earlier. I reassured them that it is very hard to tell who will abuse a child—you certainly can't tell by looking at someone—and that they had done the best they could by stopping Josh's involvement immediately when they felt something had gone on. I supported the good parenting I saw them do. Nevertheless, the issues of responsibility for the abuse and subsequent guilt were ones we would return to frequently. Often, when parents can get past some of their guilt, they can take back the responsibilities of parenting, e.g., setting limits and administering consequences. At this point, I reassured them, helped them process their guilt, and then asked them to help me with some limits around Sarah's talk and play about sex. I asked if they would remind her that it was okay to talk about her experience and other sex behaviors, but now we needed to try to keep that conversation for our sessions. They were to tell her "talking to Sandy is the best place to talk about it." They agreed to try.

Later that week, I had my second individual session with Sarah. John brought her (I had asked that they share the job of bringing her to the appointments as their work schedules would allow). In the brief parent consultation time I typically schedule along with individual appointments, he reported that there was more talk about penises at home, "penises, penises, penises, point to the ceiling." He was quite upset about this. I again encouraged him to direct Sarah to discuss these things only in our sessions.

However, Sarah did not repeat these phrases in our sessions, usually playing instead. Sarah chose the SAC dolls, Josh and Sarah, from our last play for this session. When she brought Josh out she took down his pants and said "him stick up him penis and Sarah get mad. She no be your buddy no more." With that she sat Josh down. It was clear she had internalized my comment from the previous session, adding her own affect. She repeated this sequence a few times and I repeated her words, affirming her and reaffirming her statements. She then chose to color some balloons, making mad and sad balloons and talking about her parents being mad and sad at her.

She session ended with a challenge. I told Sarah that it was time to stop and she refused to stop. She would not pick up toys, would not leave the room, and would not comply with my directives. So I picked her up and removed her from the room and told her she could not disregard my requests and that we were in fact done with our session. Sarah screamed and yelled as I did this, and I wondered what kind of resistance she would present to her mother for the next session!

After processing the intensity of her response and the level of repetition I was seeing, I began to suspect that there had been multiple incidents of sexual play, over time, with Sarah. In my experience, this level of reaction is related to the intensity of the abuse. I was beginning to believe that more had occurred than one or two exposures. I knew I would have to communicate this at some time to the Smiths and I was worried about the impact this news would have on their anger and guilt. Sarah's behavior also reminded me of the impact that such early abuse has on young children. Although Sarah could not verbalize what she was experiencing at the time it occurred, she had very clearly stored the memory and was able to play it out. I have learned from Sarah and many other young children that abuse experienced preverbally is not assigned to oblivion but is most often retained and sometimes played out when, verbally and developmentally, the child is ready.

The next therapy session was preceded by a collateral contact with the day-care center. Sarah's lead teacher told me that Sarah exhibited numerous behavior problems. That week they had found her lying in a cupboard with one of the boys. He had his hand in her pants and she had been undressing. Sarah had also stripped naked in the bathroom.

We talked about these behaviors as probably having their origins in the earlier abuse and I suggested that the day-care teacher handle Sarah's behavior by informing her that "the rules" in the center were that she must keep her private parts covered and that she could not be naked there. Staff members should be firm about these rules, but kind. Day-care consultation is necessary in these cases because behaviors certainly raise the possibility of rejection by other adults or peers. The emotional impact of these behaviors on caregivers cannot be overlooked.

Session four was held with both parents, who were very ashamed of Sarah's behavior in the center. They knew she was already a behavior problem there and worried about how her behavior reflected on them as parents. The session ranged over the topics of parental limits of responsibility, grief and loss issues, current behavior problems and limits. We talked about Sarah's bedtime problems and made some plans to deal with them.

The fifth session was held with Sarah alone. Rosemary informed me in our time together that in the last week Sarah's acting out had markedly decreased, and she had been better behaved at home and at day-care. Sarah had told her parents after day-care one day "I don't pull my pants down."

During our session we played with the tea set. Sarah set up a tea party for us and again used the Josh doll. As we sat down to eat, Sarah turned to Josh and told him he was bad and he had to sit down. Then she gave him these rules: "Josh, you no put your penis in kid's bottoms. You can't do that, I not be your friend anymore!" Then she had Josh sit apart from our tea party until Josh "knew the rules." Sarah decided he knew the rules after 15 minutes and she let him come back. Toward the end of the hour, I read *It's My Body* (Freeman, 1984) to her and she listened quietly. We ended the session by making Play Doh spaghetti. No more sexual play was initiated or discussed. Sarah helped to clean up and left without incident when I told her it was time to end.

Our sixth session, several weeks later, found Sarah's behavior improved. She still talked to her dad about penises at bedtime and he found this upsetting. I suggested that he listen quietly, but not reinforce this discussion by reacting very much. He needed to continue to encourage Sarah to talk about this in therapy instead of at bedtime. John reported that their behavioral management of Sarah was more consistent and was resulting in more compliance from Sarah around bedtimes and other limits.

My time alone with Sarah that session found her making negative comments about Josh for the first time. Earlier during the week, Sarah told

Rosemary that Josh pinched her and had told her not to tell her parents. Sarah told me "Him stick out him penis and me not yike that." She said he had done this in her room, "in my bed," "him took him pants down, penis stick out." After this verbalization, Sarah directed me to put the Josh doll's penis in the Goldilock doll's crotch. At the end of the session she spontaneously took the Josh doll and told him to apologize to the Goldilocks doll. She said, "Josh, you can't put penis in Goldilock's part. You listen to the rule, Josh!" The session ended.

One month lapsed between this session and the next, our seventh session. Mutual vacations contributed to the time lapse. Therapy had begun in May and run through July. It was now early September and the Smiths reported a wonderful vacation with no sexual talk and no mention of sexual incidents. John and Rosemary were able to set a structure for Sarah and maintain it. Their processing of guilt and loss in the interim had helped free them to provide the needed rules and limits for Sarah. Things were going well for everyone.

The first session after vacation was with Sarah alone. Early in the session, she again chose the Josh doll for play, and said "him put him penis in a vagina [while pointing to her own], him can't do that." In response to my questioning, she indicated that he hadn't put it any other place on her body. Then she spontaneously told Josh that he "can't get mad at me like that." For the rest of the hour, she abandoned the Josh doll in favor of nonsexual play with the dollhouse.

Collateral contact with the day-care two weeks after Sarah's visit indicated that she still had some behavior problems. However, Sarah had made no mention of any sexual content, and no sexualized behavior had been observed.

Sarah's eighth session was a week after contact with the day-care. During this session she told me three things she wanted me to tell Josh not to do: 1. "Tell Josh not to use dirty words." 2. "Tell Josh not to tell kids to take their pants down." 3. "Tell Josh don't hurt nobody." After this brief instruction to me, Sarah turned to the dollhouse and for the rest of the session played quite appropriately with no unusual or problematic themes. Rosemary reported only a few behavior problems. Although therapy had resumed, there was no talk about sex. By all accounts, Sarah was looking very good. Therapy had now occurred over a five-month period, with stable behavior for the last two, and although there had been sexual content to therapy sessions, it was minimal and appropriate. I stopped regular sessions at this time and shifted to a "call as necessary" agreement with her parents and phone follow-up within a month.

John and Rosemary had experienced a difficult time with their guilt in the course of therapy. They had been able to feel less guilty, but the had also gotten more in touch with their anger and felt some compensation for their loss was due. They had talked in therapy about initiating a civil suit and now, after September, they sought legal assistance in bringing a civil suit against Josh. I wrote a letter to the attorney documenting my involvement and my opinion regarding the nature and extent of sexual contact.

I initiated phone follow-up in late October. Things were continuing to be fine. However, two months later, Sarah returned to therapy. There had been no sexual talk or play and behavior problems had been quite manageable until Sarah was found by day-care staff in the bathroom with a boy. Both had their pants down and they were hugging and kissing. Sarah told her Mom that his pants were down and his penis was in her vagina. This triggered a regression and Rosemary told me, "Sarah is talking about sex all the time again." Needless to say, both parents were upset, and I wondered what I had forgotten to do in therapy that would have Sarah acting out in this manner.

Further inquiry into the incident indicated that Donny, the boy with whom Sarah was involved in sexual play, was new at day-care. He had just been adopted by a family after a termination of parental rights had been completed. He had a documented history of physical abuse, but the adoptive family was unaware of sexual abuse, at least until now. Sarah was four years, five months when she returned to therapy for the second time.

Phase 2

The first session of this second round was held with John and Rosemary alone. They vented their anger and frustration at the day-care and the recurrence of the abuse and then pretty quickly pulled themselves together to deal with this latest problem.

The second session began as a conjoint meeting with Sarah and her parents. In the session, when discussing what had happened, Sarah told her parents that what Donny did was naughty and what Josh did was naughty. John carefully affirmed his daughter's observations. John, Rosemary, and I began adult-level discussion about some aspect of this incident. While we were talking I became aware that Sarah had gotten the Josh doll out of the bag and was holding it up near her face and talking quietly to it. She had removed the jeans, leaving the underwear on, and she was holding the genitals near her face and pulling the elastic on the underwear out, peeking in the pocket she created and then letting it snap back. Not wanting to draw undue attention to this play by having everyone focus on it, yet wanting to know what was going on, I asked Sarah's parents to leave so I could play with Sarah alone.

When her parents left, I asked Sarah to show me what she was doing.

She repeated the sequence of behavior and in a singsong voice announced "find the animals, find the animals." She told me that this was a game that Josh used to play with her. I was impressed that at four years, five months, this child could clearly, with appropriate affect and intonation, replay what had happened to her most probably prior to age three. After I understood the behavior, I asked what we should do about Josh's game and Sarah suggested we tell Josh the rules for touching again. I supported Sarah's ability to be in charge of the rules and her boundaries.

The third session of this phase was about two weeks later. Donny had been removed to another classroom and her parents reported no more problems at day-care and no more comments about sex or behavior problems at home. Sarah initially had us say the rules about Josh again, and then she initiated normal, nonsexualized play for the remainder of the hour. This was our last regular session, and I relied on phone follow-up as needed for the next few weeks. Sarah was functioning well with progress maintained.

Phase 3

Six months later, two weeks prior to her fifth birthday, Sarah returned again. Three weeks before Rosemary's phone call, Sarah had told her mother that she needed to see me. The parents had not followed through with a phone call. Then at day-care Sarah had again been found with Donny. He was lying down, his penis was out, and Sarah was piling rocks on top of it. John and Rosemary were incensed that Donny had been placed back in her group without their knowledge and contrary to the promises that had been made to them by the day-care staff. Donny, who had been back in Sarah's group for four days, had not been involved in any therapy. The Smiths were assured that Donny would be removed again. Sarah had been drawing pictures of penises at home and John described her as "acting sexy" by "wiggling her butt." (Sarah had also just been terminated in speech therapy. She had proven a difficult client, but some progress had been made. Her voice quality was better, as was her fluency and her articulation.)

I had expected the sexual material to be settling down now as she was about to enter kindergarten and begin to approach latency. Both my experience and the literature suggest that overt sexuality begins to submerge at this time (Rutter, 1980). Sarah's first individual session was marked by her anger. She strapped on a holster gun and said she was gonna shoot Josh if he did it again, and she "wanted" the police to come. She then had the Josh doll pee, and repeated this three times. She initially asked me to hold Josh's penis while he peed. I suggested it was Josh's job to hold his own penis while he peed, not mine, and stated further that this was a private thing and not something to be done with others. Sarah seemed to assent to this.

The second session, one week later, coincided with Sarah's complaining of tummyaches for a few days and not wanting to go back to day-care. Sarah was saying that "Donny is bothering me." Rosemary called the day-care and learned that Donny had been put back in her class again. The day-care staff felt that Sarah should learn to control her behavior and that Donny had a right to be in that class, too, as it was a better placement for him. John and Rosemary removed Sarah from the day-care center after this last betrayal. She was placed in an in-home setting with a firm but pleasant mother who had several other children, ages six, five, four, two, and two infants. This day-care provider was quite clear regarding rules for behavior and was quite firm with Sarah.

Individual playtime again began with the donning of a holster and guns. Sarah took the Josh doll out again and took his penis out and she helped him pee. I was again clear about this being a private job. I told Sarah that Josh was to do his peeing alone and that he was not to show his private part. It was his job to hold it himself. It was not Sarah's job to hold it. Sarah turned to me and said, "He's gonna do it again." I asked her what we should do about that and she said, "Put him in the chair for seven minutes." We did this and Sarah had him sit there until "he learned the rules." The rest of the hour evolved around Josh wanting to come out with his penis and Sarah keeping him in line with her guns. Rosemary's individual consultation time during this session focused on the fact that the bedtime problems were back in full force. Sarah was not getting to sleep until 10 p.m. most nights. We discussed handling these problems by being firm but clear and insisting on compliance.

The third session found Sarah much more relaxed at home and in my office. Her parents reported that she was adjusting very well at her new day-care home and that, furthermore, she was falling asleep by 8 p.m. with no problems. They were setting consequences for her behavior and they were pleased with the results. Alone, Sarah's play centered around the dollhouse, the toilet, and Josh. He was going to the bathroom, and Sarah would smile at this activity. She said to me toward the end of this play, "He's gonna show his penis again," and she smiled. I was concerned about Sarah's apparent pleasure at this.

Session four was with the parents. Further improvement in behavior was reported, with Sarah going to bed without a parent lying down with her. She was also doing very well at day-care. However, Sarah was talking to the neighborhood children about Josh. Rosemary had told her not to but instead to direct her concerns to me or herself or John.

I took this case to a full staff meeting for consultation. My impression was that Sarah found the peeing sexually stimulating and that playing it through did not seem to lessen the intensity. Sexualized behaviors had recurred because of lack of promised controls. I felt it was now time to put controls on in the session and that I needed to help Sarah put this stimulating material away and get on with the task of preparing for kindergarten entry. In our staff meeting we reviewed possible causes for her behavior — the violation of the rules at her day-care, her parents' problems with rules, Sarah's own ambivalence about this material — and we decided that therapeutically it was time to "put away" the sexual behavior in the session. I had always felt that children played out issues until they were resolved and that it was not "good therapy" to direct kids to put material away while it was still surfacing in play. But in Sarah's case the play seemed not to be resolving anything. To be able to function, Sarah needed a clear reiteration of structure and appropriate procedures.

Session five was planned to be with Sarah alone for the "big put away," but during the initial parent check-in time, Rosemary indicated that during the week Sarah had tried to stand up to pee and she had gotten all wet. It was as if she was experimenting with not having a penis. It dawned on me then that I had not done any sex education with this child and that the deficit might be part of the penis focused behavior.

Together Rosemary and I used the SAC dolls and explained that boys have penises, but girls have vaginas. We explained these as very special places that Sarah could be very proud to have because that meant she could grow babies some day when she was grown up, just like her mother grew her. Not having a penis was not a loss; having a vagina was a special and wonderful thing. Sarah was very interested in this and attended well. Later she expressed great pride in her newfound anatomy.

When alone with me in the sixth session, Sarah chose to play with Josh, a girl, and a baby doll. Josh had to sit on a chair until he could care for the baby correctly. Sarah said Josh was going to go to the bathroom and take his penis out and it was going to point up. I said he could not. I said he was not to do that anymore. I then had Josh tell Sarah that he could do the peeing alone, that it was his private part and he wanted to be alone with it, and she should be alone with her private part.

The seventh session of this third phase began with Sarah's choosing not to play with the dolls but instead to draw rainbows. We did this for a while and then I brought Josh out and together we formally put "Josh and his private parts" away in his bag.

I was to see Sarah two weeks later, but she had started school and we could not find an appointment time. Rosemary reported that she was doing very well, no sex talk or actions had been noted, and she was enjoying school and doing well with the adjustment. Phone contact three weeks later again found her to be doing well, with no behavior or sexual problems. Sarah's energies were focused on the new adventure of school and her adjustment to it.

The three discrete phases of therapy included a total of 19 sessions, four of which were with the parents alone, two that involved Sarah and one or both of her parents, and the remaining 13 individual.

SPECIFIC TECHNIQUES USED IN THERAPY

Techniques used included the process of play therapy coupled with frequent use of SAC dolls, parent consultation, behavior management techniques to support the parenting process, and consultation to the day-care regarding the handling of sexually acting out children.

OUTCOME OF TREATMENT

Near the end of Sarah's treatment, I decided to leave my private practice and take a position at Children's Hospital of St. Paul as codirector of a regional child abuse resource center. I was unable to schedule a farewell meeting with Sarah, but told Rosemary of my change and asked her to relay it to Sarah. I did not hear from Rosemary for about a year. Then she called me to say that she needed help again. This time there were no sexual concerns or problems, and there hadn't been any since Sarah left therapy the previous fall. Now Sarah was telling her friends she was sad and wanted to die. I referred Sarah to one of my colleagues in private practice.

It appeared that the Smiths' behavior management skills had declined without regular maintenance and that Sarah was again out of control at home and having problems in school. There were no additional sexual concerns. The results of my colleague's evaluation indicated a need for a referral to a neurologist, who diagnosed Sarah as having both a learning disability and an attention deficit disorder. Because of a family history of Tourette's syndrome, Sarah could not be put on medication and a program of special services was instituted. IQ testing revealed an overall average IQ, but with wide scatter. At last report, Sarah was again stabilized behaviorally, she was getting specialized assistance in school, and her parents were getting support from school and the therapist as needed. It was also about this time that the civil suit begun many months ago was resolved and Sarah and her parents were awarded damages for the sexual abuse. The family was also planning to adopt a child in the near future, and Sarah was about to become a big sister.

OBSTACLES TO TREATMENT

There seemed to be two obstacles to treatment, besides Sarah's relatively young age and delayed expressive language development. The first was the parents' reaction to the molestation, which interfered with their parenting of Sarah. In addition, in an effort to deny that abuse occurred, they were seemingly reluctant at times to pursue therapy as intensively as they might have.

The second pertained to the day-care center's relative insensitivity to Sarah's needs, even after seeing very clearly Donny's impact on her sexual behavior. This rekindled Sarah's problems and also added to her parents' frustration, further interfering with their parenting.

OTHER SYSTEMS INCLUDED

Sarah's day-care center was the only other system involved, since Child Protection Services were not ongoing and the civil litigation required only minimal involvement from me. Overt sexual behavior expressed by children is usually a problem in day-care or school settings, and it can often lead to staff and peer rejection of the child. Teaching the staff at Sarah's day-care to handle sexual acting-out behavior was critical to preserving Sarah's placement there. I volunteered to do two sessions of on-site consultation regarding sexual abuse, its signs and symptoms, and methods of intervention. This helped give the day-care staff some perspective on Sarah's behavior, helped them not to react against her, and helped them cope in a positive way with problems she presented.

MISTAKES

When you've completed a therapy case and look back across several intervening years, it's easy to see where you've made mistakes and where, with new knowledge and more experience, you'd do things differently. My biggest worry with this case was that I'd made an error in having Sarah "put away" the sexualized play with Josh. Fortunately, I've been able to hear about Sarah through my colleague and I periodically talk to Rosemary (she is now one of our center's volunteer support parents for new families coming in with sexual abuse cases). The abuse issues have not resurfaced, so from an overt behavioral perspective terminating when I did seemed warranted. I think that sexual issues will be played out over time as Sarah matures and adjusts to her history.

My approach to this case would be relatively unchanged, although more careful assessment of Sarah at the very beginning might have demonstrated how entrenched her preoccupation with Josh was. This case did prompt much new learning on my part, however. When Rosemary's calls about Sarah's new acting out would come, I would wonder, "Now what did I do wrong last time that this is happening again?" Eventually, I could see that maybe I had not made some great mistake, but that it was a matter of particular circumstances bringing new aspects of the case to light. I came to give myself greater permission to see therapy not as a one-time thing with these kids, but rather as a process that may need to be ongoing over a wide developmental span.

THERAPIST'S REACTION TO THE CASE

From Sarah's case, I learned that I can give parents permission to feel okay even if a problem around the abuse occurs again. These are not easy issues, and we cannot control the environments of our children so that situations that raise old ghosts are never encountered. The issues do come up, and we do need to help our children cope. John and Rosemary taught me to respect the courage it takes for parents to face and deal with the reemergence of issues that they thought were finally in the past.

I get very frustrated with systems that will not investigate abuse allegations made by preverbal children and with systems that are able to provide little safety for these children when they are at risk. Sarah's ability to verbalize what happened, even with speech problems, argues for the need to believe very young children.

Even after many years of work with these difficult cases, I still learn constantly from the children and parents I see. As I have developed a greater respect for the complexities of these situations, I have come to respect the fact that there may be many ways to effectively treat these cases, depending on the style of the therapist and the match with the child. The last thing I learned with this case was to remember the importance of staying in touch with my colleagues for regular case discussions. There is no clear body of knowledge on which to rely in treating these cases, and colleagues' experience is often crucial.

4

Treatment of a Ritually Abused Preschooler

ANN M. UHEREK

I believe my reaction to the horrific sexual exploitation of children is similar to that of most therapists who work in this area. It bothers us a great deal and we oftentimes have difficulty putting words to our feelings. We sometimes take these feelings home with us. Continuing to work in a therapeutic manner with these children requires a great deal of effort and skill on our part. Because we are sensitive to their victimization, we work hard not to revictimize. But yet some of what we do, e.g., uncovering abuse, talking about shame, is distressful to the child.

Recently child sexual abuse therapists have begun to see occasional cases of ritualistic sexual abuse in which satanic elements seem to be a central part. This requires us to go several steps beyond the initial awareness that terrible sexual abuse does exist to a realization that it is not only horrific but almost beyond one's personal framework to understand.

Dr. Uherek does us a service by writing about this case, not only because she guides us through the gradual unfolding of the abuse but also because, in the same way that the parents needed to be supported regarding their reaction to the abuse of their child, we as therapists do as well. Parents have depressive reactions and worry about whether their child will ever by normal again,; we do, too.

Several key points emerge from my reading of this case. The first is the clear bind the therapist has in balancing the dual role of extricating information from this child so as to provide legal intervention and also providing therapy at the child's own pace. It is very easy for the child to associate the therapist with aversive feelings and so feel that she is not a safe, trustworthy individual. The child may then resist coming to therapy. However, we do often wear two hats; if we feel wearing our investigatory hat has resulted in severe damage to the relationship with the child, we need to refer the child elsewhere for treatment.

A technique I use for getting around some of this is to explain to the child that every session has a "working" portion and a "play" portion. We then negotiate to "work" a certain time period, and I help the child process reactions to the "work." This has been very helpful to me in balancing these multiple roles.

A second issue pertains to dealing with one's own countertransference to a child who has been so traumatized. Our reaction can interfere with therapy, either because we find it hard to ask the child to talk about the experience or because we feel hopeless in helping the child overcome such terrible abuse. Good case supervision can help to correct these negative reactions.

Finally, we often cannot complete the therapy at this developmental juncture. Whether or not therapy will be needed at different stages of the child's life cycle is commonly asked. For many children we need to anticipate that further therapy will be needed and to plan appropriately. — Editor

RITUALISTIC CHILD ABUSE is a phenomenon in which sexual, physical, and emotional abuse occurs in the context of bizarre and unusual rituals, torturous "games," and cult or satanic worship activities. In many cases, the children are victims as well as participants as "abusers" of other children. In effect, an effort is made to teach or indoctrinate the child into the "abusing group." These children often present in treatment as highly conflicted with a wide array of symptoms. The identification of victims of this type of abuse is still relatively new and specialized. The majority of health professionals are unaware of this form of child maltreatment and thus fail to recognize signs of ritualistic abuse in the histories of their patients. In addition, child victims of ritualistic abuse are usually too terrified to disclose their experiences, so most cases go unreported. However, several adult survivors of this type of child abuse have come forward and have provided us with insights into long-term effects on the personality (Antonelli, 1988; Marron, 1989; Smith & Pazder, 1980; Spencer, 1989). As recent surveys of the country by organizations interested in ritualistic abuse, such as the American Professional Society on the Abuse of Children (APSAC, 1990) and Believe the Children (1987) indicate, reports of ritualistic abuse are increasing and continue to occur in many areas of the country.

AUTHOR'S THEORETICAL ORIENTATION

In my private practice of psychology, I have found that a significant number of the children referred to me have been victims of abuse. Evaluation and treatment with these child victims often must be structured so as to

meet external requirements, such as legal mandates for child abuse reporting and the possible use of clinical material from therapy sessions in the
trial of the abuser, as well as the individual needs of the child.

When I am asked to interview children who are possible victims of abuse,
I pay careful attention to the environmental stimuli I present in my office,
as well as the child's behavior with me. In short-term evaluation cases, I
limit the child's access to specific toys and materials (e.g., drawing materials, anatomical dolls, playhouse and family doll figures) and tend to be
more active and focused in asking questions and eliciting information.
Since abused children often avoid the topic of their abuse experiences
through random, frenetic play, a child who has access to all of the toys
may spend much time "building and crashing" blocks or playing with
trucks. Other children avoid the topic through a careful inspection and
reorganization of all the toys in the room, resisting my interventions and
effectively using up all the time available for discussion. So, when time is
limited and I want to see just how immediately accessible the information
on abuse may be, I limit access to distractions from the topic of abuse.

In the case of a child who comes in for treatment and has already been
evaluated for abuse by others competent in the field, I am generally much
more nondirective, allowing the child to explore my playroom undisturbed,
with free access to toys and drawing materials. Observations of a child's
behavior during the first five to ten minutes in a structured playroom sup-
plied with a wide variety of toys (e.g., materials useful in expressing aggression, loose and more creative materials, small objects for obsessional and
compulsive play) provides me with valuable information about how the
child copes with an ambiguous, unstructured setting and what defenses they
use to manage anxiety.

In addition, I watch to see how easily the child opens up to me and
whether he makes use of my presence for comfort or reassurance when
he is uncertain, anxious, or frustrated. An immediate negative response,
excessive fear, or a guarded and defensive stance may indicate emotional
difficulties. Anxiety and immediate negativity often characterize the initial
interactions with children who have previously been harmed by significant
adults in their lives. Even if they start out with a positive attitude, as soon
as my exploration of issues touches upon any material associated with
conflict or anxiety, they may react negatively. Anxiety is often expressed
by young children as fear. Thus, the immediate nuances of the relationship
between the child and the therapist and the various changes that occur in it
are valuable sources of information regarding the presence of issues to be
worked through.

In the therapy session children express fantasies, wishes, and actual experiences in a symbolic way through play and games. In general, the thera-

pist's task is not only to pick out the meaning of the separate symbols in the play but also to assess the whole behavior during the session. Each observation and interpretation must then be fit into the scheme of reported and observed behavior outside the session. Single elements can be interpreted only in light of the whole treatment situation, which includes the sequences of play in the individual session and the connections made between bits of play as they have occurred over time.

I look at how children change their games in the sessions and what means they use to express the content of memories and fantasies. Repetitions of the same "play thought" are considered preoccupations, which need to be interpreted and clarified to relieve anxiety. The intensity with which the games are played and the urgency of the play also reflect a child's underlying emotional state. All of children's behavior is considered to have a method and some meaning. However, while play may be young children's most important medium of expression, children talk as well, and the things they say have as much value in helping the therapist understand their view of themselves and their world as the statements of adults in psychotherapy.

Verbal communication between myself and the child is also important in establishing a therapeutic alliance. In the beginning, the child does not understand why he is seeing a therapist. There is no motivation for treatment. But the relief from anxiety that the child feels after his fears and abuse experiences are acknowledged creates a motivation for treatment. When I make a comment or interpretation about what I see in his play, the child typically acknowledges my words with pleasure or some sign of relief — if I am right. Correct interpretation of the play tends to have rapid effects. The child will elaborate and expand his play and reveal even deeper levels of feelings. If I am wrong, however, I will be ignored, corrected, yelled at, or even chastised for my stupidity.

A number of issues separate ritualistically abused children from those who are victims of physical and sexual abuse within the family or by pedophiles outside the home. In addition to symptoms characteristic of children who have been sexually and physically abused, several specific preoccupations and behaviors are unique to this population, including:

1. Preoccupation with urine and feces, including references to putting these substances on the face or in the mouth; difficulties with toilet training associated with fears of feces and urine.
2. Aggressive play that has a marked sadistic quality; mutilation themes dominate their play and they act out severing, sawing, twisting or pulling off body parts, including harming animals; or discussion of animals being hurt, mutilated or killed.

3. Preoccupations with death and questions that are notable because of their bizarre quality (e.g., whether we eat people after they are dead); fears of their own death or that of loved ones (e.g., fears that something foreign was put inside their body that will kill them).
4. Fear of going to jail, being tied up or caged.
5. Preoccupations with the devil, magic, potions, supernatural powers, crucifixions.
6. References to people visiting the school who are not school personnel. These may include talk of "my other mommy, my other daddy . . . " References to people in scary costumes, especially monsters, ghosts, devils, dracula.
7. References to sexual activity with other children at school. Statements that the child witnessed sexual acts between adults, adults and children, people and animals, etc.
8. Atypical and unusual school outings, e.g., going to people's houses not associated with the school.
9. Marks and bruises on the child with no explanation; unusual bruising or cuts, particularly marks made in patterns.
10. Excessive fear of visiting the doctor's office; talk of "bad medicine," pills or injections; fears of blood tests and questions whether the child will die from the blood test or whether someone will drink the blood; statements that someone else was forced to ingest blood, urine, feces, human or animal body parts.

Frequently, the events ritualistically abused children describe do not make sense in terms of everyday living, yet the children do not present as excessively involved in fantasy or generally out of touch with reality. Also to be noted as unusual is the amount of "primitive" material that is presented almost immediately and played out in therapy (e.g., use of urine and feces to hurt or punish someone; sadistic fantasies and talk of genital sexual interactions such as oral copulation, genital fondling, and talk of anal and vaginal penetration with various body parts and objects). While this type of material may emerge in play therapy after months of intensive treatment, children who have suffered ritualistic abuse often present such "primitive material" in the first one or two sessions, with little work on the therapist's part to reduce resistance and decrease inhibitions. Also, whether the interview methods were directive or nondirective seems to make little difference in eliciting the "flow" of primitive material and descriptions of abuse.

CASE DESCRIPTION

Stevie, an attractive four-and-a-half-year-old boy, attended a neighborhood preschool five mornings a week for approximately six months. His mother brought him in at the suggestion of her pediatrician because he appeared extremely anxious and was having frequent nightmares about skeletons and people poking him. He was also very afraid to take a nap and was reported to become "violent" when he woke from a nap. He frequently asked his mother before going to sleep, "Will you be here when I wake up?" Stevie's mother also stated that every time she left him at school he would scream and cry and hang onto the gate. He would frequently try to climb the fence to get out. Although she attributed this behavior to normal difficulties adjusting to school and separation from her, there was little significant change in his behavior even after six months.

Stevie was reported to have had a change in temperament since he started at the preschool. His mother said that he seemed "angry inside" and was very irritable. He also exhibited severe temper tantrums over small events, a problem never present before. While attending school, Stevie would often plead with his mother to keep him home, saying he would be "good." His mother attributed this to Stevie's desire to stay home like his younger sibling. Stevie also exhibited a recent increase in clingy behavior and a desire for physical contact (e.g., at a friend's birthday party, he refused to leave his mother's side and sometimes insisted on sitting on her lap). He also asked to hold his favorite blanket again, which he had stopped taking with him at age three and a half. The mother was unable to determine any reason for the change in his behavior, other than his attendance at the preschool.

Both parents are college graduates, and Stevie's father is self-employed as an architect. His mother left her position at the marketing department of a large firm when Stevie was born. In the past year, she had started doing some temporary work as a consultant in marketing to various companies, but she was still very much available to her children as a primary caretaker. There were no reported deaths, moves, or major changes in the family to trigger the recent separation anxiety and fears of loss expressed by this child.

Stevie was reported to have been completely toilet trained by age three. However, in the past few months he had become somewhat encopretic. He reportedly had one to two bowel movements a week, but he would hold his feces in until he was in pain. And at this point, according to the pediatrician, the fecal matter would become hard and painful for him to pass. He also complained about his anus, that it "hurts" or "itches." While at the preschool, he reportedly never went to the bathroom; he would hold it in until his mother picked him up and then she would have to go straight home so he could go to the bathroom. Stevie's mother said that about two months ago he had a red rash around his anus. Both parents attributed it to leakage from holding his feces in too long. But then, a month ago, Stevie unexpectedly had a large bowel movement while playing in the bathtub. He said that he bent over and "it just came out." His reaction was one of being very embarrassed and apologetic about it.

Teachers at the school complained that Stevie was "always wandering off" and seemed "resistant" to them. The mother stated that she repeatedly spoke to Stevie about how he was to follow their directions, but this apparently had little effect. The mother also noted other unusual behavior while Stevie was at the school. He would always meet her at the gate with his sweater or jacket on and buttoned to the throat. Even if he were sweating and it was a hot day, he would refuse to remove it. However, at home and at other settings (e.g., the park), he would quickly remove the sweater if it was hot.

Stevie was also reported to have interesting, repetitive play at home. He tended to identify with the "bad guys" rather than the typical "good guys." "Skeletor," a figure who represented evil in a cartoon show, was his hero. Typically, Skeletor would torment and threaten the good guys, ridicule them for their weakness while pitting them against impossible and hopeless situations, and then kill them off. There was never any resolution of the battle or conflict in his play, only repeated scenes of torment and death. Stevie also made statements that the "police are bad." He told his mother when she asked about this that he was afraid, and that "I don't want the police to get me."

PSYCHOLOGICAL ASSESSMENT MATERIAL

Stevie's developmental history was obtained through use of the Child Behavior Checklist (Achenbach & Edelbrock, 1983). Results indicated a normal pre- and postnatal course, with the exception of a slight delay in the acquisition of language due to frequent otitis between the ages of one to two years. The Child Behavior Checklist obtained from the parents also indicated a marked increase in behavior problems from earlier months, including significant toileting, sleep, and impulse control difficulties, and recent expression of unusual and bizarre ideas and behaviors. Informal assessment was conducted during the therapy via drawings and interviews with the parents.

COURSE OF THERAPY

Phase 1

Stevie was seen in my private office, a large carpeted room set up with a couch, two chairs, a desk big enough to crawl under, and a large cabinet containing blocks, games, art materials, and two drawers full of toys (e.g.,

He-Man figures, trucks, dolls, small animals, puppets). I generally start out by telling the child that I am a "talk doctor" and that I see lots of children who talk to me about things they are mad or sad or upset about. I tell them that their parents wanted them to come see me because they were concerned that maybe something was making them upset and that maybe I could help them to feel better. In this case, Stevie's mother was present during his initial interview because he exhibited fearfulness at separating from her. This is not generally the case for children his age, but I was sensitive to his fear and wanted him to feel as comfortable as possible with me.

I introduced Stevie to my toys and told him he could play with whatever he liked. I was approaching this case as a therapy case, rather than as an evaluation for molestation, because Stevie had already been seen by his pediatrician, a physician I knew was quite competent and thorough in exploring issues of molestation, and no disclosures had been made. Also, the history from the mother and father, with whom I had met alone earlier, indicated symptoms of distress (anxiety and fear) but no actual reports or obvious evidence of abuse experiences. In any case, I thought his symptoms warranted some therapeutic intervention.

Stevie was clearly avoidant in his behavior during the first session. He made little eye contact and clung to his mother. It was immediately apparent that I would have to "woo" this child into trusting me. Stevie played with a variety of toys in the beginning with a distracted, preoccupied manner. Until I encouraged him to take a look at the dollhouse, there was little focus in his play. He then identified two Fisher Price cages as "jails" and stated that he was putting "bad teachers in jail." He volunteered that the teachers had "hurt the kids" and said one teacher "kicked and spanked me and I spanked her back." He showed intense interest in black plastic figures with devil-like heads which he found in the bottom of a toy box. He identified them as "bad guys" but would not elaborate. There were no further disclosures in this session.

I suggested to Stevie, in front of his mother, that if he remembered anything about school that made him feel bad this week, he should tell his mother. I told him I would see him in a week; he seemed pleased about that because he "liked my toys."

Stevie came in for subsequent play interviews alone. The disclosure process was not "neat and tidy," but consisted of small bits of information shared while he played with the toys and I listened and gently asked questions, such as "Did that happen to you?" (e.g., when he exhibited something with toys), or repeated his statements with a questioning inflection. The following excerpt from my fourth session reveals how the initial sessions proceeded.

Stevie came into the room alone. He spent the initial ten minutes examining and discussing the toys. After a while, I commented on his play of the previous weeks (putting people in jail) and asked why he did that.

THERAPIST   You put the teachers in jail. Why?
STEVIE   They were bad teachers.
THERAPIST   Who was?
STEVIE   (Gave teacher's name)
THERAPIST   What did she do?
STEVIE   I don't know. I don't remember.

He then played with the He-Man toys, setting up adversarial action scenes in which toys were tied up. One figure telling another he must undress perked my interest, as this was an unusual aspect of a typical He-Man scenario. I decided to ask about it.

THERAPIST   Stevie, did anyone ever take their clothes off at the school?
STEVIE   Only the girls took their clothes off. The teachers made them. They tied them up.
THERAPIST   They tied them up?
STEVIE   Only their arms were tied . . . Everybody laughed at the girls . . . but they cried.
THERAPIST   Who tied them up?
STEVIE   (Teacher's name) tied them up.

Stevie continued his play with the He-Man action figures and said he liked Skeletor best, that he "liked bad guys." When he played out scenes of the good guys being attacked and defeated, I asked, "Who could help them? The police?" Stevie responded with an adamant and angry statement, "Policemen do bad things. Yeah, they do! I know they do! Police are bad!" Stevie then repetitively presented himself as a "bad guy" in his play, i.e., using the bad guy as the main actor and having him win at his evil deeds.

I deliberately introduced the idea of the police in this session because in an earlier session he had appeared very anxious and distressed at a casual mention of police as "protectors" and "someone children could talk to if anyone had hurt them." Piecing together Stevie's comments and reactions, I was increasingly aware that strange and unusual events had occurred at Stevie's school.

In treating victims of ritualistic abuse, it is important to involve the parents as soon as possible and to expand the "keeper of the secrets" role to include trusted adults in the child's life. The effectiveness of this type of abuse in "implanting evil" (Wooden, 1981) and turning the victim against him- or herself, society, and traditional Judeo-Christian religious beliefs depends on secrecy. With a child this young, it is also important to have active family involvement in the treatment process. Out of the child's earshot, I instructed his mother to be a neutral but receptive listener for any disclosures he might make. Stevie's mother was very anxious regarding what he had said about teachers at the school. I asked her to not press him for disclosures and told her that if it did come out that he was abused at school, she would have to be the "best actress she had ever been" to conceal her own emotional distress from him. This suggestion was based on my perception that Stevie was very attached to his mother and I feared that he might inhibit any disclosures of abuse to protect her from emotional upset.

During the fifth week, between sessions five and six, Stevie told his parents that he saw the teachers from the school hurt animals, that they "cut up the baby duck." He initially said, "something bad happened when they said good-bye to Lucky Ducky at the park." The parents knew the children had gone on a field trip to a nearby park to set a pet duck free on the pond. When they asked if this was when the event occurred, Stevie said, "They were afraid of the big ducks because they would bite them, so they only hurt the little ducks." He said that he saw the teachers put the baby duck's head under the water until it died. "I saw them hurt the duck's neck."

Stevie also made reference to going on a picnic with the school "in a jungle" and seeing a man with a fat stomach there. He said, "Something bad happened," but appeared frightened and refused to say any more. Later, he referred to a "house in the jungle." On another occasion, Stevie saw a younger child crying loudly in a restaurant and volunteered to his mother that he never cried like that " . . . only at school when people were hurting me." He appeared in a "bad mood" during the week, more irritable and easily upset.

At the next session, I introduced Stevie to anatomically correct dolls. He was very interested and immediately demanded that I undress every doll. He then began to pull on the male's penis and to "shoot the pee pee" and torment the doll with a stick. He said, "I'm going to screw him," and pushed the stick into the doll's penis, bellybutton, mouth and ears, saying each time, "He's screwed." Stevie said the dolls were "bad boys," and that they "poop and peepee on the floor." When I asked if these events happened to him, Stevie nodded "yes." After discussing his feelings and obtaining his permission, I reported his disclosures to his mother. Stevie was initially upset about this, but then said okay. He volunteered that "They threatened to kill you, Mom, if I told the secret. The mean man will hurt the police." When we asked about "the mean man," Stevie referred to a man he called the "singer man," who hurt him in the bathroom, touching his bottom and his penis. This "singer man" was apparently someone who came into the classroom to sing songs and play games with the children, thus his name was "singer man" to Stevie. The mother had not known about this person before this session.

Subsequent sessions led to more descriptions of "games" played at the school in which children removed their clothing, defecated, and smeared feces on one another. They sang a "yuckie song" referring to feces, being "bad," and liking it. As the therapy progressed, I could sense that a disclosure of further abuse and a more outrageous event still untold was about to be revealed by the level of Stevie's anxiety when he entered my playroom. For example, for several weeks he would go through a "safety" ritual consisting of closing the shades on the windows in my office, locking the door and listening to see if anyone was in the outside hallway, then insisting that we crawl under my desk in the dark. There, he told me of going into a "house" in which he was forced to eat feces, was tied up and urinated on by adult males, and had his penis pulled and stretched after he was taken into a small, closet-like bathroom. He played out with dolls being tricked by bad guys into doing bad things such as oral copulation of adult males.

His play and verbal disclosures dealing with the smearing of feces and sexual molestation were of particular interest to me, given Stevie's symptoms of encopresis. On the one hand, he appeared in his play to take delight in "making poo" and the wild release in the regressed and primitive activities at the school. He was also anxious and confused, since there was little tolerance for such behavior in his home. He looked to me for reassurance frequently during these disclosures. I discussed with Stevie his mixed feelings of worry and release. He appeared to be excited by "making messes" and doing forbidden acts with the sanction and encouragement of adult authority figures.

Stevie described experiences of seeing the girls take their clothes off and having their pictures taken "when they were making poo poo." He said, "We were laughing and the teachers were laughing." He referred to this as the "poo poo game" and described it as an experience of wild acting out accompanied by an intense emotional discharge. Immediately following, however, he said, "When the kids took their clothes off, they became bad guys." This appeared to be a reflection of his own confusion and ambivalence regarding the activities in which he had participated at the school.

Phase 2

Stevie became frightened and anxious during sessions 10 through 20 (two-month time span), and a corresponding regression and disturbance occurred in his behavior at home. He had an increase in nightmares and refused to sleep alone in his room. He insisted on sleeping in the living room on the couch because it was closer to his parents' room and the family dog could sleep next to him on the floor and "protect him." He became very clingy and regressed to using baby talk. He also developed a stutter at times and exhibited nervous tic behavior, such as pulling at the crotch of his pants and blinking. He also began to wet on himself during the day, but would refuse to go into the bathroom, particularly in public places.

Needless to say, his parents were very distressed by this deterioration in his behavior and questioned the usefulness of the therapy if his behavior was getting worse instead of better. However, their active involvement in the treatment process, which I had encouraged from the beginning, not only facilitated Stevie's disclosure of abuse but also allowed for their developing a trusting relationship with me. We were, in effect, cotherapists working to help their son recover. In addition, I was able to educate them as to the link between the abuse he was disclosing and the symptoms he was exhibiting. Having this information on "why he was acting the way he was" helped them to tolerate his behavior problems and work with them more effectively.

At this time of major regression in Stevie's behavior, which was considered an indication of the massive anxiety he was experiencing, emotional support as well as appropriate limit-setting was considered crucial. I did not want the regressed, infantile behavior to be reinforced by the parents so he would stay at this level because of the attention or "secondary gain" he received. On the other hand, an angry, frustrated response by the parents might increase his anxiety and further destroy his trust in adults. We developed an incentive program with stickers to encourage more mature functioning in the home (e.g., rewarding sleeping in his own bed), while regressions were responded to in a neutral fashion with continued support and reassurance offered to deal with his anxiety.

At this point, I was also hearing about other cases of ritualistic abuse in the area. I started to experience a great deal of anxiety and outrage about the events Stevie was describing. At times, it was difficult to believe him or to restrain my disgust and anger towards the perpetrators. I knew that I still had not gotten the "whole story" from Stevie and I did not want to inhibit his disclosures. Yet it required a number of consultations with more experienced child therapists (e.g., senior child analysts and supervisors I had used earlier in my training) to convince me that what I was hearing was "real."

Later, I also came to realize that the fear and sleep disturbance that I was experiencing were mirroring, in part, Stevie's experience as a victim of abuse. This insight and my own struggle to deal with conflicting emotions prepared me to help Stevie recover from his fear in this phase of our work together. I believe my heightened empathy for his emotional distress, due to my own response to his disclosures, also helped me to avoid countertransference feelings of irritation when he regressed or acted out and aided me in guiding his parents in developing a therapeutic response to him.

Stevie's treatment continued for several months before there was any inkling that there may have been satanic cult rituals involved in his abuse experiences at the preschool. Disclosures of this type were triggered quite by accident in his sixteenth session. In this meeting, Stevie played out being angry with a puppet who, in previous sessions, had symbolized the victim of abuse. He said, "That's what happens when you're bad . . . they turn you into a circle." I asked what he was referring to, and Stevie said, "Like when you wipe your feet, a rug on the floor, the circle one . . . you go to where there are wizards." He appeared extremely anxious. I waited, and he said, "It's all black and dogs are chasing cats. The wizards put black in your eyes . . . they close your eyes and black was in front of my eyes."

Stevie then got out of the drawer a puppet with a cone-shaped hat which he said was a "wizard's hat." Stevie took an action figure and said he was punishing him by putting him in a box, that "people went inside a box." He then appeared to go through an abreaction of a traumatic experience. His voice was fearful and panicky, he fell on the floor and lay flat, flapping his arms like flying, and he began to plead with the "wizard" to let him "out," let him "come back." He said he "didn't want to be a circle anymore." He began to chant something that sounded like, "circle, circle, circle seven, circle, circle, circle, sin." Stevie was so involved in this experience that he did not respond immediately to his name and my verbal efforts to calm him. I touched him on the forehead and said, "Stevie, it's over, you are safe, you can come back now."

After several repetitions, Stevie finally sat up and hugged me and began to sob. He spoke then of "spells" and said that the "kids turned into a circle." Then, in play, while directing the wizard puppet to talk to a bird puppet, he had the wizard shove a stick up into the bird and demand he "fly around." Stevie would become disturbed periodically in the play and lapse into silence with his eyes staring into space or look blankly at me as if he were somewhere else. When I asked, "Did they put a stick in your bottom?" he said, "Do you know about that?"

In later sessions, Stevie spoke of "strangers wearing masks" and people with "green on their body and face." He drew a picture of a "bad guy" who had a green face "like the Incredible Hulk" who came to the school sometimes. He said that the "secret" was that there are "creepy ghouls" who touch the kids and make them "yucky"; "the ghouls are green and yucky all over." He referred to teachers who "wore ugly clothes" and a green wig. He also called a stranger "Mr. Poo Poo Face" because "he always puts poop on his face" and indicated that he directed the abuse against the children. Stevie also spoke of persons wearing "horns" and casting spells. These "spells" were designed to trick children into doing bad things. For example, the spell-caster said, "By the power of thunder and lightning, I will make you lose your mind." The affected children then were to do whatever the spell-caster directed.

Stevie spoke and drew pictures of dancing naked around a fire with the teachers. He said teachers referred to Satan or the Devil as all powerful. They "tried to show us we can walk on fire and we don't get dead if we are like the Devil." Stevie reported being shown movies at school "that we didn't want to watch." The movies showed lots of fighting and violence and policemen in roles that were "bad." Stevie said he didn't really believe them, but that the teachers were "trying to teach us to do bad things."

The teachers' efforts to indoctrinate the children into a belief system in which good is punished and bad acts rewarded was a frequent theme in this phase of treatment. Stevie often used dolls to demonstrate an adult directing a child to hurt another child. For example, the adult said, "Now here, Shorty, look at me. Say yes, you'll be a bad guy," and then he hit the child and made him hold another child and orally copulate him. The child "abuser" then said to the child victim, "Now, don't move; I'm going to do things you don't want," and proceeded to beat and molest him.

In another session, he played out a scene in which he and other children were directed by the teachers to hit one child who was singled out for abuse by the group. He said there was a rule, "If you don't hurt the other kid, you don't get a snack." He continued, "We had to punch him in the eyeball and poke him with a needle. I had to hurt him."

Stevie was highly conflicted regarding his role as an abuser. He said the abused child "never got snack" and anyone who refused to hurt somebody was at risk of being singled out himself for abuse. Teachers said that the resistant child "didn't like us." They would encourage the larger group of children to punish the resistant child by saying, "Let's get rid of him . . . it's time we put an end to him." Later, however, the children would be punished for being "mean" to each other. Stevie said that he was "glad," that he "liked to beat up" the child who resisted. This was an apparent expression of his own aggressive and sadistic impulses, which, as in most preschoolers, were not completely under control.

As these "gang abuse" scenarios occurred everyday, the children eventually began to hate each other. The majority of children allied as a cohesive gang against the one angry and resistant child "traitor." As Stevie presented his experiences, it appeared that often a child was asked or coerced to participate in hurting helpless animals or tormenting the classmate chosen as the special victim that day. Then, after the abusive events ended, this same child was chastised and criticized as a "bad boy" for doing "mean things." The child was made to take on the guilt for what the teachers planned and directed him to do.

The abusing teachers' involvement with the children was intense; it appeared as if they projected the unconscious and repudiated contents of their own psyches (e.g., sadistic impulses, primitive anal preoccupation) on the children. Then they may have viewed the children and their actions as dangerous and in need of degradation, repudiation, and destruction.

In Stevie's case, because of fear of his own destruction, he collaborated in the destruction of his own personal integrity. He committed acts that he knew were wrong and that were the exact opposite of what his parents approved of (his mother had indicated to me that she closely screened his television viewing to prevent exposure to violence, aggression and sex). As a result of his collaboration in the abusive acts, Stevie found it difficult to develop any self-esteem and a view of himself as "good," even though the abuser constraints and pressures were removed, now that he had been removed from the school. Although he had not become a total "believer," he protected the teachers and maintained secrecy about their acts for a long time, while at the same time blaming himself.

Stevie reported being given "red medicine" that made him sick. At other times, he referred to drinking a "poison" that turned him into a bad person inside. He also interpreted signs of anxiety (e.g., heart beating faster) as signs of dying. For a long time, the source of this fear was unclear. Only after Stevie felt that he could exercise some free will and nothing bad would happen was I able to gain his trust and learn of the explicit threats made to intimidate him and control his will. For example, he observed killings of animals and was told that he and his family would be likewise tortured and killed. He was told that it would be futile to tell because "no-one will believe you." He appeared to have been subjected to rituals such as "magical surgery" in which objects were supposedly planted inside his body and he was told that they indicated his belonging to the teachers' cult and would also be a source of his death if he ever told their secrets. Mind-altering drugs appeared to have been used to alter his perception and decrease his resistance to the assaults and programming by the teachers.

Stevie compulsively played out a belief that "bad guys always win" as a reflection of his indoctrination at the school. However, he gradually became more open to discussion about "good guys" being acceptable and attended to my empathizing with the pain a good guy might experience if he were forced to be "bad." Slowly, as he began to disclose his own experiences of abuse and denied his pain less, his identification with the "bad guys" lessened. However, as this "identification with the aggressor" was a source of feelings of power as well as a source of self-protection, it was slow to change.

An area of particular difficulty for Stevie was achieving some mastery over his sadistic and aggressive impulses when such behavior had been actively encouraged and modeled by powerful adults at school. Preschoolers are in a developmental phase when sadism is at its height (Klein, 1930). Even normal sadistic fantasies may give rise to anxiety and a fear of the "badness" inside oneself. However, in normal development, when there are no external events to feed these fantasies and exacerbate the anxiety, these feelings subside and the child develops a sense of himself as basically good, despite occasional sadistic thoughts. Involvement in actual sadistic activities during this phase increases the child's anxiety and internal sense of being "bad." Stevie was clearly struggling with these self-concept issues and overwhelming feelings of anxiety and guilt. In treatment, it was necessary to actively confront his negative self-concept and work through his feelings of guilt.

Excrement often plays a large part in the sadistic fantasies of the young child. The child may fantasize destroying enemies in secret ways by means of urine, feces, and flatus. According to Abraham (1927), the omnipotence of the functions of the bladder and bowels is a precursor of the omnipotence of thoughts.

At the preschool, Stevie underwent attack by magical substances (feces) as well as by words (being called "bad"). Given his age and involvement in magical thinking, these actions provided a climate of terror in which he became highly sensitized to the lessons being taught. Even if abuse was intermittent, every day the child felt unsafe in that environment. The unpredictability of the abuse kept anxiety high. The abusers were dominating, appeared extremely powerful, and utilized objects and experiences that had particular meaning for this age group. They used primitive rituals that tapped directly into the children's unconscious fantasies to reinforce their lessons regarding sadism and evil. They engendered an unquestioning belief and obedience to their rules and demands, which had a much more immediate impact on Stevie's psyche than day-to-day home experiences. In addition, the teachers often suggested to Stevie that his parents knew about their actions and agreed with them. This was accomplished by conversations with the parents in front of Stevie and oblique references to the rituals and abuse (which Stevie understood but the parents did not). Lies about the parents' disowning Stevie if he ever told were also used to make a wedge between Stevie and his parents.

The presence of symptoms and Stevie's verbal expressions of distress indicated that his "soul" had not been destroyed. Shengold (1979) used the term "soul murder" to describe traumatic abuse experiences so overwhelming that the person's mental apparatus is flooded with feeling. Massive and mind-distorting defensive operations are required for the person to continue to think and feel. The victim tends to react by shutting off all emotion, in effect saying, "What is happening is so terrible that it must not be felt and cannot be registered." He becomes like a robot, a mechanically obedient automaton. I have seen this phenomenon in other child victims of abuse who protect themselves by a magical robot identity and belief that as a robot they are invincible, rather than helpless and powerless. Stevie, however, had no such protection. Instead, he presented confusion and "spaciness," a general fogging of his thinking processes. He was caught between two worlds: There was pressure from his family to become socialized and repress libidinal and aggressive impulses, while at school he was encouraged to act out his impulses and obtained feelings of omnipotence from his role of abuser/actor. During treatment, Stevie acted out his impulses by repetitively tying up his younger sibling and abusing action figures in the play session. When confronted with his sadistic and abusive acts toward his sister, he expressed an extreme sense of remorse and often did some self-punitive act (e.g., banging his head or scratching himself) as an apparent act of retribution.

Since Stevie experienced sexual molestation as well as sadistic torment from his abusers, there were additional sexual problems. Stevie described a process in which several children in the school were seduced and treated "special" while being molested. For example, he played out an unusual "beauty show" in which the children were lined up and told to show how "pretty" they were. To show your prettiness for a girl was to "show your vagina." Pictures were reportedly taken of the children exposing their genitals. Stevie played out scenes in which he and the other boys had to strut around and show off as powerful males to female teachers who made admiring remarks, e.g., "Wow, look at that. Look how big he is." He was encouraged to masturbate in order to "show off" his penis to the adults. He was also directed to touch the adults (breasts and genitals), and they fondled him during these "beauty shows."

Stevie was confused and conflicted in his feelings about these experiences. On the one hand, he became highly eroticized by these experiences and was easily aroused by a variety of circumstances once the abuse ended. It appeared that he had difficulty discriminating between erotic and nonerotic relationships. He would try to fondle his mother's breast or smell his sister's genitals, and he appeared to become sexually excited by climbing on his father's back (e.g., began to hump him).

The original mode of sexual abuse (homosexual, oral-genital, etc.) became highly cathected. Since much of early sexual behavior is a learned response to stimuli, Stevie gave evidence of gender role-reversal in his play. He was apparently used as a sexual object for male abusers. In his play, then, he frequently put himself in the "female" role. In general, he appeared confused regarding issues of gender identification and appropriate sexual behavior.

During the middle phase of therapy, Stevie went through a period of compulsive masturbation. His tic behavior (e.g. pulling at the crotch of his pants, eye blinking and head jerking) also appeared to be linked to his molestation experience. Having to masturbate male adults and fondle female teachers likely engendered much anxiety in Stevie. In addition, his own feelings of guilt associated with masturbatory activities were activated.

Melanie Klein (1932) has described the strong sense of guilt that frequently accompanies masturbatory activities in children. Rather than having a "moral" basis, such guilt may be a reaction to the destructive impulses that find expression in the masturbation fantasies (i.e., semen having a symbolism similar to feces and urine in primitive aggressive and sadistic fantasies). The child's guilt may produce a desire to display masturbatory activity to the people about them, from whom they would expect criticism and possibly punishment. Compulsive masturbation may develop and occur in public despite the likelihood of an angry response from parents. In other cases, sexual abuse experiences may produce a too complete suppression of masturbation (as a defense against the anxiety associated with the abuse), leading to a tic or a touching phobia.

Stevie developed both symptom complexes: compulsive masturbation and tic behavior. His masturbation behavior had the biggest impact on the family system. His parents reacted with criticism, disappointment, and anger. My interventions resulted in a lessening of intensity in their disapproval, but they were unable to ignore the behavior completely. Stevie was directed to masturbate only in private (e.g., his bedroom). However, his public masturbation behavior continued for quite a long time, despite the negative consequences imposed by his parents.

The fact that Stevie was at an age when oedipal feelings and wishes are intense was also considered a complicating factor in his reaction to his abuse experiences. It is not unusual for four-year-old boys to play out fantasies about using their penises sexually with their mother or as instruments of aggression and destruction in the battle with their father. However, when Stevie engaged in such play in the therapy session, he would become paralyzed with fear and anxiety and regress to a whimpering, crying baby. His anxiety associated with memories of sexual molestation and his own guilt about oedipal wishes at times made it difficult for him to use his penis in any way, even to urinate. At other times, he would urinate in his clothes or on the floor without any regard for consequences.

Urine appeared to be symbolic of his rage and a "poison" used for retaliation.

Phase 3

Stevie had to be taught appropriate ways of dealing with his anger and aggressive impulses. At first, it was necessary to encourage the open expression of anger. It was interesting to observe that, as he became more verbally aggressive and angry in the home, his problems with encopresis, daytime enuresis, and tics gradually disappeared. Behavior management programs focusing on appropriate ways of dealing with anger (e.g., reinforcing verbal or written expressions, enacting consequences for assaults against others) were useful in the latter stages of treatment.

After Stevie's disclosures of his role in perpetrating abuse on others, he seemed freed, less troubled and more self-accepting. His play changed as well, and he became a "good guy" (e.g., He-Man in his action scenes). He also began to incorporate news of his successes at home and areas of competence in school work into his therapy sessions. Greater psychological "energy," which was needed for his continued development and learning, was suddenly available and not tied up in defending against the memories of abuse. This, to me, was the most significant indication that he had made progress in treatment and was ready to terminate.

SPECIFIC TECHNIQUES USED IN THERAPY

Stevie was initially only able to disclose his experiences of abuse and his feelings of fear and anxiety through reenactment scenarios with toys in play therapy. Eventually, he was able to establish a trusting relationship with me and began to express his feelings directly to me, as well as to question abuse experiences and associated "teachings" of the abusers and to seek information and reassurance from me. The development of this trust and attachment to me was necessary for Stevie to accept my identification and interpretations of conflicts he was experiencing. It was also considered crucial that he be able to disclose his own involvement in the molestation of other children. Such a step was considered essential to freeing Stevie from his guilt and anxiety and allowing a return to normal functioning.

Regular consultation with the parents around behavioral techniques to manage Stevie's aggression and fears was important to his recovery. A behavioral assessment of his functioning in the home was obtained through interview with the parents on a regular basis throughout treatment (once or twice a month) to evaluate his progress and identify further issues to be addressed in treatment.

OUTCOME OF TREATMENT

Stevie's treatment lasted approximately 18 months. He had two recurrences of symptoms (e.g., nightmares and anxiety reactions) in the three years after he terminated regular therapy sessions. In each case, consultation with his parent and a short period of therapy (one to three sessions) was all that was needed to help him stabilize emotionally and resolve the symptoms. He was making good progress in school and the memories of abuse appear to be "fading." In my last contact with him, Stevie just wanted to play and talk to me about school. In playing a game with me, he was competitive and appropriately aggressive, with little evidence of conflict regarding these issues.

OBSTACLES TO TREATMENT

Stevie was one of a number of children reporting abuse at his preschool. In most cases the children were fearful of speaking to police due to the belief taught them by the abusers that "police are bad" and fears of retaliation by the abusers if they told. Consequently, after my suspicions of abuse were reported, I experienced pressure from the investigating authorities and parents to obtain details about the abuse for law enforcement purposes. This desire for details was, at times, in conflict with the therapeutic process and respecting the child's right to control his rate of disclosure. Sometimes I would push too hard for explicit details and Stevie would resist my pressure and "shut down." Several weeks would pass before he would feel comfortable again talking with me about the abuse he suffered. I also found that information that was important to investigating authorities was not necessarily important to Stevie. Many details needed to apprehend and prosecute an abuser (e.g., color of eyes and hair, date and time of incidents, specific number of incidents) were not important for discovery of the trauma and the exact meaning it had to Stevie. As a therapist, I felt it was my role to follow the child's lead and try to understand what he had experienced and what he was currently feeling.

I also knew that the criminal justice system needed Stevie's and my cooperation to prosecute the alleged offenders. In this case, problems developed when Stevie made disclosures of his abuse at the school to me but was fearful of speaking directly with law enforcement personnel. I tried to bridge this gap by meeting with Stevie and a police officer in a safe environment (i.e., my office). However, this effort interfered with the treatment process, since Stevie later substituted rote repetition of disclosures made to police for exploration of his feelings. This resistance was particularly difficult to work through because I had presented him with signs of approval when he made disclosures to the police. In retrospect, I would advise that greater separation between the investigation process and the therapy be maintained.

OTHER SYSTEMS INVOLVED

Unlike cases of incest, in which there is a great deal of family dysfunction, in this case the parents presented little evidence of psychopathology. The family was intact and Stevie had a very healthy attachment to his parents and other family members. The family system here was the theater where the effects of the extrafamilial abuse were played out. Although the parents played an active role in promoting Stevie's recovery, they were not immune to their own stress reactions as a result of his abuse.

During the course of therapy, the parents gave evidence of post-traumatic stress disorder. The father, in particular, had intrusive thoughts and preoccupations with retaliation against the abusers. He complained of concentration problems at work and difficulty sleeping. His mood was frequently irritable and he felt "on edge." Stevie's mother reacted with tearfulness, guilt that she had chosen that school for him and that she had not removed him sooner. She also had sleep disturbance and noticed an increase in somatic complaints (e.g., stomach distress, headaches, tiredness).

I had attempted to prepare the parents for stress reactions as soon as it became apparent that Stevie suffered abuse. Information on post-traumatic stress disorder as a "normal" response to extraordinary occurrences seemed to decrease their fear and anxiety about their own changes in psychological functioning. They were also less defensive and more open in sharing their symptoms of distress, so I could help them mobilize their supports (e.g., friends, extended family members) and develop more effective coping strategies. I remember saying to the parents at one point, "Since you have removed Stevie from the school, the actual 'trauma' for him is over. However, the trauma for you is just starting. As Stevie continues to disclose what he has suffered, you might find yourselves having more symptoms as a result of your trauma."

As a member of the larger community where the abuse took place, I found it particularly difficult to maintain a neutral position and not become overinvolved in the investigation and prosecution activities. It felt as if I had a dual role to play. On the one hand, I was asked to remedy the emotional trauma of the sexual offense suffered by my patient, Stevie. On the other hand, I felt an obligation to support society's need for a legal remedy to the alleged offense.

The investigation of this case seemed to be particularly difficult for law enforcement personnel, since a majority of disclosures and details about the crime occurred in the context of therapy sessions. Members of the judicial system cautioned me against asking any leading questions; yet they often wanted me to obtain disclosures as rapidly as possible. There were also concerns regarding preserving the "purity" of Stevie's testimony. The parents were cautioned not to talk to other parents about the case or to allow Stevie contact with other children from the school, due to the investigating officers' fears of a "contagion" effect that could be used by the defense to discredit the allegations of abuse.

Notwithstanding the precautions taken and the numerous efforts made to substantiate Stevie's allegations, in the end the case rested on his testimony and that of other children who attended the school. Four-year-olds are not considered "good witnesses," and the District Attorney and investigating officers decided that they would not pursue the prosecution of the abusers in this case at this time. They hoped that as the children got older they would become better witnesses. I consider this to be a somewhat naive view. Details fade over time, and if therapy is effective the victim becomes less preoccupied with the trauma and therefore more likely to forget significant aspects of the experience. With the passage of time, the memory also becomes affected by the personal meaning attributed to the experience by the victim. Consequently, actual events later recalled may be confused with the child's fantasies of how the events "should have happened." This unconscious distortion of the truth over time would further complicate the prosecutor's efforts to try the case after a significant amount of time has passed.

Mistakes

As mentioned earlier, my mistakes primarily took the form of balancing my role as Stevie's therapist with the desire to be an ally and aid to the police and the court. Greater neutrality with Stevie was needed until I had fully explored his views of his experiences and his affective responses to the abuse and the various people involved. My need to push him to disclose the abuse and his desire to please me was in conflict with his loyalty to his perpetrators, arousing more anxiety in him than was helpful to his recovery. Balancing my roles in this case was not an easily resolved dilemma.

Therapist Reactions to the Case

Stevie's treatment aroused a number of countertransference issues in me. At first, there was a strong tendency to deny and disbelieve what Stevie presented. His parents also attempted to deny the experiences he reported. I found myself in the strange position of defending the reality and validity of disclosures that I was not even sure I believed! But then, once the repetition of disclosures and revelations of increasingly more details made the reality of the events more obvious and certain, it was difficult to contain the parents' and my own "need to know."

Finally, a problem that developed and increased with the number of disclosures made by Stevie and by other children seen from the same school was my own anger toward the abusers and my desire for justice and revenge. Since Stevie did not always feel angry with the abusers, I had to be ever watchful that my own emotions did not interfere with my being "present" for and supportive to him.

The decision to not prosecute was very discouraging and frustrating to the parents of the victims. In the aftermath, it was apparent that politics also played a role in the decision. The District Attorney did not want to make an unpopular decision, but also did not want to spend a lot of taxpayers' money prosecuting a case that might be lost because of the age of the primary witnesses and the lack of substantiating evidence. As I had several times been told by various law enforcement personnel that it is a "waste of time" preparing a case for prosecution when the victim witness is under age six, this decision was not a surprise. Still, as a therapist for abused children, I find it chilling that there is no protection under the law, i.e., no justice, for child victims of abuse.

The community as a whole became polarized into two groups: those who believed the children and those who found the allegations preposterous, within a few days of the first news leaks regarding the abuse allegations. In the end, the school was closed under pressure from the Department of Social Services, which licenses preschools, but no charges were filed against individual perpetrators. Parents, law enforcement and mental health professionals mobilized to form groups to change the laws so children could be considered credible witnesses in our courts. Efforts were also made to network with other groups around the country dealing with ritualistic abuse cases. As for Stevie, he said to me in one of our last sessions that "It's not really safe, Dr. Ann, because there's still those 'strangers' around."

5

Cognitive Therapy With a Young Victim of Sexual Assault

LUCY BERLINER

Lucy Berliner clearly elucidates a PTSD formulation for her 11-year-old client, whose presentation is certainly consistent with these criteria. A cognitive-behavioral approach, combining relaxation training, positive self-statements, and an examination of critical beliefs, is a systematic approach that could be used much more often with traumatized children than is currently the case.

A unique feature is Berliner's use of rituals to promote the child's sense of safety. My experience is that the creation of rituals is a very appropriate mechanism for developing emotional self-regulation in traumatized children. Peter Steinglass' work with alcoholic families has found that predictable family rituals buffered against the emergence of alcoholism in future generations (Steinglass, Bennett, Wolin, & Reiss, 1987). Perhaps this is true for sexual abuse as well.

Gabriela's premature termination of therapy appeared to be a shame-based reaction related to her victimizing a friend and points to the need for therapists to help the victim identify contributors to the sense of shame.

The salience of sexual issues in sexually abused children is also underscored. Gabriela was bothered by her parents' sexual intimacy and her own sexuality. These were issues that needed addressing both initially in therapy and certainly as she moved into adolescence.

What brought about Gabriela's acute psychotic depression after what appeared to be a "typical" amount of therapy for children who have been sexually abused? I believe that a core issue had not been addressed at that time — the impaired mother-daughter relationship. Gabriela rejected her mother as a sexual being and had not resolved the betrayal stemming from her mother's not having protected her from victimization.

On the one hand, Gabriela's mother appeared to be sensitive and responsive, bringing Gabriela promptly to treatment when she disclosed and providing some modicum of support to her throughout the therapy. However, careful reading indicates that Gabriela's mother actually missed appointments and placed Gabriela in vulnerable situations. Additionally, Gabriela could not identify with her mother's sexuality for fear of the resulting sexual victimization.

Gabriela's fragility at the end of treatment is evidenced in her exaggerated response to a girlfriend's rejection. The negative mother-daughter dynamics persist, with Gabriela's being able to get away with rejecting school. Later cycles of therapy appear necessary for a final resolution.

The therapist was trying to correct mother and daughter issues using individual and group therapy. A family-based approach, emphasizing the repair of the mother-daughter relationship, might have been more efficacious, particularly if begun early on. This might have been done by having Gabriela and her mother each attend an equal number of individual therapy sessions, and maybe even having Gabriela's mother attend a few extra "since she was older." This might have allowed Gabriela to believe that her mother paid her dues "for not protecting me" and enabled the development of a conjoint therapy relationship. These sessions would have allowed a more overt exploration of Gabriela's distress about her lack of protection; also, her mother could have been more overt about her regrets, and Gabriela could have begun to see her mother more accurately and choose elements other than sexual ones with which to identify.

A total of 39 individual therapy session, 10 group therapy sessions, and inpatient hospitalization brought Gabriela to a positive but tentative adjustment. — Editor

AUTHOR'S THEORETICAL ORIENTATION

Sexual assault is considered a traumatic event or series of events with direct and specific negative effects. The experience itself involves aversive feelings and thoughts, which become associated with the memories of the abuse or certain evocative stimuli. These effects can be characterized within a post-traumatic stress disorder formulation and are specifically manifested as intrusive thoughts, nightmares, flashbacks, heightened physiological arousal, hypervigilance, exaggerated startle response and fears. In other words, children usually experience distress during the actual abuse which is then conditioned to associations with the abuse.

Sexual abuse experiences not only feel bad when they are happening but also have meaning that the child must process. As with other significant life events, there is a need to explain and understand why it happened (Taylor, 1983). Sexual abuse is developmentally abnormal, coercive, and illegal; it usually occurs in the context of a relationship, frequently with a person who is important in other respects. Ideas and beliefs about oneself, the world, and others are affected by victimization (Janoff-Bulman, 1986). Children's understanding of why they were abused has implications for their sense of self and relationship to others. These impacts may be noted in terms of impaired self- esteem, negative self-concept, diminished sense of personal efficacy, loss of trust in others, and disturbed sexuality. Finkelhor and Browne (1985) have conceptualized these impacts as resulting from traumagenic dynamics. Children may also learn to behave in age-inappropriate, antisocial, or aggressive ways because such behavior was modeled or reinforced.

Dealing with the sexual assault experience is likely to produce discomfort. Post-traumatic Stress Disorder (APA, 1987) encompasses a range of avoidance coping responses, including withdrawal, psychic numbing, dissociation, and amnesia, as well as behavioral avoidance of individuals or situations. The meaning of the event may also be experienced as painful, and psychological processes such as denial, repression, accommodation, identification with the aggressor, and self-blame may be employed in self-protection.

Avoidance temporarily reduces anxiety and discomfort but does not alter the power of the memory or meaning to evoke distress. Failure to confront directly and master the experience may be associated with long-term psychological effects. Coping responses primarily characterized by avoiding or disconnecting from the experience, while adaptive in a situation where more direct control is not possible, can become maladaptive when applied to other life experiences. In some cases this may mean that the trauma re-emerges intact at subsequent developmental junctures (e.g., see Gelinas, 1983). These maladaptive coping strategies may also become integrated into personality structure or presage other significant mental health disorders (e.g., see Briere & Runtz, 1987).

The currently available empirical evidence supports the view that sexual abuse experiences are correlated with significant mental health disturbance in adults (Bagley & Ramsey, 1986; Saunders, Villeponteaux, Lipovsky, Kilpatrick, & Veronen, 1987; Stein, Golding, Seigel, Burnam, & Sorenson, 1988). Children evaluated at the time of abuse do not generally exhibit significant disturbance (see, e.g., Cohen & Mannarino, 1988; Gomes-Schwartz, Horowitz, & Cardarelli, 1990); however, a greater percentage than average exhibits elevated behavior problems (Friedrich, Urquiza, & Beilke, 1986). Thus, it can be inferred that the process of coping with the experience is critical in predicting subsequent adjustment.

A PTSD formulation has been proposed clinically (Goodwin, 1985) and from empirical findings (Wolfe, Gentile, & Wolfe, 1989). McLeer, Dellinger, Atkins, Foa, and Ralphe (1988) report that 48% of a sample of sexually abused children meet diagnostic criteria for PTSD; indeed, most of the children had at least some of the symptoms. A possible explanation for the fact that even more children in the McLeer et al. study did not meet PTSD criteria is that, while almost all sexual abuse situations are experienced as disturbing, most are not felt to be life-threatening and produce moderate rather than severe levels of fear and anxiety.

There is also support, from studies of both child and adult victims, for the idea that cognitive adjustment is a significant variable. (Gold, 1984; Silver, Boon, & Stones, 1983; Wolfe, Gentile, & Wolfe, 1989). Negative attributions may evolve into an attributional style, eventually producing lowered self-esteem and depression. What the children believe about why they were abused may be related to the degree they generalize from the abuse experience to other aspects of their lives as they get older.

Sexual abuse experiences must be addressed with children as individuals and within their specific life situation. Although age has not been shown to be a factor in predicting seriousness of impact, all treatment must take place in the context of the developmental process. The normal expectations and tasks of the developmental stage of the child determine the type and focus of the therapy. For example, certain content areas are more developmentally salient for adolescents than for younger children, e.g., forming appropriate sexual relationships. Similarly, the therapeutic modality depends on age and stage, with greater use of play and nonverbal approaches with younger children. In addition, the child's personality and history indicate the strengths and weaknesses that will factor into the treatment process.

There is evidence that aspects of family functioning and relationships (Conte & Schuerman, 1987) and organizational structure (Friedrich, Beilke, & Urquiza, 1987) are associated with level of impact. Families where incest has occurred have disturbances in family structure (Saunders & McClure, 1987). Level of maternal support for the child victim has been correlated with child adjustment (Everson, Hunter, Runyon, Edelsohn, & Coulter, 1989; Gomes-Schwartz, Horowitz, & Cardarelli, 1990). This suggests that treatment must focus on the family as well as the individual child. Family intervention targets level of support for the child following disclosure and aspects of family functioning that contribute to the parents' capacity to be available to the child.

This conceptualization requires a directive therapeutic approach which is abuse-focused and emphasizes mastery of the experience. But since dealing with abuse experiences can be painful, exposure to difficult material must be titrated, so that discomfort stays at levels that are manageable and aversive associations to therapy are not created. Strategies for anticipating and managing anxiety should be taught. In addition, in therapy children learn to recognize different emotional states, are given an environment that facilitates ventilation, and are taught strategies for appropriate expression outside of therapy. Distorted or inaccurate beliefs about victimization, the child's role and the offender's motivation are identified and corrected.

The therapeutic relationship models genuine adult interest and concern and teaches appropriate physical and interpersonal boundaries. The therapist not only assists the child in preparing for out-of-therapy events such as criminal justice intervention but also acts as an advocate for the child in that arena. Treatment occurs primarily in an individual or group modality.

THE CASE

Gabriela* was 11 years old when she disclosed abuse after watching an Oprah Winfrey show on sexual abuse. She told her mother that she had been sexually abused over a period of two years by a teenager. He was the son of her mother's best friend and frequently babysat for Gabriela and his younger sister. The abuse took place between the ages of seven and nine, when the family lived in another state. Her mother believed Gabriela and immediately brought her for treatment.

Abuse History

The abuse had begun as a game but progressed to include full vaginal and oral intercourse as well as sexual fondling. On at least one occasion the offender had tied Gabriela up, blindfolded her, and put a knife up to her neck. He committed similar acts, although not intercourse, with his sister and made Gabriela engage in sexual acts with her friend, his sister. This was not revealed initially. Gabriela said she was afraid to tell because he had threatened to kill her, her sister, or her mother. Concern for her friend, as well as being far enough away to feel relatively safe, motivated telling. The medical evaluation revealed scarring, no hymen, and a grossly enlarged vaginal opening.

Both Gabriela and her mother were interested in pursuing criminal prosecution and the case was reported to Child Protective Services (CPS) and law enforcement. A local detective conducted a courtesy interview for the out-of-state- police department. In spite of our significant efforts to advocate on Gabriela's behalf, both CPS and law enforcement in the other state failed to conduct a thorough investigation. As a result, the other girl denied all abuse and was left in the home with the offender; criminal charges were never filed.

---

*Acknowledgment is given to Gabriela (the name she chose) and her mother for permitting publication of this case study and for the opportunity to assist in recovery.

Family History

Gabriela was living with her mother, younger sister, and stepfather at the time of disclosure. Over the course of the next year her mother and stepfather separated. The stepfather had assumed a significant parental role for Gabriela and continues to do so in spite of the separation. She regularly spends weekends with him. Gabriela's own biological father has never been involved in her life and does not seem to be important to her. His relationship with her mother was reportedly abusive. Her sister's father was part of the family for about four years and two children were born—her younger sister, now eight, and a boy who died of SIDS. According to Gabriela, she never liked the first stepfather and claims she was thrilled when her mother decided to divorce him. She continues to be negative about him when he is involved with her sister. She has been told by her mother that he raped her during the marriage. She still has feelings of grief over the loss of her brother.

Her mother's family lives in the area but there is a history of conflict between her mother and grandmother. Gabriela's mother is adopted, as was her biological father. The grandmother is a high-profile community activist. Gabriela's mother is also involved in various causes on behalf of the poor and disenfranchised. The family is African-American and politically and culturally attuned to societal inequalities and the lack of social justice. These activities consume much of the mother's time and energy. These activist values have been strongly transmitted to the children.

Developmental History

Gabriela's developmental history was not remarkable. She has no significant physical disabilities, nor has she suffered serious illness or injury. She has always done grade level work, although she experienced delays in pre-academic skills and was in a prefirst program for one year. She has generally been a mediocre student. During parts of the treatment period she did have significant school adjustment problems and completely stopped performing at school, failed classes, or refused to attend. At the beginning of treatment she had only one close friend, and both girls were somewhat eccentric outcasts at school. She has not been involved in any particular activity or sport.

ASSESSMENT

Assessment consisted of interviews with Gabriela and her mother and stepfather. During the interviews an abuse history was taken, including Gabriela's thoughts and feelings about what happened. Her family history and current level of functioning were evaluated by talking with her and her mother. Mental status was determined by observation. Symptom level and areas of concern were assessed using a self-report Impact Checklist, which consists of 105 items (SAC, 1986). She responded to statements about thoughts, feelings, and behaviors by endorsing whether she experienced them "never," "sometimes," or "a lot of the time."

Gabriela endorsed items indicating high levels of fear, especially abuse-specific fears, such as being afraid around men, having bad dreams and nightmares about the abuse, suddenly feeling panicked, having flashbacks and memories, and feeling generalized anxiety. She also endorsed items relating to cognitive difficulties, such as having trouble concentrating, daydreaming, getting confused, not being able to complete things or make decisions. She said she had trouble with her moods a lot of the time, including feeling sad, alone, worried about the future, having a lot of anger, not enjoying things she used to, having guilty feelings, and thinking about suicide. She also reported sexual fears and concerns, such as having thoughts about sex that bothered her a lot and hating and fearing the idea of sex.

Her mother initially said she did not have concerns about Gabriela's adjustment in school, with peers, or in the family. She did notice some preoccupation with sex. She completed a comparable Impact Checklist and agreed for the most part with Gabriela's self-assessment of difficulty with cognitive aspects. She described Gabriela as often having difficulty concentrating, daydreaming, appearing preoccupied or spaced out, and not finishing things she started. She had also observed that Gabriela was scared around men and shy and uneasy with the opposite sex. In addition, she endorsed a number of items relating to Gabriela's not having a good sense of herself, such as trying too hard to please, blaming herself for things, having a little belief in her own abilities. She did not see Gabriela as depressed, although she did note emotional upset.

Abuse-related fears and anxieties were the predominant areas of distress as reported on interview and the checklist by Gabriela and her mother. The three aspects of PTSD — recalling the experience, avoiding the experience, and increased arousal — were evident. There also appeared to be maladaptive cognitions noted in feelings of guilt or apparent low self-esteem. Additionally, both agreed that sexuality was an area of concern.

It was decided that therapy would initially focus on the abuse experience itself, decreasing discomfort around the memories and developing strategies for managing anxiety. Inaccurate or negative attributions would be identified and corrected. Questions concerning sexuality would be explored and reassurance provided about expected post-abuse and normal developmental variations in sexual thoughts and feelings. Both Gabriela and her mother expressed crisis-related concerns about disclosure and intervention. They were interested in initiating legal action but did not know what to expect or what steps to take. They had a variety of questions and apprehensions about the scope and consequences of reporting, both for them and for the offender and his family.

<h2 style="text-align:center">COURSE OF THERAPY</h2>

Initial phases of therapy concentrated on establishing a relationship with Gabriela and addressing immediate issues around system intervention. Gabriela related well from the beginning; she was friendly, talked openly, and was cooperative with questioning. Initially, she did have difficulty describing the abuse experience and was hesitant and embarrassed. She appeared somewhat depressed and expressed affect consistent with topics. At times it seemed as though she did not fully understand the questions.

The first issues of concern had to do with abuse-related fears. She described feeling afraid that the offender would come and get her and identified numerous ways in which this fear intruded on her life, including fears at night, flashbacks, and thinking that she had seen him. She was also very afraid about the idea of going to court. The approach to addressing the fears included listing all abuse reminders and situations that evoked anxiety and developing specific strategies to combat and overcome them.

She was instructed to make up reassuring self-statements and to find ways in which her environment could be made to feel safer. For example, Gabriela was specifically preoccupied with fears that the offender would be able to enter her home at night. Among the efforts to address this were rearranging her room, establishing a ritual of checking the house before bed to ensure that doors and windows were locked, and learning procedures to calm herself if she awoke frightened at night, including controlled breathing and telling herself that all entrances were locked, that her parents would protect her, and that no one could get in without making noise.

After a few sessions Gabriela refused to come to therapy. Based on her statements to her parents, we surmised that she preferred to avoid thinking and talking about the abuse. Early efforts to reduce anxiety associated with coming to therapy sessions apparently failed. Shortly after this time she began to act up at school and to get into arguments at home. Her parents used these behavioral difficulties as justification for the need for continued therapy. Eventually Gabriela agreed to resume counseling.

At this point sessions were oriented around system intervention. A joint interview was conducted with the detective; it was here that she revealed her involvement in sexual acts with her friend. The direct contact with law enforcement evoked affective associations to the memories and allowed opportunity to explore her beliefs and feelings about the abuse: why it happened; who was responsible; why she did not tell; what she feared; how she thought it would affect her future; what she hoped would happen. She generated a list of her biggest worries and fears, which included the friend's being mad at her for telling and sad if her brother was removed, the offender's coming and finding her and killing her, having to go to court, her mother's being disappointed in her if she didn't go, being abused again, becoming an offender, and her friend's thinking she was an offender. Anxiety was managed by labeling it "memories with feelings" and developing a plan to address each concern by correcting inaccurate beliefs and allowing expression of the associated feelings. In therapy, relaxation techniques were learned and practiced for use during anxiety-producing situations.

Education and clarification about the process and dynamics of victimization were predominant in addressing these worries and fears. Information about offender psychology and the process of engaging and maintaining victim cooperation was presented. She was able to identify the various manipulations and elements of coercion that made her participate and not tell. With assistance she explored why she behaved the way she did and how it was consistent with what she knew at the time and what she feared. A part of each therapy session was devoted to allowing expressions of her acute feelings of guilt about her involvement in sexual acts with her friend and grief over the loss of the relationship.

Gabriela also focused on the sexual component of the experience. She described her distress around both her own and others' sexuality. She reported being disturbed by knowing that her parents had sex or overhearing them making love. Her mother confirmed that this seemed to be evoking anxiety for Gabriela. In response to this, her bedroom was moved to another location in the house. She was acutely aware of the physical consequences—an enlarged vaginal opening—resulting from the assaults and described exploring her body. She was both excited and repelled by this activity, as well as worrying that it was wrong.

Weekly therapeutic sessions consisted of providing information and clarification about normal development, sexual feelings, and masturbation. The internal conflict posed by the abuse effects of premature sexual knowledge, experience, and arousal was addressed. Her differentness was reinterpreted to be potentially positive if reserved for the appropriate time in life. Some therapy time was devoted to simply allowing expression of her feelings about sex and sexuality.

Periodically, the focus of one-to-one counseling would be on current issues of adjustment at home and at school. Gabriela would have trouble getting along and be upset or her parents would bring issues of concern to sessions. When efforts to proceed with intervention were frustrated by the lack of response from the system, sessions were spent ventilating frustration and anger. Gabriela's fears of the offender and worry for her friend would resurface intermittently. Her mother also expressed rage at the failure of the system and frequently spoke of initiating her own legal response, although this never actually materialized.

Gabriela also attended 10 sessions of a time-limited victim group during this period. She was reported to be verbal and appropriate in discussions about abuse and related well to other children. She missed several sessions and during the last couple of sessions, when the topic had to do with sexuality, sex education, and body-image, she had some difficulty. She was described as having trouble attending to tasks and being distracted. During the discussion about body-image, Gabriela said she liked everything about her body and then drew a monster-like self-portrait, indicating continuing ambivalence.

Gabriela's attendance at individual and group sessions was not consistent. She had 14 individual sessions and 10 group sessions over the first year of treatment. Although her mother always expressed support for therapy, she was often unable to arrange to bring Gabriela for appointments. The stepfather was the one who usually brought her to sessions. Gabriela participated in two group series, although she missed most of the sessions during the second course. Gabriela always seemed eager to come to individual treatment. After a while sessions became sporadic and would be scheduled in response to a specific request from Gabriela or when something happened to cause concern.

For example, her mother and stepfather separated and this produced intense anxiety for Gabriela. She expressed great concern about losing the relationship with her stepfather and a joint therapy session was held to reassure her about the meaning and outcome of her parents' decision. She was pleased that it meant seeing her mother more, although she did exhibit an increase in anxiety symptoms at home and some bedwetting was reported.

During the following school year there were a number of occasions when problems at school or home led to a counseling appointment. There was an incident of sexual harassment by some boys at school and a witnessing of an attack on a boy that evoked abuse-related and generalized fears. Once she requested an appointment to talk about her own sexual feelings, exploratory masturbation, and questions about her sexual identity. These concerns came up in relation to experiences with and feelings toward a girl friend, with whom she had discussed masturbation and whom she once caught masturbating. She also described having sexual feelings toward girls, which disturbed her.

In each case a problem-specific counseling session was held. The fears or sexual concerns were identified and related to the abuse experience, information and reassurance provided, distorted or inaccurate beliefs challenged, strategies for managing anxiety or clarifying disturbing thoughts reviewed, sources of support identified. Gabriela appeared to respond well and, according to either her own or her parents' report, associated problems dissipated.

A couple of months passed without sessions. Gabriela had transferred schools, and the anxiety symptoms appeared to have subsided. Then her mother called and said that she was reporting suicidal intent and having a lot of physical complaints which were medically evaluated and found to be without physical origin. An appointment was scheduled; however, before it occurred Gabriela's mother came home to find her attempting to hang a noose from a light fixture after having written an explicit suicide note.

She was referred immediately for inpatient psychiatric care at the Children's Hospital. Upon admission Gabriela was hallucinating and was actively suicidal. She had loose associations and was cognitively disorganized. She spent three months as an inpatient on a children's unit and a subsequent three months in a special psychiatric foster home and in day treatment before her transition back home.

During the hospitalization Gabriela was medicated with first antipsychotic and then antidepressant medication. The vivid hallucinations persisted for some time and were of figures dripping with blood beckoning her to do something to kill herself and join them. In spite of the severity of her suicidality, Gabriela rather enthusiastically joined the unit milieu, eventually becoming a strong member of the group. She began to express intense anger toward her mother. In family sessions Gabriela would provocatively and dramatically tell her mother how much she hated her. She was very resistant to discharge planning and repeatedly refused to return home. She begged to stay longer on the unit and threatened to commit suicide if forced to return. the diagnosis upon discharge was major depressive episode with psychotic features.

The discharge planning process was complicated. The hospital staff continued to encourage her and work toward a return home, planning follow-up with a special mental health center program for children discharged from psychiatric units. The state Department of Social Services was involved and sought the mother's approval for state involvement with conditions to fulfill. The unit asked this therapist to provide individual therapy. Gabriela had originally rejected that aspect of the plan but later agreed.

This was a very difficult period for Gabriela's mother. She tended to see Gabriela's resistance to returning home as primarily resulting from the comfortable situation she found herself in on the unit. She took a strong position that Gabriela return home as rapidly as possible. She was skeptical of the medication regimen and to some extent downplayed the seriousness of her daughter's distress. She was hurt by Gabriela's rejection of her but tended to see it as partially manipulative. As a social activist she insisted on a direct role in decision-making and questioned the need for state involvement. However, she agreed to and complied with all recommendations.

Following discharge to the specialized foster home, Gabriela resumed regular individual therapy. On a much more regular basis she attended 25 sessions over the next eight months. She was pleasant and cooperative but regularly asserted her hatred of her mother and reluctance to return home. She spoke fondly of the unit and her relationships with the other patients. She frequently stated that she would be suicidal if forced to return home. However, she made no suicide gestures or attempts and talked rationally about the consequences of self-destructive behavior, which would include restriction of freedom. She had no history or inclination toward acting out and she ruled out such options as running away.

Her feelings of belonging when she was on the unit became an important therapeutic focus. She often talked about how accepted she felt and how much she enjoyed the group activities. She reported encountering other children she had known from school and discovering that some of them had been abused as well. As she put it, she did not feel that she was an outsider as she always had before with peers. She was helped to make sense of her pervasive feelings of differentness, which stemmed in part from the abuse experience. The hospitalization experience was defined as a vehicle for breaking the isolation and providing an opportunity to gain skills and form age-appropriate relationships in a safe and highly structured environment.

On the issue of her feelings toward her mother, I sought consultation from my colleagues on staff on how to proceed. Gabriela had related how her hospital therapists and staff and the foster mother had repeatedly said she didn't really hate her mother. She always responded that she really did and had all her life and nothing could change it. It was advised that, rather than challenge Gabriela's assertions, I should accept and explore them.

Gabriela was asked to identify all her reasons, specifically, for this hatred. The resulting list contained the following statements: "she is not the motherly type; how she looks [her mother is an extremely attractive woman]; when I was little she was a stripper and maybe a prostitute; it seems like she would have sex with any man; she acts like a 'whore' and a 'dumb broad' around men" (e.g., she giggles, sits on their laps). Gabriela saw this behavior as contradicting the values her mother claimed about being independent and not letting men push women around.

It was apparent that most of Gabriela's negative feelings were associated with how her mother acted as a woman and a sexual person. Gabriela's mother is, in fact, a very beautiful woman whom men find compelling. For example, the stepfather had left his wife of 18 years within three weeks of meeting her. The issue of identification coupled with antagonism toward her mother was explored in depth with Gabriela. She said how she wished her mother appeared more as a mother than a woman. Gabriela was able to figure out that her own fears of sexual development were related to her feelings toward her mother. She consistently spoke of how she wished to halt her growth of breasts and body hair, that she would like to jump to being an adult. She conspicuously dressed in oversized and baggy clothing and acknowledged attempts to cover up her changing body.

Gabriela's focus on her mother's qualities as a woman dominated her view of her mother. She was harshly critical of her mother in the role of parent, perceiving her as inadequate and as having priorities other than the family. Her mother's active involvement in school, work, and causes contributed to Gabriela's sense that she was not the primary recipient of her mother's energies and concern.

Whether this alienation or the basis for it preceded the sexual assault experience was impossible to determine. However, the sexual abuse clearly exacerbated the relationship problems in two very important ways. First, like most abused children, Gabriela felt she was unprotected, although she knew her mother had no explicit knowledge of the abuse when it was occurring. However, her mother's focus of time and energy away from the family contributed to Gabriela's being left with the offender and to her sense of mother's unavailability. The second aspect had to do with the increased salience of sexuality and accelerated sexual experience. Gabriela's fears and revulsion about sex, which derived from the abuse, conflicted with her mother's overt sexuality. The identification with her mother associated with psychosexual development and puberty forced Gabriela to think excessively of growing up in terms of becoming a sexual person.

As she talked more about the sexual aspects of her own development and her perceptions of her mother, the affective intensity of dislike diminished. Permitting expression of the feelings without direct challenge had the effect of reducing their potency. Having an explanation for the source and strength of her negative feelings made her more comfortable, although the feelings persisted. She described rejecting all efforts by her mother to show affection and continued to say she looked forward to being 18 and being able to leave home. Gradually she reported that her suicidal feelings decreased in intensity.

Concomitant with this treatment, Gabriela entered a new school. She developed a crush on a boy and a new circle of friends. She became increasingly estranged from her former best friend, preferring her new friends, a more mainstream group of kids. She was obviously more confident and was able to talk about her newfound social competence. Insight was facilitated about her transfer of self-esteem and social skills from the unit into the school setting.

Gabriela's interest in the boy provided a therapeutic opening to explore age-appropriate sexual feelings. She was clear that she did not want an explicitly sexual relationship but enjoyed the flirting, the junior high girl games of having friends ask him whom he liked, writing notes, checking on him, and acting silly. She was able to talk about how much fun the fantasy and the games were when they took place in a safe context. She knew he was too shy and immature to even respond to this attention and gained a sense of comfort and ease with the situation. Her prior confusion about her own sexual orientation disappeared.

Gabriela said that she continued to have suicidal thoughts when around her mother and felt estranged from her. But she said she would never try to kill herself because she would miss her school friends and was really enjoying her peer relationships and school activities. As she adopted a style of compliant distance at home, conflict diminished. She became less preoccupied with her discomfort with her body and said she rarely thought about masturbating anymore. This state of affairs persisted over several months.

Then Gabriela experienced a setback at school when a girl rejected her and caused a split in the social circle. She quite suddenly stopped doing school work and started to find reasons not to go to school. My efforts and those of her parents to place this experience in perspective and to help her devise strategies to handle it were not successful. She eventually stopped going to school and made two minor suicide gestures. Yet she did not exhibit the depressive symptoms of the year before and was not hospitalized. The situation turned into a power struggle with her mother; in fact, Gabriela seeming to almost enjoy her power to manipulate and infuriate her mother.

This turn of events was interpreted as evidence that Gabriela's sense of herself was still quite fragile and not yet robust enough to cope with the ordinary vagaries of adolescent relationships. However, although she withdrew from the school environment, she was not depressed. The school refusal and aggressively defiant and noncompliant behavior at home appeared to be primarily a function of dysfunctional family patterns which were not directly related to the victimization of Gabriela. Although family therapy was suggested, the family did not follow through after an initial appointment. About six weeks later, when the new term began, Gabriela returned to school and resumed her peer-focused but adequate functioning. The remainder of the school year passed relatively uneventfully.

TREATMENT OUTCOME

The course of therapy so far with Gabriela has produced significant improvement and could be considered successful for the direct effects of sexual assault. Over the two-year period of intervention Gabriela's abuse-related fears diminished and generalization to other situations was contained. She no longer expressed significant fears of men or teenage boys or of potential sexual situations. There was a decrease in anxiety-related symptomatology. She became able to talk about and remember her abuse experience with a minimum of affective discomfort. Her understanding of sexual abuse situations is accurate, she says she does not feel responsible, she is aware of the process of grooming and has ideas about how she would handle a potential abuse situation. Anxiety about and distaste for her own developing sexuality have been reduced and her attitudes and behaviors have assumed normal developmental qualities (e.g., interest in agemates).

Negative beliefs about herself that might produce low self-esteem or depression appear to have dissipated. She recognizes that she is capable of relating with confidence and competence with peers and at school. She is able to say that kids like her. Even though she has suffered a relapse, it was not nearly as severe as the previous year and has been resolved within a relatively short period. She seems to have successfully translated the experience of social acceptance in the hospital to a more normative setting. Future successes in this environment will reinforce a growing positive sense of self. She no longer expresses stigmatized feelings about having been sexually abused, but rather identifies with the large group of other children sharing the common experience of victimization.

Her developmental process seems well on its way to a normal course. Her activities and interests are age appropriate and prosocial. Fortunately, she was never tempted to join a delinquent subculture or engage in antisocial or destructive behaviors, which might have made return to a path of positive adjustment more difficult. Even during the relapse period she never escalated the behavior to seriously destructive, antisocial, or self-destructive level. She maintains a strong sense of values about right and wrong, respect and empathy for others.

The most problematic remaining area pertains to her relationship with her mother. It is not surprising that this would continue to be unsettled, given the specific nature of their relationship independent of the abuse. Gabriela has always been focused on her mother and wished for greater closeness and more of her time. She both admires and resents her for her attractiveness and her activism. There is no positive model for mother-child relationship in her own mother's history, which limits her mother's capacity to respond to Gabriela. The competitiveness is intergenerational.

Gabriela's mother chose not to continue family therapy with the mental health center or to initiate it elsewhere during the year following the hospitalization. However, the current problems have made family life uncomfortable enough that she is now prepared to engage in family treatment. They have begun this process.

The victimization-related effects seem to be adequately treated for now. The experience has been integrated emotionally and cognitively. Gabriela is not far off-track in relating to her peers; she is in the correct grade and is not involved in or drawn to the dangerous activities of substance abuse, early sexual activity, or antisocial behaviors. However, as with many abused children, Gabriela's victimization is not the only problem for her and her family.

OBSTACLES TO TREATMENT

The primary obstacles to treatment were the logistical and management problems in maintaining regular attendance. These are common problems in working with children. In this case it did not appear to be active resistance but a matter of other activities or the lack of a vehicle interfering with consistent involvement. This can be especially problematic in treating sexual abuse cases because children do not always exhibit significant distress that would signal the importance of regular therapy. Many of the concerns these children have relate to internal processes and there is a natural tendency for them to want at times to avoid dealing with the subject matter. In the absence of overt disturbance and particularly where the child is resistant, participation in therapy may seem unnecessary to the parents.

Avoidance may also be a problem for the therapist who must identify issues for therapeutic intervention. To some extent, in order to engage a child in therapy there must be an interest and willingness to talk about and work on something. If the child is presenting as if everything is going fine, therapy may be reduced to weekly chats about how life is going. While some children may appreciate simply having the relationship, therapy may come to seem irrelevant or useless.

However, it may be part of the nature of sexual abuse effects that issues surface and become salient only when there is an event or a developmental shift. Therapy may have to be episodic and responsive to the process of growing and changing and not something that can be accomplished over a single time period. In this case the more immediate abuse-related fears and anxieties were quite accessible. The more complicated feelings about her mother, which had their origins in the preexisting relationship and are part of an evolving process, could only be addressed when forced to the surface.

SYSTEMS INVOLVED

The other systems were significant both in issues of case management and in terms of therapy content. Clearly, the failure of the legal system to respond adequately negatively influenced both Gabriela's and her family's beliefs about individual power, justice, safety, and the efficacy of social institutions. These were already significant concerns for the family in terms of their values and perceptions of society as generally oppressive, racist, and exclusive. Gabriela is African-American; the offender is white. Not only were these views reinforced, but there was no opportunity to feel as though reporting the offense had led to any positive outcome. They could not feel as though the friend was now safe, the offender was neither punished nor helped, and the relationship between the two families was permanently severed.

I was similarly disturbed by the ineffectiveness of my efforts to promote system involvement. Numerous attempts to advocate proved useless. These included making phone calls and writing letters to the police department, the victim witness advocate, the Department of Social Services, the juvenile division, and the prosecutor's office. At each step there were delays, lost information, a failure to follow through, inadequate approaches and a lack of interest. It was disheartening and made it difficult to combat the victim's and family's anger and frustration, which I shared.

The other systems related to the hospitalization and the involvement of the numerous mental health professionals and ancillary staff, as well as the state Department of Social Services. The hospital staff were extremely competent in treating Gabriela's psychotic depression but also facilitated Gabriela's expression of anger toward her mother. The issues for me during this period centered around maintaining the confidence of both the family and Gabriela by not allying with either the hospital or Gabriela's mother. This was possible because my relationship with Gabriela was always clearly identified as individual and victimization-focused. The hospital staff primarily addressed other issues and focused on the immediate concerns around depression and the emerging feelings toward her mother. Although these feelings were related to the abuse, by separating the treatments it kept both Gabriela and her mother from feeling threatened or resistant toward me. It was explicitly stated that family therapy would be done elsewhere.

MISTAKES

There may be a question about whether family therapy should have been more strongly pursued. There clearly were and continue to be significant issues around family relationships. However, the resistance from both parties did not make it an attractive endeavor and, until the problems more specifically surfaced, there was insufficient motivation for engaging in what will undoubtedly be a long and difficult process.

For me either to have shifted a focus onto the family or to have insisted on concomitant family therapy would have seriously jeopardized the therapeutic relationship with Gabriela and diminished parental support for Gabriela's involvement in victimization treatment. Since Gabriela has done significant work on the relationship with her mother in the context of individual therapy, there has been some progress in this area.

This issue frequently arises in sexual abuse cases and has major implications. Abuse-focused therapy can really only be done individually or in group; however, it is obvious that in many, if not most, cases family issues are extremely relevant to treatment. Yet, it has been my experience that to insist on addressing other family issues almost invariably means that the family becomes less cooperative with victimization therapy. This can result in disruption of the therapeutic alliance with the child or termination of therapy altogether. Sometimes the parents seek to shift the focus onto those issues, but most often when it occurs that is in terms of seeking behavioral management and control over the child and not in evaluating and changing structure within the family.

I strongly believe that an essential ingredient of recovery is the opportunity to work on the experience directly and separately. After all, it is the child who had the victimization experience. However the family was affected, it was not in the same immediate and personal way. Family members and others usually wish to avoid the explicit aspects of the experience or want to push the focus away and beyond the abuse as quickly as possible. There is often a message that recovery means forgetting or even the implication that the child is using the abuse to get attention or void responsibility.

These views reflect the society-wide avoidance and denial of the intense and long-term impact of abuse experiences. Since children are never truly voluntary patients in the sense that they must rely on adult willingness to allow them to participate in therapy, it becomes the victim specialist's duty to make that possible.

Perhaps greater emphasis on regular counseling sessions would have accelerated the recovery process and prevented the deterioration into psychosis. That episode was clearly related to intense ambivalence in her feelings toward her mother that had not surfaced in individual sessions. Perhaps the depth and long-standing nature of the feelings made such an extreme reaction necessary and inevitable. In retrospect, I might have paid more attention to the ways in which the parent-child relationship was inextricably connected to the child's feelings and perceptions about the abuse and its effects.

THERAPIST REACTIONS

Overall, this has been a very rewarding and challenging therapeutic endeavor. It made a great deal of difference that Gabriela, her mother, and other family members were likable and mostly cooperative. There was a basic commitment by the family to Gabriela and her welfare, which made hope and progress possible. Had her mother doubted her or minimized the seriousness of the abuse or had there been a fundamental lack of love or attachment, treatment success would have been severely compromised. Without those elements, intervention may be simply an exercise in patching and filling in to help the child survive but not truly move forward.

Since Gabriela is only 13, many years remain before successful adult adjustment is achieved. It is not only possible but likely that there will be setbacks and crises. However, treatment of children cannot be measured just by adult outcome. It is assumed that dealing successfully with pieces of the process will lay the groundwork for continued progress. It is also likely that positive results along the way will have a mitigating effect on the potential long-term harm that might have resulted without these steps.

The most rewarding aspect of this case has been the continued perception by the family that participation in this type of treatment was beneficial. Both Gabriela and her mother express positive attitudes and are compliant with the treatment regimen. This reinforces my view that individually focused victimization therapy can produce a positive outcome even when other significant issues are extant and that, when the focus and purpose are specifically identified, both the victim and the parent are able to see the value and appreciate the importance of the victim having a therapeutic context devoted primarily to the child and the victimization experience.

6

Treatment in the Absence of Maternal Support

ALISON J. EINBENDER

Dr. Einbender presents a familiar case. The child comes to treatment in the absence of family support regarding the abuse allegations and the child's continuing needs for treatment. Many children understandably refuse to engage in therapy when put in this dilemma. They will deny the abuse allegations even though earlier statements had been quite clear and specific. Compounding this case further is the presence of an overtly rejecting mother who eschews psychotherapy due to her cultural background and who is also physically abusive.

Sarah's therapy had to contend with the misguided interventions of various professionals. The initial in-home counseling following Sarah's physical abuse by her mother, Kim, resulted in making Kim even more coercive toward and less supportive of Sarah.

Sarah's early behavior was a conflicted mixture of dependency and needs for control. Too often we negatively interpret children's needs for control in these situations as manipulative and aggressive. I believe it is more helpful to think about their behaviors as a way to manage their incredible anxiety about the intimate therapy situation.

Given Sarah's fragility and preoccupation with sexuality, the need for a female therapist was clear. She had become overly aroused during the evaluation by the male psychologist and would have faced constant difficulties with emotional regulation with him as the therapist. Using small toys as transitional objects enabled the therapist to maintain emotional contact with Sarah; this is crucial when issues of betrayal and trust are salient. Dr. Einbender's home visits were also important in furthering the relationship, both providing support to Sarah and also allowing her presence to be felt by Kim.

A common therapy question pertains to physical closeness with sexually abused children. Dr. Einbender's clear discussion of these issues is important in this regard. She allowed hugging and even lying down on the floor side by side. However, it seems as if she was very sensitive to the fact that this alternated between being helpful and somewhat upsetting to Sarah. Sarah would ask for physical contact by getting hurt and in so doing was allowing for opportunities for physical contact that were presumably safer. It is interesting to see how Dr. Einbender's extreme tolerance of Sarah's physical behavior with some gentle limit-setting resulted in Sarah's gradually being able to define greater and more appropriate limits. Too often therapists set very rigid limits on physical contact and boundaries. When given time and gentleness, these limits can be internalized in a less punitive manner. As an example, witness Sarah's being able to go to the bathroom by herself.

Dr. Einbender allowed a very gradual uncovering of Sarah's sexual abuse experience, given the facts that Sarah had already discussed this in her evaluation, that she was safe from her father, and that she was so prone to overexcitement within the sessions.

We often don't see children's behavior outside of the therapy setting. The guardian ad litem's comments about Sarah's behavior at the zoo, on other outings, etc., was instrumental in letting Dr. Einbender know the full range of her behavior and in opening up the therapeutic targets.

Sexually abused children are often rejected, and we need to deal with their rejection by caregivers and care providers. For example, Sarah was rejected from an afterschool day-care provider because of her inappropriate sexual behavior and because her intensity seemed to greatly bother the daycare provider.

Progress could be seen, however. Sarah's response to Dr. Einbender's second vacation was much more appropriate, suggesting that their attachment had become more secure.

The importance of emotional regulation is underscored, as Sarah became better able to contain the intensity and duration of aggression expressed toward her father. She internalized some capacity for self-control and was able to contain this aggressive activity. — Editor

AUTHOR'S THEORETICAL ORIENTATION

The therapy I do with children is guided by a blend of perspectives, including family systems, psychodynamic, object relations, and developmental theories. The systemic model appreciates the multiple reciprocal influences and demands of one family member upon another, as well as of one system upon another (Minuchin, 1974). Psychodynamic and object relations theory examine the way in which relationships with significant others affect the child's developing sense of self (Bowlby, 1973; Winnicott, 1986).

A developmental perspective also is crucial in understanding a child's psyche (Fraiberg, 1959). Although this may seem obvious, it is often overlooked by parents and professionals, leading to serious misinterpretation of children's symptomatology. For example, young children tend to communicate their feelings behaviorally rather than verbally. I have seen children who were labeled "oppositional" for refusing to visit a relative, yet who later were discovered to have been resisting these visits because they were being sexually abused but were afraid to tell anyone.

My therapy with sexually abused children is guided by my understanding of how children at various developmental stages cope with trauma. Because individuals of all ages typically respond to trauma by regressing to a previous level of functioning, I carefully assess sexually abused children for signs of regression in a number of areas, including sleep, toileting, anxiety levels, peer relations, school functioning, and ability to tolerate separation from significant others. Sexually abused children sometimes act out these issues directly in sessions through behaviors such as seeking out a high degree of physical contact with the therapist or needing to go to the bathroom midsession when anxiety-arousing material has emerged.

Whether therapy for sexually abused children differs from general child therapy is an interesting question. Other types of childhood trauma, such as the death of a parent, physical abuse, or neglect, can produce symptomatology similar to that of sexually abused children. In addition, there is great variability in how children respond to sexual abuse, due to variability in premorbid factors (such as the child's age, intelligence, prior adjustment, socioeconomic status, and family structure), the nature and extent of the abuse, and the events that transpire after the abuse is revealed. For these reasons, it is difficult to generalize about therapy with sexually abused children.

However, a few observations can be made about how therapy with sexually abused children differs from general child psychotherapy. Because the law requires that any suspicions of child sexual abuse be investigated, these cases always involve multiple systems. Typically the child's family, social services caseworker, and pediatrician are involved. In addition, legal professionals (lawyers, *guardians ad litem*, and judges), therapists, and foster care parents may be involved. This necessitates that therapists working with sexually abused children be highly skilled at recognizing and managing systemic issues, since these issues can sabotage treatment. The case which I will discuss illustrates this point.

Therapists who work with sexually abused children need to be able to talk explicitly about sexuality with the child, the family, and with the other professionals involved. Given our culture's taboo against freely discussing sexuality, most therapists need to learn a language and develop a comfort level for talking about sexuality to help the child and family talk about what happened.

Because child sexual abuse violates one of the most basic taboos of our society, therapists working in this area must deal with feelings that are elicited by this issue. Some sexually abused children directly act out their sexual confusion in the presence of the therapist. Therapists may find themselves confronted in session with challenging situations, such as a child masturbating, trying to undress him/herself or the therapist, or seeking physical intimacy with the therapist in a sexualized way. Setting appropriate boundaries while ensuring that the child does not feel rejected or humiliated requires delicacy. Moreover, children respond as much to the affect and tension level of the therapist at such moments as they do to what is actually said and done.

Additionally, the therapist may experience intense feelings and counter-transference issues towards the child's family members and the perpetrator(s). These cases can elicit powerful feelings of rage and powerlessness, as well as rescue fantasies, in the professionals involved. It is important that therapists recognize and deal with their feelings so that they do not negatively affect the therapy. Consultation with colleagues as well as personal therapy can be useful in this process. Therapists also need to be aware that the personal reactions and biases of all professionals involved in a case may skew their judgment at times.

Lastly, although this is true of psychotherapy in general, it seems particularly true that trust is a difficult issue for many children who have been sexually abused. This gets expressed in the therapy in many ways, such as a child's being overly concerned about privacy and whether others can overhear what is said in the therapy room. It also means that sexually abused children often take longer to form a trusting relationship with the therapist that is secure enough to allow them to begin to explore the actual abuse. This requires great patience from the therapist, who may feel pressure from the system (e.g., caseworkers, parents) to "make the child deal with the sexual abuse" before the child is ready to do so.

DESCRIPTION OF CASE

Sarah, a six-year-old Asian-American girl, was referred to me for psychotherapy by a male psychologist following his court-ordered evaluation of her concerning her long-standing history of sexual abuse by her natural father. As a result of the evaluation, Sarah was made a dependent of the state and visitation between Sarah and her father was suspended pending his evaluation and treatment. She was ordered to obtain psychotherapy, and her mother was required either to participate in family therapy or to take a parenting class.

Sarah's history of sexual abuse first came to light when she was four and a half years old. Between the time of her initial disclosure and my eventual work with her, a complex series of interactions between her family, the legal system, and social services had occurred.

After the initial referral, Sarah revealed to her caseworker and a detective that there had been repeated sexual assaults by her father, during which he had had oral, anal, and vaginal intercourse with her. It also seemed probable that the abuse may have been accompanied by threats and physical violence. Although the initial medical/gynecological examination found no abnormalities or physical signs of abuse, the physician referred Sarah to a female therapist at a local sexual abuse treatment center for further evaluation (Finkel, 1988).

The therapist was convinced from Sarah's statements, behavior, and extreme fearfulness of her father that she had been brutally sexually assaulted by him. She therefore urged that visitation with him be restricted until he had completed treatment. She stated that, during her first contact with Sarah, "she lay wiggling on the floor like a worm that had been stepped on." She described Sarah as "hyperactive and extremely distractible," and recommended that Sarah receive a psychological evaluation to assess her emotional functioning, academic abilities, relationship skills, and reality testing.

The therapist was also concerned about Sarah's poor relationship with her mother, Kim. Apparently Kim frequently hit Sarah on the face, was ambivalent about her, and did not believe the allegations.

PSYCHOLOGICAL ASSESSMENT MATERIAL

The male psychologist who evaluated Sarah determined that she was not psychotic and that she had above-average intelligence and academic abilities. His contact with her teacher corroborated the fact that she was highly motivated and that her academic performance was excellent. He viewed this as a good prognostic indicator of her ability to continue to succeed academically and to benefit from psychotherapy.

The psychologist's behavioral observations of Sarah and the test results were indicative of sexual abuse. He described the high level of inappropriate, sexualized affection-seeking behavior that Sarah demonstrated towards him: "She repeatedly wanted to kiss and hug . . . [me] on both occasions that I saw her, and her efforts at affection-seeking seemed to make her increasingly nervous and upset, to the point where in the initial interview she actually urinated in her pants as a result of a high level of anxiety." He noted that she had included explicit genitalia on the figures in her drawings. The projective measures (the Rorschach, TAT, and drawings) indicated that Sarah was markedly depressed, anxious, and impulsive. She had low self-esteem and she was extremely ambivalent about the issue of dependency. He reported that she was angry and that she had a strong tendency to internalize her anger. She viewed her mother as a "weak" and helpless woman and her father as a "bad" man who had done "bad" things to her. He echoed the recommendation of the sexual abuse counselor that Sarah's contact with her father be prohibited until both he and Sarah had completed psychotherapy.

The psychologist had concerns about Sarah's relationship with her mother. The mother's responses on the Achenbach Child Behavior Checklist (Achenbach & Edelbrock, 1983) indicated that she denied the sexual abuse and viewed Sarah as an ungrateful, disobedient child. The psychologist recommended that both Sarah and her mother obtain psychotherapy.

Sarah came with her caseworker for the initial interview with me. Her mother had refused to attend the session. The caseworker provided background data. Sarah's mother, Kim, was Asian and her father, Mike, was American. They met when Mike was stationed in Asia. Sarah was born after their move to the United States. Mike left town abruptly after Sarah's abuse disclosure, and Kim divorced him. The caseworker pointed out, however, that Kim still did not believe Sarah's reports of the abuse. She explained that Kim's refusal to participate in Sarah's therapy was reflective of her cultural belief that going for therapy meant that a person was "crazy." Kim had strong objections to Sarah's participating in therapy, but the therapy had been ordered by the court. Despite Kim's opposition to therapy, she seemed to need help in parenting Sarah. She complained continuously to the caseworker about her frustration and difficulty in disciplining her daughter.

A letter from an Asian counselor who had briefly treated Kim explained that Kim had a seventh grade education and that she was not fluent in English. Kim was under considerable stress because she was separated from her native culture, family, and friends, and because she was divorced (which was a disgrace in her culture) from a husband whom she felt had publicly humiliated her. Kim apparently had a strong desire to return with Sarah to her native country, but was limited in doing so by her finances and by her knowledge that, as a divorced woman, she would be ostracized there.

The counselor stated that Kim was distrustful of all of the "helping professionals" with whom she had interacted since the disclosure of the abuse. She had experienced her contact with each of these systems as punitive, and was outraged that she had been ordered to participate in therapy or a parenting class, given that she "had done nothing wrong." The counselor recommended that no further attempts be made to engage Kim in psychotherapy for herself or her daughter.

In the intake session, my first impression of Sarah was of a very pretty, nicely dressed girl who was extremely active and verbal. She separated easily from the caseworker and seemed very eager to engage with me. She repeatedly asked if she could again see the male psychologist who had evaluated her. Her initial behavior was an interesting mixture of anxiety, intrusiveness, and compulsivity. For example, she quickly switched from one play activity to another. She used hand puppets to talk to me and had them repetitively kiss me on the face and neck. She eventually did some drawing, and then perseverated in trying to replace the colored pens in their original order. Sarah's affect in that first session was anxious and artificially cheerful. She showed distress only at one point in the interview, when she talked about being hit frequently by other children, both at school and in her neighborhood.

Soon after, I contacted Kim and arranged a home visit, accompanied by a female interpreter. I felt that it was vital for treatment planning that I get to directly assess Kim's and Sarah's relationship, as well as Kim's stance towards me. Kim seemed pleased to have the chance to speak with the interpreter, someone from her native country. However, she avoided me and refused to answer the questions I had the interpreter pose to her. Sarah and Kim seemed physically and emotionally distant. Sarah never approached her mother while I was there, although she repetitively begged me to play with her in her room. Each time she did this, her mother chastised her, telling her that she was a "bad girl" to interrupt and that she should "shut up."

After we left, the interpreter explained that Kim believed that Sarah had fabricated the incest report and blamed Sarah for the breakup of her marriage and the subsequent financial stress and cultural humiliation it caused her. She restated her refusal to participate in the therapy and said that her only goal for Sarah was for her to learn to be more "obedient."

COURSE OF THERAPY

My original goals for Sarah's therapy were tempered by her mother's refusal to be involved. It was clear from the home visit that their relationship was disturbed and that they were both emotionally deprived. It was also clear that Kim was not going to support or validate Sarah's feelings about the abuse. Therefore, my primary goal was to build a trusting, safe relationship with Sarah, so that she could express and resolve her feelings and behavior related to the abuse. My long-range goals were:

1. to build her self-esteem;
2. to intervene in the cycle of scapegoating she experienced at school;
3. to teach her appropriate, nonsexualized ways to express affection;
4. to support her continued academic progress in school;
5. to allow her to express her feelings toward her mother; and
6. by educating her, to help prevent the possibility of future sexual victimization.

My weekly sessions with Sarah were held in a therapeutic playroom, which had a one-way mirror that adjoined an observation room. A microphone hung from the ceiling, making it possible to videotape sessions.

Phase 1

A potential threat to the therapy arose between the first and second sessions. Due to the caseworker's suspicions of physical abuse, Sarah had been placed in a children's shelter for three days and Kim had been arrested and put in jail overnight. Subsequently, the caseworker arranged to have a family crisis intervention worker go to the home three times per week for one month to help Kim and Sarah improve their relationship.

I was worried from the outset about the family intervention, given the complexity of the issues involved, as well as Kim's negative feelings about the mental health system. The counselor's final treatment summary confirmed my concerns. Her intervention had been based upon an individual rather than systemic viewpoint. She had viewed herself as Kim's agent, and she had used behavioral reinforcers to try to get Sarah to conform more readily, and without protest, to her mother's expectations. This approach overlooked the dynamics of their relationship related to the incest, such as the possibility that Sarah might be furious with her mother for her inability to protect her from the abuse and for her unwillingness to believe it had occurred. In addition, the counselor noted that she had "taught Sarah to gracefully lose a game without crying." This disturbed me because I believe that deprived and abused children need to experience more, not less, success in order to build self-esteem, and that they should be given opportunities to win whenever possible.

Sarah's relationship with me went through many changes during the course of therapy. In these first sessions, she seemed desperate for a relationship with me. She repetitively asked in each session how much time we had left together and resisted parting from me at the end of sessions. Sarah had a great need for physical contact and affection, which she expressed in a variety of ways. She insisted upon hugging me goodbye at the end of sessions. At times she sought contact indirectly by engaging in risk-taking behaviors, such as climbing on furniture, which had the effect of bringing me nearer to ensure her safety.

Sarah also began to exhibit regressive behavior in the therapy sessions. This manifested in her wanting to play with babydolls and also in her attempts to sit in a small toy highchair. I commented on these behaviors and told her that it was all right to act like a baby during our time together if she wanted to.

In one session, Sarah drew a very poignant drawing of a little cat. She then told me to close my eyes and she colored over the entire picture with a black crayon. She then told me that the cat was very scared because it was lost. I asked who would find the cat and she said that she and I would do so together. I felt that she was letting me know through this picture that, at least on an unconscious level, she understood that I was there to help her.

In these early play therapy sessions, Sarah frequently had us pretend to be co-teachers who were also sisters. She cast me into the role of the "new" teacher, while she assumed the role of the well-established teacher whose task was to introduce me to the class and to train me. It was striking that in her play she put herself in this position of power relative to me. I felt that this represented her desperate need to be in control of some aspect of her life. From her teacher's reports and from her play, I had the strong sense that school was perhaps the only place where she experienced a positive sense of herself, through her good academic achievement and her teacher's positive regard for her. Not surprisingly, her stated goal was to become a teacher. However, her play also indicated that she was struggling to bind her anxiety through being compulsive in her approach towards school tasks.

Following her theme of making us "sisters and co-teachers," Sarah began to express a need, which became increasingly pronounced later in therapy, for us to be "the same." Early on, she repeatedly directed me to imitate her behavior, as well as to make exact replicas of designs she drew. I interpreted this need for sameness between us as evidence of severe ego boundary confusion and a need for identification.

In these first sessions, Sarah expressed angry and fearful feelings towards her mother. She complained about Kim's hitting her and yelling at her. She fantasized about creating a family that would exclude her mother and father and include only herself and the female "helping professionals" in her life. She exhibited a great deal of boundary and identity confusion between the *guardian ad litem* and me. At times she wanted the GAL to join us in the therapy room, while at other times she worried that the GAL could overhear our conversations from the waiting room.

Given Sarah's seeming fragility and lack of maternal support, I was concerned about prematurely pushing her to deal with the sexual abuse. Therefore, I told her that I knew what had happened to her and that we could talk about it when she was ready. She clearly was preoccupied with sexual issues. In one session, she had us undress a male and female baby doll to examine them medically and she insisted that I take the boy doll. In the next session, she chose the boy doll and gave me the girl doll, but she warned me that she "might get angry because it is a boy." She told me I had to exchange dolls with her if this happened.

Sarah also demonstrated a fascination with the hanging microphone, which was to become highly significant later in the therapy. She asked to be held up to the microphone so that she could suck on it, which I did not allow. She also expressed some bizarre fantasies involving the microphone and the male psychologist who had evaluated her. She insisted that he had lifted her up to the microphone and then allowed her to fall and hurt herself. (He confirmed that nothing remotely like this had happened.) She frequently spoke of both wanting and fearing further contact with this psychologist. It seemed clear that her contact with him had triggered transferential feelings towards her father, which included great confusion between affection, sexuality, and aggression in her relationships with men.

Sarah's extreme level of anxiety manifested in sessions in a variety of ways, including her pressured activity level, somatic complaints, hypervigilance, and compulsive behavior. Her apparent hyperactivity began to quiet down in response to my tactic of assuming a pace slightly slower than hers. She complained frequently of stomachaches, nausea, and vomiting. The GAL reported that Kim had told her that Sarah had frequent nightmares. Sarah routinely interrupted sessions to go to the bathroom, particularly when anxiety arousing material came up. She was excessively hypervigilant. She wanted to lock the door of the therapy room so that no one could come in. She had difficulty trusting that people would respect the "Do Not Disturb" sign on the door.

Sarah exhibited extreme fearfulness and bizarre fantasies during one session when we heard a siren outside. She insisted that we turn out the lights and sit side by side, holding hands. When the lights were turned on, she insisted that a photograph of a shark, which was hanging on the wall, had actually bit her in the dark. She insisted that we cover up the picture, which we did. It seemed to me at that point that she may have been reliving some of the terror of the abuse. Sarah also was compulsive about having us clean the chalkboard after drawing on it. She then typically insisted that we wash our hands a number of times, to "make sure they are clean." These behaviors suggested that she was struggling with feelings of "dirtiness," which may have been related to the abuse.

One and a half months into therapy, Sarah and I had a three-week separation because of my Christmas travel plans. Before I left, I gave her a small stuffed animal as a Christmas present, so that she would have a tangible reminder of our relationship during my absence. Her sensitivity to the separation was evident in the sessions that followed my return. Her previous enthusiasm to see me was replaced by reluctance to enter the therapy room with me. Upon entering the room, she typically burst into a flurry of pressured activity, which included much nonsense baby talk. She was usually able to calm down by mid-session. Much of her play during this time continued to involve having us play-act school situations in which we were very active, somewhat frenetic, teachers who rushed around trying to do an impossible number of tasks in a short time. I felt that this type of play expressed Sarah's feeling that she and I had too little time together in which to deal with the disturbing feelings and thoughts racing around inside her. She also began to initiate games of hide and seek in sessions. She usually chose to be the one to hide. This choice of play seemed to be a metaphor for her ambivalence about wanting to be close to me, given my "abandonment" of her over Christmas break. She seemed to be testing me to see if I would continue to be there for her.

During this time, Sarah made references to difficulties she was having in relationships. She complained that her classmates hit her a lot and that she generally felt disliked by them. She also began to talk more about her relationship with her mother. Most of her comments about their relationship were negative, although she did acknowledge that her mother performed certain basic, caretaking activities for her, such as buying her clothes and making dinner. She believed that her mother hated her and she feared that her mother would send her away to live somewhere else. She also expressed a lot of anger towards her mother. It was striking that she made no references to her father during these sessions.

She continued, however, to make indirect references to sexuality during this phase of therapy. In one session, she asked if she could take the trousers off a male doll. I told her she could and she did so, and she then got quite anxious and said, "That's his butt—that scares me." I responded by telling her that maybe this reminded her of something scary and that she didn't have to play with the doll any longer if she didn't want to.

After one of the bathroom breaks Sarah frequently took during sessions, she told me that the sound of the toilet flushing terrified her, although she was unable to elaborate why this was so. It later emerged that some of the sexual abuse from her father had occurred in the bathroom. She continued to demonstrate a preoccupation with the hanging microphone in the playroom. She repetitively asked to be lifted up to touch it, scream into it, or suck on it. She also initiated an activity during this time in which she and I got out pillows and blankets and pretended we were lying next to each other in bed. She seemed alternately agitated and comforted by this activity.

Sarah became very accident prone during sessions. She hurt herself in minor ways in almost every session. This seemed to provide her with a way to indirectly ask for attention and physical contact and nurturance from me. As she became more attached to me, she also became increasingly distressed at having to separate from me at the end of our sessions. I therefore gave her consecutive reminders before the end of sessions that our time was almost over. She frequently protested or attempted to persuade me that my watch was wrong.

Phase 2

Four months into treatment, a potential obstacle to the therapy emerged. Kim told Sarah that they were going to return to her native country. The next five months of therapy after that announcement could be considered the second phase of treatment. This phase was qualitatively different than the first because of the constant threat of an impending termination. Sarah reacted to the possibility of losing me by regressing. She began hiding under the couch in the waiting room when I came to get her. It typically took a lot of coaxing to get her to emerge. I felt that this behavior reflected her ambivalent feelings towards me — her desire to possess me coupled with her fear of losing me. After being coaxed out from under the couch, Sarah often demanded to be carried into the playroom. At such times, she clung to me, made babytalk or animal sounds, and insisted on being held for the first part of the session. Sarah exhibited significant anxiety in these sessions. She routinely left midsession to use the bathroom, often to have a bowel movement, which she always reported to me.

During these sessions, Sarah began to move closer to broaching the issue of sexuality through her play. For example, she frequently commented that dolls that were unclothed were "naked." She always blushed and squirmed when she mentioned this and then quickly changed the topic. At times she filled a baby bottle with water and went wild squirting it everywhere, while shrieking that it was a "boy's peepee." She made references to "eating boy's weenies," but declined to elaborate upon this. She also made her first references to her father, all of which were negative. She described her father as a "mean man." She related her fear that he might be living in the woods near her home, waiting to kidnap her. She also had wild fantasies of elephants coming to help her escape from him. Apparently this man was so powerful to her that only elephants could stop him.

Because of Sarah's unremitting anxiety about the plans to return to their native country, I set up a second home visit. The interpreter and I met with Kim and Sarah in their home. Kim confirmed that she was planning to return to her country. She expressed continued opposition to the therapy but agreed because of the legal mandate to let Sarah continue to see me for the few remaining months before they were scheduled to leave the country.

Sarah's reaction to the threat of losing me took a variety of forms. She became preoccupied in every session with having us build a house together, using chairs, tables, and blankets. In this activity, she always had us be "sisters" who lived together in a house that contained everything we needed. This type of play seemed to represent her wish that she would never lose me. She also seemed to be desperately trying to use our relationship to gain a sense of safety and control over the uncontrollable – the threat of moving. At this time, she also gave me two pictures of herself that the GAL had taken, as if to say, "Hold onto me." Similarly, she asked to take small objects (such as bits of clay or pieces of chalk) home from sessions, which I allowed her to do.

During this period, the *guardian ad litem* assumed a more central role in Sarah's life. In addition to assuming responsibility for transporting Sarah to sessions, she also took her on outings on the weekends. Therefore, she was able to provide me with valuable observations of Sarah that I was unable to obtain from Kim. She was very nurturant towards Sarah and I felt that their relationship provided an additional source of support for Sarah. The fact that the GAL and I related well to each other allowed Sarah to experience a relationship with two adults in which she was not perversely triangled (Palazzoli, Cirillo, Selvini, & Sorrentino, 1989). This was in marked contrast to the "middle" position that she must have occupied between her parents and that she still occupied between her mother and the rest of the world.

The GAL told me that during their car rides Sarah talked poignantly about the fact that she had no friends. When I asked her to list her friends, her list was comprised of adults – the GAL, her teacher, and me. The GAL related serious concerns she had after taking Sarah to the zoo one day. She said that Sarah had "invaded other people's space by running up to them, screaming, and drawing a lot of attention to herself." Sarah also made inappropriate, sexualized comments about the animals. For example, on viewing an otter washing its baby, she screamed, "That otter is being sexy." When she was taken to the children's zoo, she attempted to kiss all of the animals. When the GAL prohibited this behavior, Sarah responded by kissing her all over her arms and neck. The GAL also related other concerns about Sarah. Sarah's afterschool care teacher had told the GAL that she could not keep Sarah in the program. Apparently, the teacher had found

Sarah lying on top of a younger boy in the boy's bathroom, with their pants down. The teacher had also expressed concern about the fact that Sarah's drawings had changed from "happy pictures to dark sinister ones, with a preoccupation with red lips."

During this phase of therapy, Sarah's increasing insecurity manifested in a number of ways. Her earlier behavior of hiding under the couch before sessions was replaced by a more active approach, in which she began searching for me as soon as she entered the mental health center. Once she found me, she would then call out, "Momma!", leap into my arms and start kissing me repetitively. When we got to the therapy room, she demanded to be rocked like a small infant. At times she directed me to fill a baby bottle with water so that I could feed her while I held her. She pretended alternately to cry and to be comforted. She seemed very much like an actual infant at these times, as she expressed primitive needs for nurturance which I suspected had never been adequately met.

As Sarah regressed, her behavior towards me became more sexualized. She was obviously confused about the distinction between nurturance and sexuality. She began to make provocative gestures towards me, for example, by trying to touch my breasts or by throwing the Nerf ball at my chest. At such times I tried to model appropriate limit-setting for her by telling her that I did not like for her to try to touch or hurt the private parts of my body. Through these and other limit-testing behaviors which Sarah exhibited at this time, she seemed to be struggling to determine how much she could trust me to help her contain her aggressive-sexualized impulses and to not push her away because of them. In setting limits I tried to be gentle yet firm, and I frequently made interpretive comments about what she might be feeling at the time. In one session, while pretending to be a baby, she sat on my lap facing me, wrapped her legs around me, and directed me to hold her hands and repetitively raise her up and lower her down to the ground, while she became increasingly excited and agitated. I was uncomfortable with this behavior because it seemed masturbatory. Therefore, I set a rule that if she wanted to be held like a baby, she had to be held the way real babies are held. She was responsive to this limit.

Sarah tried in a number of sessions to undress me or to get me to take off some of my clothes. I handled this by asking her why she wanted me to do this while setting a firm limit and explaining why I would not comply with her request. I also noted during this period that she began to be quite provocative. This was especially pronounced when she wore scanty clothing. For example, during one session when she was wearing a sundress, she pulled it up to wipe her mouth, thereby exposing her underpants, while watching intently for my reaction. When I responded by saying that she should not exhibit the private parts of her body to others, she ignored me.

During the same session, she later stood in front of the one-way mirror in the room and declared that she was "a sexy lady."

During this period, Sarah sometimes approached me in sessions and kissed me repetitively on my arms and neck. At such times, I told her that I liked her too, but that I didn't feel comfortable getting kissed. I told her that she could ask for a hug if she wanted affection. I realized the extent to which her early experience of nurturance had been blurred by her premature experience of sexuality.

Sarah's preoccupation with the hanging microphone intensified. She continued to beg to be held up so she could "suck it." For the first time, she began to behave aggressively towards the microphone, by throwing objects at it or by trying to hit it with a bat. I noted that Sarah tended to become somewhat frightened and regressed after aggressive-sexualized behavior such as this had emerged. For example, she might abruptly stop the activity and ask to be held like a baby.

Sarah continued to express upset feelings towards her mother. She began begging me to come for another home visit, which suggested to me that she wanted me to intervene in some way in her home environment. Interestingly, in one session in which we were pretending to be sisters, she called me "Mom" and then pretended to make me a meal. When I commented that the child was feeding the mother, she became confused and stated that she had forgotten we were sisters. I felt that this "slip" reflected her poorly defined relationship with her mother, which at times operated more like a sibling relationship. At other times there was a clear role reversal in their relationship, with Sarah cast into a caretaker role. This was seen in the fact (which Kim openly acknowledged) that Kim often used Sarah as her interpreter because Sarah's English speaking skills far exceeded her own.

During this period of extreme uncertainty about her future, Sarah was extremely emotionally reactive. This was seen in her difficulty tolerating the fact that I was different (i.e., distinct) from her. She expected me to know exactly what she meant and became infuriated when I didn't. She fell apart emotionally at the slightest provocation. For example, one time when she misplaced a deck of cards she had brought into the room, she sobbed inconsolably until we found it. In another session, when I enforced the rule that we would stop our water play if she got me wet, she became furious and insisted upon ending the session early.

Phase 3

Not long before treatment was supposed to terminate, Kim announced that she and Sarah would not be returning to their native country. Soon after, the court determined that the dependency and the therapy should continue.

My work with Sarah continued for approximately 10 more months, which could be considered the third and final phase of treatment.

During this phase, Sarah began to idealize me. She told me she loved me and that she wished she could be my daughter. She wrote me love notes during session and sought affection frequently, although in increasingly appropriate ways (such as sitting very close to me in sessions). Her response to my leaving for vacation during this period was more mature than at previous times in the therapy. She was able to talk directly about her sadness that I would be gone. I also noted that when I returned she was very excited to see me and was ready to engage with me, in contrast to our first separation, after which she had seemed distrustful. She told me that she had dreamed about our playing together during my absence, which let me know that she had sufficiently internalized our relationship for it to remain stable even during a separation.

Sarah continued to have us build a home of our own in every session, which I viewed as symbolic of her attempt to infuse the safety and trust of our relationship into her home situation. Her insecurity began to be expressed in less infantilized, more age-appropriate ways. For example, she became very interested in playing board games, which she manipulated so that she always won. I allowed her to do so while commenting on how good it feels to win.

I also noted during this time that Sarah exhibited a forced altruism, which seemed related to her desperate need for approval and acceptance. She insisted upon sharing her possessions, such as candy the GAL had given her, and she would never allow herself to have more of something than someone else. This was a striking behavior in a child who had been deprived in so many ways. I suspected that this dynamic was related to her feeling that she could not have more than her mother, which may have emerged from the fact that she was asked to take on as much responsibility as her mother within the home environment.

During this phase, Sarah began to assign me the role of "audience," who watched her perform "on stage." She liked to get up on top of the table and pretend to be holding a microphone and singing a song. She seemed starved for the basic infantile experience of being watched and admired. She also continued to want me to mirror her by copying her behavior.

Increasingly fearful themes emerged in Sarah's play during this period. She began to assign to me the role of a younger sister who had continual nightmares, which ended only when Sarah awakened and comforted me. I viewed this as a positive step in her attempt to deal with her fears, since she was now able to place them outside of herself and assume the role of the one who masters the frightening situation. These nighttime fears seemed to be related to the fearfulness of the abuse experiences. Sarah made two direct, factual references to her father, Mike, during this time. She told me one day that her father was "bad" because he had hit her mother. She also related to the GAL a seemingly positive memory of her father letting her sit in his lap to help him "drive" the car. In retrospect, I can see that she was continuing to inch closer to being ready to deal with him in the therapy in a more direct way.

Sarah eventually made a breakthrough in dealing with the sexual abuse. It began with a vague fantasy about her mother, and then her, getting married to "a man named Mike," whom she described as "mean and big and old." In the following session, she became more explicit. She described memories of her father's physical violence towards her mother. At times it was difficult to tell what was real and what was imagined. She told me that her father had beat her mother with a hammer so badly that her mother had gone to the hospital. She then told a story about how she had saved her mother by kicking her father "in his private parts and busting his head open." She clearly expressed how scary her father, and her parents' marital relationship, had been to her.

In the next session, she clearly identified the hanging microphone as her father's penis. She had us throw things at the microphone and she spit at it, while screaming at it (him) that he was "bad" to have hurt her "private parts." She stated that we were now hurting his private parts to get back at him. In one session, she pretended that she was choking him but she was unable to get him to die. This seemed to reflect her inability to metaphorically kill him by putting her fears and bad memories to rest. She had us play-act killing her father in very gruesome ways. She fantasized that we were hurting his penis and "popping his brain out."

Interestingly, Sarah was very clear about how much of this issue she could bear to confront in any given session. She typically stopped this type of activity abruptly by stating that she was scared and that she didn't want to talk about it anymore. At other times she dealt with the issue of sexuality less directly, by talking about male and female genitalia, bodily functions, and "bad words" she had heard at school.

In one discussion, she indirectly revealed more about the sexual abuse. She was talking about "boys' weiners and girls' pussies." I commented that sometimes boys put their weiners in girls and she replied, "Yeah, in their mouths, and they put their mouths on girls' pussies too." She then abruptly stopped the discussion, stating that she thought the GAL could hear us from the waiting room.

During this period in which we were dealing directly with her past victimization, Sarah seemed confused about what to keep private (and from whom) and what to share. I felt that her anxiety and uncertainty about this mirrored feelings she may have had while her father was molesting her. I suspected that she had struggled with whether she should be participating in the sexual activities with him and also whether she could tell anyone (particularly her mother) what was occurring. In her relationship with me, she vacillated between being provocative and setting firmer boundaries than she had ever set. There were times when she was still extremely sexualized towards me. One example was during a session when she wanted us to both take off our pants. I refused and she rolled onto her back with her legs spread wide apart and said, "look at my booty." At other times, however, she set more appropriate limits than she had in the past. For example, she asked me not to look while she pulled up her tights and she chose to have us sleep separately, rather than together, when we played house.

Some of Sarah's earlier, more regressive behaviors returned during this period. I felt that the regression was in response to dealing explicitly with the sexual abuse, as well as to the anxiety engendered by having to miss a number of sessions because of bad weather and the holidays. I noted that at times she reverted to her past pattern of calling me "Momma" and insisting that I carry her into the therapy room. She again had mid-session bowel movements, a clear sign of her anxiety. Her reality testing seemed tenuous at this time. Although she often spoke of a "boyfriend" at school who reportedly kissed her, gave her presents, but also kicked her, this was unsubstantiated by her teacher. The GAL reported that, during their car rides to the mental health center, Sarah pointed to Asian girls they passed and insisted that they were her actual sisters.

Interestingly, as Sarah began to deal overtly with her victimization by her father, she complained a great deal about feeling victimized by her peers. School had started during this time and she reported in many sessions that the kids were "mean" to her. Specifically, she said that they teased her and called her "ugly." I wondered if she was somehow inviting this type of behavior. It certainly was clear that she did not know how to defend herself, and we talked about this frequently.

During this time, the court scheduled a date for termination of the dependency and the therapy because no further harm had occurred while Sarah was in her mother's care and because she had received psychotherapy as ordered. In the final months of therapy, as the date of termination approached, Sarah began for the first time to resist coming to see me. She protested that she was missing important subjects at school to come for sessions, although this was not true. I suspected that Sarah might be voicing her mother's viewpoint and that she might be feeling a need to ally with her mother against me, given that she would soon be losing me. In addition, I thought that her newfound resistance might in part reflect her wish to take control and leave me before I could leave her.

In sessions, Sarah had us pretend to be sisters who were constantly plotting to run away from their "mean" mother. Sometimes she had us be caught by the police and put in the "child jail." She was adamant that I not tell anyone about these scenarios. It seemed that she was struggling with the conflict between her desire to run away from her mother and her desire to be accepted by her. Although at times she stated that she loved her mother, her play revealed great ambivalence. In one session, she had us pretend that I was a mother who had high blood pressure and who eventually died. I later found out that Kim had heart problems which greatly worried her and of which Sarah was aware.

In these last months of treatment, for the first time ever, Kim scheduled a meeting with Sarah, the GAL, and me at the mental health center. Her agenda was to make sure that therapy would end as soon as possible. She made it clear that she did not believe that Sarah had ever been sexually abused. When she said this, Sarah put her head in the GAL's lap and pulled her coat up over her head. Kim talked about the fact that her own mother was urging her to give Sarah away so that it would be easier for Kim to find someone to marry. However, Kim indicated that she was not yet planning to give Sarah up. It was apparent that Kim was so preoccupied with her own problems and unmet needs that she was emotionally unavailable to Sarah. I made it clear to Kim that I believed that Sarah had been sexually abused by her father and that I thought she had made progress in dealing with this. I explained that the court had ordered Sarah to complete her therapy and that therefore this was not negotiable. I did this to try to defuse Sarah's feeling that her participation in therapy was a betrayal of her mother's wishes.

After this session, Sarah seemed less conflicted about coming to therapy. She stopped voicing resistance to seeing me and instead began to express her wish that sessions would never end. In the next session, she expressed a great deal of anger towards her mother. She had us skip around in a circle, singing, "We killed our mother . . . we are so happy." She told me that her mother did not like me. I talked to her about how confusing it must be to have her mother feel differently towards me from the way she did. I also talked about the fact that her mother did not believe she had been abused by her father, while I believed she had. I explained that we were ending therapy because the judge and I thought it was time to do so. I wanted her to realize that her mother was not causing therapy to end. I wanted to try to decrease the polarization between Sarah's idealization of me and her devaluation of her mother by rightfully assuming the responsibility for therapy ending.

In the ensuing sessions, Sarah seemed to respond to the impending termination in a number of ways. Whereas she had previously had us be quite symbiotic, she made moves to become more separate. For example, she began to insist upon my remaining in the therapy room while she left to use the bathroom, rather than having me accompany her. She continued to interrupt sessions frequently to use the bathroom, which suggested to me that she was still feeling anxious. She again began to request that she be allowed to take small objects from the therapy room home with her. She cried easily and seemed to be emotionally fragile.

The GAL also reported that Sarah had regressed since our session with Kim. She said that Sarah had resumed her preoccupation with singing sexualized songs during their car rides. I noted that Sarah became increasingly difficult near the end of each session. She resisted limits I set and demands I made, for example, for her to clean up the toys. I viewed this testing behavior as her way of expressing anger that the therapy was going to end.

I had us count down the number of sessions left to try to help her to feel more in control of the separation and better prepared to say goodbye. I was concerned about the double loss of her separating from the GAL as well as from me. However, the GAL assured me that she would stay in contact with Sarah as long as Kim would allow her to do so.

During these last sessions, Sarah continued to progress in dealing with the sexual abuse. In one of the sessions in which she identified the hanging microphone as her father's penis, she announced that she had succeeded in strangling and killing him. This was in marked contrast to earlier sessions, when she had been unable to overpower him. In another session, she had us pretend that we were camping and that we had encountered deadly tarantulas. She declared that she was the only one who could talk to the tarantulas and get them to agree not to harm us. She also was able to talk about her father more realistically. She made it clear that she knew that what he had done to her was wrong. We had often talked about ways in which children can protect themselves from dangerous situations, and Sarah was proud of the fact that she knew what to do and who to tell if anyone tried to abuse her again. In addition, she no longer believed that her father lived in the woods near her house. Rather, she said that she knew he lived far away.

In planning for our last session, I decided that Sarah and I would have a party, as a ritual to mark the end of therapy. I had Sarah help me plan the food and decorations, and asked her whether she wanted to include the GAL in the party. She originally chose to exclude her, but decided to invite her to join us midsession when the time came. I have vivid memories of our silently decorating the room to make it look celebratory, while the atmosphere felt as though someone had died. I handled this by commenting that it was hard to feel like having a party and being happy when we were sad to say goodbye. She cried and agreed that she felt sad. She had brought me a piece of paper with her name, address, and phone number carefully written on it. She explained that she wanted me to write her letters. I told her that she could give letters to the GAL to send to me and I would then answer them via the GAL, who would give them to Sarah when she saw her. At the end of the session, I asked the GAL to take some Polaroid pictures of Sarah and me together so that we each could have one to keep.

OUTCOME OF TREATMENT

The GAL telephoned me the day after I terminated therapy with Sarah. She said that after she and Sarah got into the car, Sarah had told her that she was afraid she might cry. The GAL told her it was all right to cry. As they were driving away, Sarah said, "Alison is my true friend." I was very moved to hear this, since I feel that successful therapy leaves one feeling befriended. I also felt that this comment showed that Sarah had come to a very appropriate, realistic place in her relationship with me, where she no longer viewed me as her sister or mother, but rather, as her friend.

I felt that Sarah had made progress towards a number of therapeutic goals over the course of one and a half years. Her relationship with me had grown very strong and clearly was of great importance to her. She had gotten primitive needs for nurturance met through our relationship and she had progressed from sexualizing those needs to expressing them more appropriately. She had dealt directly with her past sexual abuse and she had achieved an appropriate understanding of it, as well as some knowledge about how to prevent further abuse. Her self-esteem had improved and she had continued to make good progress academically.

SPECIFIC TECHNIQUES USED

In my work with Sarah, I tried to take a supportive, praising stance with her whenever possible. This included allowing her to win games we played, so that she might begin to experience some success in interpersonal interactions. I tried to follow her play in a nondirective manner to let her know that she could raise issues when she was ready to do so. I felt that this was particularly crucial with regard to the issue of the sexual abuse. At the beginning of treatment, I did not want to overwhelm her fragile defenses and risk precipitating a more severe regression or even a possible psychotic response. I also felt that for me to pressure her to deal with the abuse before she was ready would constitute another experience of being violated. Therefore, my approach was to comment upon any sexual references she made so that she would know that I had noticed them and that I was ready to pursue the issue if she wanted to.

Given Sarah's pressured activity level at the onset of treatment, I tried to help her slow down by assuming a pace of speech and activity that was slightly slower than hers. This approach seemed helpful. I tried to respect her past traumatic history of loss and disrupted attachment by being especially careful about how I handled separations from her. I gave her advance preparation so that she would feel more in control. I allowed her to take home small objects from the therapy room (such as bits of clay) and I occasionally gave her small gifts before impending separations. Children from deprived, abusive backgrounds frequently have disturbed and sometimes primitive object relations. My hope was that these transitional objects would help her sustain between sessions the fragile sense of connection she derived from our relationship (Winnicott, 1986).

Given Sarah's troubled relationship with her mother and her mother's denial of the abuse, it seemed doubtful that she was able to get help with the insecurity and feelings engendered by the abuse. I allowed her to regress in therapy sessions while interpreting this behavior for her (e.g., "It feels safer to be a baby"). At the same time, I modeled appropriate limit setting with regard to her sexualized behavior towards me. I wanted to teach her that she could get affection without being sexual and that a person has the right to set limits about what she wants done to her body. I tried to help Sarah modulate her anxiety when sexual issues arose by reminding her that we could stop thinking and talking about them whenever she wanted. This allowed her to experience some control over that which had formerly been out of her control. Interestingly, as she progressed in therapy, she became increasingly able to self-monitor her level of anxiety by announcing when she didn't want to talk about "that stuff" anymore in that session.

TREATMENT OBSTACLES AND OTHER SYSTEMS INVOLVED

These two topics will be discussed together because of the extensive overlap between them. Most of the threats to the therapy were either caused or ameliorated by other systems. A major obstacle to treatment was the split between Sarah's treatment team (the caseworker, GAL, and me) and her mother, which left Sarah uncomfortably in the middle. Kim's opposition to Sarah's therapy was based in part on her cultural belief that psychotherapy was for the insane. Moreover, she refused to believe Sarah's reports of the abuse and held Sarah responsible for the breakup of her marriage. I attempted to manage these obstacles by making home visits with an interpreter so as to meet Kim on her own territory, where she might feel most comfortable. This accomplished little, which is not surprising given that Kim's counselor, who shared a common ethnic background, had been unsuccessful in engaging her in treatment. At times I wondered to what extent Kim's denial of the abuse was contributing to Sarah's resistance to bringing it up in therapy sessions. Sarah's feeling of security in the therapy was hindered by her mother's opposition to it, as well as by Kim's plans to return to their native country.

Without the commitment of her GAL, Sarah would not have been able to receive the treatment she needed. The GAL was a source of support to both Sarah and me. She was in close contact with significant people in Sarah's life and gave me invaluable observations and information about Sarah that Kim was unable or unwilling to provide. She had a warm, nurturant relationship with Sarah, which extended beyond merely transporting her to sessions. I am sure this helped to counteract the neglect Sarah experienced at home. The fact that the GAL and I worked well together facilitated Sarah's therapy, both legally (i.e., court recommendations we made together) and in terms of allowing her to stay out of an uncomfortable "middle" position between two adults.

A final treatment obstacle arose from the confusion of roles at times among the helping professionals in Sarah's life, for example, between the family crisis intervention counselor and me. If the hierarchy of decision-making had been different, or if communication between the caseworker and me had preceded the decision to attempt crisis intervention, I could have recommended against that action, which in the end seemed to have been countertherapeutic.

MISTAKES

In retrospect, I can see that I should have realized that any positive changes from the therapy were at risk of being undone by Sarah's relationship with her mother, especially given her mother's denial of the abuse and opposition to the therapy. I could have refused to see Sarah as long as her mother refused to participate in the therapy. However, I believe Sarah would have suffered unfairly if she had been denied treatment on this basis. Another tactic I could have taken would have been to advocate that Sarah be removed from her mother's care. However, social services had not determined that there was adequate basis for removing her from the home. I had little basis for further evaluating this issue, nor could I judge whether the trauma of separation from her mother would warrant such an action, even if removal was legally justified. Despite the obvious difficulty in their relationship, Kim was the only person who had consistently been in Sarah's life. In addition, my awareness of the variability of foster care placements leaves me unsure as to whether this would have been a better solution.

I struggled a great deal with the issue of whether to change my nondirective stance when, midway through treatment, Sarah still had not dealt directly with the sexual abuse. After some consultation, I decided to wait and to trust that she would use me as she needed to (Axline, 1947). This approach was successful with Sarah, who eventually did overtly raise the issue of her past abuse. However, in more time-limited therapies, it might be to the client's disadvantage not to be more directive.

Finally, in retrospect, I would handle the termination session differently. I feel that the notion of having a party was at odds with the sad reality of our parting. I think that a better approach would have been to spend the last session reminiscing about our memories of our time together and reflecting upon the ways in which Sarah had changed and grown.

MY REACTIONS

I struggled with many different feelings during the course of the therapy. I was frustrated with the cultural differences that functioned as a barrier to treatment. I felt angry at Kim's refusal to believe that the abuse had occurred. I also felt empathic towards her, realizing how frightened and alone she must have felt. It was clear that she was as emotionally deprived as her daughter. As Sarah increasingly turned her need for maternal nurturance towards me, I struggled with fantasies of wanting to rescue her. I consulted frequently with colleagues to help manage my countertransference towards Sarah and her mother. At times I experienced great anger towards Sarah's father, whom I had never met. I tried not to displace this anger onto others, such as the caseworker or Kim.

When Sarah behaved in a sexualized manner in sessions, I experienced a variety of reactions, including shock, fascination, and a queasy feeling that came as I began to comprehend the reality of the abuse that this small child had suffered. I found it helpful to read more about child sexual abuse, not only to gain a better understanding of Sarah but also to get some necessary distance from my feelings.

There were moments of joy when I glimpsed progress, and there were certainly times I despaired for her. It was particularly difficult to say goodbye to her, given my concerns about her relationship with her mother. I wondered whether issues related to the sexual abuse would resurface at puberty. Given her past history and the deficiencies of her living situation, I feared that she was at risk for eventually turning to alcohol, drugs, promiscuity, or antisocial behavior as a means of getting her needs met. In the end, I was left with one hope—that she had been able, because of her relationships with the GAL, her teachers, and me—to build enough of a sense of self-worth to enable her to form other healthy relationships in the years to come.

It is difficult to articulate all that I learned from my work with Sarah. I presently limit the number of sexual abuse cases I see at a given time because of the intensity of the issues and the complexity of dealing with the numerous systems involved. I have been learning to set more modest, realistic goals for therapy and to face the limits of my power in effecting change. Most importantly, perhaps, I have learned from Sarah a lesson I suspect I'll learn again and again—to be patient in therapy, to trust the process, and to know that my clients will share their hardest issues with me as they come to trust me.

7

Developing an Internalized Protector

MARILYN J. KRIEGER

The notion of internalized protector presented by Dr. Krieger is very useful. This appears to be a specific type of internalized object, more specific than a good object in being self-protective. This conceptualization explains the risk-taking behavior of these children and places it in a solid theoretical framework of object relations theory, a British psychoanalytic perspective.

Dr. Krieger presents a case that is unusual in that she has the option of many years' work with this family and frequently can meet with the child more than once per week. With hindsight we might suggest that it would have been useful for her to have used one of those weekly sessions for work with Kathy and her mother.

Note the difference in gift-giving to Sarah from Dr. Einbender (Chapter 6) and to Kathy from Dr. Krieger. Kathy rejects what is provided to her initially, but then Dr. Krieger is successfully able to utilize treats that she buys for Kathy at the beginning of each session. It is also interesting to note the ritualized quality of the sessions in the second six months of therapy, which hearkens back to the notion of emotional regulation. The ritual of cigarette smoking seemed overtly designed to prove Dr. Krieger's protectiveness. Children at this age will provide rituals if you don't provide rituals for them.

A persisting treatment issue is Kathy's sense of not being good enough. It hearkens back to Kathy's competition with her younger brothers who are already home from foster care. This persisting issue is hard to overcome in individual therapy.

So often Kathy plays both good and bad roles in her role-playing behavior during the play therapy sessions. Here it might have been helpful for Dr. Krieger to "do the dialectic." This is a technique I have developed (Friedrich, 1990) which allows the child gradually to begin integrating these good and bad opposites into something that is more mature and age-appropriate.

If Dr. Krieger had used the Untreatable Family Checklist (Friedrich, 1990, p. 106), it is likely that the poor prognosis of Kathy's mother would have been predicted and Kathy would have been permanently removed from her home sooner.

It is also important to note that, after five years of therapy, Kathy still is not done. Considering the maternal absence Kathy has experienced throughout her life, one can only hope that Dr. Krieger can see her into her early adult years. — Editor

AUTHOR'S THEORETICAL ORIENTATION

The general principles underlying my work with abused children are based in psychodynamic theory. The foundation of such an approach includes the recognition of the following:

1. the child's stage of psychosexual development;
2. the importance of transference; and
3. the importance of the child's fantasy in the experience of self and of reality and as expressed in play.

There are several additional principles that play a crucial role in my work with abused children. These focus upon a theoretical construct that I have termed the "internalized protector," defined as a part of the parental introject and developed through the child's consistent experience of her parents' or caretakers' nurturance and protection. The internalized protector serves several functions; in particular, it communicates to the child her worth and entitlement to respectful treatment from the outside world and acts as a governor such that the child guards herself against danger when separated from her caretakers.

Children from nonabusive homes experience their caretakers' protection from the typical dangers of the outside world on a daily basis. The children introject and eventually identify with the protecting/nurturing parent, as the parent sets limits or takes some action to protect the child from her own or the impulses of others. As the child matures and the internalized protector becomes a stronger psychological structure, the testing behaviors that children exhibit to establish the limits or test the safety of their environment may be less extreme. That is, the testing behaviors will be modified by the very existence of the internalized protector.

Children with histories of incest often fail to develop an internalized protector. Instead there exists the unhealthy dual introjection of and identification with an abusive perpetrator (in the following case the father) and a helpless, ineffectual, nonprotecting yet nonabusive parent (in the following case the mother). The absence of such a structure forces the child to continually test the safety of many situations, as she tries to determine who she can trust. Unfortunately, the nature of her tests may be quite irritating or dangerous. An example of a dangerous test would be seductive behavior towards an individual who does not recognize the behavior as a test and fails to maintain appropriate boundaries.

The absence of an internalized protector contributes to the difficult, destructive or directly seductive behaviors that many children with histories of incest display. Mary De Young (1984) reviewed the histories of several sexually abused children whose behavior led to "the initiation and maintenance of a sexual relationship with an adult." De Young suggested that the children's seductive behavior represented an attempt "to master the anxiety and fear created by the phobic stimuli" and thus could be considered a "counterphobic response."

In an earlier paper (Krieger, Rosenfeld, Gordon, & Bennett, 1980), I suggested that the difficult and seductive behavior in the psychotherapeutic setting of children with histories of incest be considered a testing of the safety of the therapeutic relationship. This testing can be unconscious or, more rarely, volitional and generally reflects the child's need to establish that she is safe. Clearly, there are some counterphobic elements to this behavior, as the child attempts to master the anxiety of the implied intimacy in the therapeutic environment. The child needs to know and test that the psychotherapist will help and care for the child, rather than be seduced and have the child take care of the psychotherapist. The child must establish for herself that the psychotherapist is strong enough to withstand the child's anger and impulses. The therapist's passing of the tests (i.e., maintaining appropriate boundaries and limits) gradually assures the child that her experience with the therapist is going to be different from her experience with the abusive adults. Until the child establishes this difference and feels safe within the therapeutic relationship, she will be unable to make full use of the therapeutic relationship.

Often, the child must contend with a highly chaotic family involved with the judicial and social service systems. Ideally, the judicial and social service systems function as external protectors when the parents are unwilling or unable to protect. Unfortunately, the systems' limited resources and standard legal procedures often inadvertently make the child feel that she is the one who has committed a crime (Krieger & Robbins, 1985). Consequently, the systems' own difficulties may further the child's identification with an abusive, nonprotecting parent.

An important goal in my work with abused children is to help them develop an internalized protector. One way is to communicate in word and action within the context of the therapeutic relationship that I believe they are worthy of protection. As the following case will demonstrate, this communication can take various forms, although the message must be consistent. This involves setting and maintaining limits around how the child relates to herself, the therapist, and the outside world. Since the therapist has only limited control over the external events in a child's life, the ability to exercise protective action outside of the therapeutic hour is limited. Nonetheless, every effort must be made in that realm as well.

One technique that does involve helping children cope with the external real dangers of the past and present is to directly discuss past traumas and possible ways to avoid those dangers in the future. Lenore Terr (1990) describes helping traumatized children discover an action the children could have taken which might have prevented the original traumatic event. This allows the child to realize she could not have avoided the trauma because she did not know how, and provides her with ways of coping with similar events in the future. This technique also communicates to the child that she is worthy of protection, complete with specific ways to protect, and furthers the development of the internalized protector.

Another technique that I have found useful is to enter the child's fantasy play and, within that context, introduce a protector. This is especially useful when the child is engaging in repetitive play. Terr (1990) described the characteristics of post-traumatic fantasy play of children as "monotonous ritualization," which included an element of secrecy. She observed how the repetition of the play did not abate with interpretations relevant to the trauma. The following case demonstrates how the introduction of a protector into the fantasy play leads to a change not only in the play but also in the child's behavior and intrapsychic structure.

The psychotherapy of children with histories of incest goes through several stages in which different issues are emphasized. The stages have considerable overlap and reflect the gradual and often uneven development towards an internalized protector.

1. *Testing of the therapist's integrity, ability and willingness to protect the child from her own impulses.* While this occurs throughout the course of treatment, it is emphasized in the earlier part of the work. The child may behave in an overtly seductive manner, tell her history in provocative detail, or try to cajole or intimidate the therapist into permitting rule violations (Krieger et al., 1980). The child may also behave in such a manner as to hurt the therapist or place her in jeopardy.

   During this period, it is crucial for the therapist to maintain the rules and safety of the therapeutic relationship by not complying with the child's overt wishes and requests. Once the child feels safe, she can explore her more difficult issues as well as look upon the therapist with assurance and respect. The child's observation that the therapist will protect both the child and the therapist inherently encourages the child to consider the therapist a role model for protecting oneself and facilitates movement into the next stage of therapy.

2. *Identification with the therapist and other appropriate caretakers.* This facilitates the introjection of the identified object's values and beliefs, most importantly the belief that the child is worthy and deserving of protection. During this stage the child may consciously or unconsciously mimic the behavior, beliefs, or appearance of her therapist and other caretakers. It is as if the child is literally "trying on" a new way of thinking about and relating to herself and the outside world.

3. *Introjection of nurturing and protecting caretakers; development of the internalized protector.* Once this process begins, the child demonstrates ways in which she protects herself from her own impulses and those of others. She treats herself in a way that is respectful and caretaking and avoids others who do not treat her accordingly.

In the case of Kathy, seen for five years in individual psychotherapy, we can observe these stages and trace the development of her internalized protector.

DESCRIPTION OF CASE

Kathy, a nine-and-one-half-year-old white girl, came to the attention of Social Services after her school observed her sporadic school attendance, poor hygiene, and malnourishment. Kathy lived with her mother and two brothers, ages two and three, in dirty and sparse conditions. During the Social Services investigation, Kathy disclosed her past history of sexual abuse by her own father and her current sexual activity with the janitors at a neighborhood store.

Kathy's mother, a thin and frail woman with brightly red dyed hair and a penchant for wearing at least 15 different pieces of jewelry at one time, presented as desperate, passive, and helpless. Though she had worked in the past as a cashier, her chronic ulcerative colitis had prevented her from working for the past six years. Born in Oregon, mother had been placed in foster care at age six. The foster parents then separated. By age eight, the foster mother's new male companion was living in the home and sexually abusing Kathy's mother. The foster mother did not believe Kathy's mother when she sought help with the abuse. Eventually, at age 18, Kathy's mother ran away to San Francisco and began living with Kathy's father. They were evicted from many apartments, as father's alcoholism interfered with his ability to pay the rent and his loud, physically abusive behavior brought the complaints of the neighbors.

Mother and father married shortly before Kathy's birth, when mother was 19 years old. Although Kathy reported that her father sexually abused her as far back as she could remember, she did not tell her mother until she was seven years old. Mother felt powerless to deal directly with father, but tried to protect Kathy by taking her with her when she left the house. Shortly after Kathy's youngest brother was born, father abandoned the family and has not been heard from since.

Kathy presented to the Social Service intake worker in torn, dirty clothing, needing a bath. Though never directly hostile or inappropriate, Kathy behaved in a tough, guarded manner; she was full of wisecracks. Kathy spoke easily of her long history of sexual abuse by her father, which included fondling, deep kissing, oral copulation, and attempts at vaginal penetration. He masturbated while watching Kathy undress. Kathy also disclosed that janitors from a nearby store paid her $20 for anal or vaginal sex and smaller sums for examining and fondling their penis. The police reported that the janitors said Kathy solicited them and threatened to report their involvement with her if they did not continue with their payments. Kathy had not told her mother about these recent incidents, fearful of her reaction.

Mother, fearful that a police investigation would cause her children to be removed, talked about leaving California for Texas. Not surprisingly, when the police arrived at the home several days later, Kathy recanted her story.

PSYCHOLOGICAL TESTING

Psychological testing revealed no cognitive or intellectual deficits. In fact, Kathy was described as having a "resourceful, striving, and aggressive cognitive style which allows her to grapple with complex problems, . . . highly manipulative, especially of adult males," lacking in any sense of control and self-worth, and considerably conflicted about intimacy. She saw intimacy as leading to her own demise, as those around her with whom she might be intimate were clearly stronger than she was and wished to hurt and destroy her. This was apparent on her CAT story:

> A great big lion and a tiny mouse went together in the forest. The lion was hungry and the mouse was available. The lion held his stomach and said, "Oh, rub my tummy, it hurts." And the mouse rubbed his tummy and went to kiss him. Then the lion ate him.

The psychologist suggested that Kathy's father had been both "open, loving and beckoning, and then too stimulating and somehow overinvolved and strangely interested in her." Kathy saw her mother as a younger, ineffectual sister. The evaluating psychologist recommended psychotherapy and an evaluation for out-of-home placement.

COURSE OF THERAPY, TECHNIQUES AND OUTCOME

Kathy's dangerous and inappropriate behavior, plus the psychological evaluation, led to a referral to me for twice weekly psychotherapy. My first concern involved mother's inability to exercise any control over the children. The children were often poorly dressed for the weather and out of control. One evening after my second visit with Kathy, I found Kathy alone, running up and down the street outside my office. The younger brother, out of mother's control, had run into the elevator of an adjacent office building and was now nowhere to be found. Mother told Kathy to check the street and then search each of the floors of the building, while she waited in the coffee shop. I suggested that Kathy and I return together to the building and call the building's security service. Kathy panicked, saying, "I'm not sure if my mother wants us to call the police." I called Social Services, informed them of the events, and all children were placed in foster care; the two boys were placed in one foster home, while Kathy was placed in another foster home.

During the first six months of treatment, until her 10th birthday, Kathy presented much as she had to the original intake worker. Cocky and coy, she denied any worries, spontaneously describing her "perfect" life with mother. While very protective of mother, she was not angry at me for her removal from mother's care. Instead, she admitted her preference for foster care, where she received warm clothing and had clean surroundings.

During these early therapy visits, Kathy's play and discussions overtly focused upon sexuality. With much sexual posturing, she spoke of her interest in a male classmate and her wish to "make him hot" and to "hump." Her doll play often included simulated intercourse, complete with labored breathing sounds. She spoke with bravado of her experience soliciting the janitors, described in provocative detail. Generally I limited my responses to comments about her wish to show or tell me her worries about sexuality and being close.

The suggestive and driven quality of these early discussions demonstrated Kathy's testing of the safety of the therapeutic situation, the very first step in developing an internalized protector. She needed to establish how I would respond to her history (i.e., would I be repulsed, seduced, etc.), before she could discuss her feelings. She also needed to test the safety of the therapeutic relationship. Remarkably skillful in the past at seduction, Kathy needed to see if I was any different from her parents or the janitors.

Through a repetitive play, Kathy introduced her rage and fear of both parents. Kathy, a wealthy princess, invited "Lad" over to visit. Her "butler/bodyguard," portrayed by myself following Kathy's detailed directions, sabotaged the princess's relationship with Lad. I, as myself, questioned aloud what kind of "butler/bodyguard" would behave so badly. Kathy had no answer, instead directing the "butler/bodyguard" to attempt to murder the princess. Instead of complying with the "murder," I, as myself, continued exploring the "butler/bodyguard's" motivations and the "princess's" reactions to having such a "butler/bodyguard." After several weeks of this repetitive play, I told her that I did not like even pretending to hurt her so that I, as "butler/bodyguard," could not even pretend to murder her. Kathy, shocked that I would not cooperate with her script, demanded that I repeat my reasoning several times over several visits.

My refusals to murder during this fantasy marked my second introduction to Kathy as a protector, the first being my involvement with Social Services. By not cooperating with her script, I protected her from the nonprotecting and harmful caretakers of the past represented by the "butler/bodyguard," most likely symbolizing both parents. The fact that the "butler/bodyguard" sabotaged her adult development (preventing the princess from having an appropriate love object) made him not only a nonprotector but also an exploiter; his behavior was designed not to protect the princess but to save the princess for himself. That he later attempted to murder the princess spoke to Kathy's sense of fear at the hands of her parents.

As this first six months of treatment ended, Kathy insisted that I either buy her gifts or give her things from my office. When on her 10th birthday I gave her a present, she demanded a much more elaborate one, called me "ugly bitch," and threatened to leave the office.

Giving presents to deprived children is a complicated issue. The therapist must consider the meaning of giving a gift, which occasion deserves a gift, and the practical issue of whether the therapist can realistically continue or remember to maintain this position after setting a precedent. The gift must be appropriate for the child's development, not a potential nuisance to the family (e.g., not something that makes noise), and not overtly competitive with the gifts the child receives from her family. Giving gifts strengthens the alliance between the child and the therapist and can be a concrete symbol of the therapist's acknowledgment of the child and the event being celebrated. Unfortunately, giving gifts can also shift the focus away from or diminish the importance of nonmaterial representations of the therapist's caring, i.e., the words, thoughts, and consideration the therapist gives to the child and the child's feelings.

I decided to give Kathy a diary on her birthday, even though I was aware of the potential complications. I felt it was important that Kathy experience a common interaction and come to understand her reaction within the safety of the therapeutic relationship. While other adults had given Kathy gifts, these adults had generally wanted Kathy, in return, to take care of them, often in very inappropriate, if not abusive, ways. Although Kathy had been quite insistent that I give her a birthday present, when I actually gave her the diary she unconsciously became frightened. She feared I could be manipulated, that she was therefore stronger than I, and that we were both thereby in danger of her impulses. She could not tolerate the intimacy that gift giving implied, as her past had provided little experience with true, benevolent gift giving. At that point she had to push me away by calling me "ugly bitch" and test the limits by forcing me to take a position in which I would not give in to her demands for a more elaborate present. My refusal to let her leave the office, in spite of her threats, established that I could withstand her anger. This behavior illustrated Kathy's important unconscious question: Are you strong enough to protect yourself from me and my internal world, so that I can trust you and take you in?

Kathy's need to test my emotional strength and dedication to her protection appeared in several sessions in which she ordered that I buy her cigarettes. Sometimes she simply brought cigarette stubs from the waiting room ashtray into my office, put them in her mouth and demanded a match. I repeated that I would not allow her to smoke as it was bad for her health. Defiantly, she repeated her trips to the waiting room for the cigarette stubs, only to be told to remove them from her mouth since I would not allow her to smoke. This routine became something of a game, in which she gave my speech about her health before I began. Kathy's repeating my speech, though ostensibly done to mock me, demonstrated the primitive beginning of her internalizing the concept of a protector. Our struggle around cigarettes represented my willingness to place and hold clear limits, proving my belief in her worth and need for protection.

As negotiations proceeded for her younger brothers to return to mother's care, Kathy stole small but obvious items from school. When asked about these charges, she adamantly and angrily denied them. Several weeks later, she stole an item from my waiting room. The foster parents quickly discovered the article and called me.

Kathy began the next interview by asking if the item had been returned. I told her that it had. She then read a magazine, jiggled her shoulders provocatively, and refused to discuss the events or feelings around her stealing. I told her that I knew that sometimes she wanted to live at my house and that perhaps that was one of the reasons she took my things. Kathy angrily threw the magazine down, saying, "You don't know so much.

And what if you are right anyway?" She then spoke of her confusion as to why her brothers were being returned home while she remained in foster care. My interpretation was designed to introduce her to the concept that her worries and conflicts can drive her to inappropriate or dangerous actions. My hope was that, by directly interpreting the unconscious motivation behind the action, we could talk about the feelings, instead of Kathy's acting them out.

During the second six months (10 to $10\frac{1}{2}$ years old), Kathy's rigid defense against her feelings softened. She developed an elaborate play in which Kathy, a 20-year-old famous singing and dancing television star, driving in her limousine, sees her mother and brothers. She invites them in, takes them home, and shares her wealth with them. Kathy assigned me the role of "mother" but refused to tell me what to say. Without her direction, I as "mother" commented on how I knew of Kathy's anger at me ("mother") for being unable to take better care of her. I added that I wished I could have taken better care and that she did not deserve to have been hurt. Kathy would then offer to buy "mother" a mink coat and food. "Mother" commented that it was not Kathy's job to take care of "mother" but "mother's" job to take care of Kathy, even though "mother" had been unable to do so.

This fantasy continued for quite a while before Kathy revised it. In the revision, the family members drive into a park where they are chased by wolves, have considerable difficulty, and often do not escape. Kathy resisted my attempts to introduce characters who could assist the family, e.g., passersby, park rangers.

Kathy's play depicted her belief that she was ultimately responsible for her mother and brothers, a responsibility that made her feel overwhelmed and helpless (the family's inability to escape the wolves). While she may have been relieved by my position that it was mother's responsibility to protect the child, that did not change her belief that mother—and everyone else—was powerless to save the family from the external dangers (like father). My attempts to bring in outside protectors could not yet be internalized.

By this point the therapy had a routine; at the beginning of each session, Kathy and I walked to the corner store where she bought a small item to eat. Sometimes we walked to an adjacent park. Kathy enjoyed the walks and I felt they provided an opportunity to participate in an outside activity that allowed us to experience real life events, without being too gratifying. During the end of this second six months of therapy, Kathy insisted that, if anyone asked, I was to say that she was my daughter, since she was embarrassed to be a foster child. Her embarrassment at being a foster child represented her belief that she was bad and that it was this badness that prevented her from living at home. Intellectually, she may have started to appreciate that her mother had been unable to protect her, as opposed to her not being worthy of protection, and that it was her father who was responsible for the abuse. However, she still saw herself as the powerful one, a power that made her responsible for the abuse and that she feared would be revealed by her living in a foster home. Her request also reflected her increasing identification with me.

A year had passed. Kathy was now $10\frac{1}{2}$ years old and, although mother had been able to take care of the two younger children with significant help from Social Services, Kathy's acting-out behavior seemed beyond mother's ability to control, such that Kathy had to remain in foster care. My contact with mother was limited, but mother did appear regularly for her own therapy appointments with another therapist. That therapist felt that, although mother was compliant, she remained extraordinarily passive, depressed, and unable to manage an active child like Kathy.

Kathy overtly responded to the news that she would remain in foster care with depression. She postulated that she was unable to return home because she had stolen and lied. She began a new play in which she, a movie star, "made all her money by being a 'sex maniac'." I, again being given the role of "mother" but again without direction, wondered aloud what would make a girl feel like she was a "sex maniac." Kathy angrily responded to "mother," stating, "You never tried to stop him, and you watched him whip me and didn't do a thing. And you made me take back a scarf that I had paid for because you were sure I had stolen it." Here, Kathy directly stated that mother's inability to protect her made her feel unworthy. Mother's inability communicated to Kathy that the sexual abuse was acceptable as Kathy was simply unworthy, whether a "sex maniac" or a thief. Her ability to tell me, as "mother," these feelings spoke to her continuing confidence in our relationship.

The next six month period ($10\frac{1}{2}$ to 11 years old) began with my monthlong vacation. Kathy refused to talk about her feelings about my vacation. Instead, she emphasized all the things mother bought her on her visits home and how much she missed her mother, clearly telling me that she really did not need me.

When I returned, Kathy began playing with the dolls. She had not played with dolls for almost one year. Now the play initially involved a mundane rendition of a stereotypic television family. However, over the following weeks the play became sexually explicit, including sexual intercourse and various forms of oral and anal sex between the father and mother. Kathy stated directly that her father had done "this" to her, that her mother had been unable to prevent it from happening, and that it made Kathy feel "nasty." She then had the father doll engage in sexual intercourse with the daughter doll. I commented upon how the daughter doll must feel and wondered why no one was helping the daughter. I received no answers. After several repetitions of this play, I picked up the mother doll, had her discover the activity and take action to prevent the daughter from being molested. Kathy, very confused and surprised at my self-initiated action, temporarily changed the activity. However, this play, in which the father molests the daughter and the mother takes various protective actions, became a regular activity for a major part of the next six months.

My vacation brought back feelings of abandonment reminiscent of her mother's inability to protect her from her father. It may also have made her feel that, if she were a worthwhile person, not only would her mother have protected her but I also would not have left her. My initiating a protective action with the dolls surprised but delighted her. My action strengthened the concept of her being worthy of protection. The repetitious quality of the play represented Kathy's attempt to master the traumatic event, her testing the reliability of the protection, and her integrating such protection into her emotional world as part of the development of an internalized protector.

Kathy developed a fantasy involving two gymnasts. "The Kid," a scruffy, sloppy, insolent child, competed against "Janet," a poised and mature child. While she played both girls at the Olympics, she directed me, "the audience," to applaud for the best gymnast. Her demeanor changed completely as she assumed the two characters. In spite of her pleadings, the "audience" refused to make the final judgment as to the better athlete. Instead I wondered aloud what made "The Kid" need to push people away by acting so tough, or voiced my suspicion that "The Kid" was probably sad, a sadness that she tried to hide by acting so tough. I also added that I suspected that sometimes even "Janet" became angry and had sad feelings that made it hard for her to act grown up.

The gymnasts fantasy illustrated the disparity between Kathy's real self (the abused, sexually preoccupied, and vulnerable self) and her ideal self (Janet, a girl who behaves appropriately). Her wish to have the audience judge her represented her fear that I had left on vacation, or her mother had left emotionally and father had abused her, because of her own misbehavior.

An interesting event took place towards the end of this six-month period while Kathy and I walked in the park. Kathy as Kathy, (not "The Kid" or "Janet"), was demonstrating her skill at turning cartwheels. Neither she nor I saw the man watching us. He applauded her cartwheel and offered her candy. I thanked him for his offer and quickly guided Kathy out of the park. Kathy completely complied with my actions during this interchange. As soon as we returned to the office she became overtly angry. She claimed I had treated her "like a child." She said she knew "who and what was safe" and did not need me to make that decision for her, adding that it was now my responsibility to buy her candy to make up for the candy I had prevented her from accepting. She could not yet simply take in my caring or protection.

During the next six-month period (11 to $11\frac{1}{2}$ years), Kathy was preoccupied with suggestive dance steps and lyrics. She expressed her belief that all men and women do together is either "argue and hit, or hump." She said this belief resulted from observing the relationship between her parents, as well as from father's statement that this is what relationships are about. She decided that her father was a "bad guy" who knew the difference between right and wrong but chose to do the wrong thing. This was the first time that Kathy referred to mother's sexual behavior. Given the family sleeping arrangements, Kathy most likely had observed her parents' sexual activity. Throughout the therapy, Kathy never spoke about mother's sexual behavior, telling me to "mind your own business."

Kathy complained that the younger of her two foster sisters insisted that they masturbate each other. She found this "nasty." The foster mother telephoned after she found Kathy and the foster sister engaged in sexual play. The foster mother and I devised a plan to increase the structure and limits. She held a meeting with all three girls, discussed inappropriate touching and instituted new rules preventing the girls from being alone.

At the therapy visit following my discussions with the foster mother, Kathy, afraid of my anger about her behavior with her foster sister, revealed the following nightmare:

> Kathy comes to her therapy appointment only to find my office full of frightening creatures including a tank with piranhas. I grab her hand and put it in the tank. I am so powerful that the piranhas do not hurt me.

These fascinating symbols can represent several aspects of Kathy's world. For example, my placing her hand in the fish tank could represent her activities with her foster sister. In part, the dream reflects her fear that my anger will make my office a dangerous place where I would use my power to hurt her.

As Kathy turned 12 she continued to be highly conflicted about the discrepancy between the quality of care she received at the foster home and what she would and did receive from her mother. The conflict expressed itself in angry accusations that I kept her from living with her mother and that her mother provided well for her. These accusations often followed her foster mother's buying Kathy some clothes or taking her on an outing.

Kathy's behavior improved considerably. Although in therapy she continued to demonstrate her sexual preoccupation, outside of therapy she had stopped stealing, behaved appropriately, and obtained acceptable grades in school. In therapy, her eroticized dancing subsided; instead, she asked if I could teach her several ballet steps. Kathy viewed ballet as "pretty and graceful," a controlled form of movement, especially when compared to her dancing. Since I saw her ballet interest as a displaced request for control and protection, I taught her some steps. Her request also reflected her identification with me and her wish to please me.

During this period, Kathy's therapy was reduced to once a week due to a funding change, as well as the improvement in her behavior. This change, combined with Social Services speaking to Kathy about returning to mother's care, led to a deterioration in her behavior. On one occasion, for no apparent reason, she appeared at the foster family's dinner table without pants. I interpreted this action as Kathy's fear that, once in mother's home, mother's inability to control Kathy's impulses would place her in danger. Kathy insisted that she wanted to return home so that she could assist mother. She spontaneously shifted the discussion to suggestive comments about her own "boyfriends" and a provocative denial of any sexual contact.

Although many of us involved with the case questioned the decision to return Kathy home, mother had cooperated with all the guidelines and it was believed that a return needed to be tried. Kathy, now $12\frac{1}{2}$, returned to mother's care, where she remained for approximately five months. During that period, Kathy's psychotherapy visits fell off dramatically. On several occasions, mother canceled the visits because she was without bus money, had menstrual cramps, or said that Kathy had a cold. Kathy never came to the visits on time. When she did come for her psychotherapy she was verbally abusive. I could not do anything right. She made many provocative statements about her sexual behavior. I commented that I thought she was telling me that she did not feel safe and perhaps was angry about her current living situation. Kathy responded with an increase in her abuse towards me and a flurry of positive and grandiose statements about her mother. When Social Services discovered that she had not been attending school, Kathy, now 13 years old, was placed in a group home.

The therapy sessions following Kathy's entering a group home (13 to $13\frac{1}{2}$ years old) were very difficult. The group home reported that Kathy did not want mother to visit her at the group home because she was embarrassed by mother's hair and jewelry. In therapy, she stood close to me, posturing and moving her shoulders in an intimidating manner. She shouted angrily that I could not tell her what to do and blamed me for her placement in a group home. She said that both she and her mother "hated" me and that I had "ugly hair." I doubt that it was my hair that so infuriated her. Rather, it was my inability to protect her from a nonprotective environment, i.e., a peculiarly coiffed mother who remained needy, ineffectual, and unable to protect Kathy from her own or anyone else's impulses.

Kathy, now $13\frac{1}{2}$, struggled during the next six months. The group home reported much sexual acting out and posturing. In therapy, she spoke obsessively about boyfriends and sex. Concerned about her safety and intimacy with me, she commented that a woman leaving my office building looked like "she had just had sex." She continued saying that she would never go to a male therapist because he would want to have sex. Laughingly, she said "You probably go to a therapist just to have sex. . . . Do you know how it feels to have a man's penis in your mouth?" I responded to her questions and statements by commenting that she was letting me know that it was hard for her to feel safe anywhere, even in my office. I added that it sounded like she was very confused about what was okay behavior with her body, and that she was interested in how grownup ladies behaved with their bodies. She danced erotically on our walk or in the grocery store. I commented upon her continuing to show me her worries about sexuality, but also told her directly to stop that behavior on the street or in the store, as it was unacceptable. She always laughed, but always stopped.

This sequence of material demonstrates several issues, most of which center around the safety of my office as well as her questioning my sexual drives. Her behavior asked how I handled sexuality, if I had sexual thoughts about anyone or her, or if she and I were both impulse ridden. She needed these answers to assess if I could protect and guide her. Her erotic dancing in the street again tested my ability to protect her from her own impulses.

Now quite fastidious about her dress, Kathy mentioned that once a week she washed all her clothing, even items she had not worn. In a way similar to her earlier fear about others' knowing her foster child status, she now feared that her sexual, dirty, and abused self would be seen unless she took great care to hide it. Her laundry activities also expressed her desire to be as different as possible from her mother.

Her grappling with her ideal and real self, which had appeared in her gymnast play, reappeared in a new fantasy. In this fantasy, Kathy, an actress, first makes a soft drink commercial in a very seductive manner. In the second take of the commercial, the same "actress" behaves conservatively, advertising the soft drink in a straightforward, nonerotic manner.

In the commercial play, Kathy created one character with two different behaviors, good and "nasty." In the earlier gymnast play, the two different behaviors had to be separated into two different characters. Her ability to tolerate both behaviors in one person represented her integration of her history with her present self and the development of an internalized protector. The existence of both behaviors in one person suggested that Kathy now felt greater control over her impulses. Since the internalized protector controlled or protected Kathy from her impulses, she could tolerate both feelings without becoming overwhelmed or needing to split these feelings off from herself to maintain a sense of safety.

As this period of treatment progressed, her identification with me became more obvious. Commenting on a new piece of clothing I wore, Kathy remarked, "You look good—you're dressed like a mother. My mother dresses that way." She stopped throwing her candy wrappers on the street, saying that she knew I did not like it and "that it is bad for the environment."

This identification with me and her group home counselors created a further foothold in the establishment of her internalized protector and allowed Kathy to state overtly her conflicts about returning home. Now 14 years old, she sometimes wanted to see mother; at other times, she wanted to avoid her. In therapy, she spoke of how embarrassed she would be to have a boyfriend come to her home and meet her mother. Kathy revealed that mother allows her to watch the Playboy channel on her visits to mother's home. She knew that none of her caregivers would approve of this behavior. I suspected Kathy reported this activity to test if we would take action to prevent her from returning home. In that same session, she spoke with significant disgust about a "really skinny" woman on her bus who had multicolored hair and whose pants were so tight that they outlined her genitals. Here Kathy displaced her disgust and fear of her mother's sexuality onto the bus rider and the bus rider's revealing pants.

During several visits in this sequence, Kathy complained about menstrual cramps. This was the first time that she willingly discussed her maturing body. Her willingness to acknowledge her own sexuality suggested her own increased sense of control, although it also spoke to her fears of both injury and being a woman.

Later Kathy overtly questioned how I would be as a protector in an attempt to learn ways to protect herself. Such questioning is an advanced prerequisite to internalizing a protector and could not have occurred without Kathy's earlier testing of and an identification with her care providers. For example, one day on our walk in the park, we passed a man sunbathing in a bikini bathing suit. Kathy, worried the man was looking at us, continually glanced behind to make sure that he was not following us. She mentioned how her mother always looks to see if men watch her. Kathy questioned what I would do if a man followed us.

Kathy's worry about the man's watching was reminiscent of her father's masturbating while watching her undress. The man's lack of clothing brought up issues of Kathy's sexuality that frightened her. She turned this fright into a discussion about how I would protect her from him, although unconsciously she was asking about protection from herself. Kathy frequently questioned what I would do if a man suddenly burst into my office or if a man appeared on the stairs with a gun. I connected for Kathy her worries about the sunbather, her father, and her wish for protection. I also answered her directly; I told her how I would protect her from an intruder and guided her thinking such that she could find ways to protect herself. In this sequence, she overtly tested if and discovered that I considered her worthy of protection. The repetitious quality again illustrates her slow internalization of the concept of protection.

Kathy is now $14\frac{1}{2}$ years old and her conversations demonstrate a substantial beginning of an internalized protector. Although Kathy is unable to speak directly about her fears about being with her mother, she talks continually about the dangers in mother's neighborhood and says that to go home would mean taking care of her mother. Mother told Kathy that her not coming home makes mother feel guilty and rejected.

Recently, as we were on a walk, a car suddenly turned into a driveway. Instinctively, I grabbed Kathy and knocked us both out of the car's way and into some bushes. I asked how Kathy felt about my atypical action. She replied that she liked it when I did things like that because it let her know that I cared, even if I was telling her not to do something, "like not dance dirty in the grocery store."

Kathy has been in psychotherapy for five years. In a backhand manner, she has raised the issue of termination: "I can just see it now. I'm going to be 21 years old and you will still be telling me to be careful or not to throw trash on the street." Her statement demonstrates her wish and need to stay connected and have someone watching over and protecting her. At this point, there has been a major decrease in sexualized behavior, an appreciation for the need to be protected, and some sense of an internalized protector, through an identification with myself and her other care providers. A return to mother's home may lead to a return of the acting-out behavior. Hopefully, her young internalized protector will limit the self-destructive quality of those behaviors.

OBSTACLES TO TREATMENT, OTHER SYSTEMS INVOLVED

Kathy clearly did best in the foster home. She related well to the structure that her foster parents provided. She received considerable attention and caring. It was possibly the closest experience she ever had to a normal family setting, and helped tremendously in establishing an internalized protector. At the same time, mother had complied with treatment and both mother and Kathy overtly stated their wish for reunification. While we all recognize the importance of family bonds, focusing upon reunification sometimes causes the system to overlook the limits of that particular family.

Although mother complied with her own treatment, there had been little change in mother's basic character structure. She remained a characterlogically depressed and needy woman, unable to manage an acting-out adolescent. Mother's neediness created a reliance upon Kathy to manage the household and the younger siblings.

Kathy's continued questioning and testing of what I would do if someone approached her demonstrated her need for external protection that she could internalize. When the system put her back into an unprotected environment, i.e., her mother's care, the notions that we valued and would protect her and that she was worthy of both her own and our protection became emotional fallacies.

Until very recently, directly interpreting her unhappiness or her sense of lack of protection was futile. For Kathy to have responded to such an interpretation with anything other than a negative reaction would have placed her in the public position of being disappointed with her mother. Not only would this have brought forth feelings of disloyalty but, by making the disappointment overt, such an interpretation would have forced Kathy to look at her own sense of worthlessness resulting from her father's abuse, her mother's inadequacy, and Kathy's identification with both. Thus, it was very difficult if not impossible for Kathy to make a direct statement about her wish to remain outside of her mother's care. Only through her prolonged absence from school and increased acting out could she tell us that her mother could not control her.

The school Kathy attended for two years created another outside obstacle. The school, designed for children in foster care, consisted predominantly of acting-out adolescent boys. It was difficult to assess whether Kathy actively solicited the boys' sexual attention. Yet, she complained bitterly about the boys' touching her and showed the overtly sexual notes she had received. While I wondered if a part of her complaints reassured her about her attractiveness and power, the predominant message was a plea for help and protection. When I consulted with the school personnel, they stated that they handled the situation the best they could. Eventually, she transferred to a more stable school with a more mixed group of children. She still talks about her interests in her new male classmates, but without the fervor and panic she expressed at the previous school.

MISTAKES

My primary mistakes revolved around not having more frequent contact with mother. Mother needed her own internalized protector and needed to be actively taught how to protect her child. I understood her presentation as a symptom of her neediness, her poor sense of self, her depression, and her wish to keep others away. Yet mother's inability to provide adequate care, use of Kathy as her own surrogate mother, passivity, and clear need, if not tacit demand, for others to provide for her made me impatient. I rationalized that since mother had her own various therapists, complained that it was too difficult to get to my office, and Social Services coordinated the treatment anyway, there was little need for me to forcefully pursue the collateral visits. My personal reaction led to the infrequent contact and limited my appreciation for Kathy's life. Should Kathy be returned to mother's care, it will be important for me to have a good relationship with mother so that she will support Kathy's continuing treatment.

REACTIONS

Given Kathy's mother's presentation, all of us involved in the case readily understood Kathy's negative feelings about her mother. Yet, another part of Kathy mourned her mother's helplessness and genuinely loved and wanted to help mother improve her life. Although Kathy had also developed an identification with me and her other caregivers, this identification coexisted with her identification with her mother and father. Thus, I had to continually monitor my own feelings about mother and father, so that my interpretations reflected both sides of Kathy's feelings. That is, the interpretation had to include an understanding of mother's inability to nurture as based not on malice but on mother's own unfortunate life experiences that interfered with her adult functioning.

The interpretation also had to acknowledge Kathy's wish that mother could be different. A negatively tinged interpretation would have raised Kathy's defenses and need to protect mother from me. For example, my comment when Kathy discussed her laundry activities focused upon her own need to feel clean and attractive, rather than upon the difference between how Kathy cared for herself and how mother cared for Kathy. Nonetheless, there were times when my interpretations were felt by Kathy to be a criticism of her mother. After Kathy had been returned to mother I commented that I thought she was angry about her living situation. In retrospect, I believe I was not only commenting upon her feelings but my own as well. In light of Kathy's ambivalence, her subsequent verbally assaultive behavior towards me made sense. I suspect, however, that my simply behaving in a manner that was different from mother's was also felt as a criticism of mother. Kathy's guilt around her ambivalent feelings towards mother and her identification with her made "criticisms," tacit or otherwise, very threatening.

Initially, Kathy's play was both explicitly sexual and sexually assaultive. At times it was so primitive, undefended, direct and in its way assaultive, that most observers, including myself, would become uncomfortable. I understood that part of this play represented her testing if and how I would protect her. However, I wanted to be clear that my motivation for introducing a protector was primarily to develop an internalized protector in Kathy's personality structure, as opposed to my own need for protection from this sexually assaultive play. Kathy's need to repeat this play knowing that I would reliably provide the protecting mother confirmed my interpretation of her wish for protection, as well as her inability to find protection on her own. Her wish to repeat this now altered play reflected her slowly taking in the notion of a protector. As she internalized the protector, her need for this altered, now "protecting" play diminished and eventually disappeared.

As therapists, we worry about interfering with the flow of the child's play and scrupulously avoid altering the play. When the play involves a unique fantasy or a new storyline, one must wait and see how that play develops and grows over time. A repetitive play, such as that which Kathy displayed, most likely reflects the child's inability to find a solution and her sense of helplessness. The therapist's other motives for altering the play can certainly coexist with, if not mirror, the child's own needs and provide important clues as to the child's emotional state around those issues; my need for protection paralleled Kathy's need for protection. I managed my reaction to Kathy's play by recognizing the symbolic meaning of the sexual assault in the play and then introducing a protector who would protect both of us.

Children with histories similar to Kathy's develop a way of relating to adults that can be remarkably engaging if not overtly seductive. Over the years I grew increasingly fond of this extraordinarily difficult child. Although such feelings are not unusual after working with a child for several years, much to my amazement I found myself with the fleeting thought of raising this difficult child in my home. I understood this thought as a further demonstration of how the therapist can pick up the child's feelings and absorb them into the therapist's own psyche; Kathy identified with me and wanted to live with me. It also demonstrated the skill of the sexually abused child at obtaining her needs.

8

Sexual Abuse of a Young Boy Arising During Visitation

ANTHONY P. MANNARINO

Dr. Mannarino presents a situation most of us have encountered, i.e., allegations of sexual abuse arising during visitation, with the allegations occurring in the context of a litigious separation. In treating this case, he had to play several roles: evaluator of the child, evaluator of the father, and eventually, therapist for the child and the child's caregivers.

He introduces the concept of interactional assessment, where the child victim is observed with the alleged perpetrator by a trained professional who has been requested to complete an objective evaluation. He accurately identifies the conflict that exists when one plays multiple roles, i.e., evaluator of parent and child, and appropriately raises the question of whether or not the child should be forced into taking part in the observation. Dr. Mannarino considered the best interests of the child during this observation, and ended the interactional interview when it became clear that continuing would be traumatizing to Michael. Dr. Mannarino could then lobby hard for Michael's safety to the court, using the information obtained via the interactional assessment.

Sexual behavior emerged in Michael, a common consequence of sexual abuse (Friedrich, Grambsch, et al. in press). Much of the treatment of sexually reactive behavior requires the family to think about and react to the behavior in a less reactive, less pathologizing manner. That clearly was done in this case.

Initially, Michael's mother did not want to believe that her separated husband was the perpetrator. Her behavior is actually much more common than is vociferous lobbying of one parent for condemnation of the other. The mother's restraint in this case certainly gave credibility to the numerous accusations that emerged.

An interesting secondary focus was Dr. Mannarino's correcting the parenting imbalance between the grandmother and the mother in a way that was nonthreatening and supportive. He had to deal with both mother's and grandmother's distress at having a child who had been damaged.

Dr. Mannarino outlines one of the briefer treatments described in this book. This was possible because Michael had numerous coping resources in the context of a supportive mother and grandmother, neither of whom had a previous history of sexual abuse. — Editor

AUTHOR'S THEORETICAL ORIENTATION

In my therapeutic work with children, adolescents, and their families, I am generally eclectic in my approach, with a strong systems orientation. Although I believe that individual treatment with a child can be beneficial, I feel strongly that it can achieve little success without appropriate interventions with other family members, particularly the parents. In addition, consulting with a child's teacher at school or with other relevant adults, such as day care workers or baby-sitters, is a vital part of the therapeutic process. In this way, therapy with children differs from treatment of adults, where the focus is largely on the individual patient.

This systems orientation is even more crucial in working with sexually abused children. The impact of the abuse may be significant not only for the child but also for the parents. Indeed, in many cases parents react more strongly to the abuse than the child does. Accordingly, helping parents to deal with the abuse may be as important as the treatment provided for the child. Moreover, in some cases, consulting with day care workers or preschool teachers may be appropriate with regard to eliminating sexualized behaviors, decreasing fears/separation anxiety, etc.

Complicating the treatment process in sexual abuse cases is the fact that the legal and child welfare systems are typically involved. Therapists will often spend a great deal of time talking with caseworkers, police, district attorneys, defense counsel, and judges who are involved either in the criminal prosecution of the alleged offender or in determining placement for the victim. Consulting with these various agencies and professionals is crucial in helping them to better understand the emotional needs of the child. Ultimately, how the various systems respond to a child victim may have greater therapeutic implications than the direct work a therapist does for the child and his/her family. This again reinforces the importance of a

The assistance of Ann Marie Kotlik in the preparation of this chapter is gratefully acknowledged.

systems perspective relative to individual treatment in child sexual abuse cases.

DESCRIPTION OF CASE

Michael is a six-year-old boy who was living with his natural mother and maternal grandparents, along with his four-year-old sister Julie. There was no known history of sexual abuse of any member of this family. The parents had been separated for nearly two years at the time of referral. They were not yet divorced. Michael and his sister visited with their natural father every other weekend. The father lived in a town in a neighboring state that was a two-hour drive from the children's home. The father always transported the children to and from his residence.

For about four months, Michael had been vehemently objecting to visiting his father. He was not specific in his protest, simply indicating that he did not want to go. In addition, he was experiencing sleep disturbance, which was later diagnosed as night terrors. His mother took him to the family pediatrician because of these night terrors and also because Michael had been complaining of pain in his rectal area. Upon examination, the pediatrician discovered stretching of Michael's sphincter muscle. This physical finding raised some concerns about possible abuse. Michael was therefore referred to me for psychological assessment of this issue. Visits with the father were discontinued pending the results of this evaluation. The pediatrician also filed a SCAN (suspected child abuse and neglect) report to the local child protective services agency.

PSYCHOLOGICAL ASSESSMENT

The psychological evaluation conducted in this case was critical with regard to determining the likelihood of sexual abuse and to planning the course of treatment. In many ways, it was more therapeutic and clinically significant than the actual treatment that was subsequently provided. Therefore, it will be extensively described.

Initial Sessions

In total, there were six assessment sessions. With a young child, the author believes that it is often necessary to have several meetings to establish a trusting relationship prior to any disclosure of abuse. Michael was accompanied to the initial three sessions by his mother and maternal grandmother. He presented as a bright, verbal child of average size who did not manifest any separation anxiety. Vocabulary and expressive language skills were grossly in the normal range. Michael related in a pleasant and friendly manner and was able to maintain reasonably good eye contact. Psychotic features or symptoms of serious depression or anxiety disorder were absent.

In the context of different play activities during these initial three meetings, I talked with Michael about members of his family, preschool, friends, etc. He was extremely positive about his mother, maternal grandparents, and sister. When asked about his father, he typically became rather quiet and withdrawn, although he did not express any negative feelings about his dad. He also seemed somewhat anxious when asked about his paternal grandmother, whom he saw frequently when visiting his father.

I also talked with Michael about normal touching activities, such as that which occurs during bathtime, medical examinations, etc. In addition, there was some focus on "good" and "bad" touching and on the identification of body parts, including the private parts. Michael readily provided the words he uses for his private parts and eagerly stated that his mother and maternal grandparents frequently kiss and hug him in an appropriate manner. When asked about "bad" kinds of touching, Michael became somewhat anxious and withdrawn and avoided eye contact. He also clearly tried to avoid my questions about this issue by talking about other things. However, he did not indicate that anyone had ever touched him in a way that made him feel uncomfortable or upset. He appeared very relieved when the interview was refocused on less threatening topics.

The maternal grandmother and mother provided important information about Michael's adjustment. They were very distressed by his night terrors, which lasted about 45 minutes and occurred every night. Typically, Michael would scream intensely "no, no" or "Daddy, leave me alone" while simultaneously thrashing his arms and legs. The mother reported that her son seemed terrified during these night terrors and that there was absolutely nothing she could do to awaken him. Interestingly, within four weeks of the time that visits with the father were stopped, these night terrors decreased to three or four per week and were clearly less intense.

The mother further reported that Michael had been quite aggressive with his sister Julie, often hitting her without provocation. He was also observed frequently to "dig" his fingers into his rectum and to masturbate almost every day. On three occasions, the mother discovered Michael trying to get on top of Julie while they were bathing.

The mother and maternal grandmother were very worried about Michael. They were suspicious that perhaps he had been sexually abused by his father but they also did not want to believe that this could have actually occurred. Their anxiety mounted each week. A significant part of my work was geared toward helping them to remain calm while I was proceeding with my interviews with Michael. I also strongly encouraged the mother and grandmother to not question him about visits with his father but to listen if he wanted to talk.

Court Involvement

Because of the concern about possible sexual abuse, the mother and grand-mother wanted me to write a report to the local child protective services agency which would recommend that the father not be permitted to visit with the children. In light of the fact that the parents were separated and I had never met the father, I felt that I could not comply with their request. Moreover, it was clear that the parents were not yet divorced and a final settlement, including custody of the children, had not been determined. I therefore suggested that the father should be involved in the evaluation. Moreover, it was my idea that the evaluator be court appointed and agree-able to all parties, including counsel. The mother and grandmother were upset by this suggestion, but I was able to help them to see why the father's involvement was important.

This idea was accepted by the attorneys for both the mother and father and the family court judge. Since I had already been involved in evaluating Michael, the judge requested that I remain the independent evaluator in this case. No abuse had yet been disclosed by Michael. Furthermore, none of the parties felt that I was biased toward the mother's side or towards finding abuse. Accordingly, I agreed to be the court-appointed evaluator.

The Disclosure

Michael disclosed the sexual abuse by his father during the fourth interview. This was the first interview after the family court judge had appointed me to continue with this case. I believe that the disclosure occurred at this point because Michael had begun to trust me and also because he had some awareness of the court proceedings which frightened him. He initially stated that he was afraid of his dad and did not want to see him. He felt that the judge might make him visit with his father. He then said that his father "did bad things to me." After some encouragement, Michael was able to describe acts of genital fondling and anal intercourse. By his report, the father told him to never tell anyone about the abuse and threatened to hurt his mother if he disclosed. Near the end of this meeting, Michael also revealed that the father had assaulted his sister Julie and that he had wit-nessed some of these incidents.

These disclosures made Michael very anxious. In particular, he appeared very frightened that his mother might get hurt and wanted to be reunited with her. My reassurance seemed to allay some of Michael's anxiety. I tried to explain to him that the abuse was being investigated by the authorities whose job is to ensure that this does not happen again. In addition, I discussed with him the fact that many children have been sexually abused and that it takes a great deal of courage to talk about it.

During the next session, Michael seemed fairly relaxed. He spontaneously repeated the disclosures that he had made during the previous interview. He remained, though, quite afraid about something happening to his mother. When given the opportunity to use anatomically correct dolls, Michael provided an explicit demonstration of how his father had engaged him in anal intercourse. This doll demonstration was entirely consistent with his previous verbal statements. Again I tried to be supportive of Michael and praised his efforts to talk about such a difficult thing.

After the fourth interview with Michael, I again met with the mother and maternal grandmother. They indicated that his behavior had sharply deteriorated over the past week. He seemed very angry and was often aggressive with Julie. In addition, his night terrors had worsened and his appetite had become extremely erratic. In a tearful, private talk with his grandmother, Michael had revealed that the father had been engaging him and Julie in anal intercourse. The mother and grandmother were both extremely upset when reporting this disclosure to me. They seemed shocked that these children could have actually been sexually abused and were angry at the father. They also expressed intense guilt because they felt that they had failed to protect Michael and his sister.

It was very important for me to provide support, understanding, and reassurance to the mother and grandmother. Their pain was intense. If not addressed, it could have hindered their efforts to be supportive of the children. Yet, at the same time, it was equally important for me to convey to them that it was essential for the father to participate in the assessment and perhaps for Michael and the father to be seen together for at least one meeting. Until that time, no conclusive determination could be made about the sexual abuse. The mother and grandmother expressed a great deal of concern about the father and Michael being seen together. However, I had gained their trust and they were able to remain reasonably patient and calm as the evaluation progressed.

Session with Father

For the purposes of this chapter, it would not be helpful to provide extensive details regarding my individual interview with the father. As one would expect, he totally denied that he had ever abused Michael or Julie. Moreover, he claimed that the mother and grandmother had many negative feelings toward him and were "coaching" the children to make false allegations. This is a common scenario in cases of alleged sexual abuse, particularly when there is pending custody litigation.

The more significant data relate to the planned interactional assessment of the father and the children. In the county in which I reside, interactional assessments are commonly done as part of court-ordered evaluations. In fact, in their absence, evaluations are viewed by the judge and/or attorneys as incomplete. Interactionals can provide information as to a parent's style or a child's comfort with a parent. I had hoped to gain a gross measure of Michael's willingness and/or ability to interact with his father, as this might have shed some light on the issue of visitation. The interactional assessment was not designed to establish Michael's credibility. His individual sessions had provided sufficient data regarding that issue.

I had talked with Michael about the interactional assessment during the previous individual interview and had tried to reassure him that he would be safe. At that time, he had agreed to participate but it was clear that he was quite apprehensive. When Michael arrived at my office with his sister, mother, and grandparents for this interactional, he was extremely upset and fearful. He strongly indicated that he did not want to see his father. (The mother and grandmother later reported that Michael had been very upset in the car and that they literally had to drag him into the building.) I again attempted to reassure Michael and gently encouraged him to accompany me to my office. However, not only did he resist my efforts but he actually became hysterical and begun to run uncontrollably throughout the lobby. My observations suggested that Michael was not being oppositional but that he was truly terrified of seeing his father. Accordingly, it was decided that it would not be appropriate to force him to participate in this meeting. Michael's extreme and genuine fear of his father contributed significantly to my subsequent recommendation to the court that he and the father have no ongoing contact.

Interestingly, Julie was willing to see her dad. She did not seem afraid of him and was able to interact with him in a reasonably positive fashion. The father, though, was very intrusive with Julie and frequently pressured her to hug and kiss him against her wishes. (It is worth mentioning that the mother and grandmother had reported that Julie had made some disclosures to them and the pediatrician about sexual abuse by the father. However, she never seemed afraid of the father to the extent that Michael was.)

The individual interview with the father and the interactional assessment of him and Julie were the final parts of the evaluation. Subsequently, a report was prepared and sent to the family court judge and the attorneys for both parties. In this report, I suggested that there was substantial evidence that Michael had been sexually abused by his father. I recommended that he not be forced to visit with his father for the time being, even on a supervised basis. I also strongly urged that Michael be involved in individual therapy and the mother and maternal grandmother in adjunctive counseling.

The critical decision that I was faced with at this point was whether to conduct the therapy with this boy myself or to refer him to another therapist with extensive experience in the sexual abuse field. The mother and grandmother very much wanted me to stay involved with Michael and them because of their trust in me and their reluctance "to start all over" with a new therapist. This seemed logical and reasonable. However, I was also concerned about my role as an independent evaluator. If I remained on this case as a therapist, I would not be able to conduct a reevaluation at a later date if this became necessary. My decision to continue as Michael's therapist was primarily based on the positive relationship that he and I had established. This sense of trust is essential in helping children to make additional disclosures and in encouraging them to talk about abuse-related feelings. I informed the judge and the attorneys of my desire to continue with this case. They all agreed that this would be appropriate.

COURSE OF THERAPY

Individual therapy for Michael and adjunctive counseling for the mother and grandmother continued for six months beyond the completion of the psychological assessment. In total, there were 20 treatment sessions. During the last two months, sessions were conducted every other week. There were three distinct phases of treatment in this case. They will each be described below.

Phase 1.   Reestablishment of Trust

Michael experienced a high level of stress on the day that he was scheduled to participate in the interactional assessment with his father. His mother reported that he remained quite upset for a couple of days and that severe night terrors were common again for about two weeks. Unfortunately, some of the trust that he had developed in me was lost because he came to associate me and my office with the reappearance of his father.

It took approximately six sessions for Michael to reestablish a solid sense of trust in me as his therapist. Sessions were arranged such that there was time for unstructured play, structured play, and verbal discussion. During these meetings, Michael expressed tremendous bitterness and anger toward his father. He frequently drew pictures of "voltrons killing bad guys" and would simultaneously verbalize that his father should be in jail or killed. Sometimes Michael's anger was directed at me. For example, on one occasion, he purposely spilled some paint on my clothing and then angrily stated that my shirt was "ugly" and looked better all "messed up." Several times he indicated that he was "mad" at me for "tricking" him into coming to my office when the father was present.

I attempted throughout these initial meetings to empathize with Michael's feelings and to let him know that it was acceptable to express anger verbally and through his play. One major interpretation that was made that he had felt betrayed by me for allowing his father to come to my office and that this feeling was perhaps similar to the sense of betrayal he experienced with his father as a result of the abuse. Michael did not respond verbally to this interpretation. However, he did make eye contact and seemed relieved. I then told him that I understood that it was hard to trust again after having been hurt.

By the end of the sixth session, Michael's anger toward me had totally dissipated and he seemed to feel very positively about our sessions. He continued to express anger toward his father. This was much less intense, though. Michael clearly felt more confident that he would not be forced to visit with his father. At this point, he had not had any visits with the father in nearly four months.

Adjunctive sessions with the mother and grandmother were critical in the early phase of treatment. They continued to need support and encouragement in accepting what had happened to Michael and Julie. (Julie was not in individual treatment but was a minor focus during sessions with the mother and grandmother.) The grandmother, in particular, remained very upset for weeks and needed the opportunity during sessions to express her anger, bitterness, and fears regarding how the children had been "damaged." It is worth pointing out that because of the mother's irregular work schedule, the grandmother was often in the primary parenting role for both children. For this reason, she was highly invested in them and terribly disturbed by what had occurred.

A significant focus of these sessions was on helping the mother and grandmother to deal with Michael's night terrors. The grandmother was encouraged to let the mother deal with this problem. This was designed to keep the grandmother's anxiety from escalating because the night terrors were truly horrible, and to build the mother's sense of competence as a parent. She had clearly been feeling inadequate because of the abuse and because she believed that she had not been sufficiently available to the children. The mother was instructed to hold Michael within a couple of minutes when a night terror began and to gently keep informing him of her presence. Otherwise, she was advised not to talk to him. (Formerly both the mother and grandmother had asked many anxious questions of Michael during a night terror [e.g., "What's the matter?"; "Michael, can you tell us what's happening?"] and had done this in a rather histrionic manner which seemed to intensify and prolong the night terror.)

The mother was effective in dealing with this situation. Not only did she explicitly follow my instructions regarding how to intervene with Michael, but she also managed to keep the persistent grandmother from becoming involved again. After about four weeks of treatment, Michael's night terrors had almost totally disappeared. He had only two more over the next five months of therapy and these were probably triggered by specific stressful events in his life.

Phase 2

After the first six treatment sessions, during which time Michael reestablished his sense of trust in me as his therapist, he began to make additional disclosures about specific abusive incidents perpetrated against him and his sister by his father. Again sessions were a combination of free play, structured play, and verbal discussions. These disclosures always occurred in the context of Michael's involvement in different play activities, such as drawing. For example, on one occasion he made a picture of a policeman and then said that he wished that the policeman could have protected him when his father took pictures of him without any clothes on.

In addition to more disclosures, Michael was able to express both verbally and through drawings his fears related to the father's threat to hurt him, his sister, and his mother. Expressions of these feelings seemed therapeutic in and of itself for Michael, but it was also important to provide encouragement and support. Moreover, he sometimes indicated that he was a "bad boy" because of what his father did to him. This required helping him to understand that it is the adult's responsibility whenever a child is abused.

This phase of treatment lasted about 10 sessions or two-and-a-half to three months. Michael enjoyed coming to our sessions and provided a great deal of therapeutic material to work with. As a therapist, my approach was largely nondirective and supportive. Michael needed encouragement, understanding, and occasional gentle "pushes" as he took the lead in trying to accept and resolve what had happened to him.

During this middle phase of treatment, the major focus with the mother and grandmother was related to the upcoming family court hearing, in which it would be determined whether the father would be permitted visitation with the children. They had tremendous anxiety with regard to this hearing. They were very apprehensive that the judge would not find Michael and Julie credible and/or that visitation would be permitted nonetheless. It should be mentioned that I was extremely opposed to visits between

Michael and the father based upon my evaluation and that I was willing to testify regarding this recommendation. With respect to Julie, I believed that supervised visits might be acceptable as long as a criminal proceeding was not pending. (The mother had decided not to press charges because of her concern that testifying would potentially traumatize Michael and because the case would be tried in another state where the abuse had occurred.)

The mother and grandmother were able to control their anxiety reasonably well until the time of the scheduled hearing, although the grandmother, in particular, frequently called between sessions for additional support. As it turned out, this hearing never took place because the father, through his attorney, agreed to drop his petition for visitation. The judge awarded total permanent custody to the mother and left it to her discretion as to whether the father would ever be permitted visits. This outcome provided an enormous sense of relief for the mother and grandparents and contributed to their feeling that justice had been served in behalf of the children. Their anxiety largely dissipated based on this judicial determination.

The other major issue addressed with the mother and grandmother during this treatment phase was their concern that the children were damaged because of the abuse. This notion of "damaged goods" is commonly reported by the parents of victims and even sometimes by older victims themselves. Both the grandmother and mother frequently expressed intense anger toward the father for irreparably robbing these children of their childhood. In addition, they had tremendous anxiety and sadness related to their feeling that Michael and Julie would "never be the same." In order to help the mother and grandmother deal with this issue, it was important that they understand that the children did not perceive the abuse in the way that they did. Although Michael and Julie experienced the abuse as coercive, frightening, and a betrayal of their father's trust, they did not perceive it as sexual, at least not in the sense that adults would.

An educational but supportive approach was taken with the mother and grandmother to help them resolve this matter. They were strongly encouraged to focus on the assaults as being abusive and to not focus on the sexual aspects. In this regard, I suggested to the mother and grandmother that Michael's heightened sexual interest was probably the result of the abuse and that his sexual acting out with Julie was an attempt to master feelings he did not understand. However, the emphasis was on Michael's sense of confusion and emotional upset and the behavioral manifestation of these feelings, not on sexuality per se. Through these interventions, they became better able over time to see the abuse as Michael and Julie did.

Some of the therapeutic work related to this same issue concerned the mother's and grandmother's guilt for not being aware that the children were being assaulted. To enhance their sense of parental competence, they were often given much support and honest feedback about their being good caretakers. I also emphasized that I was absolutely certain that, if they had had any real sense that the children were being abused, they would have immediately stopped the father's visits. By the end of the fourth month of treatment, the mother and grandmother had made much progress related to this theme of damaged goods. They were beginning to make hopeful, optimistic statements about the children's future. Moreover, in their interactions with Michael and Julie, they were able to overlook or ignore minor behavioral incidents, sometimes of a sexual nature, that would in the past have caused them grave concern and alarm.

Phase 3

After four months of weekly treatment sessions, Michael's fears had largely dissipated, his night terrors had virtually stopped, and there was no longer any evidence of sexualized behaviors. He had also dealt quite effectively with the fear and anger that had been generated by the abuse. Because of these therapeutic gains, it was decided to schedule sessions every two weeks, with the goal of termination. Four additional sessions were conducted, during which termination was discussed with Michael. He seemed enthusiastic about ending, as he was "tired" of talking about what had happened. I frequently informed him, nonetheless, that he could always tell his mother that he wanted to see me if he began to have negative feelings again. This termination phase went very smoothly with Michael. There was no return of any symptoms.

As for the mother and grandmother, they were somewhat anxious regarding the prospect of ending treatment. They needed much reassurance that Michael was doing well. In addition, although there was uncertainty about long-term negative sequelae to the abuse, I tried to convey a sense of confidence that Michael's future was bright and hopeful. The mother and grandmother always seemed to be reassured by my encouragement and support. They also knew that they could call me at any point after termination if they developed any concerns about Michael or Julie. As with Michael, they were able to end treatment in an upbeat, smooth fashion.

TREATMENT OUTCOME

The outcome of treatment for Michael was not empirically assessed. This is probably typical for most outpatient child and adolescent psychiatric clinics, except where there are specific treatment outcome studies being conducted. The criteria of change in Michael's case were subjective and based on my observations during sessions, his self-reports, and the feedback provided by the mother and grandmother.

By the end of the initial phase of treatment, Michael demonstrated an increase in interpersonal trust and was able to deal with and resolve some of the anger he had felt toward his father. Although he continued to be quite negative about his father, the intensity of this feeling was markedly less and there was more a sense of detachment. As treatment progressed, Michael's fears related to his father's threat to hurt someone in the family if he disclosed abuse also significantly decreased. The increase in trust and reduction in anger and fear were observed during treatment sessions in Michael's verbal statements and drawings and his manner in relating to me. These changes were also confirmed by the mother and grandmother based on their observations of Michael at home.

The mother and grandmother provided other indices of positive change. Michael's night terrors were virtually nonexistent by the end of treatment. Moreover, there was no longer any evidence of sexualized behaviors or excessive aggression with his sister. Michael's adjustment in school improved. By his teacher's report, he became less withdrawn and more actively involved in peer activities. His academic performance was consistently good. Thus, there was documentation from a number of sources that Michael was markedly improved in his affect, behavior, and adjustment. This convergence of data from several reporters, including Michael, was convincing and contributed to the mutual decision made by the mother, grandmother, and myself to terminate treatment.

The real question in this case and for that matter in any kind of child therapy, including that provided to sexually abused children, is what accounts for the positive changes that are observed. As therapists, we would certainly like to believe that we make a significant impact on children's growth. However, there are typically other environmental agents that may more likely be the source or stimulus for change. For example, in Michael's case, the fact that he no longer had any contact with his father had a major influence on him and clearly contributed to his sense of security and stability. In addition, the judicial outcome in which his mother was awarded full, permanent custody provided her and the grandparents with enormous emotional relief. This helped them to be calmer and more relaxed with Michael and Julie, which no doubt had therapeutic benefit.

The above discussion does not imply that my therapeutic interventions were not helpful. The nondirective approach used with Michael, the support given to the mother and grandmother, and the behavioral techniques employed to address his night terrors and sexualized behaviors seemed appropriate and were, in my judgment, therapeutic. However, treatment does not occur in a vacuum. Without the impact of the environmental events mentioned above, I am convinced that the therapeutic success of this case would have been significantly reduced.

OBSTACLES TO TREATMENT: COMPLEX DECISION-MAKING

In a case as complex as Michael's, there are always decisions that are made which could have been handled in a different fashion. Sometimes these decisions are made in response to various systems that affect a case or based on the personal biases of the therapist. In this section, several decisions made in Michael's case will be reviewed in order to highlight this decision-making process.

One critical decision was my agreement to be the court-appointed evaluator. In this regard, I could certainly have informed the family court judge that, since I had already established a relationship with Michael and the maternal side of the family, another professional should have been appointed as the independent evaluator. I could have then remained on the case strictly as a future therapist, if this were necessary. My decision to take on the role of independent evaluator was based primarily on two factors. First, Michael had developed a sense of trust in me as a helping professional. I was very concerned that he might be very reticent to talk to a new professional. Moreover, at that point in time, this child had not yet disclosed any abuse. Therefore, I did not feel that I was biased toward the mother's side or toward finding abuse. For these reasons, it seemed appropriate and reasonable for me to conduct an independent assessment in this case. Fortunately, throughout the evaluation, none of the parties, including counsel, ever questioned my objectivity or desire to pursue the truth about whether any abuse had occurred.

The next significant decision was very difficult from a clinical point of view. Specifically, was it appropriate to see Michael and the father together for an interactional assessment? From a legal perspective, such an assessment seemed reasonable in order to provide the court with information about their interaction. Such data could be utilized in any decision regarding future visitation. Nonetheless, I was fully aware that Michael was afraid of the father and that such an interactional assessment could be very upsetting for him.

As it turned out, this interactional assessment never occurred because, when Michael arrived at my office, it was clear that he was terrified of seeing his dad. The final decision not to force this issue seemed wise. However, in retrospect, scheduling the interaction and having Michael expect that it was going to take place may not have been the right clinical decision. My attempt to conduct a comprehensive evaluation for the court no doubt resulted in Michael's trust in me being compromised. This specific issue highlights how the demands of the legal system can be at cross purposes with respect to what is clinically optimal in a sexual abuse case. It must not be forgotten, though, that, unless an evaluator seriously addresses the judicial and legal perspectives, even an excellent clinical assessment may turn out to be meaningless and, in the long run, not in the best interests of the child.

The final critical decision was whether to continue on this case as the therapist. As mentioned earlier in this chapter, remaining as the therapist would preclude any future independent evaluations on my part. I was also concerned about blurring the boundaries between the professional roles of evaluator and therapist. My decision to continue as Michael's therapist was based primarily on not wanting him to have to talk to a different professional about the abuse. The involvement of multiple professionals in sexual abuse cases can result in children becoming oversensitized and resistant. Moreover, although scheduling the interactional assessment with the father clearly had a negative impact on Michael, it was possible to reestablish his trust because of the bond that already existed. It is worth adding that the mother and grandmother continued to have great faith in me and very much wanted me to be Michael's therapist. These factors, plus the fact that the family court judge and attorneys supported my desire to continue as Michael's therapist, ultimately convinced me that this was the right decision.

The boundary between evaluation and treatment is never rigid with children. Particularly in sexual abuse cases, it is common for new disclosures or even initial disclosures to occur well after the "treatment" process has been initiated. Thus, diagnosis is a continuous and often changing process with children. From a clinical perspective, having one professional "evaluate" a child and then continue with "treatment" is probably the wisest choice. This permits greater continuity for the child, whose sense of trust in his/her "evaluator-therapist" increases the likelihood that additional disclosures will be made and abuse-related feelings discussed and resolved.

THERAPIST'S REACTIONS TO THE CASE

My strongest reaction in this case was a sense of compassion for Michael and his sister, mother, and grandparents because of the difficult feelings and circumstances that they were forced to confront. Having young children myself, I was able to empathize with the pain they were all experiencing. I felt some need to provide protection and safety for all of these family members. Nonetheless, particularly during the evaluation, it was essential that I remain objective. Even after formal treatment had begun, I needed to maintain appropriate professional detachment, which would ultimately best serve this family. There is no doubt in my mind that having previously evaluated and/or treated nearly 500 sexually abused children helped to provide me with the right balance of compassion and professional objectivity. I truly wonder how well I would have managed my reactions in a case like this one if I had had little experience in seeing sexually abused children.

The other significant reaction that I experienced was a renewed faith in the court system. In many cases, I have been frustrated by how the courts further victimize sexually abused children. Sometimes children are forced against their will to visit with abusive parents or must be evaluated by multiple professionals in order to determine whether any abuse has occurred. In Michael's case, the family court judge showed real sensitivity to this child's emotional needs by permitting me to be the only professional involved and by later not forcing Michael to visit with his father. Although I have often felt that the court system can be unfair and cruel to sexually abused children, I felt strongly that in Michael's case justice had been served.

9

The Treatment of
Young Abused Sisters

ANONYMOUS

With this chapter, we have another case to put side by side with those of Boat and Uberek. Each of these cases describes "unspeakable acts" committed on children. Given that these sisters are such young children and they already exhibit a profound attachment disturbance, the authors provide numerous helpful pointers to us about the importance of connection and attachment in children.

A number of rich clinical vignettes are also presented. For example, they were sensitive to the needs and fears of these children and arranged to meet them in the home of the foster parents. Beginning the relationship in a more secure context helped to build a working treatment relationship more quickly. In addition, they utilized food as a reinforcer and a normal vehicle to nurture children. In so doing, they came to be viewed in a more positive light and the child-therapist relationship could better weather some of the naturally occurring storms that were part of treatment. The therapists also used photos to solidify a visual representation of the relationship. This again is developmentally sensitive and strongly recommended. In a treatment outcome study I helped to conduct in a day treatment center for preschoolers, each child receiving therapy had a picture of him- or herself and the therapist taped into his/her locker so that he/she could have a visual reminder of the therapist several times a day. The child valued the gift of a picture; in addition, an internalization of the relationship was facilitated.

As is often the case, the therapists seemed to work harder than the foster parents of these two girls. Many foster parents are compromised, and the frustrations stemming from this fact can fuel negative countertransference towards the child unless the origins are discussed in supervision.

The utility of small group therapy is also a powerful tool for children. Although these authors used it with a sibling pair, I have used it with good results with unrelated sexually abused boys who have been deficient in social skills. Before children can be expected to work in group therapy, they have to have success relating as a dyad. I recommend a recent book on "pair therapy" by Robert Selman and Lynn H. Schultz for guidelines in using dyadic therapy with isolated, socially unskilled children (1990). To foster psychosocial and personal development, pairs of children are asked to carry out challenging activities together and, with the help of a therapist, reflect on the success of their mutual efforts.

Despite the biological relatedness of these girls, it is interesting to read about the individual differences in their behaviors and in utilizing therapy.

Finally, psychological testing, particularly the projective testing utilized, clearly captured much of the interior world of these girls and was also useful in documenting improvement in a systematic way. — Editor

Introduction and Theoretical Orientation

It has been our observation that, regardless of the occasional media blitz surrounding a sensational child abuse case or the reports of continuously climbing victimization statistics, adults in our society do not want to believe that child abuse occurs — let alone that it occurs in the family. The denial of incest seems to hold true even of our professional colleagues who work in health and mental health fields with adults. At the beginning of each new case, we as "child people" also find ourselves hoping that this particular child has escaped, that the allegations are not true, that the child has not been drugged and sodomized and starved and devastated.

This chapter on the treatment of young abused girls — Molly and Suzi — is being written not at the beginning or at the end of the case but from somewhere in the middle. At this point in time we find that we are believers. We believe that these little girls, who show up in our offices each week in beautiful matching outfits and black patent leather shoes, were pervasively neglected, psychologically terrified, and repeatedly physically and sexually abused. As we reflect back over the past two years and try to look forward to the next generational cycle when these children become mothers, it is still tempting to use denial — if not for them at least to protect our own children and theirs from the same fate.

Several things have made our work with these children unique. First, the week in which the referral phone call came from an out-of-state social worker, a letter came from the editor of this book asking if we would be interested in participating in the creation of a casebook on the treatment of abused children. Thus, woven throughout the treatment, the supervision, and the haunting visions that wake therapists in the night have been the additional threads of reflection and reading and action necessary to communicate our experience with these children to you. The decision from the beginning of the case to commit ourselves to write about our work has provided a meta-layer of supervision which we believe has enriched our work and our understanding.

Second, the treatment team has been composed of two women trainees and a senior faculty member at a university medical center. Although both therapists had had extensive work with a broad range of adult psychotherapy patients, for each this was the first child case. Midway through the first year we tapped another experienced clinician, who agreed to work collaterally with the caretakers and consult with us. Even before the end of the first year of treatment, it became apparent that the needs of the children would extend far beyond the arbitrary educational training assignment of the therapists. The therapists decided to reschedule their workloads and to make the necessary accommodations in their personal and interpersonal lives in order to maintain a continuity of treatment for these children. This decision, above and beyond the call of educational duty, reflects simultaneously our judgment about the compelling needs of the children for continuity in psychotherapy and the compassion of the therapists.

Third, beyond the common history of tragedy that all abused children share, these girls carry yet another biopsychosocial legacy with them — and that is of being siblings. Sibship offers both a strength and a vulnerability (Kahn & Lewis, 1988). There is the opportunity for a reality check with another who has shared the same — albeit violent — experience; there is also double confirmation that the abuse is deserved. One of our assignments as we began to get acquainted with the girls — who were very similar in appearance and less than a year apart in age — was to facilitate the continuous and normal individuation process. Another task was to determine their unique experiences from the past, and finally, to counter the nearly inevitable replay of abusive victimization by the stronger, more assertive sibling of her sister.

Cognitive developmental theory has provided a framework for our therapeutic interventions (Harter, 1983). Young children are, by definition, in a period of rapid growth. Abuse dramatically interrupts some developmental lines and distorts the development of others. Cognitive developmental theory alerts a therapist both to the developmental sequencing of such phenomena as cognition, motivation, and affect and to the structural differences within each step that give a child the power to reorganize experience. From this perspective, growth is not just more but truly different. Thus, the child's sense of self, as well as the child's understanding of parental intention and behavior, evolve. The therapeutic use of play rather than free association as a mode of communication is clearly linked to a child's cognitive limitation and capacity. This perspective also highlights the need for the therapist to be actively didactic rather than merely interpretive in order to facilitate a child's movement to the next developmental level.

The therapeutic treatment model employed here is a modification of the group treatment model that evolved out of work with young abused children whose therapists were mental health professional trainees (Steward et al., 1986). At the time the girls were referred to us there were no available therapy groups for them to enter. That was fortuitous, for these children, as sisters, presented unique dynamic needs that we felt could be best served by a judicious combination of individual and group treatment. Therefore, the model was augmented quite explicitly by the decision to offer each girl her own therapist, who was with her in both individual play therapy and group sessions. Other components of the original model were incorporated, including group therapy techniques, joint supervision of therapists, regular home visits and consultation to caretakers.

Treatment goals, set to address both the wounds of the past and the girls' unique needs for the future are defined in Table 1.

Our therapeutic work with these children has also been influenced by the clinical literature (Fagan & McMahon, 1984; Kluft, 1985) suggesting that children repeatedly victimized early in childhood are vulnerable to the development of multiple personalities, which manifest in adolescence and adulthood as a psychological defense against the trauma of abuse. Cognitive developmental theory defines young children as preoperational thinkers

TABLE 1
Treatment Goals

1. To help the child translate thoughts and feelings into words.
2. To support the child's ability to say "no" and to ask for help.
3. To allow the child to experience some adults as caring, able to listen, to comfort, and to set limits.
4. To help differentiate and limit the child's beliefs in their own power to evoke violence and destruction or to initiate separation from a valued adult.
5. To support social and emotional skills necessary for peer interaction and peer learning.
6. To support an increasingly realistic sense of competence.
7. To support mastery of normal psychosocial development.

From Steward et al., 1986

who easily separate their world of experiences into distinctive categories—
"good vs. bad," "yummy vs. yucky," "mine vs. yours." It makes sense
psychologically that a repeatedly victimized young child would assign the
traumatic experiences into a "not me" category (Sullivan, 1953); eventually
the part of the child who is "not me" might be given a new name and
even splinter further into many fragments of personality as development
continues. In the first session, one of the girls announced that she was
going to change her name—and you can believe that caught our attention!

Most therapists are familiar with the theoretical model presented by Finkelhor and Browne (1985), which articulates the sequelae of early child
abuse: traumatic sexualization of the body, a sense of betrayal, stigmatization of the self as bad, and the feeling of powerlessness. Their thinking has
influenced our work as well. In each individual case, however, the therapist
must seek to move the model in order to ask just what a child—in our case
just what each of these two children—thinks about herself, her body, and
her relationship with others. The child's unique vocabulary of words and
actions needs to be mastered—a slow, deliberate process, and one both
dangerous and difficult to intuit. Just how does one begin?

We have found that particularly in the diagnostic phase of treatment,
which is not tidy but does exist, it has been helpful to loosen the linear
thinking of our common expectations, so that we can believe the unbeliev-
able and think the unthinkable. The first opportunity in this case to do so
was particularly poignant, as our young patients and their therapists slowly
shared the knowledge that the children had experienced the death of an
infant sibling and the destruction of their family, while subsequently one
of the therapists created a new family constellation by giving birth to her
first child. Thus, mourning and hope had to be dealt with both separately
and together.

CASE DESCRIPTION

Suzi and Molly are sisters, born 10 months apart, who were referred to us
for treatment by the welfare department in another state. The children were
placed with foster parents in our community following the violent death of
their younger sister. The current placement appeared to be a stable one, as
the foster parents had no other children and intended to adopt them. We
have no information on the girls' early developmental, social, and emotional milestones until after their parent's divorce. At that time the father
and his 12-year-old son from a prior marriage left the household. Molly
was just three, Suzi was two years old. Reports to health and welfare
agencies increased shortly after a new stepfather moved in. The girls' father
was contacted by the concerned authorities. He was on military duty, sta-

tioned abroad and had neither the room nor the time for the other children. The girls were first placed in protective custody after Suzi reported that the bruises on her face, neck, and buttocks were caused by the stepfather. They were returned to their mother's custody under informal supervision by welfare, but it was ineffective, as the mother angrily refused to let social workers into her home, moved frequently, and eventually left the state.

The girls were again taken into protective custody when Molly was five and Suzi was four years old, after their baby sister was beaten to death by their mother and stepfather. The residence was found to be filthy and reeked of urine and feces. The girls were very dirty, their heads had been ritualistically shaved, and the few clothes which they had were dirty and smelled of excrement. They had no bedding, and their mattresses were stained with urine and blood. Subsequent physical examination revealed that both girls had been repeatedly sodomized, and subject to frequent, severe physical punishment. We are still in the midst of determining the psychological environment of the home, but there is no doubt that the children's physical, social, and emotional needs were neglected, and that they were aggressively subject to physical, sexual, and emotional abuse. The mother and stepfather were jailed.

The girls, spirited away by police to an emergency foster care home in the middle of the night, touched the hearts of local social welfare staff. These good people immediately mobilized personnel and agency resources to provide them with everything from clean clothes, to arranging for a private funeral service for their sister, to aggressively seeking permanent placement and long-term psychotherapeutic treatment. The warmth, skill, and compassion of that staff undoubtedly lessened the trauma for the girls and increased the possibility for their healing significantly. In addition, it was clear that the prognosis for the girls was strengthened by the staff's ability to respond immediately to their needs during the height of the trauma in which they lost both a sibling and a family. The power of that positive interactional process between the girls and the welfare staff enhanced the transition to the foster parents and the therapists. The staff have continued to maintain contact with us and, beyond the fact that they hold legal jurisdiction over the children, they have made important and unusual resources available to us. Our work with the girls has been therapeutically richer and more effective as a result of their commitment and skill.

Reviewing the written case material, we found that the children did not have the benefit of Hartmann's (1939) "average expectable environment" or Greenspan's "adaptive environment" (1979). They were not even held or rocked or fed by Winnicott's (1987) "good enough mother." Enormous distortion has been described in interpersonal relationships within the family in which these abused children grew up. Generational boundaries were broken and role reversals were abundant (Minuchin, 1974, 1984). For example, it was the adults in the family who played, not the children. The game of Dungeons and Dragons captured the attention of the caretakers, while the children worried about finding enough food to eat. The adults often dressed in costumes and alternately threatened the children as witches and ghosts or neglected them entirely. Younger siblings were not to be protected and loved by their older siblings; rather, they were despised. What the children in this family learned about the intentions of persons in roles of social authority were also distorted. Policemen were the "bad guys" not the "good guys," thus, at one point in treatment the girls were terrified by the therapists' suggestion in play that the police be called to rescue the doll in distress.

PSYCHOLOGICAL ASSESSMENT

There are no psychological assessment data available on either the biological father of the girls or the stepfather. However, a court ordered psychological evaluation of the mother was completed during the investigation following the death of her daughter. She described herself as being raised in a dysfunctional family. She was sexually abused during childhood, and severely depressed as an adolescent. Psychological testing revealed the mother to be of superior intelligence but severely constricted in the use of her cognitive skills by a passive-aggressive personality disorder with narcissistic and schizoid features. The tragic translation of this evaluation is simply that, although this woman knew that her children were being victimized by her new husband, she was unable to mobilize effectively to protect them.

Informal assessment of the children by their respective therapists occurred over a four-week period, when Molly and Suzi were both five years old, and was reported in the clinic intake evaluation. The health and general nutrition of each of the girls appeared to be good. There were no distinguishing physical characteristics or deformities. Gross motor coordination appeared to be age adequate; fine motor movements appeared somewhat clumsy, a delay that may have been partially a function of deprivation of normal play experience and materials. Speech was normal, though both girls frequently reverted to baby talk or unintelligible gibberish. Suzi was initially very friendly, cooperative, and affectively buoyant. She rarely expressed feelings of anger or fear, though over time she exhibited increasing dependency on her therapist and demanded full attention. Molly, by contrast, initially held her therapist at considerable emotional distance, preferring parallel to cooperative play, and quickly introduced a full range of negative emotion, including anger, fear, and anxiety, often expressed in a harsh, loud voice. Formal psychological testing was not available until the end of the first year of treatment. Those data are reported below, in the sequence in which that information became available to us.

COURSE OF THERAPY

The initial plan for the psychotherapeutic treatment of the sisters included weekly individual therapy for each child, group therapy approximately once a month, and home visits every two to three months. Weekly joint supervision was provided to the therapists. In addition, the foster parents were encouraged to seek supportive counseling with a therapist at our clinic. One unusual but critical early event in the course of therapy was an "investigative visit" by the therapists, approximately two months after therapy was begun, to the site of the original home from which the sisters were removed on the night of their baby sister's death.

First Therapeutic Contact: A Visit to the New Foster Home

The therapists made arrangements with the foster mother so that the first contact between the girls and their therapists occurred during a visit to the foster home approximately a month after placement and four months after the girls were removed from their mother's custody. We wanted to demonstrate to the girls that there was a cordial and supportive, rather than hostile or secretive, link between the foster parents and the therapists. We wanted to address any fears they might have about whether the presence of the therapists automatically signaled that they were going to be moved again — fears often voiced by young abused children at the sight of strange, new adults in their lives.

Finally, we wanted to see the girls interacting with one another and with their foster parents in this new home environment — a setting less pressured and formal than the offices at a big medical center. During the visit the therapists also had the opportunity to assess unobtrusively the adequacy of the home situation in terms of space, sleeping arrangements, toys and books, and other play materials.

The therapists found the home to be neat and clean with a warm atmosphere. Initially there was lively interaction between the foster mother and the girls, as well as open expressions of physical affection. During the visit the sisters displayed competitive behavior with one another. Each regressed to baby-talk, and angrily challenged the other; but they shared some happy, excited moments as well. Early in the visit, Suzi asked one of the therapists,

"Are you going to take me away?" Only temporarily reassured, she later asked her foster mother if the therapists were going to take both sisters with them when they left. Gradually, as the girls warmed to the therapists, the foster mother seemed to withdraw, signaling to the therapists that she might still be insecure in her new foster parent role and threatened by the attention the girls were giving the therapists. While the foster father was not home during the first visit, he has been present at subsequent visits. Home visits have been scheduled periodically every two or three months and are seen as an important component of psychotherapeutic treatment.

First Psychotherapy Session

In the initial psychotherapy session the sisters were seen together in the playroom with both therapists present, so that all four persons could continue to get acquainted with one another. As in most initial play therapy sessions, the children were introduced to the room as a safe place. They were free to explore the toys and equipment and shared the making and eating of popcorn and juice. It is our policy that nutritious snack food is always available for children in the playroom. It is both symbolically and actually nurturing. For children who have been maltreated and/or neglected food is also powerfully rewarding. The opportunity for the child to help prepare snacks provides an early, positive link with the therapist. A child's differential response to food is often a useful barometer to his or her currently felt need for emotional support, compassion, and caring.

During the session, Polaroid photos were taken of each sister with her individual therapist. Duplicate sets were made so that each could take home a picture of herself with her therapist, while the duplicate pictures were hung "permanently" on the playroom wall. We have found that children value the pictures of themselves with their therapist. We believe that these pictures facilitate object constancy and enhance the relationship between child and therapist. The picture provides a concrete reminder that they have a very special friend. Some children look at and talk to the picture when they are feeling stressed during the week between therapy sessions; some like to look at it as they talk to the therapist on the phone. As they come into the session some children check to see that the picture is still on the playroom wall, as if to confirm that the relationship with the therapist is still real.

Near the end of the first session the sisters were told that sometimes all four of them would get together, and sometimes each would meet with her own therapist.

Getting Acquainted: Early Individual Sessions

Molly, the older sister, was aggressive, bossy, and angry throughout much of the first six months of individual treatment. She held her therapist at a distance, rarely seeking or accepting physical contact. Initially her play was quite defensive and brittle. For example, she seemingly randomly selected toys and then compulsively stacked them into color-coordinated groups. When she began to play out family scenes, she always either assigned the therapist to the father role—and sent "him" off to work while she played alone with the babies—or called the therapist "darling" and scolded, yelled at, and punished her for crimes unknown. On several occasions she cried that she wanted to kill "darling," and once she admitted that she was afraid that the therapist might kill her. She refused to talk about the molestation, about her mother or stepfather, or about her sister.

In sharp contrast, Suzi, the younger sister, was affectionate and sought physical contact with her therapist from the initial home visit, when she climbed into the therapist's lap. Her play themes consistently reflected her experiences of physical punishment, sexual abuse, and her mourning of the separation from her mother and baby sister. She has spontaneously told her therapist of nightmares about her baby sister's death. In play, the therapist has often been assigned the role of mother, while Suzi is the daughter who always has a new boyfriend. The boyfriend is sent to jail because "he hit her because she would not kiss him." In one session she had a baby who had "an ouchie" because her old boyfriend had hit the baby. When asked about the old boyfriend she said, "My daddy, your husband, killed him, so he died and went to jail." The theme of babies being hurt by the boyfriend led the therapist to ask if Suzi had ever been hurt by the stepfather. "No, this is just a pretend game!"

It became clear to the therapist that Suzi was confused about the concepts of jail and heaven. She knew that her mother and stepfather were in jail, but she didn't know why. When asked to draw a jail, she drew a black square and filled it all in black. She then scribbled over it with brown crayon saying "Jail is all black and brown." She also often spoke of her baby sister who died, once reporting that "she is in heaven, and we just don't know how to get her out!"

The timing of the individual sessions was designed to further the individuation of the sisters. They arrived together with their foster mother. They were always seen on the same day, and their sessions were 50 minutes back-to-back consecutively. Thus, the foster mother had time alone with each child. We talked with the foster mother about this and made several suggestions about how she might use the time to give each child special attention—which she acknowledged was difficult to do when they were together at home. We envisioned that the foster mother might want to read a favorite storybook, take a child on a walk through a nearby park, go over to the hospital cafeteria for a special treat, or to pack a lunch and have a little picnic. Much to our disappointment, she has not yet used that time for special interaction with either child. Sometimes she has even brought along other children whom she is babysitting; other times we have found the free sister has fallen asleep or is involved in isolated play in the waiting room.

The Investigative Visit to the Site of the Sisters' Former Home

Following the initial referral, the transmission of written records from the welfare, health, and legal agencies took approximately one month. After a careful review of the written materials, several long-distance phone calls and reflection of the data from the first two months of psychotherapy, it became clear that it would be extremely helpful to visit with the social service staff who had immediate and intimate contact with the sisters at the time of their removal from their home. It also seemed important to visit the home itself—something routinely done in the investigation of an abuse case by legal and social welfare staff, but rarely done by therapists. The trip took two full days but was judged to be well worth the investment for the therapists. We met and talked with the social services staff, reviewed police records and saw dozens of color photos taken by police, read hospital records and the younger sister's autopsy report, and visited the sisters' former home.

The police accompanied us to the home. It was empty, and had been "redecorated"; the high fence at the front of the property had been cut down, although the basic structure of the house and yard had not been changed. Further confirmation of the bizarre state of the home, which we saw in the police photos, came from the real estate agent who showed us the home. She complained that when the house was vacated it had been a mess and that although she had cleaned and repainted it, the "damn blood is still seeping through the walls." One of the plainclothes policemen, who accompanied us to the house, scuffed at the rug in the bedroom with the toe of his boot, revealing the trap door to the root cellar, which the children had described to us as the "black hole"—where they had been placed for punishment. One critical function that the home visit played for us was to help us to help the girls to separate fantasy from reality. Although we did not find the "box of blood," the "skeleton," the "ghosts" or Satan, who the girls believed lived in the cellar, we did find five dice, a dragon's head and many small trinkets used in the Dungeons and Dragons games, along with the spiders and mice. It was frightening enough for us to go down there, let alone to think of the children being imprisoned there.

The trip presented us with the horrifying, but critically important, task of integrating all of the new information we had gathered. Henry (1971) observed that dysfunctional families distort not only interpersonal relationships but also space and time. Police photographs of the home showed the closets were empty (they were used for punishing children), while clothes were scattered in the middle of the room. Blood and feces were on the wall and floors, not in the bathroom; sheets were used to convert people into ghosts, not to make mattresses into beds. The "black hole" that the children described was not fantasy, as we adults initially suspected, but a real place—and after we found it, our understanding of it helped them cope with their reality of it. Mealtime, an anchoring point that establishes the rhythms of nurturing in many families' lives, was a random, harsh, sparse event in the lives of the girls. As we began to understand that children had been punished for eating and that they believed their baby sister had died because she grabbed some food from the adult table, the girls' use of the food available to them in the therapy room took on new meaning.

Psychological Assessment of the Sisters

The formal psychological assessment of the children was conducted by a child clinical psychologist who was informed that the children were victims of abuse and who knew the identity of the children's therapists. However, she did not know any of the specific details of the case. Thus, she was sensitively aware that the children might be psychologically distressed but "blind" to any information which might pull the data in one direction or another. Each child was tested individually, and seen twice.

The battery included the Stanford Binet Intelligence Scale, Form L-M, a measure of intelligence: three different drawing tasks which focused on the human form: the Draw-a-Person Test, Kinetic Family Drawings and the Outside/Inside Body Book and selected cards from two projective tests: the Tasks of Emotional Development (TED), cards (LG-2, L-G-6), and the Projective Storytelling Cards, cards (87-A3, A5, A6, A14, A15, A21, A24). We agree with Browne and Finkelhor (1986) that, in order to test for specific and diverse sequelae of abuse, special sexual abuse outcome instruments need to be developed. Thus, two of the instruments named above are relatively new assessment tools. The Outside/Inside Body Book, a drawing test developed to monitor changes in body image as a result of acute and chronic illness (Steward, 1987; Steward et al., 1982), appears promising for clinical use with abused children. The face validity of the Projective Story Telling Cards (Caruso, 1987) is high, as these cards depict different constellations of parents and children in potentially sexually evocative interaction. However, reliability and validity studies and comparative studies between abused and control children have yet to be published.

Molly was six years, four months and Suzi was five and one-half years old when they were tested. On the Binet, each child scored solidly within the average range. Their patterns of successes and failures were similar. Each demonstrated a solid mastery of language, comprehension, perceptual and fine motor skills. The average scores, however, mask the emotional turmoil that still characterizes each child's life and the markedly different ways in which the girls displayed their upset during the testing. Molly revealed her experiences of victimization and loss primarily through her drawings, while Suzi dramatically burst into tears and climbed into the lap of a stranger to seek comfort in the middle of the vocabulary subtest.

All three of Molly's drawings of people demonstrated distortions. Even the most complex figure that Molly drew, a self-portrait, when scored developmentally using the Harris-Goodenough scoring system (Harris, 1963) yielded a total of 11 points, and a standard score of 75, far below what is predicted for a child her age of average intelligence. In fact, a drawing like Molly's might be expected of a child nearly two and a half years younger. As predicted by Di Leo (1973), there was a regressive shift in terms of form quality when the child moved from a single drawing of a person to the creation of figures for a family drawing. In fact, not only were the figures in the family drawing more primitive than the drawing of the self, but there were also numerous signs of emotional disturbance (Koppitz, 1968).

Molly drew her mother, herself, Suzi and her father, in that order. There were numerous distortions, particularly of the drawing of the mother, which was broken into four separate pieces. A set of vertical lines was identified as "the back"; moving right and downward on the page, Molly drew a circular head (with facial features extending beyond the boundaries of the face) to which arms attached, a circular torso with belly button, and finally two legs. In looking at this drawing, we were reminded that Molly had watched "mommy's baby die," referring to her observation of the spontaneous abortion of a child prior to the birth of the baby sister. None of the four figures had a complete torso; too few fingers and toes were drawn, eyes dominated the faces, and belly buttons were drawn near the bottom of the open torso.

Thematically, although there was no closure to the torsos in the family drawing, all of Molly's drawings were full of circles/holes, places where daddy "wiped his muscle." She completed the face of the Outside/Inside Body Book with huge circular eyes, two large circular nostrils, and two circles inside the ears. The torso of the clothed child was inappropriately decorated with a large circular belly button and a penis prominently breaking through the pants. There was no attempt to identify the drawing of the child with the self or to make it feminine, a common omission in the drawings we have collected of abused girls. The inside of the body was void of the critical internal organs which fascinate most six-year-olds and which they typically include in their drawings — such as a heart, brain, blood, or stomach. Molly's body was essentially empty; she sketched only broken lines representing bones. One interpretation would suggest that Molly continues to demonstrate a deprivation of inner and outer self.

As primitive as these drawings are, they represent increased complexity and evidence more human likeness than Molly's first long, purple diagonal line done a year earlier, which she described to her therapist as "me and Suzi."

Suzi revealed her experiences of victimization and loss through editorial comment, disturbed content, and selective silence. All of this was as often elicited by the seemingly neutral items from the Binet as by the explicitly sexually provocative Projective Storytelling Cards. For example, "a stove" is to "cook with a pot, NOT TO BURN LITTLE CHILDREN." During the vocabulary subscale, in response to the request to define the word "roar," she suddenly became very sad, then burst into tears and cried, "I lost my sister; she died!" She wept nearly inconsolably for several minutes in the tester's lap. The projective cards were presented during the second assessment session with Suzi and, much to our surprise, the usually talkative child clammed up. She rejected several cards outright and threw one card back with the comment, "He's ugly." When she did tell a story, the child was repeatedly "getting in trouble" and threatened with punishment. However, even when she minimally responded to a card, there was no doubt that her perception of the interaction was accurate, i.e., "a little girl is on a dad." We assume her guarded response were partially a function of the explicitness of the pictured interactions between the child and adults and partially a function of having experienced the "breakthrough" of too much sadness during the first assessment session.

In Molly's stories appropriate parent-child touch was prohibited (as when a child wanted to touch the pregnant mother's dress/tummy to feel her baby), but the little girl was allowed to play "on the dad when it was wrong and the daddy laughed." The TED card which often elicits stories of nurturing maternal behavior instead yielded a story about a child helping the mother cook " . . . and the kid wasn't done and the mom slammed the lid on her fingers!"

THERAPEUTIC PLANS: SHORT AND LONG RANGE

As we indicated at the beginning of the chapter, we are writing about this treatment case from somewhere in the middle of the process. Thus, rather than discuss treatment outcome further, it seemed appropriate to reflect on the case at this point using both short-range and long-range lenses.

The Development of Molly's Themes: The First Two Years

Molly remained aggressive and bossy and continued to hold her therapist at a distance. Her play was generally isolative. Molly would often go to the wooden slide, climb the stairs, remove the wooden platform at the top of the stairs, and crawl down into the "hole." She would reappear and drag various small animal toys and a telephone with her. With the help of the telephone and a tape recorder Molly was able to tell a story about a little girl who always went to the doctor and the hospital and whose mama suddenly left her. Molly started crying out, "Mama, mama, where are you mama? Don't leave me, please come back." Despite the interpretations by the therapist, Molly was unable to make a connection to her own experiences with her biological mother.

Molly, who had been described as "the little mother," was obsessed with the food available in the playroom. For the first several months she insisted on our making several bowls of popcorn, into which she poured handfuls of salt. She would rarely eat it, but she did squirrel it away in the refrigerator for the next time. Each week she would religiously check "to see if it's still there." This routine diminished over time and now recurs only at points of stress.

Generally, Molly's anxieties were triggered by outside events. For example, when sister Suzi was scheduled for a tonsillectomy, a doctor's play kit was introduced into the playroom. She was quite skilled with all the instruments, requested that her therapist pretend to be pregnant and sick, and would "check her into the hospital . . . for several weeks." Several times she frantically administered CPR on a playroom doll, requesting the aid of the therapist, imitating the paramedics' behavior with her dying baby sister. The doll *always* died. Another event was triggered by the physical punishment of a classmate at school. Apparently he was taken to the principal's office and spanked. Molly was quite disturbed and worried that she too might be punished. What kind of punishment might this be? In the past she had been punished by "daddy's" violent sexual abuse. Did she fear the principal would punish this way too? Molly was allowed to repeatedly play out this punishment theme. The therapist reinforced her newly developing ability to defend herself against inappropriate physical contact and her understanding of appropriate means of punishment. In addition, the therapist contacted both the foster mother and the school to reemphasize the importance of nonphysical means of punishment with these vulnerable children. This intervention took on new meaning when Molly was recently discovered by her foster mother inserting a pencil into the rectum of a young neighborhood girl. The foster mother brought this to the therapist's attention, which provided the opportunity for further discussion regarding body boundaries. Emphasis was placed on directing energies toward self-stimulation and self-touch and away from victimization of others.

The Development of Suzi's Themes: The First Two Years

Suzi continued to display affection toward her therapist and persisted in centering her play around mother-child games, with Suzi always as the child. She repeated play themes centering on food. She would repeatedly offer to make her therapist coffee or a meal, and then never deliver. She rarely made popcorn or initiated requests for food for herself. She often pretended that the doll children were being taken for ice cream, but when they arrived at the store, the ice cream would be gone. In her play, children were frequently punished for no apparent reason. Hunger, food, and punishment had been fused in her mind—"I was hungry, it's bad to be hungry." As with her sister, much of her therapy focused on differentiating appropriate from inappropriate punishment.

Several weeks prior to undergoing a routine tonsillectomy, Suzi became preoccupied with playing doctor. Although she denied any fear about the impending surgery, behaviorally she exhibited regression and anxiety, with frequent nightmares and stomachaches. Using a toy doctor kit, she and her therapist play-acted step by step the experience of undergoing a tonsillectomy. With permission from her foster mother, the therapist spoke to the surgeon (who was unaware of Suzi's abuse history) to alert him of her special needs. Recommendations included the following:

1. making arrangements for foster mother to remain at Suzi's bedside until she was completely anesthetized and to be present upon awakening in the recovery room;
2. carefully explaining each step of the procedure to be performed;
3. keeping an awareness of Suzi's intense feelings of personal violation; and
4. respecting her increased sensitivity to bodily exposure.

To an abused child, undergoing even the simplest medical procedure can trigger extremely frightening fantasies. We believed that it was essential that the medical team be aware of the history of abuse so they could do whatever possible to allay her fears. Despite the intervention, many of our recommendations were not heeded. Several weeks after her tonsillectomy, Suzi again requested to play doctor, at which time she voiced her fear that while she was anesthetized her mother and stepfather would "come do what they used to."

Gradually, throughout her second year in therapy a strong focus on religious imagery emerged. Suzi is being raised in a religiously conservative foster home, which is both supportive and confusing for her. This monologue of hers is a poignant example.

My sister is dead. I have dreams where I see Jesus holding my sister in His hands. Jesus is in heaven with my sister. Satan is bad. Satan is inside me. He's in my heart. I feel him in there. He's like a snake and when he puts his tongue in and out like a snake I can feel it in my body. He tells me bad things like to disobey my mother and God tells me good things like to obey my mother. I try not to listen to Satan and I try to listen to God. Satan is a snake like the snake that used to talk to Eve and told Eve to eat the poison apple. He's a bad snake.

Is this Satan she is learning about in a religious class the same snake that used to live in her cellar and torture her sister? If Jesus is holding her sister up there in the sky, will He give her back? These are questions which Suzi has asked repeatedly in subsequent sessions. While the introduction of organized religion may provide some security for her, it is also exacerbating her profound difficulty distinguishing reality from fantasy.

SPECIFIC TECHNIQUES USED IN THERAPY

Group Therapy

There is no doubt that the chemistry of the group sessions has been significantly different from the individual sessions — with far more spontaneous discussion of the specific experiences of abuse than either child expressed alone.

The group recreated enough of the context of the abusive family so that elements of the experience they shared as sisters could emerge more readily. The therapists observed not only the natural playing out of the dominant role of Molly and the subordinate role of Suzi, but also shifts in dominance and, more importantly, the powerful interplay of the two as they stimulated one another's memory and rehearsal of their abusive experiences within the family. The girls surely provided more pieces of the puzzle when they were seen together than either provided separately. For Molly, it was only in the joint sessions that she would talk about the abuse. As in the individual play sessions, tape recorders and telephones seemed to enhance the interaction and eased the retelling of the horrible events the children had experienced.

As a general rule, joint sessions have been used just prior to and following events in which the therapists knew that the children would both participate, and which were anticipated to be affectively charged. Examples of such events were a "family trip to Disneyland" (perfectly well-intended family vacations are easily misinterpreted by children who have been multiply placed as a cue that they are about to be moved again); birthdays and other significant holidays (Halloween, for example, is a particularly difficult time for many ritualistically abused children, such as Molly and Suzi, for whom witches and ghosts are real demons to be fought). The joint sessions were videotaped for later review by the therapists and supervisor.

The most stressful event which the sisters faced, to our knowledge, was a return trip to the house where they had lived with their mother and stepfather and in which their baby sister had been killed. The trip was at the request of the legal system, to determine the children's memory for the events which happened in that house and to determine whether or not either of the children would be called to testify. Both girls expressed their fears about going back to the old house. Suzi said, "We have to tell some people about the bad things daddy did." Molly whispered into the toy telephone to her mother, "Mommy, I want you back. They're taking me back to ask me questions." The group sessions that prepared the children for the trip and "debriefed" them after they returned home proved to be powerful. Because the therapists had actually visited the site, they could prepare the children for the physical changes in the house (empty house, no furniture), guarantee the children that neither the mother nor stepfather would be there, and reconfirm that their baby sister would not be there either.

It was during the joint sessions that the meaning of some of the unique sexual vocabulary of the girls was demonstrated and finally understood. For example, although Suzi had been talking with her therapist about "doing privacy" for several weeks, it was not until the children were together in a joint session that they revealed its meaning by actually demonstrating the sexual act of intercourse, first with dolls and, stimulated by that, immediately thereafter with one another. This gave each therapist the opportunity to teach the appropriate meaning of the word "privacy" by incorporating it frequently into play themes. In addition, the therapists helped each child identify boundaries of sexual behaviors and physical bodily contact (i.e., good touching vs. bad touching).

Entering the Third Year

Following the second summer break we entered the third year of therapy, in which we are seeing more prominent changes in the children. During the summer, several events took place. The children were moved to a new foster home and also from a private to a public school. There is also a foster baby in this home. The current foster parents seemed to be experiencing personal and interpersonal stress.

Dramatic changes in each sister were noted by her therapist immediately upon resumption of therapy. Molly was bright and energetic and for the first time showed a genuine eagerness to engage with her therapist. She seemed distanced from her new foster mother and her sister and became worried that her therapist would die or abandon her. Suzi, on the other hand, showed decreased signs of affection and was more guarded and defended. She tended to exclude the therapist from her play. Her play now demonstrated the increased chaos in her home environment. It has been several months since themes of punishment, food deprivation, or issues of sexuality have emerged.

There are many factors contributing to the changes observed. Life is rarely simple for young abused children and certainly the external environmental changes have significant impact. It appears that Molly is individuating from her sister and developing increasing dependency on her therapist, while Suzi's experience of this is contributing to increased anxiety, fear of abandonment, and guardedness with her therapist. The focus for both girls has temporarily moved away from traumatic experiences of past abuse to struggling with issues concerning their present circumstances.

Breaks in the Course of Therapy

A six-week break was scheduled each summer. Six weeks prior to the interruption of therapy, we began discussing it with the girls. In order to help them understand the concept of six weeks, we used a piece of paper folded into six equal pieces. Each week the therapist would bring out the paper, help the child check off a box, and count the remaining boxes. At the last session each child was given a new sheet with six new boxes to take with her; with the help of the foster mother she was to check one box off weekly, as had been modeled in therapy. They were each told that their therapist would be contacting them each week over the course of the break. The contacts were in the form of a combination of cards with short notes on them and phone calls. The girls were very responsive to these contacts, and the re-initiation of therapy went smoothly as a result.

Therapeutic Plans: The Next Few Steps

Sexuality education. We are searching for sexuality education materials that will be appropriate to the needs of these children, whose bodies have been sexually stimulated, and used to stimulate adults, but who have not been effectively discouraged from public acts of self-stimulation or discovered the private role of pleasuring the self (Amsterdam & Levitt, 1980). Most curriculum materials, created for sexually naive youngsters with the purpose of discouraging the first abusive assault, are not appropriate for these children. They need to reclaim their bodies, define their body boundaries, and explore the different sources of internal and external self (Goldman & Goldman, 1988).

Our offers to work with the new foster parents on this issue have been rebuffed until just recently. They have been jolted into the necessity to confront the issue by the report of the girls' abuse of neighbor children. We hope that the therapists and foster parents can work together to direct energies to self-stimulation and self-touch and away from victimization of others within the context of continuing development of what Erikson termed the "somatic ego."

Decoding emotions. Although most young children prefer to use facial cues rather than situational cues to interpret social situations (Gnepp, 1983), current research findings suggest that abused children are at a disadvantage. Camras et al. (1988) have found that abused children and their mothers pose less recognizable facial expressions than matched control children and their mothers, and that abused children have more difficulty recognizing both "pure" and masked emotional expressions on faces than nonabused children. It has been our observation that the girls often misread the intention and emotional states of their therapists — or assign them harsh, incongruent affective roles in play. Using the work of Ekman and Friesen (1975), our therapists will begin to work with mirrors — large full body and small hand mirrors — to demonstrate/practice both more accurate self-expression and reading of the emotions of therapists. Therapists will continue to explain very clearly the behavioral cues which they are using when they infer the child's emotional state ("When I see you crying, it makes me think you are sad." "When I hear that shouting voice, I think you are angry," etc.) (Carroll & Steward, 1984).

Physical activities in treatment. "The ego is first and foremost a bodily ego" (Freud, 1900). Winnicott (1972) suggested that healthy feelings of the self have their origins in and are based upon parental attitudes towards the child's body. Especially because of the girls' parents' negative, hurtful, coercive use of the children's bodies, we believe that the children's resultant attitudes toward their own bodies have been critically impaired or otherwise compromised. Rhythmic physical activities with music, exercise, dance, ai-kido (the only nonaggressive martial art) all contribute to awareness of body boundaries and to continuous development of body image (Schilder, 1935). The therapists, utilizing their individual talents, will begin to introduce rhythmic activities into the treatment hour. While this will increase the structure of the therapy hour somewhat, it will also provide regular attention to the body in a nonviolent, noncoercive manner.

Therapeutic Plans: Long Range

We believe that it is important to identify developmental periods when the girls, because of their history of sexual abuse, will be particularly vulnerable to cognitive and emotional distress and potential revictimization. These include menarche, dating, pregnancy, early parenting, and anniversaries of traumatic events. The caretakers will need to be alerted to anticipate these potentially stressful periods and urged to make psychotherapy available.

Reentry into therapy just prior to menarche is advised, for there are several critical issues that must be dealt with at that developmental period. The salience of the physical self in adolescence provides a therapeutic opportunity for new learning and for the surfacing and correction of distortions from the abused child's past. At the simplest level, many girls have learned so well the lessòn that others have control over their bodies that they don't handle even the mechanics of healthy menstruation well, nor do they take appropriate responsibility for themselves when they experience early signs of physical illness. In addition, many adolescent girls who were abused as children believe themselves to be sterile — and thus risk unwanted pregnancy. A therapist is often an effective advocate for the necessary OB/GYN referral, as well as a helpful interpreter of the meaning of the results of the examination. Reentry into social-sexual intimacy as a partner, rather than a victim, is enormously difficult for the adolescent who was sexually abused as a child, and we believe that access to both a male and a female therapist can be extremely useful.

If/when either of the girls becomes pregnant, we recommend that she seek psychotherapeutic treatment during pregnancy and through the first year of the child's life. In therapy, she would be encouraged to learn to care for herself and her fetus during pregnancy, learn to mother the infant affectionately and skillfully, and thus interrupt the affectively and experientially driven generational recycling of abuse. Anniversaries of traumatic events, one of which will occur when her child is the age she was when she remembers being removed from her mother's care, should signal the advisability to touch base with a therapist yet again.

One of the implications of this life cycle perspective to the treatment of young abused children is that we do not believe that we can "cure" these beautiful little girls now for all time, nor do we believe that we can effectively "vaccinate" them now so that they will never be vulnerable again to physical and sexual abuse. We do believe that it is our responsibility to alert their caretakers now, and to alert each of them when they become older, to the necessity of seeking formal therapeutic relationships to strengthen their ability to cope with the inevitable intrapsychic and interpersonal stress they will experience as they mature.

THERAPISTS' REACTION TO THE CASE

The therapists, reflecting now after three years, can spot some issues worth reviewing. Parenting has become a central focus for each therapist. Each has reached back into her own childhood experiences of being parented, and each has reached forward as a parent now. The pregnancy of Suzi's therapist has been a focal point of her personal and therapeutic life. For Molly's therapist, her role as an adoptive parent has surfaced with a new perspective as a result of work on this case.

Suzi's therapist reflected,

> The issue of my pregnancy was first brought up by the foster mother in the waiting room in front of the children. When she asked about it, Suzi's first comment was, "If you're going to have a baby, does that mean you're going to need to find a husband?" From that time on, Suzi was very preoccupied with my pregnancy and at virtually every session made some comment about it. This seemed to have opened up a whole series of personal questions about my home life: Did I have a husband? What was his name? What color car did he drive? Suzi seemed to be concerned that my husband would be upset by the things she told me in therapy.

We know that the issue of pregnancy is of importance for these children for a number of reasons. They had observed their mother during her pregnancy with their baby sister and they had watched the spontaneous abortion of an earlier pregnancy. Also, they are aware that their foster parents had wanted children but were unable to have them. Suzi was apprehensive, "After you have a baby, will you still see me?" She offered the opinion that when her foster mother has a baby, her foster parents will still keep her, hoping to influence the therapist to make the same judgment.

When the therapist returned after the birth of her baby, Suzi had very few questions or comments about the pregnancy or the baby. She was curious about whether the therapist and her husband kissed, kissed on the lips or on the cheek, and whether or not they had "privacy" (i.e., sexual relations), but at that point she was unwilling to explain the concept. Suzi later explained that she was frightened that if she talked with her therapist about "privacy" the therapist's husband would be angry.

The pregnancy of the therapist raised important issues for the therapist as well as for the children. Every pregnant therapist worries about how much of the details of the birth of the baby should be brought into treatment. Should child patients be told the sex and name of the infant? Should children be allowed to visit her and the baby at home? These questions have reasonable answers. There are also questions for the pregnant therapist which have no answers, such as how to protect her soon-to-be-child from the horrors of abuse that her patients have experienced. The mandate to be the "perfect parent" hangs over the head.

Molly's therapist reflected,

Working with Molly has certainly been challenging in many ways. While my cotherapist continued to report in our joint supervision that Suzi was responsive, cuddly, and interactive, Molly was unresponsive, closed, and rigid. My expectations were that, because the girls were sisters, they would behave similarly and perhaps I was at fault for not eliciting a warmer response in her. However, after 18 months, she was finally able to show some trust, including me in her play and telling me that she loved me. I gradually came to realize how really different these two children are.

Although we will never fully understand the reasons for their differences, there are some factors which could have contributed to their differing personalities and coping styles. We know that the girls were both physically and sexually abused, yet it is important to note that Molly was more often victimized sexually, while Suzi was physically abused more frequently. The girls were given different social assignments by their biological mother. "Molly the mother," as the oldest child in the home, was made to feel responsible for her siblings, and thus took on the fruitless task of attempting to protect them.

The most jolting experience of this case for me was the visit to the town where the abuse took place. Viewing actual photos, talking to social workers, and climbing down into the "dark hole" made a curious, barely believable story about two adorable girls a shocking reality. That trip gave me a sense of what these children experienced and thus enabled me to be more effective in therapy.

The horrors of this case and I suppose the horrors of child abuse cases everywhere have made me a more aware mother of my own children and at times more suspicious and guarded because, after all, these things really do happen.

10

Psychotherapy Meets Fundamentalism in the Treatment of an Adolescent

JUDITH A. COHEN

The presentation of an adolescent in this book is useful because it illustrates the longer-term consequences of sexual abuse and its interference with normal development. This perspective helps the reader realize that sexual abuse affects a variety of key adolescent developmental milestones, especially peer formation and the emergence of sexuality.

Dr. Cohen articulates a carefully managed case in which she tried to advocate for an adolescent in need of psychotherapy with a family that was avowedly fundamentalist and did not believe in the need for therapy. Her advocacy is impressive. After direct appeals to the family failed, Dr. Cohen engaged in what has been termed "therapeutic triangulation." By pulling in leaders in the church, she was able to gain their support and effectively mobilize for Cara. It was very difficult for Cara's parents to object to her treatment given the support of the church.

It is important for therapists to enlist support for the child from wherever they can get it. If it is not available from the parents, the child can obtain it from alternative parents, such as Della in this case. Studies of resilient children point to the critical role continued social support plays in their development.

Cara, an adolescent, demonstrated separation anxiety that is usually seen in much younger children. Her separation anxiety was evident in her relationship to Della, her school refusal, and her competition with her "sister", Margery. This certainly underscores the primacy of attachment variables, not only with young victims, but also with older ones. It is likely that Cara's mother never could have a secure, committed relationship with Cara, given the demands of a controlling, insecure husband. Thus, the sexual victimization occurred in a vulnerable child whose resolution of her abuse was compromised by attachment difficulties predating the abuse.

Finally, Dr. Cohen provides further support for a PTSD formulation, particularly the phenomenon of revivification. Cara saw her two perpetrators and was reminded of her previous abuse. However, therapy helped her to better regulate her affective arousal when she saw them several years later, and her distress was less severe. Cara's continued avoidance of adult sexual intimacy also fits with a PTSD formulation, in that one diagnostic criterion is the avoidance of situations that remind the victim of the stressor. —Editor

AUTHOR'S THEORETICAL ORIENTATION

Generally my therapeutic style is eclectic. I typically combine behavioral, cognitive, psychodynamic, and supportive modalities in whatever ways seem most applicable to the particular situation at hand. This is probably related to the fact that I see most problems as being multifactorial in their origin. I have found this to be particularly true in my treatment of sexually abused children. I conceptualize sexual abuse as an event (or series of events) that may affect a child in a variety of ways. There is a huge diversity in how different children respond to this experience. In this way it is similar to other life events, such as parental death or divorce, relocation to a new city, etc.

We have very little empirical knowledge regarding the specific factors that mediate the development of psychological problems in these children. However, my clinical impressions are that certain personality and systemic factors may be crucial in this process. For example, I have found that children who are believed and supported about the sexual abuse seem to recover much faster than those who are doubted or blamed. Children who are protected from further abuse, ridicule by peers, and reprisal from perpetrators seem to do better than children who are exposed to these additional stressors. And perhaps most importantly, there seem to be some children who, for whatever reason, simply seem more impervious to traumatic events than others. This may be related to their own coping mechanisms and cognitive styles or a variety of other personal qualities.

In devising a treatment plan for a sexually abused child, I try to incorporate aspects of all of these. For the child herself or himself, I generally combine cognitive therapy, assertiveness training, relaxation or desensitization approaches, and insight-oriented treatment modalities. When group therapy is available, I encourage children to participate in it with other abused peers, to decrease their feelings of isolation and being different. I also work whenever possible with family members, to increase their under-

The assistance of Ann Marie Kotlik in the typing of this manuscript is gratefully acknowledged.

standing and ability to effectively protect and support the child. It is important to address other problems the child may have which are unrelated to the sexual abuse. The need to protect the child from future abuse frequently necessitates systemic involvement with police, child protective services, legal advocacy networks and the courts. All of this makes working with these clients much more complex and time consuming than work with other populations. However, I believe therapists who restrict themselves to treating only one aspect of the child, or are limited to using only one modality significantly, diminish their ability to respond to the multiple origins of the problem.

Description of Case

When I first met Cara, she was a 16-year-old junior in high school. She was referred to me for individual and family therapy by a local rape crisis center. Cara is the only child born to strictly observant fundamentalist Christian parents. She was still living with her parents at the time she started therapy, but was spending much of her time talking on the phone and visiting with Della, a 45-year-old family friend and member of their conservative religious sect. The family lived in a small house in a middle class suburb. Father worked in a managerial position in a small company, and also served as an elder in the church, which required several extra hours of speech-writing and service weekly. Mother was a homemaker. To my knowledge, Cara was the only member of her family who had ever been sexually abused.

Cara had been raped repeatedly between the ages of five and twelve by two teenaged male cousins. Cara was frequently held or tied down as each cousin raped her in turn. They warned her to never reveal the abuse to her family, telling her that she would be punished if she told and that her parents would hate her if they knew what had happened. Cara was fearful of reprisal from her cousins, as well as being blamed and punished by her father, so she did not disclose the abuse for several years. When she was twelve years old, the older cousin moved away from his parents' home, and the sexual abuse of Cara stopped.

Cara first disclosed the abuse to Della four years later, when she was 16 years old. They were at a religious convention together when Cara saw the younger of the two perpetrators there. He came up behind her and grabbed her, fondling her buttocks. Cara said, "At that moment, everything came back to me—I remembered everything they had done to me and I was scared. I thought, 'I'm going to go through this the rest of my life with them. What next? This time I might get pregnant.'" Someone asked Cara to get something from the car and her cousin volunteered to go with her.

Cara said, "I knew what he'd do if I went out there with him." She refused to go.

Later that night, Della asked her what that had been all about. Cara was very embarrassed but Della encouraged her to talk, and the whole story came out. Cara made Della promise to never tell anyone. Della felt strongly that Cara's parents should know what had happened to Cara, but she was also concerned about Cara's emotional upheaval and wanted to support her. Eventually, Della persuaded Cara to tell her parents. Della accompanied her at Cara's insistence. Cara described that while she was disclosing the abuse to her parents, her father insisted on leaving the television on, as he was watching a program. He "half-listened" while Cara talked about the abuse, and did not say anything in response, but continued to watch television. Mother disbelieved Cara at first, saying, "If this really happened, why didn't you tell us before?" She implied that Della was "putting ideas" into Cara's head, and Cara felt that her mother resented the fact that Cara had confided in Della rather than herself. Mother's attitude toward the abuse was "nobody got hurt, it's over now, so what's the big deal?"

Cara felt betrayed by her parents' response, and turned to Della for support. Shortly after this occurred, Cara disclosed the abuse to a school psychologist. He recommended counseling, but the parents did not comply and the school did not pursue this. Apparently, the school psychologist did not file a child abuse report because the cousins had never been in a caretaking role.

After her disclosure Cara began to lose weight and became more isolated and withdrawn. Della noticed this change in Cara and became increasingly concerned. She invited her to call or visit whenever she wanted to. As time went on, Della became worried about Cara's overdependence on her. Cara was calling her literally morning, noon and night, and begging Della to let Cara live with her. Cara frequently threatened to hurt herself if Della were to become less available. Because of these issues, and also because Cara had lost almost 40 lbs. in four months (although she had been about 30 lbs. overweight prior to that), Della convinced Cara's parents to bring her for a psychiatric evaluation at a local rape crisis center. Although Cara's parents were very much against her growing relationship with Della, they agreed with her that Cara was in need of an evaluation. They and Della accompanied Cara to the evaluation. The evaluator was concerned about the severity of Cara's depressive symptoms and felt her treatment was beyond the scope of what was available through the rape crisis center. For this reason she was referred to me for therapy.

At that time I was working as a child psychiatrist in the outpatient child and adolescent treatment clinic of a large metropolitan university medical center. For two years I had also been working with a group of researchers examining the impact of different types of treatment on recent victims of rape and had become known to the rape crisis center staff.

INITIAL ASSESSMENT

I initially saw Cara with her parents to evaluate what immediate interventions would be most appropriate. During that meeting, her father, George, presented as a very controlled and authoritarian man to whom Cara and her mother deferred in all matters. He appeared to have very inflexible ideas about what Cara needed and the meaning of the sexual abuse. While he clearly said that his nephews were wrong and responsible for abusing Cara, he also implied that Cara was somehow impure as a result of having had sexual intercourse. He explained this in terms of the teachings of his religion. (I later learned from other elders from the church that this was not an accurate representation but rather father's own rigid interpretation of the religious teaching.)

The mother, Martha, was very quiet and appeared torn between her loyalty to father and her desire to support Cara. She would not oppose anything father said, although I got the impression that she did not share his feelings. She did not seem to understand the extent of Cara's emotional traumatization, but said that she loved her daughter and wanted her to feel better. Both parents were adamant about not wanting Cara's relationship with Della to continue. Their objections were based almost completely on their idea that it was "improper" for Cara to live anywhere outside of the parental home or to prefer any other adult to her own parents. Father, in particular, seemed to care much more about the "proper" thing and maintaining a commendable appearance to the religious community than about Cara's needs. Mother seemed more concerned about Cara, but would under no circumstances contradict her husband. (This is consistent with the stance of the family's church that the husband should be the dominant member of the family.)

The parents provided a developmental history at this meeting. Cara was the product of a full-term, unplanned pregnancy. The parents described Cara as having virtually no problems throughout her childhood; she was a straight A student from first grade through the present time. Cara had few friends, and usually played by herself rather than seeking out peers. However, both parents viewed this as a positive rather than negative attribute. They expressed satisfaction that Cara did not associate with nonreligious children, as this could lead her to exposure to impure behavior such as smoking, drugs and alcohol, etc. Apparently in the family's church there had been few children Cara's age and those who were close in age did not live near her. Cara had been moderately overweight since the onset of puberty (around 11 years old), but the parents had not been concerned about this (mother was mildly overweight as well).

Both parents were ambivalent about whether Cara really needed professional help; father's response was for Cara to "study the scriptures to cleanse" herself. He expressed a suspicion during this initial meeting that Cara did not need any therapy and that her symptoms and Della's insistence on getting an evaluation were all merely part of Della's plan to steal Cara away from them. Despite their doubts, the parents agreed to further family sessions on the condition that their insurance completely cover their bills.

I met with Cara individually for part of this initial session. She had been very quiet during the family meeting, answering only direct questions and then as briefly as possible. She sat hunched over, covered by a coat that was much too big for her, which she did not remove during the session. She rarely made eye contact and was on the verge of tears during most of the session. Alone with me, she became more verbal. She said that her father "has always come first with my mother. I never counted." She said when the family did something together, "I was like a dog, I just followed them around." She said she never felt free to discuss her feelings at home (often when father was writing a speech she was not allowed to talk at all for two to three hours at a time because he demanded total silence). She said, "I suffered in silence."

Cara described a fantasy family to which she frequently retreated while alone in her room. She pretended to be part of this family and carried on elaborate conversations and activities with them. Cara said she got comfort and support from this fantasy, much more than she did from her real family. (I was somewhat concerned whether this fantasy was actually part of a psychotic process, but it became clear as I got to know Cara that her superior intelligence and imagination had merely allowed her to make the fantasy elaborate enough to seem real; Cara was always sadly aware that it was merely a fantasy.)

Cara seemed sad that she was not allowed to have friends at school (because these peers were not members of her church). She said she had many male acquaintances at school, but "all I'm good for is helping them with their homework." Cara said female peers were more interested in boyfriends and other "secular" things, which as a fundamentalist Christian she was not allowed to discuss. When she was younger, Cara said she was terrified of playing with other children because of what her cousins were doing to her. She was afraid other children might hurt her, too. She also felt that she was "so different" from other children and that, because she had been abused, they would never like her.

Cara endorsed many depressive symptoms, including decreased appetite and weight loss, sleep disturbance, suicidal ideation, poor concentration, frequent crying, and feelings of worthlessness. She denied significant post-traumatic stress disorder symptoms, such as flashbacks, nightmares, numbing of responsiveness to the outside world, or impaired memory or concentration. Cara said the only person who made her feel worthwhile was Della and, if her parents had their way, Della would soon be taken away from her, too. If that happened, she said she would just as soon be dead. Cara agreed to return for therapy with her parents and individually.

Routine psychological testing indicated that Cara's IQ was in the very superior range (Full Scale IQ on the WAIS-R was 131). On the PIAT, her total test grade equivalent score was 12.9+ (standard score 118, percentile rank 88). The tester noted that in his opinion "had this child been tracked into a more academically enriched environment than she has currently been pursuing, her scores would have been even higher."

No legal or child protective action was ever taken with regard to Cara's abuse. At the time she came to me, both cousins had left the state. They had not technically been in caretaking roles when the abuse occurred. The family was unwilling to take legal action against the cousins, as they considered that to be "vengeful" and also because it would bring shame on the family and, more important, to the family's church. Thus, aside from Della, Cara had had virtually no support available to her.

I met with Della later that same week as part of my initial evaluation. Della presented as a short, attractive, matronly-looking woman who was very verbal in her support of Cara. She told me her hope was that Cara would be able to live with her parents and be happy, but she was not sure this was possible. She described Cara's parents as unloving, unsupportive, and unable to communicate with Cara. She had offered that Cara could live with her and her husband temporarily, an offer that thrilled Cara but was completely unacceptable to her parents.

Della had a grown married daughter with whom she had regular contact and a very good relationship. Della's husband worked in a blue collar job. He and Della had little in common and lived largely separate lives in the same home. He was not an active member of the church at that time, whereas Della was very involved in all aspects of her religion. It appeared that, while Della's main motivation was to support Cara, Cara also provided her with closeness and companionship which she welcomed.

My initial assessment of Cara was that she had been severely sexually abused and that she was currently manifesting severe depressive symptoms. It was not clear to me whether her depression was due more to the disclosure and renewed focus on the sexual abuse or to the present lack of social and familial support. My guess was that both factors were significant and were synergistic. My immediate goals were to enhance the parents' understanding and support of Cara and to begin to relieve Cara's depressive feelings and symptoms.

COURSE OF THERAPY

I saw Cara for a total of 145 sessions over a three-year period. Initially, Cara and her parents had agreed to meet with me for family therapy as well as Cara being seen for individual treatment. During the first week of therapy, Cara began staying overnight at Della's house, begging her parents to allow this. They at first reluctantly agreed, but father soon became angry and refused to permit it. He said, "Cara is hurting us [parents]; she is in need of discipline, not therapy." The parents did in fact appear to be hurting, and were reporting difficulty sleeping. We tried to focus on positive ways the family could spend time together. Father was very inflexible about this, saying his "fatherly obligation" to Cara was to study the Bible with Cara and "help her get a better understanding of God." Mother seemed agreeable to doing other activities with Cara, but father was not; mother as usual deferred to her husband.

At that session, father said, "you haven't seen me angry yet!" He described that when he was younger he "put a pitchfork through a horse" and once shot a dog out of anger. He did not seem able to understand that Cara was frightened by his authoritarian manner and that she needed positive rather than negative incentives to return home.

Cara in fact felt her father was a hypocrite because he had never had Bible study with her in the past (it was actually Della who suggested Cara begin study group when she realized Cara had never participated in this at home). Despite this, Cara agreed to return to her parents' home, and they agreed to spend more time with her. I acknowledged to Cara in our individual sessions that this was giving priority to her parents' needs rather than her own. We agreed that, if her parents did not show some changes in their ability to be more positive towards her, I would support her living elsewhere (although that would not necessarily be with Della).

Once Cara returned home, her depressive symptoms markedly worsened. The parents refused to continue in therapy as soon as she came back to their house (they had participated in three family sessions altogether). Cara told me that, once she was back, her parents treated her exactly as they had before therapy began: they expected her to comply with their wishes but otherwise spent little time with her. Cara said, "The only reason they want me back is because the 'Biblical family arrangement' is important to them. They don't care about me, only how it looks to everyone." The parents had not only demanded Cara's return home, but also set stringent limits on the amount of contact she was allowed to have with Della. Although Cara was compliant with these conditions, father soon changed his mind and prohibited any contact at all between Cara and Della.

Cara then became increasingly depressed, was losing weight rapidly (12 lbs. over three weeks), was not sleeping at all, and was actively suicidal. She drew a picture at this point which demonstrated her preoccupation with death and her feeling of being "a captured butterfly" (see Figure 1). She said she "felt like a prisoner". Although I tried to sympathize with her parents' fear that they would lose Cara to Della, I felt strongly that they were handling the situation in a very destructive way. I asked them to come in to meet with me but they refused, saying, "We'll work this out as a family." At that point I was actively trying to convince the parents to hospitalize Cara. The parents suggested a meeting between myself and another church elder, saying they would trust his opinion regarding hospitalization. When I explained to this elder that I was concerned about Cara's potential for suicide, he agreed that hospitalization was a reasonable recommendation. Cara's parents then agreed to hospital admission.

Cara was hospitalized for four weeks on the adolescent unit of the university psychiatric hospital. During that time, I continued to be her primary therapist. Although use of antidepressant medication was strongly considered, Cara's improvement in the hospital was so dramatic that medication was not started. Cara occasionally called her mother but refused to talk to her father. She said "he made me feel so bad about myself," and she felt that he would always view her as blemished because she had been sexually abused. Unfortunately, my experience with her father led me to believe she was accurate in her assessment. Cara wanted her mother to defend her and felt betrayed when mother remained loyal and obedient to father rather than advocating for Cara. I tried on several occasions to help mother understand this, but these attempts were unsuccessful.

On several occasions while Cara was hospitalized, I spoke and met with two elders from the family's Kingdom Hall. (This was with full permission of the family.) They explained to me the primacy of the nuclear family unit and stressed that Cara's spiritual needs could best be met in that setting. They were, however, extremely flexible and supportive once they understood the negative impact Cara's father was having on her. They assured me that in the eyes of their religion, Cara's purity was not in question, that she had been the innocent victim of violent behavior and was to be comforted and supported rather than needing to be "cleansed". They agreed that, if father could not accept this, he was misguided regarding the Bible's teaching and that this could be detrimental to Cara's spiritual growth.

Father was not present at these meetings but he did speak to the elders privately on many occasions. They concluded that father was indeed unable

FIGURE 1

to be appropriately supportive of Cara at that time. After several meetings between the elders and myself, it was agreed that Cara would be allowed temporarily to live with Della upon her discharge from the hospital. I expressed the strong opinion that her parents needed therapy if the family was ever to be reunited. The elders agreed that this was desirable. However, Cara's parents refused to see me or even to speak with me on the phone, as they perceived me to have "helped Della steal our daughter from us."

Cara meanwhile was joyful about the elders' decision. Her depressive symptoms had resolved within several days of entering the hospital; her sleep and appetite improved, her mood and weight stabilized, and she reported renewed hope for the future. Della had given her some new clothes as gifts during her hospitalization and for the first time since I had been treating her Cara began to attend to her physical appearance. She was discharged to Della with parents' very reluctant agreement.

Once Cara left the hospital, I began to see her in weekly individual outpatient therapy. Her parents continued to refuse any involvement in therapy. (I had offered them the opportunity to see a different therapist if they preferred; this was also refused.) My goal had been to attempt a family reconciliation at some point, but this did not seem productive unless Cara's parents were willing to make some changes in their perceptions of the abuse and Cara's needs. Cara informed me that her father had relinquished his duties as an elder, and shortly thereafter her parents stopped attending weekly meetings at their church. Cara felt guilty about this, but also relieved, as she was sure the elders would not send her back to live with her parents if they had lapsed in their religious duties. From the time of her leaving the hospital until years afterward, her parents refused to speak with Cara unless she returned to live with them. They gave away her belongings to other children, including items Cara had carefully collected and treasured since her childhood. Efforts by myself and various elders to modify their decision were flatly rejected.

Forming a therapeutic alliance with Cara was not difficult. She was extremely bright, articulate, and insightful, and was also hungry for understanding and support. Had I met Cara a few years earlier, I'm sure she would have been more guarded and withdrawn emotionally and had more difficulty in being able to trust a therapist. However, she was "ripe" for therapy at this time and welcomed an outlet for her emotions.

Cara had many difficulties after she came to live with Della. I believe that the double betrayal of chronic sexual abuse by her cousins and emotional distance and eventual rejection by her parents greatly impaired her self-esteem. Because of the strict rules of her religion, many positive emotional outlets available to other children were denied Cara. For example, she was not allowed to interact with most of her peers; thus she had few friends on whom to rely or from whom to derive positive self-esteem. Scholastically, Cara could have received a scholarship to almost any university in the country. Her grades and SAT scores were superior; she came in second in a state-wide academic competition, and she was valedictorian of her graduating class. Yet none of these achievements was allowed to be a source of pride or accomplishment to Cara because her church discourages personal achievement, particularly among women. Cara elected to become a secretary rather than go on to college for this reason.

Although she had become very attractive in her physical appearance, this was not allowed to be the source of any positive self-image or pride either. Thus, many typical sources of self-esteem for adolescents were not available to Cara. I frequently felt frustrated by this, and had many talks with Della about the problems this posed to Cara. At the same time I came to recognize that her religion served as a great source of fulfillment to Cara; one of her proudest and happiest moments during treatment was when she was baptized. Nonetheless, poor self-esteem, insecurity, and fear of betrayal were ongoing issues for Cara in therapy.

Soon after coming to live with Della, Cara developed severe separation anxiety symptoms. She became panic-stricken if Della left the house for more than a few minutes. She had nightmares that Della was dying (exacerbated by minor health problems which Della developed). The smallest comment was misinterpreted and distorted in Cara's mind to represent rejection by Della. We devised several techniques to deal with this. I encouraged Della to make special time to spend alone with Cara, but also advised her to go about her usual activities despite Cara's attempts to disrupt them. Cara and I explored her fears and used cognitive and behavioral techniques to counter them. Della was able to reinforce this with reassurance and consistency in her interactions with Cara. After several weeks, Cara's symptoms subsided, although it took her many months to really trust Della's commitment to her.

Cara developed extreme jealousy towards Della's daughter, Margery. Margery and her husband Richard lived several miles away, but frequently visited and called Della. Cara envied Margery for her ease with others and for "having had Della all those years to love her." Cara felt like an outsider in the family compared to Margery. The reality was that Margery did everything she could to welcome Cara into the family and treat her like a sister; Cara herself was too insecure to feel accepted and always felt like a "second fiddle" to Della's "real daughter." This was very stressful to Della, who felt that Cara was forcing her to choose, when Della loved both girls equally.

Finally I suggested several joint meetings between Margery and Cara, to which Margery readily agreed. Cara had described Margery as a "beautiful, thin, perfect" girl who was universally adored. Margery in fact was short, mildly overweight, and not as attractive as Cara. She was completely supportive of Cara's living in Della's home and expressed astonishment that Cara viewed her as being problem-free. Margery disclosed several of her own perceived shortcomings to Cara, and over time Cara became much more realistic in her perception of Margery. In fact, the two became very close, which was extremely beneficial to Cara.

Margery and Richard actively included Cara in their social activities; the couple were in their mid-20s and most of their friends were other young married couples. Cara became more comfortable socializing with these people over the next few years, but her feelings of being "an outsider looking in" persisted throughout therapy. I suggested that Cara begin group therapy with other sexually abused adolescents, but Cara and Della both felt this was not a good idea. They were concerned that the other members of the group might smoke or be sexually active or have other "immoral" behaviors, and Cara did not want to associate with such people. Thus, she remains somewhat socially isolated to the present time, although her social skills and comfort have certainly improved. I did not know how else other than group therapy to treat this persistent feeling of being different in Cara, which is so typical among sexual abuse victims (Briere & Runtz, 1987).

Cara got a good secretarial job after graduation from high school. After a time, she perceived that she was being taken advantage of by her employer; her conscientious perfectionistic work was rewarded by receiving even more work to do. Cara worked hard in therapy trying to understand why she always needed to be perfect. Once she identified this as part of her fear of being rejected, she was able to relinquish this need to some degree. She became appropriately assertive with her employer and in fact quit that job to get a much better one. She continued to do very well at work, getting frequent raises and promotions. However, she remained socially isolated from most of her coworkers, despite being well liked by them.

Another area of conflict was the issue of Cara's sexuality. This was complicated by her religious sect's views of sex and sexual feelings, which I had a great deal of difficulty accepting. As Cara and Della explained it to me, an unmarried person is not to have any sexual thoughts or feelings. If they do occur, the appropriate response is to overcome them. To me this did not seem developmentally realistic or healthy. I could understand the proscription against nonconjugal sexual activities but felt the obliteration of such feelings was an unreasonable expectation. Cara in fact did experience sexual "urges" at times. She had in the past masturbated to orgasm, having masochistic fantasies which were for her uncomfortably similar to the sexual abuse she had experienced. She stopped this activity once she came to live with Della, by using "will power."

Cara frequently said she did not wish to ever marry or have children because she did not want a child of hers to ever be abused, and also because she never wanted to have to "cater to a man." Upon further exploration, she admitted that she was afraid of ever trusting a man, and marriage would require that. She was afraid she would have to marry anyway, however, because she kept having "unacceptable sexual feelings" and marriage (i.e., conjugal relations) was the only acceptable way they could be satisfied. I explained to Cara on many occasions that her feelings and urges were normal for someone her age. She maintained that they may be common, but that did not make them acceptable. In this particular case, I believe her religious training was not helpful in her attempt to resolve the sexual abuse. Rather, it gave her an excuse to avoid confronting the sexual nature of the abuse or her own subsequent sexual feelings.

Because of her social isolation and the religious prohibitions against ever spending time alone with one male, Cara has not had an opportunity to develop a trusting relationship with a man. Her experiences with her cousins and her father have made it even less likely that Cara will be able to do so. All of these factors together make me doubt whether Cara will ever have a fulfilling relationship with a man. She seems to have accepted this at times, yet other times she wonders what she will do when Della eventually dies and she is left alone. She has resisted further exploration of this, saying she would dedicate herself to religion at that point.

Cara had an anniversary reaction about one year after she was admitted to the hospital. At this time she began having recurrent dreams where people told her "you are incomplete." She also dreamed that her parents and Della had new babies, and that she was "kicked out to live on the streets." Della provided constant reassurance during this period, and Cara was able to use cognitive and behavioral methods (i.e., thought stopping, reality testing tasks, relaxation, etc.) to counteract her anxiety. These techniques are described in detail by Wheeler and Berliner (1989). Cara gained insight into her feelings of having been damaged (more psychologically than physically) by the sexual abuse. She came through this period with a strong determination to "not let them [perpetrators] win. If I feel like a regular person, then I've beaten them." She focused more as time went on on the positive aspects of her life and her areas of competence. Della taught her homemaking skills, which Cara had assumed she could never master, such as refinishing furniture, doing laundry, learning needlecrafts and cooking. Cara derived significant feelings of competence from these.

During the final months of therapy, Cara's uncle, the father of the perpetrators, died suddenly of a heart attack. Cara debated whether to go to the funeral or not, and finally decided that going would help her obtain closure on many of her feelings about the abuse. Her parents did not attend because they heard Cara was coming. However, both of her cousins were present. Cara "felt nothing" when she saw them there and was very proud and relieved about this. The rest of her extended family was very warm towards her, after having had little contact since Cara had moved in with Della. Cara said she felt a lot of tension and conflict resolved internally after the funeral because "it's really over." Cara also told me she had planned to "punch their faces out" if either cousin made any sexual overtures to her. She was relieved that this did not happen, but also felt a great sense of victory that she was no longer afraid of them.

At this point, Cara began to improve rapidly. Although she had not been significantly depressed or suicidal since her hospitalization, Cara had often been dysthymic during treatment. However, the funeral of her uncle proved to be a turning point in this regard. Cara became increasingly cheerful and upbeat and was able to navigate the ups and downs of daily living with much greater ease. She became less needy of constant support and reassurance, and she herself eventually suggested termination of therapy. After several months of less frequent treatment (every two to three weeks), we agreed on a termination date. Cara was able to express sadness about losing me, but also felt that she no longer needed therapy.

We terminated treatment as planned, and Cara has continued to do well in the two years since. When I contacted her with regard to writing this chapter about her, she was very enthusiastic. She came in to talk with me about it and brought me up to date on her situation. She has continued to work as an executive secretary for a large company and is still living with Della. She had had no contact with her parents until a few months ago. At that time she learned that her mother was having surgery, and with Della's encouragement, Cara telephoned her mother. They talked for two hours, mostly about what each had been doing over the past five years. Neither broached the subject of the sexual abuse or what happened to the family as a result. Cara's father was not mentioned (Cara intentionally called at a time when she knew her father would be at work).

Cara felt no desire to renew an ongoing relationship with her parents and felt that "Della is more my real mother than Martha ever was." However, she did feel good about having "broken the ice" and ended the five-year silence which had seemed so unnatural to her. Cara continues to be euthymic, and is actively involved in activities related to her church. She is still socially isolated, and her close friends are all women around Della's age (Margery and Richard have been out of the country for several months, involved in missionary work). She describes herself as "happier than I've ever been."

Specific Techniques Used in Therapy

As noted above, a variety of specific interventions were used at different times. These included: behavioral techniques such as thought-stopping and progressive relaxation therapy; extensive cognitive therapy to reframe why the abuse happened and why her parents reacted the way they did; role-playing to integrate ambivalent feelings about herself (Briere, 1989) as well as to try out new interactional strategies; family therapy (including Della and Margery in Cara's sessions at different points); and psychoeducational interventions to educate Cara about aspects of normal sexuality. Unfortunately, coordinating therapy for Cara and her parents ceased to be an issue, as they dropped out of therapy after only three sessions. I occasionally met alone with Della to offer support at stressful times and to discuss parenting issues when Cara's demands became excessive. Della and Cara were both flexible about this, and Margery was cooperative with whatever was suggested. This made coordination of therapy relatively easy.

OUTCOME

Cara improved significantly in many ways, as discussed above. The ongoing issues are related to her relative social isolation and lack of ease regarding heterosexual relationships. These are both exacerbated by religious restrictions. Cara's affect improved markedly, as measured by her self-report and Della's and my own observations. Her neurovegetative symptoms and suicidal ideation cleared up quickly and did not recur.

The most negative outcome related to Cara's family situation. Her parents withdrew completely from her, and neither my efforts nor those of the church elders were successful in reengaging them. They remain completely dissociated from their church; my assumption is that they blame both me and the religious hierarchy for "taking their daughter away" from them. In reality, their own behavior resulted in Cara's estrangement; I believe she would have welcomed any genuine understanding or support they could have offered. Even given her father's rigidity, if her mother could have defied father enough to reach out to Cara and take her side, I believe Cara would have preferred to remain at home.

TREATMENT OBSTACLES

Obviously, Cara's parents' attitudes were a huge obstacle in the beginning of therapy. This was eventually managed by placing Cara outside the parental home (which had its own negative consequences for the family). The attitudes of their religious sect towards the absolute sanctity of the nuclear family were also an obstacle, but this was removed through the flexibility of the elders with whom I worked. Nevertheless, their attitudes about dating and sexuality were an obstacle which I did not overcome. I accepted these standards in my treatment of Cara, which I believe prevented her from resolving some of her issues related to trust, intimacy, and sexuality. On the other hand, this acceptance allowed her to feel integrated into her religion, and she derived a great deal of comfort and support, as well as an abstract sense of belonging, through this.

OTHER SYSTEMS

Child welfare was never involved in Cara's case, nor was the criminal justice system. This made Cara's situation somewhat unusual. I don't believe criminal prosecution would have been possible at the time Cara first came to me; not only had the abuse ended four years previously, but both perpetrators had been minors at the time of the abuse, and they had both left the state. I'm not convinced that legal action would have been therapeutic for Cara, given her negative religious attitudes toward disrupting the family and seeking revenge. She eventually resolved most of the abuse issues intrapsychically, without the benefit of external punishment of the perpetrators.

WHAT I WOULD DO DIFFERENTLY

I considered from the beginning the possibility of seeing Cara's mother independently of the parental couple. I believe Martha could have gained insight into Cara's feelings and provided significant support for her, if she hadn't been so concerned with pleasing and appeasing her husband. My reasoning for not suggesting this at the time was that it would be perceived as an attempt to undermine the parental coalition or to force Martha to choose sides. In fact, that would have been the case to some important degree.

Perhaps it was doing him an injustice, but I essentially wrote off George as having potential to make significant changes. Thus in my mind it came down to Martha's choosing to support Cara against George's wishes or to remain allied with George and ignore Cara's needs. She chose the latter, and I did not actively attempt to change her mind in this regard. I did point out Cara's feelings and needs, but I did not confront mother with statements of what she needed to do. I frequently do exactly that in these cases, becoming very directive in urging the mother to unilaterally support the victim. This reflects the fact that my training and approach have always been primarily child-oriented rather than family-oriented (when a choice had to be made). I'm not sure why I didn't do this in Martha's case. It would certainly have enraged George; perhaps I felt she could not have stood up to his anger. But I wonder whether that would not have been a chance worth taking; had Martha been able to defy her husband and stand up for Cara, Cara may have chosen to remain with her parents.

On the other hand, it's possible that taking a family orientation approach (i.e., focusing on the interrelationships within the family rather than on the needs of one member) would have been more beneficial to the family. I have my doubts whether it would have been optimal for Cara. It's obvious that the results of my approach were not beneficial for the family as a unit or for either of Cara's parents individually as far as I could tell. I think if Cara had been less depressed, I would have been more balanced in weighing the child's needs vs. the family's needs. If I had done this, perhaps the outcome would have been more favorable.

PERSONAL REACTIONS TO THE CASE

Although I had treated many sexually abused children and numerous dysfunctional and unsupportive families, becoming Cara's therapist presented
a new challenge to me. I had never treated a child belonging to a strict
fundamentalist sect and was largely unfamiliar with the beliefs and practices of this group. It quickly became clear to me that, because of the
parents' very strict ideas about family, obedience and sexuality, I would
have to significantly modify my usual approach in order to not contradict
their standards of morality, yet still find ways of helping Cara to take
control of her life and develop feelings of competence and positive self-
esteem. At many times during the course of treatment, I felt these were
mutually exclusive goals. As a child psychiatrist, I had generally put the
child's best interests first; I now had to confront the alternative philosophies
of placing the needs of the family as a unit, or the tenets of the broader
religious group, ahead of Cara's needs. I was often unsuccessful in this;
other times we managed to find compromises we could all live with. I
learned to choose my battles, to be as flexible as possible on most issues,
and to stand my ground on the points I thought were most critical to Cara's
well-being. Throughout this process I found the elders of the church to be
utterly committed to helping Cara and her family; I found them to be much
more flexible as a group than I had believed they would be based on my
interactions with Cara's father.

During the initial stages of therapy, I clearly allied myself more with
Cara than with her parents, because of my need to protect and advocate
for her. I suppose I felt that the parents had always put their religion
and the father's needs before Cara, and there was no one in the family
who put *her* needs first. I did not feel this need to protect Cara with Della;
at many times I encouraged Della to set reasonable limits on Cara's demands. This was because I believed Cara was receiving adequate support
and understanding in that situation, whereas she was not in her parents'
home.

Overall, I feel the case went well in treatment. I believe many of Cara's
unresolved issues stem more from long-standing familial patterns than from
the sexual abuse (although the two are certainly related). Most of my usual
avenues of intervention were blocked with regard to improving Cara's social
interactions. I came to accept this eventually, although I feel personal regret
that so vibrant and intelligent a person as Cara will probably never reach
her full potential either vocationally or interpersonally. Despite this, I feel
a great deal of satisfaction in the improvements Cara made and in her
increased level of overall happiness.

11

The Role of the Extended Family in the Evaluation and Treatment of Incest

PAMELA C. ALEXANDER

Given the frequency with which families either "permit" the emergence of incest or fail to support the victim following the abuse, it is important for treatment specialists to think as clearly as possible about these families. At the same time, it is also important to realize that Dr. Alexander is discussing only one type of incestuous family, the enmeshed type. There are a variety of other family types, some of which are articulated elsewhere (Friedrich, 1990).

Early on therapists learn the notion of parallel process. For example, what occurs within a family may mimic what occurs between the therapist and his or her supervisor. In this case, the enmeshment and collusion present in this incestuous family is paralleled by Robert's therapist, who is not open with the adoption agency about his having a history of incest with his nieces.

In addition, Robert, a minister, had molested his siblings when younger. While many individuals dismiss sibling incest as minor, recent research by Michael O'Brien, of PHASE in St. Paul, Minnesota, indicates that sibling offenders offend longer, more severely, and have more victims than do adolescent offenders of nonsibling victims (O'Brien, 1990, personal communication). (It is important to remember these findings when reading the Bentovim and Ratner case in this book.)

Dr. Alexander demonstrates considerable bravery in her lengthy family sessions with the extended family. However, the initial discussion of secrets is the critical first step in reducing the collusion evident in the family. Her inclusion of dialogue clearly illustrates the gradual unfolding of secrets and triangles that have long existed in this family. — Editor

AUTHOR'S THEORETICAL ORIENTATION

My approach to the treatment of the sexually abusive family rests on two assumptions. The first is that there is a circular and reciprocal relationship between the family structure and the sexual abuse. In other words, certain dysfunctional kinds of family structures are associated with the occurrence of incest. This is not to say that it can always be determined which preceded the other—the family structure or the abuse. While some family structures seem to "permit" the occurrence of abuse, others seem to organize around the severely pathological behavior of the perpetrator. In either case, certain commonalities of family structure can be observed. In describing these commonalities, I will be focusing primarily upon the "enmeshed" incestuous family in which the perpetrator turns to children within the family to seek sex and affection instead of seeking relationships with others outside the home (Authier, 1983; Trepper & Barrett, 1986).

Exploration of the enmeshed family with sexual abuse will inevitably reveal secrecy, social isolation, and an attempt to avoid overt conflict through triangulation (both across generational boundaries and with outsiders) (Alexander, 1985). Furthermore, the incest plays a reciprocal reinforcing role in maintaining those family characteristics through the effects of secrecy. Therefore, in order to effectively protect the children within the present generation and to preclude the development of future incest, it is imperative that treatment focus both on stopping the abuse and on changing the family structure.

The second assumption that will be illustrated in this case presentation is that long-term maintenance of treatment gains (including the elimination of the abusive behavior) necessarily has to rely upon resources within the family. Although a focus on resources is applicable to all families (Karpel, 1986), there are several reasons why it is especially relevant to sexually abusive families.

First, present approaches to the treatment and social control of sexual abuse have not yet reached the level of efficacy that can assure the long-term safety of the victims. For example, although individually-oriented methods of treatment with the perpetrator may be highly successful while he is in treatment, recidivism rates for abuse are still unacceptably high once treatment ceases. Similarly, efforts to encourage the breakup of the family to protect the children in the home do not seem to protect the children from the courts' definite tendency to grant visitation rights to the perpetrator (Sirles, 1987). Therefore, treatment programs cannot afford to neglect the potential of the family to monitor the perpetrator's behavior and to maintain behavior changes instituted in a more structured treatment setting.

A second reason why a focus on family resources is relevant to the problem of sexual abuse is because the very same family rules and patterns that are associated with the abuse can often be used as forces for healing and prevention. For example, the secrecy and avoidance of conflict described earlier are frequently manifestations of an intense loyalty and need for relatedness in the family. Helping the perpetrator and other family members to express this loyalty and relatedness in more adaptive ways (including the active protection of children) can be a means of introducing specific treatment gains into the family context. On the other hand, a therapist's inattention to these family rules and forces could easily result in the sabotage and undermining of treatment gains. For example, inadvertent permission for scapegoating of the perpetrator (either by the therapist or certain family members) can set the stage for other family members to protect him and even exonerate him from his accountability for the abuse (Gelinas, 1986). Therefore, the intense loyalty that is frequently seen in abusive families (Cotroneo, 1986) can either become a barrier or a pathway to long-term progress in treatment.

The case that is presented below is meant to illustrate the principles of family structure and family resources that can be observed in working with sexually abusive families. The focus is on one element of what is assumed to be a multidimensional approach to treatment. Just as it is short-sighted for treatment professionals working with perpetrators or sexual abuse victims to ignore the family (its contribution to the abuse, its experience of the abuse, and its resources in dealing with the abuse), it is equally myopic for family therapists to not make use of behavioral approaches, therapy groups, and other perspectives on individual treatment. However, since I was not involved in other aspects of treatment for this case, I will limit my discussion to the family sessions.

This case presentation is also circumscribed, in that it is based upon an evaluation of a perpetrator. Although the goals of evaluation and therapy are ostensibly different, the overlap is substantial, since one of the purposes of evaluation is to assess an individual's responsivity to treatment. Therefore, the family sessions described represent both an assessment and a model for this particular family therapy approach. Because the primary purpose was to evaluate the perpetrator and because of other reasons given below, the victim of the sexual abuse was not included in the work conducted. She was, however, seeing her own individual therapist and would have been involved in these sessions at a later point if the evaluation had been formalized into therapy.

DESCRIPTION OF THE CASE

Robert Edwards was a 33-year-old white male. He was the third of five children with two older sisters, one younger sister, and one younger brother. Robert was in the ministry, as was his father. He had been married for 12 years. He and his wife were in the process of adopting a baby girl from a church-affiliated adoption agency of which Robert, as a minister, had been supportive during its formation a number of years earlier. Robert and his wife were approximately one month away from completing the standard six-month probation period before the adoption would be complete.

According to Robert and to hospital records, he had been accused of fondling his 14-year-old niece. (This apparently was not an isolated example.) His niece had pretended to be asleep at the time and had then reported the behavior to her mother (Robert's sister Ellen) who had then called their father. The elder Mr. Edwards told everyone in the family who knew of the abuse to keep quiet about it, and he encouraged Robert to check himself into a psychiatric hospital. Upon admission, Robert was diagnosed as depressed, with secondary diagnoses of histrionic personality disorder and passive-aggressive personality disorder. Hospital records noted that Robert participated in a variety of therapy settings, including individual, marital, and group therapies, although interventions did not appear to be specifically related to the sexual abuse. It was noted that Robert's emotional insight lagged relative to his cognitive insight. Therapy appeared to focus primarily upon Robert's depression and, more specifically, his high need for approval and his guilt over his own anger. Whether the lifting of his depression and guilt was appropriate given the abuse was apparently not questioned.

Robert's hospitalization was significant in demonstrating the dynamics operating in the family and how it interfaced with outside agencies. Not atypical for families with sexual abuse, this was an extremely patriarchal family with a strong emphasis on maintaining a facade of role competence. Robert reported that he had entered into the ministry in order to gain his father's approval. Denial was almost institutionalized within his family by the emphasis on outward social propriety. For example, although Robert later reported a long-term history of sexual exploration and acting out between himself and several of his sisters (older and younger), this had remained a well-kept secret up to this time.

Robert's therapist in the hospital decided to not reveal to the adoption agency exactly why Robert had been hospitalized. This decision was made by the therapist even though, coincidentally, the therapist served as the consultant to the adoption agency. The therapist also warned Robert to discontinue any further contact with his siblings, with the rationale that they would not understand. The effect of this move was to ally the elder Mr. Edwards with his son against the inquiries of three of the other siblings (Jim, Tammy, and Ellen). On the other hand, Robert's older sister Susan chose to ally herself with Robert against the other three siblings. The stress on the family was also exacerbated by the sudden death of the elder Mrs. Edwards, who had apparently served the function of peacemaker in the family. As a result of this stress and unresolved conflict, one of Robert's brothers-in-law (Tammy's husband Howard) anonymously informed both the adoption agency as well as Robert's district supervisor as to why he was in the hospital.

This initial description of the Edwards family illustrates three characteristics common to sexually abusive families:

1. the structural problems of the family which contribute to and permit the occurrence of sexual acting out;
2. the reciprocal role of the incest behavior and also, inadvertently, of treatment providers in reinforcing the structural problems;
3. the cognitive process which serves as the mechanism linking the family structure to the behaviors of the individual family members.

As noted by Larson and Maddock (1985), incest is a manifestation of a system that is "relatively closed, undifferentiated and rigid in both structure and function" (p. 28). The maintenance of the tight external boundary of the Edwards family did not come from physical isolation (Tierney & Corwin, 1983), but from a strong facade of role competence and apparent emphasis on moral and religious values. This family needed to present itself as without problems. This tight external boundary contributed in part to the development of the sexually abusive behavior, in that the emphasis on role competence not only encouraged Robert to seek a vocation that was, in his own words, highly stressful to him, but also prevented him and his wife from dealing more openly with their marital conflict. On the other hand, this family structure was also reinforced by the abuse, in that there now was an even more important secret to be kept from outsiders.

This discrepancy between the Edwards family's public and private faces was also indicative of the Edwards family's excessive use of denial, i.e., their ability to keep secrets even from themselves. Although the family was imbued with a strong moral/religious emphasis, this frequently took the form of righteous indignation. The triangulation and indirect communication within the family simultaneously fueled this moral superiority and prevented the family from openly confronting any violations of their norms. Therefore, although it later emerged that the teenage cousins within the family had long talked among themselves about Uncle Robert's flirtatious behavior, none of their parents had ever confronted him.

Triangulation was not only rampant among the siblings' families but also occurred between the generations. After the niece disclosed the fondling to her mother, the mother, instead of discussing the matter with her own husband and then with Robert, went directly to her father. In other words, the elder Mr. Edwards was so central in his family that all communication (certainly between siblings, but even between spouses) proceeded through him. A sense of loyalty and respect for this patriarch's decisions and judgments seems to have precluded the siblings' handling their own conflicts among themselves. The father's centrality also emerged in later therapy sessions.

OTHER SYSTEMS INVOLVED

Just as the incest behavior itself reinforces the structural problems described above through its effects on secrecy, the agencies and individuals responsible for treatment of the incest frequently find themselves triangulated by the family into repeating many of the same structural problems. The effect, of course, is to reinforce the denial and the conflict that permitted the sexual abuse in the first place. For example, in this case, Robert's individual therapist chose to cut off any further communication between Robert and his siblings and to keep the abuse from important agencies in the community.

There are several ways in which these decisions mirrored the behavior of the family. First, at the level of the boundary between the family and the community, it reinforced the Edwards family's emphasis on secrecy and its facade of role competence. Second, at the level of subsystem boundaries, it communicated to the niece and the rest of the family that it was fitting and proper to attend to the needs of the adults as more important than those of the children. Finally, it reinforced the family's natural tendency to triangulate between subsystems. The most important triangle resulted from the therapist's intervention to decrease communication between Robert and his siblings. This served not only to increase their level of conflict but also to set the stage for another round of intergenerational triangles.

With respect to Robert and his family, the cutting off of communication between Robert and his sibs occurred at a time, around their mother's death, when the need for cohesiveness was heightened. Kahn (1986), for example, has noted that the sibling subsystem becomes especially important with the death of a parent, in that it allows the children to maintain an ongoing sense of family. This rupture also occurred precisely at a time when the sibs were trying hard to have an influence over each other — Robert in convincing his brother and sisters of his basic goodness and they in making sure that the abuse wouldn't recur. However, the lack of opportunity to communicate was understandably interpreted by all as a message that resolution was not possible. Therefore, the conflict increased. The elder Mr. Edwards responded to the apparent alliance of most of the sibs against Robert by allying with Robert. This included inviting Robert and his wife Jan to come and live with him, since the complaint to Robert's district supervisor resulted in his temporary unemployment. In his compliance with the therapist's recommendation, Mr. Edwards effectively discouraged any of his other children from visiting his home while Robert was there (i.e., most of the time). Needless to say, what could always have been characterized as sibling rivalry in the Edwards family for their father's attention increased greatly.

The description of this triangle also illustrates the way in which the family structure is translated into the specific behaviors of the family members. In other words, family structure is a reflection of family members' perceptions and expectations of each other. Bogdan (1984) noted that order, pattern, or structure can be identified in family interactions precisely because the behavior of each individual is cognitively consistent with the behavior of every other individual in the system. Figure 1 demonstrates how family members' beliefs were based directly on their perceptions (accurate or inaccurate) of each other's behavior and how each family member's beliefs were

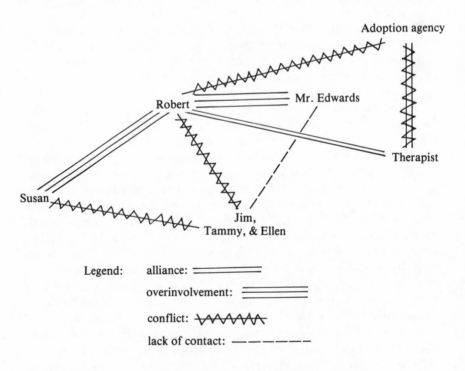

FIGURE 1. *Triangulation within the Edwards family*

then responsible for his/her own behavior. It also illustrates the intransigence of such a triangle.

This interplay between cognitions and behaviors was important primarily in its effect upon the potential for future abusive behavior. Robert was allowed to externalize blame for his problems with the adoption agency instead of acknowledging and accepting his own responsibility for the negative consequences of his behavior. In his attempt to support Robert, Mr. Edwards worked even harder to keep the abuse secret and minimized his approbation of Robert's behavior. Finally, Robert's sibs' demands that he accept responsibility for the abuse and that he exhibit more appropriate behavior in the future were dismissed by Robert and Mr. Edwards as being self-serving and resulting only from the conflict. Therefore, what *could* have been a resource for treatment in terms of ongoing support and confrontation of Robert's behavior by his siblings was unfortunately inverted into a barrier to change.

In addition to this primary triangle, the family's inability (both inherent and imposed) to resolve the conflict resulted in a second set of triangles — among the therapist, the family, and the adoption agency. Much of the intensity of the adoption agency's reaction to Robert was fueled by intermittent phone calls from Robert's brother-in-law and by the agency's anger at its consultant, Robert's therapist. The therapist's decision thus ended up reinforcing and exacerbating the family's innate tendencies to triangulate as an alternative to conflict resolution. Some of the triangles present within the family at this point are illustrated in Figure 2.

PSYCHOLOGICAL ASSESSMENT MATERIAL

A referral was then made to me by the adoption agency. I met with Robert individually and with his wife for a total of five sessions. In these sessions we explored his history of sexual acting out within his family of origin (he denied any contact other than with his sisters), the couple's problems of communication and conflict resolution, and Robert's history of conflict with members of his congregation.

Robert was administered the MMPI, the Thematic Apperception Test, and the Rorschach. He was somewhat defensive; nevertheless, the test profile was judged to be valid. Although there was evidence of depression, negative self-esteem, and withdrawal from social contacts, Robert did not appear to be experiencing an undue level of psychological distress.

Test results suggested that Robert's preferred tendency was for action and affective involvement. However, at present he was withdrawing, suggesting an avoidance or discomfort with processing affective stimuli and with displaying emotion. He appeared to be using extreme denial to deal

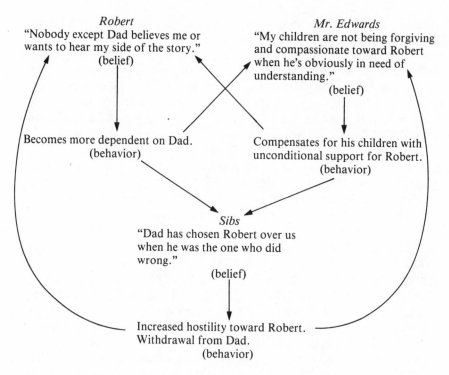

FIGURE 2. *The interaction between beliefs about others' behavior and the justification for one's own behavior.*

with unwanted emotions. Not only was he backing away from his preferred style of coping, but his repertoire of coping skills was too inadequate to provide him with an effective alternative strategy. Consequently, Robert was attempting to simplify and showed a reluctance to deal with complexity. He not only displayed an avoidance of responsibility, but passively fantasized about problems simply disappearing. Although his thinking was unconventional, there was no evidence of a thought disorder. On the other hand, his idiosyncratic thinking was consistent with his impressions of people, which seemed to be based on non-real or imaginary experience. In summary, Robert appeared to be relying upon a passive, almost childlike tendency to simplify and to wish that problems would go away.

COURSE OF THERAPY

A number of questions remained after the formal testing and after I had seen Robert and his wife alone. The most important question concerned Robert's tendency to externalize blame. On the one hand, this was obviously a poor sign of his prognosis for taking responsibility for the abuse. On the other, he *had* been encouraged by his therapist and by his father to avoid assuming responsibility with the adoption agency and to avoid contact with his siblings. Robert, in essence, was exhibiting a "circle the wagons" mentality learned from his father. Therefore, this externalization of blame could also have resulted from his lack of opportunity to resolve the conflict within the family.

A second question concerned the role of the siblings. Did they have the potential to establish the norm that any kind of fondling and seductive behavior between adults and children was inappropriate and forbidden (as opposed to being seen as a continuation of sexual experimentation from their childhood)? Or was their focus on the abuse simply a means of slandering Robert in their father's eyes?

Finally, a third question concerned the role of Mr. Edwards. Was he able to step out of his position of centrality and allow the siblings to resolve their own conflicts and develop their own norms for the family's behavior? Or was his discomfiture with conflict and his focus on public appearance going to inhibit him from genuinely exploring the problems in his family and establishing a new set of mores? With these questions in mind, I invited Robert, his wife Jan, Mr. Edwards, and all of Robert's siblings and their spouses to attend a family session. I also invited a cotherapist to work with me during the family sessions.

Initially, the adults in the family decided they did not want their children involved in these sessions. This seemed to be an appropriate demarcation of generational boundaries, since the conflict between the siblings over Robert's alliance with his father needed to be resolved before the family could establish clear norms regarding sexuality. In other words, the siblings' issues as children were distracting them from their issues as parents. Furthermore, the secrets regarding the purported history of sexual acting out among the siblings as children needed to be explored. Finally, the niece who had been fondled was being seen by her own therapist. However, other considerations will be discussed as to the importance of this generation's involvement in subsequent sessions.

SPECIFIC TECHNIQUES USED IN THERAPY

As will be illustrated in the selected transcripts below, the therapists had several simultaneous goals for the family sessions:

1. to eliminate the secrecy which allowed the sexual acting out to continue;
2. to attempt to decrease the triangulation, which allowed the family to avoid conflict and confrontation; and

3. to explore potential resources in the family which could be used and developed to mitigate the potential for abuse in the future.

Family Session 1

Present were Robert, his wife Jan, his father Mr. Edwards, his older sister Susan and her husband Sam, his older sister Tammy and her husband Howard, his younger sister Ellen, his younger brother Jim and his wife Betsy, my cotherapist, and myself.

Initial remarks by therapists included framing the family's presence as an indication of their commitment and intent to resolve conflict. Also, the rationale was presented that sexual abuse occurs primarily in families in which there are secrets. Since there was such a great tendency to scapegoat Robert, although not necessarily because of his responsibility for the abuse, it was important for the therapists to walk the fine line between holding Robert responsible for the specific abusive behavior and confronting the family's style of triangulating and avoiding conflict.

TAMMY   It has hurt us all so terribly bad and to my understanding he [Robert] still does not seem to feel it was so terribly bad. I love my Dad and I lost my Mom and I lost my Dad because I took a stand against what he believed because he thinks Robert hung the moon and he doesn't. He did something wrong and he needs to stand on his own two feet and admit what he did and not lean on his Daddy and let him be his crutch.

Although Tammy is expressing legitimate concern about Robert's behavior, it is difficult to separate out her reprehension at his behavior from her envy of his apparently favored position with his father. Since her feelings must also be equally apparent to Robert, her remarks come across to him as self-serving (whether or not they actually are). In this way, the triangulation is distracting everyone from the abuse.

HOWARD   (Tammy's husband and the individual who, unbeknownst to the rest of the family, made the call to the adoption agency) Are you aware that our daughter was involved in an incident with Robert? Two and a half years ago, she came to us and said that Robert made an advance. She was a young child at the time—11 years old. We didn't really want to believe it. We decided that we would say nothing to anybody. I did, however, call Robert's boss and made him aware of it.

THERAPIST   I really appreciate your saying this tonight with Robert here because that to me is much more straightforward and I appreciate your being that open.

I reinforce him for talking about this directly and in front of Robert.

* * * * *

THERAPIST   (to Jim) How can this (issue) be resolved?

JIM   It sounds like a bunch of excuses. I don't think he should preach. On Thanksgiving, Robert was at Dad's house when there was an understanding he wouldn't be there. I'm still in the family too.

A long discussion about Mr. Edwards' involvement with Robert follows. Concern is expressed that Robert will be a financial drain upon his father. Also, questions are raised as to whether Mr. Edwards is being as supportive to his other children as he is to Robert.

The siblings and their spouses are still more concerned at this point about the implications of Robert's behavior for their own ability to get attention from their father than about the implications of Robert's behavior for the safety of their children. Their concerns as children are taking precedence over their concerns as parents.

* * * * *

MR. EDWARDS   It bothers me because trust was broken and we agreed not to talk about it. We needed to listen to the professionals for Robert's sake.

Although the advice of Robert's therapist becomes a convenient excuse, it is apparent that Mr. Edwards has established quite explicitly a norm of secrecy and the appearance of propriety.

* * * * *

The therapist returns to Jim's dilemma about Robert's not taking responsibility.

THERAPIST   What would be a sign to you that he was taking responsibility?

JIM   For him to get a job. All I can hear are excuses.

THERAPIST   How would that feel to you now if Robert came out and said to you, "I was wrong. It was my behavior and I apologize"?

JIM   That would be real easy to say. At this particular point, I probably wouldn't believe it.

Jim is emerging as a potential resource within the family for several reasons. Robert has previously identified him as the sibling he would most like to become closer to. Jim is also the most consistently confrontive of Robert, even though, ironically, he is the only other family member without a teenage daughter. Aside from identifying this potential, this two-and-a-half hour first session mainly served to highlight the points of conflict. Because the family was also uncomfortable with the lack of resolution, they agreed to a second session.

Family Session 2

JIM (to Robert) I had just told Daddy a week before this happened that you were doing good, that I felt closer to you and everything.

Therapist encourages Robert to respond.

ROBERT I don't know what to say. I never felt like he was very much interested in what was going on in my life.

THERAPIST What's he saying now?

ROBERT He's saying he was. Is that right?

JIM It wouldn't make any difference if you were my brother or someone else.

ROBERT I'm hearing you say I wasn't any different from everybody else and I wanted to be your big brother.

Robert needs to acknowledge what Jim is saying, but also needs to feel supported by him in order to do this. Therefore, both the confrontation and the support are essential.

THERAPIST How will he get to know you well enough to trust that it won't happen again?

ROBERT I think it would take talking and being around each other and that.

MR. EDWARDS (interrupting) I think if all of this group could have been with Robert like I've been, they would feel that this wouldn't happen again. If they could see the suffering and the heartbreak and the sorrow and the remorse, because somewhere down the line he got the feeling that none of them loved him anyhow too well.

THERAPIST (interrupting) Okay, but the question is legitimate.

It is important to keep Mr. Edwards out of this triangle, since his involvement and attempt to support Robert actually undermine Robert's rapport with his sibs. This is also an example of how Mr. Edwards is reacting to the others' anger at Robert by protecting him and actually excusing him for his behavior. As opposed to Mr. Edward's unconditional support of Robert, the question about responsibility suggests the ongoing conditional nature of trust. Karpel (1986) has noted that one family rule and potential resource existing in most families is the concept of respect and the inference that it is earned.

THERAPIST   (to Jim) I tie that back to your question in the beginning: "How do I know that it's not going to happen again, that things are going to change?" And I guess when I think about that in real concrete terms, I guess where I am with it is, if you see Robert interacting with your daughter (presently two years old) in the future and are uncomfortable with that, where are you going to be with Robert? Are you going to be able to say to Robert, "You're making me uncomfortable"? That's how I tie it all together.

Here the therapist rehearses and models parental protection of children.

* * * * *

TAMMY   Daddy can't say "no" to Robert. He can say "no" to me but not to Robert.

(Mr. Edwards disagrees.)

JIM   That's the way I feel. You can say "no" to me because of my views about what he did and not say "no" to him after what he did. I didn't do anything.

THERAPIST   Is it all right for people to be angry in this family?

MR. EDWARDS   Oh, yes. I can understand. I was angry, too.

JIM   The reason I didn't show any compassion was from the very first week, it was going to be covered up. He was going to go back into the pulpit. From the very first week — he would never have seen the hospital if it hadn't been pushed.

Here Jim challenges Mr. Edwards' decision to keep things secret.

* * * * *

JIM   (to Robert) One more question. At the time you went into Sandy [the niece], were you conscious of what was going on? Did you know what you were doing?

ROBERT   Basically.

JIM   So you made a conscious decision to do what you did? Or did you not know what you were doing?

ROBERT　No, I basically guess I knew what I was doing.

MR. EDWARDS　I know where you're coming from with that. I told you Robert didn't know *why* he did it and you interpreted it as Robert not knowing what he was doing. I still don't know why he did it and I don't think he does.

THERAPIST　I'd like for you [Robert and Jim] to continue right where you are and, Robert, I'd like you to speak for yourself.

JIM　Making a conscious decision, as far as I'm concerned . . . when I think of a sickness . . . ever since this started, I said I don't buy somebody being sick, because I know right from wrong.

THERAPIST　Are you arguing with Robert or with your Dad?

JIM　I don't know, with anybody who will listen.

THERAPIST　I think you need to talk to Robert about this and keep it clear whom you're talking to.

JIM　Well, at one time, I guess I did misunderstand that—I thought you had said that you didn't remember what happened—and what you said was you didn't know why. I can understand that. But you still made a conscious decision to do what you did to Sandy.

ROBERT　Yes and no. It just happened.

JIM　You couldn't stop yourself?

ROBERT　I really don't know. I guess if I could have, I would have.

JIM　That's my point. If you made a conscious decision to do something, and you could not stop yourself from doing it, then how can you stop yourself the next time? If something clicks to make you want to do something, what's going to stop you? Do you see what I'm saying?

ROBERT　I hear where you're coming from.

This interaction illustrates Jim's dilemma about responsibility: if a behavior is acknowledged to be conscious, then the person is taking responsibility but is also "wrong" or "bad." If a behavior is labeled as uncontrollable, then the person is "sick" but hard to control in the future. Although one would expect this focus on responsibility to emerge from someone in the ministry, neither Robert's district supervisor nor his father has posed it. Instead, both of them have rather readily interpreted Robert's behavior as a sickness. The tension arising from Jim's commitment to this stance is actually healthy and essential in maintaining expectations for appropriate behavior in the future.

JIM　Can you understand why I can't see . . . a lot of thoughts that have come to my mind or reasons for not trusting you have come from the very start where, right after this happened, you were going to be well enough to go back into the pulpit and I could not see it because of the respect and automatic trust I give to that position. I never had a chance to show any compassion because I was always trying to make Daddy understand that you could *not* get back into that position and if anybody ever did find out, they'd be after me for knowing and not telling if something else happened.

OUTCOME OF TREATMENT

The following observations were noted by this second family session. First, Robert seemed to be much more open, less defensive, and more willing to assume responsibility for the abuse in the face of continued questioning by family members. He also seemed more willing to acknowledge and grapple with the complexity of other family members' perceptions and expectations of him, particularly Jim's. Second, a history of abuse (or possible interpretations of sexual abuse) among the siblings when they were children was discussed. Third, the importance of open family conflict was stressed repeatedly and appeared to be endorsed by the family, in that very few issues were sidestepped or denied. Fourth, the loss of their mother's role as family peacemaker was acknowledged and could help pave the way for the additional issue of unresolved family grief. Fifth, several family members seemed to be beginning a process of conflict resolution with their father — this process reduced some of the conflict with Robert as he moved out of the role of family scapegoat. Furthermore, it left their legitimate confrontation of Robert untainted and separate from the previous issue of envy. Finally, family members seemed to be realistically grappling with the notion that the mental health profession *could not* provide 100% assurance that abuse could never happen again. This realization seemed important in empowering the family to assume responsibility for the protection of their own children and to reinforce the family dictum that future abusive behavior would not be tolerated.

On the other hand, much remained to be accomplished. It was still important to meet with the cousins not only to confirm the specifics of their interactions with Robert, but also to assess their perceptions of adult protectiveness and their comfort with going to their parents about any future sexual overtures by Robert or anyone else. Similarly, it was important to work with the adults to help them concretize 1. what "sexual abuse" means (especially given their experience with behaviors they could define as simply "sexual exploration") and 2. what they needed to do to assure adequate protection of the children in the family.

As a function of these observations, the recommendation was made that, with continued therapy (including the continued involvement of the extended family), there was a good prospect that Robert could be trusted in a parental role. However, the adoption agency was unwilling to extend the period of probation in order to allow for a better assessment of Robert's potential to act responsibly as an adoptive parent. Understandably, the adoption agency's reasoning was that this was not a typical situation of custody in which the risk of abuse to the child is weighed against the adverse effects to the child resulting from the permanent disruption to the home. Although the Edwards' infant had been in their home for five months, the question of bonding had to be countered with the question of whether *any* risk of abuse was justifiable for adoptive parents. Therefore, the adoption agency made the decision to remove the infant permanently from the home.

As soon as this decision was reached by the adoption agency (shortly following the second family session), Robert's animosity toward his siblings escalated rapidly and he refused to meet with them any further. It is obviously impossible to know whether sufficient resolution of conflict and continued confrontation of inappropriate behavior would have been achievable with more therapeutic contact.

At this point (several years after the termination of the case), Robert is no longer in the ministry and his father has remarried. Several months ago, Robert substituted for his father at a church service while his father was out of town. Upon hearing of this, one of Robert's sisters threatened to report him if he didn't turn in his credentials, which he thereupon did. There has been some level of resolution achieved between Robert and his younger brother. Tammy and Howard came to see me about a year ago to report that they had discovered that their 24 year old son had been sexually abusing his teenage sister for several years. (By the time they saw me, they had already reported this to the authorities and, although their son received treatment for drug abuse, he had refused with their consent any treatment for his abusive behavior.) All of this is to say that this was a very disturbed family and that conflict remains. On the other hand, resources did and do exist in the family (especially in the relationship between Robert and Jim) and perhaps, under other circumstances, could have been availed of further.

OBSTACLES TO TREATMENT

There are a number of factors that made working with this family particularly challenging. First, there was a potential for becoming entangled in the very same type of triangle between agencies and individuals that had created problems in the first place. On one hand, Robert's individual therapist was very gracious in allowing me to step in to make an evaluation for the adoption agency. On the other hand, when conflict between family members became intolerable, they exhibited a tendency to blame all of it upon this therapist. Although I personally believed that some of his decisions had unfortunate consequences, it was apparent that his decisions fit in well with the family's tendency to exploit any potential triangles. Therefore, it was essential in the family sessions to prevent the family from scapegoating the previous therapist.

A similar potential for triangulation existed between the therapist and the adoption agency. The adoption agency had become so distrustful of psychological intervention that there was a question for me of whether *any* recommendation or intervention with the Edwards family was to be given credence.

It was also important to clarify for Robert and the family exactly whom I represented — namely, the adoption agency in making a recommendation to them about the potential for further abuse. Since the agendas of family members differed radically with respect to the adoption, it was simultaneously necessary and challenging to establish the trust of different people who were in overt conflict with each other. Therefore, these sessions required a strong commitment to the concepts of neutrality and multipartiality (Gelinas, 1986), recognizing that the multipartiality included individuals and agencies not in the room.

With respect to the Edwards family itself, the main obstacle to treatment was the loyalty to the rigid rules of the original nuclear family. The denial and secrecy in the family were institutionalized by the patriarchal structure and the strong commitment to the appearance of decorum and religious values.

A final obstacle to treatment was the missing link provided by the deceased Mrs. Edwards. She appeared to be essential to the fragile peace which existed in the family and it is not unlikely that the conflict and secrets would not have surfaced on this occasion had she still been alive. Furthermore, the family had not been permitted to sufficiently grieve her absence and much of this was even literally attributed to Robert, since his presence at her funeral reportedly precluded several of the others from staying. Therefore, it was not clear whether what was being seen was actually a substantially different family organization from what had existed previously.

MISTAKES AND THERAPIST'S REACTIONS TO THE CASE

It is with respect to missed opportunities that my main reaction to this case is concerned. The other goals that I would have liked to have accomplished with this family (even working under the aegis of evaluation rather than therapy) would have required me to act sooner than I did to get the whole family involved. By the time I met Robert and his wife and certainly by the time I met his extended family, the level of conflict within the family and between the family and the adoption agency had escalated to a fevered pitch. Although there are advantages to working with families who are in crisis, decisions that were being made may have precluded the need for an evaluation.

With respect to different subsystems, it would have been useful to have arranged for a session just between the siblings (Robert, Susan, Tammy, Ellen and Jim) and perhaps just with Robert and his younger brother Jim. Much of the conflict between the siblings was exacerbated by their spouses (certainly Howard). In retrospect, this may have been due to Howard and Tammy's own need to find an outward focus for the problems existent within their own nuclear family. One way to mitigate the disruptive effect of the spouses while keeping them feeling left out would have been to have them observe the sibling subsystem interacting from behind a one-way mirror.

I also regretted that my cotherapist and I were not permitted to meet with the teenage cousins together. First of all, the cousins' report of Robert's actual behavior towards them was vital. Furthermore, it would have acknowledged to the family the primacy of the children and could possibly have strengthened the mutual support and protectiveness of this subsystem. It also would have been useful in exploring any other occurrences of sexual abuse. Unfortunately, the parents in the family remained adamant about not involving the children. In retrospect, this may in itself have been a prognostic sign about the adults' willingness to discuss the abuse openly and to provide adequate protection for their children. On the other hand, to the extent that they perceived me as primarily responsible for assessing Robert, they might have been more willing for a session with their children to be conducted by another therapist.

Several attempts were made to follow up with Mr. Edwards in an attempt to compensate for some of the centrality that he gave up in these sessions. He was left to grieve by himself for his wife and initially seemed amenable to our intervention on this issue, although he then missed several scheduled appointments.

Finally, in retrospect, it might have been useful to involve someone from the ministry in the work with this family. Although their religious values may have reinforced their need for a decorous appearance to outsiders, they were also an important resource in the family. This was demonstrated most vividly by Jim's stance. It is possible that this dilemma could have been strengthened even further by the participation of someone in the ministry.

In conclusion, this case has been presented to illustrate two primary points: first, structural problems (as evidenced by secrecy, triangulation, and indirect communication) abound in the sexually abusive family; second, these same strong forces necessitate an effort to work *with* the extended family rather than against it or in spite of it if long-term changes are to be maintained. It remains a goal and a challenge for family therapists to identify those forces and to turn them into resources. Through reference to certain therapeutic decisions, accomplishments, and missed opportunities, an attempt has been made in this chapter to demonstrate the importance of attending to the extended family in the treatment of intrafamilial sexual abuse.

12

Sibling Abuse in a Reconstituted Family: A Focal Family Therapy Approach

ARNON BENTOVIM   HARVEY RATNER

Practitioners in the United States are usually unaware of treatment programs for sexually abused children and their families in other countries. Dr. Bentovim and his team in London have worked in this area for some time and have an accomplished record. However, it is useful to draw contrasts between the typical management of sibling incest cases in the United States and the management of Drs. Bentovim and Ratner's case. As in the family described in Chapter 11, pathological dynamics are evident. While Alexander's case showed enmeshment, the combined family described here is characterized by numerous emotional cutoffs. Loyalty to each other and the incest taboo are absent.

The process of treatment outlined here is quite different from what is typical in the United States. In the U.S., Gabriel would probably have been referred to a program for adolescent sex offenders. That did not happen; rather, he was treated within the family context. Very little attention was given to his acts of sexual abuse in the family sessions. I believe he remained at risk for further offending as a result.

In addition, while American practitioners usually work with sibling offenders by combining individual offender theory and family dynamic theory, Dr. Bentovim's purely family systems approach considers almost exclusively the systemic complications and contributions to the abuse. However, until empirical data exist on adolescent offender treatment outcome, it is premature to argue relative efficacy of these different approaches. The authors now themselves favor the addition of group work to the family approach described here, to attend to the risks of further offending by boys such as Gabriel. — Editor

AUTHOR'S THEORETICAL ORIENTATION

This case is drawn from a series of sexual abuse cases treated using a specific family therapy approach: focal family therapy. All of the cases were referred to the Institute of Family Therapy, London. Therapists were supervised as a group in family therapy training run by Dr. Bentovim.

Simultaneously one of the authors (A.B.) was in the process of establishing the first comprehensive sexual abuse treatment service in the United Kingdom at The Hospitals for Sick Children, Great Ormond Street, London, in 1981. Family therapy theory and techniques formed the basis of the approach developed at the hospital. Groups for children and young people of various ages, nonabusive parents, abusive parents, couples, and caretakers were also established. Thus the comprehensive treatment approach linked family systems work with group work to reverse traumatic effects and help families to establish a caring context for their children or to establish them in a new family if required (Bentovim, Elton, Hildebrand, Tranter, & Vizard, 1988).

The work at the Institute of Family Therapy, London, differed in that cases were often self-referred, since the institute is a voluntary agency in comparison to the hospital. Being a statutory agency, the hospital required child protection actions to be taken as a precondition for referral.

Since the work was carried out by a training group, each case was treated using a standardized family therapy approach to test its effectiveness. Attention was paid to child protection issues, and no child was left in a context where re-abuse could occur. Statutory agencies were involved as appropriate. However, the approach was to see the whole family, as well as subsystems of the family, towards achieving a defined therapeutic goal.

The case to be discussed is one where a 16-year-old boy in a reconstituted family abused the nine-year-old daughter of his stepfather when she visited at weekends and holidays. There is a growing concern about the abusive behavior of young people of this age, since adolescence is now known to be a nodal point for the establishment of an inappropriate sexual orientation towards children. Reconstituted families appear to be clear risk situations, since young people are thrown together who do not have an established relationship.

Focal Approach to Family Treatment

The approach to treatment used was the focal approach. This has developed over a number of years (Bentovim & Kinston, 1991). The basic premises are as follows:

1. The approach is developmentally orientated and considers the health of the family in the context of its lifestyle within and across generations.
2. Therapy is explicitly offered, and the approach is oriented to any possible pathology in the family while not ignoring the family strengths.
3. The family is viewed as a system which has human beings as its components embedded in a social context. Thus, societal attitudes towards men, women and children are represented within the family and manifested through the personal histories of parents.
4. Traumatic events are regarded as the prime originator of disturbances that bring families to professional help. Traumatic events and stressful relationships, e.g., abusive activities, can occur in the family of origin or the current family, at an individual, family, or societal level. Such events are frequently associated with intense anxiety and helplessness. They frequently cannot be talked about and are represented by repetitive patterns of action that are dysfunctional, reflecting the feelings of helplessness. Once initiated, such actions can continue and be maintained contextually. They can restrict later development. Such patterns can include sexually abusive attitudes towards children.
5. We therefore hold that therapeutic work has to change such patterns of actions, as well as deal with the original traumatic experiences. In other words, the family has to both change its way of being and gain an understanding of how the dysfunction arose.

Central to the approach is the development of an approach to describing families and bringing together observations and information gathered during an assessment process. This results in the making of a focal hypothesis to explain pathological actions and relationships. A desired outcome for treatment is defined in systemic terms. Techniques of intervention and ways of creating therapeutic change are dictated not so much by a particular orientation but by what seems clinically relevant to achieve the goals to be defined. Many different interventions may be employed to achieve specific goals, including work with the whole family, subsystems, parents, siblings, and individuals, whether alone in one-to-one work or in group contexts.

Ethical views (Bentovim & Jacobs, 1988) would indicate that care must be taken of the least powerful, most dependent member of the family. It is not acceptable for any practitioner to believe that a child, in particular, can be sacrificed for the good of the rest of the family, especially the adults. Strengthening the individual to assist him or her to take a different role within the family, providing that family members can accept appropriate responsibility for what has gone wrong, is an important aim in working with sexual abuse.

Context for Work

The case to be described was treated directly by Mr. Ratner, one of a supervision group of four trainees, and supervised by Dr. Bentovim. The family was seen by a single therapist in front of a one-way screen, with telephone contact available. The therapist could take breaks during the session, either being called out by the supervisor or coming out spontaneously. A longer break was taken near the end to devise a specific intervention. The session was followed by a period of evaluation and planning.

In addition to utilizing the initial sessions to join with the family and initiate the therapeutic process, we gathered information to devise a hypothesis integrating what was known about the family. History was not explored in detail, but sufficiently to trigger responses that might be connected with presenting problems. As will be noted during the work with the case to be reported, a wide variety of therapeutic approaches was used.

DESCRIPTION OF CASE

Carla referred her family to the Institute of Family Therapy on the advice of her private individual therapist. She reported that both she and her husband Paul had been married before. The current family household consisted of herself, Paul, and her three sons by her first marriage, Gabriel, 16, Rafael 13, and Mauricio, 11. On alternate weekends Paul's children by his first marriage, James, 10, and Sandra, 9, would come to stay with their father and his new family (see genogram in Figure 1). A month before the referral, Sandra told her mother, Gina, that Gabriel was sexually abusing her: he had been going into her bed at night. It was not known how long the abuse had been going on. Carla also referred to problems with her other two boys, that Rafael was "bored all the time" and Mauricio was "very aggressive."

On contacting the family by telephone the therapist learned that Sandra's mother, Gina, had initially contacted Carla, telling her that Sandra said Gabriel had been cuddling her when he had no pants on and had come close to penetration. When Carla confronted Gabriel, he admitted it. Carla said that Gina was happy for Sandra to continue to come to her father's house if Carla could guarantee to supervise Gabriel; Paul had decided to take his children away for the weekends instead. So at the time of referral Gabriel had no contact with Sandra.

The therapist also learned that Carla and Paul had been married only

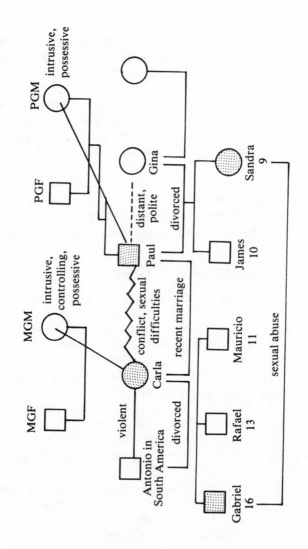

FIGURE 1. *Paul and Carla's family*

nine months, although they had lived together for some months previously. Carla reported said they were having marital difficulties, especially sexually, and both were seeing individual therapists. Carla said she had come to England from South America six years earlier and had had problems with her boys since then (for example, stealing). A child guidance clinic consultations had been helpful. Carla felt Paul cut himself off and used her as a baby-sitter for his children. Paul expressed confusion at what had happened and difficulty in believing it to be "real." However, he took the need for protection of Sandra very seriously. The family was invited to attend the institute. Paul was asked about inviting Gina but he said, after consultation with his therapist, that he did not want his ex-wife and family to attend. Gina subsequently wrote to the therapist indicating that she would be prepared to bring her daughter at a later date in order for her to be helped to lessen any sense of guilt or responsibility. Gina's feeling was that "the less that is made of this with respect to her, the better for her."

Psychological Assessment

No formal psychological assessment of any of the family members was performed.

Course of Therapy

The First Two Sessions: Assessment Phase

The first session was attended by Paul, Carla and her three sons. Gabriel admitted to touching Sandra only "once or twice" on her bottom and said that his penis had been exposed. Paul had not spoken to Sandra about this at all. The boys all said that they disliked Sandra, that she caused problems and fought a lot with James. There was much discussion in the session around the boys' missing their own father and Paul's distant role in the family. Paul clearly felt unable to discipline the boys, and he accused Carla of giving Gabriel money to go out with girls. He said that Gabriel had committed the abuse as an act of revenge on him. Paul said he enjoyed his country weekends away with his own children. Despite all this, there was some evidence in the session of cohesiveness in the family, for example, the ability to share a joke.

Another remarkable feature had to do with language; while Carla (whose basic language was Spanish) was having difficulties understanding some of what was said, Paul frequently used abstract and vague language that she could not follow. Cultural issues as such were not explored. It was clear that Carla was unsure about how to deal with Gabriel; she referred to her and her husband's different expectations of parenting, that his tended to be freer, hers more "structured."

In the final intervention, as a way of joining with the family, we used Paul's description of himself as "confused" as a description of the family as a whole, as it grappled with "new family" issues and adjustments to English society. Gabriel's act of revenge on Paul was linked to his longings for his own father so far away, but framed as a challenge to Paul to be drawn more into this family. Confusion extended to boundaries and what behavior was appropriate and therefore created a context in which sexual abuse could both occur and be kept secret. It was not safe for Sandra to come to the house. It was, therefore, imperative that the police and Social Services be informed. Either Sandra's parents could make a formal complaint or Carla could invite the Youth and Community Section Police to talk to Gabriel, to help Carla get the "rules" right. Carla's responses to the question of police involvement was to say that she would prefer to get divorced.

We added that it would be necessary to see Sandra and James at some point, to work on issues of guilt and responsibility, and to see Gabriel and Sandra together. We asked to see Paul, his ex-wife, and their two children at the next session. Only at the end of the session did Carla refer to the fact that Gina had been considering sending Sandra to live with Paul.

Between the first and second sessions the therapist had contact with Gina, who felt it was too early for Sandra to be seen. Police and Social Services were contacted, interviewed the family and subsequently held a case conference at which they decided not to put Sandra's name on the Child Protection Register. The therapist was informed that this decision had been reached, as it was felt the family had taken adequate steps to protect her from the risk of further abuse.

The second session was attended by Paul, Carla, Gabriel, and Rafael. It transpired that Gina had refused permission for the police to interview Sandra, but a social worker had met the family. Carla had spoken to the Youth and Community Section. Sandra continued to be protected by the family agreement that she and James did not come to Paul's house, but he took them away alternate weekends. Asked about how things were at home, the family described a pattern of Carla arguing with everyone and the boys and Paul therefore retreating to their rooms, except Mauricio, who "smashes things."

These references to expressions of anger and to closeness and distance led us to an exploration of historical issues, in accordance with focal family therapy's aim of relating past issues to current functioning. To begin with, a structural move was made, moving family members around so that Gabriel could talk to Rafael about how life had been for their family back in

South America, as Gabriel, the eldest, would remember it best. Gabriel proceeded to describe massive arguments between their parents over petty issues; he said their father began drinking, but there hadn't been any violence. Rafael spontaneously related this to the similar situation he thought he saw between Paul and Carla, and Paul confirmed this.

Carla was encouraged to talk about what she had seen in Paul's first marriage. (Carla had been friendly with the family through her sister Ursula, whose daughter Rebecca was very friendly with Sandra.) She described a set of polite relationships, so distant that Gina's lesbian partner had had to tell Paul that his marriage was at an end. Although this portrayed Paul as a quiet, calm person, Carla insisted that she saw a fiery side in Paul, not unlike that of her first husband. Paul agreed that Carla was the opposite of Gina.

There was then a discussion of their families of origin. Paul said that he had been jinxed by his intrusive, possessive mother and that in marrying Gina he had aimed for as completely an opposite person as he could find. As for Carla's parents, he talked about the dependence of Carla's father on her mother, which Carla confirmed.

The information we gathered from this discussion enabled us to talk to the family in the final intervention about how the confusion of the present family with regard to the marital relationship and parenting issues was compounded by efforts "not to repeat the mistakes of the past." We said that in this context Gabriel's abuse of Sandra and Mauricio's difficult behavior were perhaps their unconscious attempts to create a crisis that would force Paul and Carla to resolve their differences rather than split apart. The whole situation would take a long time to sort out.

Creating a Focal Hypothesis

From the initial information obtained from the total family complex, we can construct a focal hypothesis, even though this needs to be modified with further information. There are a number basic steps to the creation of a focal hypothesis:

- How is the symptom connected to the general interaction of the family?
- Can this symptom be restated in a family interactional form or as an expression of family meaning?

In this case one first of all had to consider the sexually abusive pattern between Sandra and Gabriel. It could be speculated that the abusive actions were taken to "unite" the two families, i.e. Gabriel's mother and Sandra's father. It may alternatively have been a means of reducing a degree of competitiveness between Gabriel, the oldest, near-adult son, and Paul, a new man in a sexual relationship with his mother. Perhaps Gabriel, confronted by his mother's new marriage, abused his stepsister as a way of acting out his own sexuality. His abuse was a way of appearing to accept his stepsister through his sexual interest in her, yet of retaliating and expressing resentment and grievance against his mother and/or Paul through his abusive actions, which clearly took on an addictive character.

Sandra's secrecy may have been connected with both the oppressive threats and control by Gabriel and also her fear of matters going wrong in her father's new family. She may also be accustomed to a rule of secrecy as a response to the atmosphere created by her mother's previously secret lesbian relationship.

What is important for the hypothesis is to make sense of why secrets were broken at the time they were. On the one hand, there was the threat, as we learned subsequently, that Sandra's mother was thinking of sending her to live with her father and his new family. At the same time Paul and Carla, who had married relatively recently, were becoming increasingly conflictual in their own relationship. Paul was withdrawing further from Carla when Sandra revealed the abuse. Gabriel could also be involved in a conflict of loyalty, being opposed to Paul's being a part of the family but recognizing Carla's wanting him and her need to become settled in England. Once the abuse was revealed it had the effect of increasing Paul's involvement with Carla because of a need to create protective childcare arrangements. Carla took greater notice of Gabriel and Paul became very concerned for Sandra. Through the painfulness of the situation they became united.

The revelation of sexual abuse meant that professionals were drawn into the family. This included the Institute of Family Therapy, as a potentially effective "distance regulator" for a family registering a sense of failure and need for help. Breaking the taboo of silence, therefore, may well have occurred at a point when the strains of the remarriage for the parents were considerable and the fears for Sandra very real. Revealing the fact of abuse produced the effect of putting the adults in touch with parenting responsibilities and concerns.

Next we ask:

- What is the function of the current interaction?
- What would happen if the current interaction were not present?

The therapist has to infer from a variety of clues what the interactional consequences to the family would be if the current interaction were not present, that is, what might have happened if the fact of the abuse had remained secret and the pattern of family life continued in the way that it had been previously. It seems likely that, as Paul and Carla would have become increasingly concerned with their own marital differences, i.e., sexual problems requiring individual therapy, there would have been an increasing amount of conflict between them. There might have been violence. Paul might have withdrawn further and further from Carla, who thus would become more isolated in a foreign country. Sandra would have become increasingly distressed and confused, and would have developed various post-traumatic symptoms, adding to the strain on Paul and Carla's marriage.

Still in pursuit of a focal hypothesis, we ask:

- What is the disaster feared by the family that maintains current interaction?

Quite clearly, the interactional consequences described above present as a dangerous situation for family members. Sandra revealed abuse to her mother after she had watched a child protection program on the television. Yet, clearly it was at a time of increasing stress in the family. It could be hypothesized, therefore, that it was the unconscious realization and awareness of danger that triggered her telling.

The feared disaster appeared most likely to have been a universal fear of separation and marital breakdown. Paul would feel alone and a failure, both in his second marriage and especially sexually. Carla would have been faced with the failure of a second marriage and her attempt to integrate into English society. The boys would have faced the loss of a potential second parent, Gabriel would have been drawn back to his father in South America, Rafael would have become more withdrawn, and Mauricio would have become more disruptive and uncontrollable. Sandra and James were in danger of losing their only father figure.

To attribute an awareness of such feared disaster to Sandra, which would then lead her to speak about abuse as a way of drawing attention to these issues, is difficult to demonstrate; however, such awareness is a frequent factor leading to disclosure of abuse. It should be noted that the parents had already been going to individual treatment for their own sexual problems. In other words, the fear of failure in this second relationship was already staring them in the face. When the facts of abuse were revealed, an additional failure had to be faced, resulting in the parents' bringing in a family agency to help them.

Our final question is:

- Is there a plausible link from current events to original traumatic events and stressful experiences?

It is necessary to make a plausible link between the above steps and salient traumatic events and stressful experiences in the past life of the parents as individuals in their families of origin and in each of the families they formed before they came together. Both had considerable experience of failure, mother having to leave her first husband because of his arguing and drinking and father having been confronted with his first wife's lesbian relationship and the subsequent dissolution of his marriage. Therefore, both parents have in their history experiences of failure and loss that they would not wish to repeat. There was no significant history of sexual abuse revealed.

In addition, both parents were particularly sensitive about the issue of control. This seemed to linked to their sexual problems and fear of violence, leading to the understandable and considerable response to Gabriel's sexually abusive behavior. Both parents were particularly sensitive about the other's control of them. Each parent's sense of helplessness seemed linked to his or her experience of an intrusive, controlling mother. Both therefore felt very vulnerable to either feeling out of control or being in control, leading to conflict between them about who was to control and be controlled.

Intrusive parents are identified with, or the helpless role is perpetuated. It may well be that these models enacted by the parents, reacting against their former marriages, are acted out by themselves and their children.

Each of the parents had dealt with control issues from the family of origin differently. Paul had initially married a woman, Gina, whom he perceived to be more distant; then he married one he saw as more emotional, Carla. It is a common observation that a first marriage often attempts to reverse what is perceived as the traumatic and feared disaster of the parental relationship, e.g., a more distant partner is substituted for an intrusive mother. Perhaps later, with more maturity, it becomes possible to take on the more emotional, and perhaps more intrusive, woman, with a feeling that such an issue can be faced and dealt with. Fears are inevitably aroused that the new partner will be as controlling as the parent, and ordinary demands may be perceived as attempts to control.

Carla had initially sought a far more controlling husband, perhaps unconsciously reversing the helplessness of her own father, but she clearly found his violence and control oppressive. She then recreated her own family of origin script by marrying a man, Paul, who appeared more distant, but who would, she now feared, repeat the process out of his own sense of frustration with her.

Bentovim and Kinston (1991) have pointed out the shared and disparate beliefs and meanings that can trigger conflict when parents create a second family. In this family some issues were held in common, e.g., both parents had controlling, possessive, and intrusive mothers; some were different, so that fathers could be passive/distant/dependent or violent/controlling. These spouses also brought their previous attempts to deal with these early relationships to their new marriage, as well as their expectations of partners. Bentovim and Kinston (1991) have described such patterns in terms of the enactment or the reversal of previous ways of dealing with stressful relationships. Byng-Hall (1989) described such responses in terms of replicative or corrective scripts. The children become inducted into the meaning systems or scripts in various ways. Gabriel seemed to model himself after and recreate his father's controlling, violent patterns of behavior. Yet, he, Rafael and Mauricio, perhaps in reacting to the traumatic loss of their father, were also seeking the consistency of a new parent and had hoped that their stepfather could provide a different model.

Summary of Focal Hypothesis

In this case we hypothesized that maintaining secrecy about abusive behavior preserves the fragile togetherness of marital relationships. Revealing abuse then brings in professional caretakers and draws the parents' attention from their marital and sexual difficulties to a need to develop a collaborative parenting approach, which means resolving issues of control, violence, and possessiveness. There is a fear that facing such issues will result in marital breakdown and losses, which have characterized both parents' previous marriages.

Changes to be Achieved with Therapeutic Work

For therapeutic work to be successful, the following concrete changes need to occur. Paul and Carla should be able to make appropriate childcare arrangements, whereby Carla helps Paul to develop appropriate relationships with his stepsons. Paul has to resolve, between Carla and Gina, his contact with his own children, so that they are protected from the possibility of further abuse. Gabriel has to take full responsibility for abusing Sandra and to work on his abusive pattern. Sandra must be enabled to talk through her experiences, to understand that she is in no way to blame, and to resolve her traumatic responses. Paul and Carla will have to resolve their marital difficulties, especially their respective fears about being violently controlled.

Family Sculpting

At the start of the third session the family reported that things had been quiet and that Mauricio had become upset when Paul went off for a weekend with his own children. The family members were asked to sculpt themselves as they saw themselves now and in five years' time. Sculpting is the use of nonverbal methods to represent patterns of relationship (Byng-Hall 1982). Each family member demonstrates the patterns of closeness and distance and the shape of relationships both now and as imagined for the future. A future sculpt can be a powerful way of creating emotional intensity in a session, especially for a family with communication difficulties.

The family members acknowledged the impact of the various sculpts, as they revealed distances and splits. Paul referred to the "two systems" he was in, saying that he wanted to keep the first, his two children, as far away as possible. The boys, meanwhile, saw Sandra and James as a part of their family. In a very moving moment, Gabriel demonstrated how difficult it was to "face three ways at once": toward his real father, toward his mother, and toward Paul. The therapist pointed out how each person tended to line his or her family sculpture up as a parade in front of the therapist, as if the therapist was being incorporated as a crucial member of the system, and he provocatively asked if the family needed a "therapist, social worker, policeman, whoever." Mother, in particular, acknowledged the problem, saying "the family is very complicated."

Attention was drawn to the fact that while mother was close to her boys, they were thinking of their father. This was reframed as helpful: by "bringing in" their father, the boys helped their mother remember how violent men can be, so that she thereby maintained her distance from Paul, who in turn feared being "jinxed" by an overly close woman.

Creation of a Therapeutic Metaphor

In the final intervention, some of the ideas of the previous session regarding the confusion of boundaries in the new family were repeated, with added emphasis this time on the reframing concerning the role of the boys' own father in keeping Paul and Carla separate. The previous notion of the sexual abuse disclosure as creating a crisis to push the parents to resolve their problems was expanded into a metaphor of a "fire-break." This metaphor was devised with the deliberate aim of connecting with the cultural background of Carla and her children. They were told that in some rural areas where people have homes near forests there is a fear of fire, and these people seek to protect themselves with a fire-break; they burn the area around their homes so that the real fire will not reach them. In other words, a "small" disaster is created to avoid a greater one of major destructive power. The family immediately took to this image. The parents were told that the boys needed to be convinced by them that there was no need for the boys to seek to regulate closeness and distance between the spouses.

Meeting with the Parents

At the fourth session, two weeks later, the therapist met with Paul and Gina. Gina had decided to participate in therapy after all because she was concerned about the symptoms of "nervousness" that Sandra was developing, e.g., tearing up paper, stomachaches. She accepted our earlier argument that it would help Sandra if Gabriel accepted responsibility for what had happened, but she requested a prior meeting in order to discuss the course therapy was expected to take.

In the session Gina said that Sandra was unhappy about the continued separation of the two families; also, Carla's sister Ursula had stopped letting her daughter Rebecca see Sandra. The therapist questioned Gina as to whether Paul kept the children separate in order to protect Sandra or to keep his two "systems" separate. She said that it had begun as the former but then became something Paul and Sandra shared; Paul said he wanted to keep his children separate from Carla because he did not approve of her child-rearing ideas.

As a final intervention, the therapist suggested that Paul wanted to keep Sandra separate from Carla because Gina would not approve of Carla's methods of disciplining Sandra and would therefore prevent access. As regards Sandra herself, the parents were in a bind, as the continued separation could only encourage the girl to feel she was in some way responsible for the abuse, while the parents continued to tell her it wasn't her fault. The therapist asked how long the separation could continue. He proposed that it would be better to "bring it out in the open" sooner rather than later. The parents then agreed to a meeting between Gabriel and Sandra.

Exploration of Parental Styles

At the fifth session, two weeks later, we again saw Paul, Carla and her boys. Although all family members reported that there were fewer arguments between Paul and Carla and that Paul was more involved as a father to the boys (Carla went so far as to say "our family is better now"), there were still issues being raised as to acceptable levels of emotion. Paul, for example, referred to an incident in the last two weeks in which Mauricio had ended up with "half his bedroom in the garden," by which, it turned out, he actually meant a couple of items of clothing. Carla blamed Paul for overreacting. The therapist chose to refer to Paul's learning from Carla "how to go over the top," as they usually reported that it was Carla who overreacted, while Carla spoke of her fear that Paul might one day really explode and be more dangerous than the boys' real father. This directly confronts the fear that "emotion" will take over and the need to be able to own one's "opposite" denied aspects.

While Paul and Carla were preparing a family trip to South America, where Carla would see her parents and the boys would spend time with their father, there were further discussions comparing Carla's two husbands. Carla said that her husband had been furious that she had remarried, accusing her of taking the children away from him. Rafael said his father would not believe that Carla could allow Paul to have some control over her boys. His father would believe that Carla had become "depressed and unhappy." The therapist was able to suggest, therefore, that, although Paul felt Carla was "letting him in more" as stepfather to the boys, it was good for the ex-husband that the two families (Paul's and Carla's) were not properly joined. The therapist took advantage of Carla's slip of the tongue in referring to her ex-husband as her "new" husband to say that there was indeed an issue around newness in this family: could Paul be a new husband to her, or would all men be the same? Even Gabriel was behaving abusively. It remained for Carla to decide whether Paul could be different from her ex-husband or whether she would have to "rescue" her boys from Paul as she did from her former husband.

Apology Session and Exploration of Abuse

The sixth session, three weeks later, was the critical one. The therapist began by interviewing Paul, Gina, Sandra and James, in preparation for the "apology session" with Gabriel and his mother, who arrived later on. The purpose of this was explained as enabling Sandra to understand that what Gabriel did to her was not her fault, and she was therefore not to blame for the subsequent separation of her and James from Carla's family.

As this was the first meeting with Sandra and her parents, it was important to go over the exact details of what had happened in the abuse. Paul was shocked to hear that the abuse, instead of being a recent occurrence, had in fact been going on for over a year, and, while he thought there had been nine incidents of abuse, Sandra said it had happened 30 times. A lot of the abuse had occurred in the daytime when Mauricio was watching TV and Paul and Carla had gone out. When it came to the actual details of the abuse, Sandra said that Gabriel would pull down his trousers, but she had not seen his body because he had come under her bedcovers. He had told her to drink his "wee" and had offered her sweets and money each time, and she once took 50p. She wouldn't say anything more. She was crying throughout this interview. Her mother explained that what she had learned so far was that Gabriel had attempted vaginal penetration but hadn't succeeded, but there had been fellatio. Sandra had revealed the abuse while watching a "Kidscape" sexual abuse program with her mother; she said she hadn't told her father about it in case he got angry with Gabriel. Paul cried, blaming himself for allowing the abuse to continue for so long; Sandra asked him not to cry and comforted him.

Following some discussion about how Sandra could continue to be protected in future, Gabriel and his mother came into the session and Gabriel was asked to speak openly about the details of the abuse. He admitted to "15 to 20" occasions of abuse. He said he didn't know why he had done it, but referred to his "pleasure" in getting her to touch his penis, and said of the fellatio that "I thought that was what was supposed to happen." He denied penetration and added that he thought James knew what was going on, which James denied. Gabriel took full responsibility for what happened and, at the therapist's urging, apologized to every person in the room. It seemed to the therapist that this necessitated considerable effort and pain on Gabriel's part; there was not the least suggestion that he was going through the motions or acting a part. His mother and Sandra were in tears. There was a sense of ceremony about this; it was an intense, moving occasion. Gina stayed behind after the session, wanting to talk further. She felt the session had been very helpful, but she refused the offer of further family therapy and said instead she would follow the social worker's suggestion of having Sandra seen individually at a child guidance clinic.

OUTCOME OF TREATMENT

Follow-up Session Review

The seventh and final session took place three months later, after the family had had its extended holiday in South America. Carla said she believed that the boys appreciated Paul more since the trip; Rafael and Mauricio did not refer to their time there as pleasurable. Indeed, Mauricio appeared to have been confused by it all and mentioned a fight with his father, while Gabriel was at pains to defend his father.

Paul was more positive in this session than he had ever been before. Despite Gabriel's expressed attachment to his father, Paul said he wanted the family members to discuss things together, including Gabriel's future educational plans.

Carla reported that Gina had stated that she is now happy to have Sandra and James resuming visits to the family, but Paul firmly put forth his view that the family needed to be closer and stronger before he would allow it.

In the final intervention, the therapist stressed that the family appeared to be engaged in "ordinary" stepparent problems. The spouses held out hope for each other in resolving past mistakes and assuaging fears. A good deal of time was needed to resolve these matters. Therefore, Paul's decision not to let Sandra and James back was right, and it was helpful to Carla and her sons to know that it was his decision, not a response to pressure from Gina. It was suggested that the family could contact the institute if further consultation was needed, but not for at least three months.

At the end, Gabriel made an emotional plea. He sounded in pain as he said that he wanted to be closer to his natural father, while he felt the other four (i.e., Paul, Carla, Rafael and Mauricio) were "going away." Carla said Paul's integration into the family was a threat to Gabriel. The therapist sympathized with Gabriel's situation, explaining to him that he was dealing with the painful situation of all children whose parents get divorced. He went on to say that Rafael and Mauricio needed a father now and Gabriel could also benefit from Paul's knowledge and experience of the world to help in his own career. When the problems of split families are not resolved, someone gets hurt, as he had hurt Sandra. In retrospect, we thought that perhaps he was also indicating that he needed help in his own right.

Follow-up at One Year

The therapist spoke to Carla and Paul and discovered there was still no contact between Gabriel and Sandra. Paul felt disappointed that Gina had stopped Sandra from going to therapy when Sandra became upset; he felt that Sandra was still affected. They reported increased marital satisfaction for themselves and better family relationships, with Paul having developed an improved stepfather role to the boys. Gabriel had a French girlfriend.

Three-Year Follow-Up

This occurred through a chance meeting between Carla and the therapist. She reported that there was virtually no contact between Gabriel and Sandra, apart from a chance encounter in church. Carla reported that Sandra had greeted and smiled at each of the boys, including Gabriel. Gabriel by this time was attending university; he still had the same girlfriend. Mauricio was doing well in a boarding school. Carla reported that Gina and Sandra did not get along and that there was some doubt about whether any further therapeutic help had been given. She had learned, however, that Gina herself had been sexually abused in childhood. She also reported that James was becoming a very difficult adolescent, part of a delinquent gang and in danger of being expelled from school. He was also involved in acts of vandalism on trains. She reported a continuing good relationship with Paul.

Obstacles to Treatment

There were no major obstacles to treatment as far as Paul, Carla, and her children were concerned. Although there were some meetings with Gina, Sandra, and Paul, there was resistance from Gina about the possibility of Sandra's needing treatment. Because the family was being treated in a family therapy agency, specific treatment for Sandra and Gabriel was not offered. Consequently, Sandra was seen at a child guidance clinic. Unfortunately, when that broke down because there was no contract for work between Sandra, her mother, and the clinic, it meant that any work between Paul and his children could not be supervised or coordinated by the treatment team. The follow-up work, although limited, appears to indicate a great deal of disturbance between Gina and her children. The positive relationship between Paul and his children did not appear to be sufficient to outweigh the failure in dealing with Sandra's own treatment needs and James' confusions.

OTHER SYSTEMS INVOLVED

Agency Issues

As has been mentioned, the parents were asked to make contact with the police. Had they not done this, it would have been the therapist's responsibility to have done so. The family's arrangements to protect Sandra seemed to us to be adequate, but we could not pretend to be the only judges of that.

During the course of treatment two case conferences were held at the local Social Services Department. The therapist worked closely with the police, the social services area manager, and the social worker, although he was unable to attend the case conferences. The conferences did not place Sandra's name on the Child Protection Register; the social worker who interviewed Sandra felt that the family's protective arrangements were adequate as long as therapeutic work continued at the institute.

Changes in our treatment approach since our work with this family include a greater focus on therapy for individuals, in addition to family work. We would now see the children along as a first step to establish the degree of abuse and the extent of abusive behavior. The extent of abusive behavior revealed by Gabriel appeared addictive in quality and a long-standing source of arousal. Although one could hypothesize that he identified with his violent, abusive father and had become aroused to his stepsister in the context of a new family, we did not establish his abusive cycle and arousal pattern in sufficient detail. Now we would suggest group work to help him deal with these issues and understand his use of power and threat to silence Sandra, as well as the traumatic nature of his behavior. He did make a start through his important apologizing session, but this work needed to be extended.

Sandra was already revealing post-traumatic symptomatology. Unfortunately, her mother withdrew her from individual treatment when she became distressed at sessions. This failure is of very great concern, since it is only too common for such a traumatic pattern to recur in a variety of ways: for instance, restriction of life plans, problems in future sexual relationships, and inability to relate to peers, both girls and boys. There may be traumatic sexualization, betrayal, powerlessness, or a sense of stigma.

We do not know whether involving the criminal justice and childcare system would have improved treatment for both Gabriel and Sandra. In our growing experience, the firmer the connection between statutory agencies and therapeutic agencies, the more likely it is that the therapeutic agency will be able to deliver effective treatment services to individuals and family members.

The fact that Paul was determined to maintain the distance between Sandra and Gabriel was protective to her. However, this did bring about a traumatic separation within the original family unit. This could have been beneficial if therapeutic work had been done in a thorough enough way; however, in this case separation was the only protective mode.

There is a very real issue here about the role of a family therapy agency in working with sexual abuse. It would have been far better if there been a somewhat stronger child protection or criminal action here, as well as the coordination of the family therapy with specific treatment for the children.

THERAPIST'S REACTIONS TO THE CASE

Although the therapeutic work in this case was not ideal as far as meeting the needs of the abused child and the abusing young person for specific help, it did reveal the way in which a focal family therapy approach could help a therapist make a helpful assessment of the family problems and put sexually abusive behavior in context. It was a positive experience for the team to be able to apply appropriate techniques to create new meanings and different relationships. In the process we learned that family-systems-based interventions can have a powerful effect on relationships. Nevertheless, traumatic events occur at a very individual level. While other family members can assist and support individuals with traumatic reactions, those individuals do need specific help with their peers to overcome the traumatic responses associated with long-standing abuse.

13

Therapy With a Sexually Aggressive Young Boy

WILLIAM N. FRIEDRICH

Therapy with sexually aggressive children is usually very frustrating. This case and that of Dr. Johnson (Chapter 14) clearly illustrate the fact. More so than the typical family of a sexually abused child, the families of sexually abused and sexually aggressive children are compromised in all areas of parenting. As a result, I have worked with only a few sexually aggressive young boys and their families where I truly felt success at the time of termination. The most common outcome was a premature termination of therapy with little initial resolution of any of the large number of presenting issues, including parental chemical dependency, parental histories of victimization, physical abuse, and poverty. All of these issues were present over and above the child's victim/victimizing status.

The few success stories I have had were characterized by my awareness that, although therapy later on in life was necessary, during our time together the family was motivated to persist in therapy and important treatment issues were resolved, at least initially. I wrote this case to show that therapy can be successful, although the more typical course of psychotherapy with sexually aggressive young children is marked by pitfalls, premature termination, and wranglings with legal and social service delivery systems.

This case, however, also underlies the importance of resilience in children. For several reasons, Bobby and his mother were able to focus on the therapy and make appropriate changes. A key to their success was that Bobby's mother hadn't been physically abusive to him. She certainly was not very available emotionally, but she wasn't shaming of him or completely negative towards him.

Another treatment issue that is underscored is the importance of disclosure. Sexual aggression is driven not only by learned sexual behavior but also by unresolved sexual abuse. When disclosure of Bobby's victimization occurred we turned an important corner in treatment. —Editor

AUTHOR'S THEORETICAL ORIENTATION

The sexually abused child is a developing organism within a larger family system. Abuse at one phase of development, if unresolved, carries with it the potential for creating new problems at other stages of development. Thus, a child sexually abused as a preschooler may begin to sexualize interpersonal relationships as peers become more important in early elementary school.

The sexual abuse of a child, particularly incestuous abuse, represents betrayal of a relationship and a disconnection in attachment. Often, disrupted attachment precedes the abuse and makes the child more vulnerable to abuse (Friedrich, 1990). The parent-child attachment is the paradigm for social development, along with its attendant outcomes, including social skills, the capacity for empathy, and the capacity for self-observation. When these basic attachment relationships are disrupted, the child has a significantly higher risk for psychological disorder. When sexual abuse is added to disrupted attachment, the likelihood of significant psychological problems is greatly increased.

To the extent that abuse at an earlier age is unresolved, the child organizes his/her internal thinking and interpersonal relationships around the traumatic experience. The world increasingly becomes viewed as a dangerous place in which victimization and victimizing are the norm.

The child and the child's system may carry within themselves the potential for adaptive coping and a more positive outcome. Certain child factors, including intellectual abilities, verbal expressiveness, and social skills, are critical to success in therapy, as are supportive parent-child relationships and the absence of a sexual abuse history in the parent. Psychotherapy works best when it maximizes these coping resources in the context of a therapeutic relationship that facilitates two very important processes: a high regard and valuing of the individuals involved, and appropriate maturity demands, which create an expectation for change and promote evolution to a more positive and appropriate way of functioning.

Recent research on sexually aggressive young children indicates that their sexual abuse experiences have been more severe than the average, that disruption in parent-child relationships is routine and that there is a greater likelihood of these children's having witnessed significant aggressive interaction between caregivers (Friedrich & Luecke, 1988; Johnson, 1988). Sexually aggressive young children are also quite likely to have been physically abused.

DESCRIPTION OF CASE

Bobby was nine years old at the time his mother was urged to contact me by the school principal and Bobby's fourth grade teacher. He was the only child of Betty, age 39, and was the product of a long-term affair that Betty had had with a former employer. Although Bobby's father was aware of his existence, he provided neither emotional nor financial support.

Bobby was referred primarily because of aggression towards his agemates and younger children in the school. He was particularly sadistic in his behavior, frightening kindergartners repeatedly; his tying up of a five-year-old, mildly retarded kindergartner was the direct precipitant of the referral. He stole from children in his classroom, and the previous year had twice been caught smashing the lunches of children while he was alone in the hall.

He was reported by his mother to have no friends. The quality of their relationship at my first interview, which was conjoint, was marked by a constant, quiet struggle between the two of them, with Bobby becoming increasingly verbally abusive of her as Betty talked about his numerous behavior problems to me.

Betty was the older of two girls born to her mother. Her father was an itinerant minister who never married her mother but was also presumed to be the father of her younger sister. She and her mother did not have a close relationship, and Betty frequently was the primary caregiver in the family, given her mother's recurrent depression and her younger sister's seizure disorder. She had graduated as the valedictorian of her high school class and had completed four years of college, with a major in library science. Betty had worked as a reference librarian since her graduation. She had no regular contact with her younger sister, and her mother had died three years earlier. Betty reported no close friends, had not been involved with a man for several years, and admitted to increasing problems with binge drinking. She had recently experienced her first blackout.

When queried about sexual abuse in an early individual interview, Betty, in a very unemotional manner, described rather clinically that she had been molested over a four-year period between the ages of 8 and 12 by her father on his infrequent visits to her mother. Molestation began with genital fondling and moved to digital penetration, oral copulation, and mutual masturbation. Betty had never obtained therapy for either the abuse or her drinking problem, which she also blandly acknowledged as "pre-alcoholic."

Bobby was a moderately overweight boy appearing his stated age. He became extremely angry with his mother, attempting three times, twice successfully, to punch her on the chest and shoulder when she informed me in our first session about his molestation, between the ages of five and seven, by a single man, John, who lived in their apartment building. Bobby had reported the abuse to her after the man had moved out. A medical examination and interview of Bobby when he was seven years old had determined that he had been sodomized on a number of occasions and forced to commit fellatio. Although this abuse had been reported, and some effort had been made to locate Bobby's abuser, there had been no trial as of the date that they were first seen. Bobby had not received any therapy for the abuse, other than a brief group experience with a primary focus on safety.

Although Betty stated that Bobby "is all I have," their relationship was extremely negative and highly ambivalent. She stated that she had difficulty managing his behavior around the home, that he was physically aggressive with her on a frequent basis, and that at times he behaved in a sexually inappropriate manner with her, e.g., spying on her in the bathroom, opening the shower door, grabbing her breasts, and lifting up her nightgown. She was unaware of Bobby's having been sexually aggressive with any children. Her only positive comment about Bobby was that he was intelligent and apparently was doing reasonably well academically in school.

PSYCHOLOGICAL ASSESSMENT MATERIAL

After the initial appointment, Betty completed an MMPI, which I obtain from the parents of all children who see me for therapy. In addition, an extra three hour evaluation appointment was scheduled for Bobby and myself, where I completed the Wechsler Intelligence Scale for Children-Revised, selected academic achievement subtests from the Woodcock-Johnson Psycho-Educational Test Battery, the Rorschach, the TAT, and Human Figure Drawings, including the Draw-A-Person and Kinetic Family Drawing. Betty also completed an Achenbach Child Behavior Checklist (Achenbach & Edelbrock, 1983) on Bobby, and a teacher report form of the Achenbach was obtained from Bobby's fourth grade teacher.

Betty's MMPI profile was significantly elevated and suggested a depressed and anxious woman who was alienated both from herself and other people. Her capacity for affection and empathy appeared limited. However, she did not appear overtly angry and appeared to have a moderate level of emotional resilience. Her response to the McAndrews, an MMPI-based alcoholism screening measure, indicated a very high likelihood of alcoholism.

Bobby had never been tested at school since he had not been an academic problem. He obtained a WISC-R Verbal IQ of 127, a Performance IQ of 121, and a Full-Scale WISC-R IQ of 125. These scores are in the superior range and above the 92nd percentile. His scores on the math and reading clusters from the Woodcock-Johnson were at a similar level, 124 and 119, respectively, and suggested that he was one-and-a-half to two years more advanced academically than his current grade placement. This suggested that, despite his earlier abuse, he was able to focus on school and achieve at the predicted level, a finding not characteristic of sexually abused children (Einbender & Friedrich, 1989).

His Human Figure Drawings were of extremely small figures, and his Kinetic Family Drawing captured most accurately his perception of his relationship with his mother. He drew his mother sitting on a sofa "reading, she is always reading," flipped the page over, and then drew a picture of himself "watching TV." The fact that he and his mother were not on the same side of the paper suggests the estrangement that existed between them.

His Rorschach was remarkable for the degree of oppositionality it suggested in a young boy who was extremely anxious and depressed and whose self-perception was quite negative. Although no sexual content was noted, considerable aggressive content was indicated. This may sound paradoxical, but the depression evident on the Rorschach was encouraging to me, in that it suggested a boy who was not yet as hardened to life as he had every reason to be.

He was overly elaborate in his response to Card 13MF from the TAT, a picture stimulus card depicting a clothed male standing in proximity to a partially undressed female lying down. He mentioned that the woman had been raped and then "sliced open." In response to Card 1, a picture of a boy sitting with a violin in front of him, he reported that "he'll learn to play the violin very well. But then he'll burn it. His Mom wants him to learn and that will make her mad. He'll burn it after he learns to play it."

Betty reported on the Achenbach Child Behavior Checklist that Bobby was significantly elevated on eight of the nine narrow-band factors, including anxious, depressed, uncommunicative, obsessive-compulsive, social withdrawal, hyperactive, aggressive, and delinquent (see Table 1). His internalizing and externalizing T-scores were 81 and 86, respectively. (T-scores of 70 and above are at the 98th percentile and higher.) The Achenbach completed by his teacher reported significant elevations on aggressive, unpopular, and socially withdrawn. His internalizing and externalizing T-scores were 71 and 73, respectively. His teacher did indicate that Bobby "could be an excellent student if he wasn't so angry."

TABLE 1
Scores on Child Behavior Checklist Over Time

Scale-Mother Report	Time 1	Time 2	Time 3	Time 4	Time 5
Schizoid/Anxious	72	68	77	63	59
Depressed	75	69	86	69	60
Uncommunicative	85	75	85	73	67
Obsessive-Compulsive	80	70	90	67	63
Somatic Complaints	57	57	72	55	55
Social Withdrawal	88	79	92	73	62
Hyperactive	85	73	87	68	65
Aggressive	90	75	91	70	65
Delinquent	79	68	81	68	65
Internalizing	81	70	85	66	60
Externalizing	86	74	89	68	61

Scale-Teacher Report					
Anxious	68			61	
Social Withdrawal	72			69	
Unpopular	80			67	
Self Destructive	63			60	
Obsessive-Compulsive	63			59	
Inattentive	69			60	
Nervous-Overactive	61			61	
Aggressive	78			68	
Internalizing	71			61	
Externalizing	73			61	

COURSE OF THERAPY

Several events came together that facilitated Betty and Bobby's beginning and initially pursuing therapy with me. Betty had recently decided that she needed to do something about her drinking, and Bobby's behavior had escalated to the point where it was scaring even her. Although school was only one month into fall semester, she was responding regularly to phone calls from the teacher. There was talk of placing Bobby in a program for emotionally and behaviorally disordered children. Approximately one month into our therapy, I found out that two nights before my first session with Bobby and Betty, Bobby had held a steak knife to his mother's face after she had told him it was time for bed.

That session, I asked about Bobby's aggression towards Betty, and her disclosure of the knife incident in the conjoint session infuriated him, causing him to punch her arm repeatedly. I was able to set limits on his aggressive behavior in this session, doing so by physically moving him to another chair in the room when Betty was unable to get him to comply. His in-session aggression dropped off markedly after this, adding further evidence that this needy boy desired approval from me and was already invested in the therapy, both signs of a good prognosis.

It wasn't until approximately 18 months of therapy had elapsed that Betty could state, "I needed to make a decision—get some help now, or spend the rest of my life visiting him in the penitentiary."

Therapy sessions for the first phase (14 months) of therapy were typically weekly, and 90 minutes long, with the first 45 minutes either an individual session with Bobby or a conjoint session with Bobby and Betty, and the second 45 minutes being the opposite. In addition, Betty had approximately 25 individual sessions with me during this same time period, usually an hour in length.

This first phase of therapy was characterized by my efforts at forming a therapeutic alliance with Bobby and Betty, motivating Betty towards assuming a more positive and active parenting role, frequent telephone consultation to Bobby's school and two school visits, and exploring Bobby's abuse history.

Because Betty was frightened by Bobby, she was initially motivated for the first time to work on their problems. However, she had to overcome her chronic depression and passivity in order to stay motivated and involved in the parenting of this very demanding boy. Initially, I helped Betty to establish a token economy which would allow her to reward Bobby for prosocial behavior towards her and at school. He could earn TV privileges with his behavior, along with food rewards, Betty's purchase of wildlife magazines for him, and mutual activities.

The token system was set up for two reasons. Betty had no handle on parenting Bobby and needed a clear structure. Secondly, Betty had never been perceived by Bobby as rewarding of him. For me to push Betty into behaving more firmly, and hence more punitively with Bobby without first trying to inject more positives via tokens into the relationship, would have doomed us to failure. As it was, I had difficulty, particularly in the first several months of therapy, getting Betty to be consistently reinforcing of Bobby, since her lifelong pattern with Bobby had been to avoid him.

Tokens were earned at various points during these first 14 months for the absence of verbal and physical aggressiveness, compliance with bedtime and TV rules, and the completion of small chores in their apartment, e.g., taking out the garbage, vacuuming the floor, making his bed.

The token system broke down several times during this phase and frequently needed adjusting. The first two times it broke down were due directly to Betty's binge drinking. This was made the focus of our individual sessions, and Betty was encouraged to begin attending AA which she initially resisted quite actively. Even after she began attendance she rarely went more than twice a month.

In my weekly sessions with Bobby during the initial phase, I was struck repeatedly by his aggressive insensitivity. At our third session, he placed a fairly large tack on my chair, causing me some pain and even more chagrin when I sat down on it. The previous session, he had spent considerable time elaborating on "how to hurt other people." I had responded to him in both of these sessions by telling him stories of "boys who worried that people wouldn't like them, so they did something to make the person not like them."

Bobby was very difficult to like. Although extremely bright and very verbal in a pseudomature manner, he was overweight, socially awkward, and extremely intrusive regarding personal boundaries. He often stood too close to me or touched me, usually when anxious, and attempted to steal several small toys from my office.

He generally refused to speak about his sexual abuse experiences, but could be engaged in elaborate and drawn-out games during the sessions (e.g., chess or checkers) or in discussions of murderous activities directed at other people (e.g., teachers). I told him at the beginning of the therapy and several times during the first six months that I expected the two of us to talk in detail about his sexual abuse experience and that I wanted him to let me know when we could do that. He usually responded with a stony silence. I even went so far as to create a reinforcement schedule to encourage disclosure, i.e., earning small toys from my office, etc., but Bobby continued to stonewall.

Significant improvement was made in Betty's parenting relationship with Bobby, now 10 years old, and his overall behavior at school had also improved by this time. Then I received calls from both Betty and the Child Protective Services worker on the same day, saying that Bobby was being accused of molesting two children, a four- and five-year-old brother/sister pair who lived in the same apartment building. This had prompted very angry and rejecting outbursts by Betty directed at Bobby.

During our session the next day, what I had perceived to be a growing and increasingly positive relationship between the two of them fell apart in front of me. Bobby was again physically aggressive towards his mother, and Betty stated twice that "he is disgusting. I can't live with him." My efforts at reframing these new developments as "a new challenge," "Bobby's finally letting us know how much he has been hurting," and "he's going to be talking about what happened to him the same way you need to," seemed to go unheard by both of them.

Bobby's outburst of sexually aggressive behavior towards these two children marked the beginning of our second phase of therapy. In retrospect, my work with him at this time represented our first true therapy. His behavior also reactivated Betty's memory of her own molestation, and for the first time she began to talk about her sexual abuse experience in something other than a clinically detached manner. The time elapsed during the second phase represented approximately six months of weekly individual sessions for both Bobby and Betty, with frequent family sessions added on an as needed basis.

I began this phase of therapy by telling Bobby that his aggression with the two neighbor children told me that he "had to talk to me about what John had done." Bobby responded by beginning to cry and whimpered off and on for much of the rest of the session, disclosing little information. I reassured him repeatedly that I was safe, that I would still like him, etc., but this triggered only silence punctuated by tears.

Because I did not want to lose what I viewed as a therapeutic moment, I informed him that he could not leave until he talked to me more directly and extended the session an additional 40 minutes. I offered Bobby the opportunity to draw pictures or talk directly about the abuse he had experienced. He chose to talk in the third person, recounting to me a story of "a little boy" who got tired of being alone in the apartment while his mother was at work, and who began regularly to watch John work on his car in the apartment parking lot. This evolved into John's giving him ice cream in the apartment and then initiating "man stuff," which initially included exhibitionism by John to Bobby. Bobby told me that he used to go to John's apartment "almost every day." I asked him to give me an estimate of the number of times John had been sexual with him, and although Bobby did not respond to this question at that time, he came in to the next session and handed a piece of paper to me with the number 125 written on it. When queried he said, "I don't remember all of them but I figured out that number because of how long he lived there."

Further interviewing over the next several sessions revealed that the majority of the sexual abuse had consisted of exposure by John and mutual masturbation. He could recall two instances each of sodomy and fellatio.

Much of the next several months was spent helping Bobby to elaborate on his abuse, to speak about it in the first person, and to explore his conflicted feelings about John, whom he had grown to like. His in-session letters to John began as angry letters, then became more complex, a mixture of anger, hurt, and loss, and then finally angry again. Once I felt that he was moving towards some resolution of his abuse, I turned the focus of the sessions to a chronicling of his abuse of the three younger children, how they felt now that he knew how he felt, and discussions of alternate behavior.

This phase marked a truly depressive period for Bobby. He had difficulty with sleeping, he lost a significant amount of weight, he had difficulty concentrating in school, and his grades suffered. He cried on several occasions during the therapy and initially rejected any comforting or soothing words from me. However, his mother reported that he was more aggressive at home, and our family sessions concentrated on supporting Betty's efforts to be firm with him regarding limits but also positive with him, offering praise as appropriate. She seemed to have no sense about how to be a parent to Bobby, and we initiated a token economy again with considerably more success than before.

During my work with Betty, she also became quite depressed, experienced her first panic attack, and reported numerous sleepless nights and nightmares. As a reference librarian, she had access to a large library of psychology textbooks, and she frequently brought into the session a psychotherapy book that she was reading at the time. Rather than view this as resistance, I loaned her copies of Finkelhor (1979), Herman (1981), and Meiselman (1978) from my library.

Betty also was much more candid about her prior relationship with Bobby, describing what appeared to be long periods of emotional and physical neglect of him, leaving him in the apartment unattended, and feeling like he was completely unlovable. These disclosures activated much guilt, along with urges to drink. Her AA attendance increased considerably at this time.

Towards the end of fifth grade, Bobby's depression lifted somewhat, and I arranged for him to begin a 16-session social skills group for latency age boys in another facility. This marked the entrance into the last phase of therapy, which continued over approximately the next eight months. Bobby's and my relationship became more mutually positive, and I began to look forward to my sessions with him. He was beating me regularly in chess, but using the structure of the game as a way to talk about feelings. I used a feeling list as a way to help teach him about other people's feelings, and he and I did considerable role playing of feelings with each other. This reflects my belief that empathy is lacking in sexually aggressive children and needs to be facilitated, with the first step learning to identify feelings. He enrolled in a school-sponsored chess club and did extremely well in his age category. Teacher reports were uniformly much more positive and, although Bobby remained somewhat isolated in school, he began to go fairly regularly with one classmate to city-wide chess meets and the two of them occasionally did things together on weekends.

Betty continued her therapy with me, although on a less frequent basis, and more of our contact was during the conjoint sessions with Betty and Bobby, where the focus was on supporting their developing positive relationship. I pushed Betty to talk about her own upbringing and its parallels with Bobby's and routinely cast Bobby as a junior image of Betty.

The total length of treatment spanned 29 months. During that time period, I had 95 individual sessions with Bobby, 58 individual sessions with Betty, and 77 conjoint interviews. In addition, Bobby completed a 16-week social skills training group that focused on generic social skill issues. Their local HMO reimbursed 20 sessions per year, and the remainder were billed on a sliding scale.

SPECIFIC TECHNIQUES USED IN THERAPY

This family differed significantly from other families of sexually aggressive young children in that Betty was not physically abusive of Bobby. Rather, her neglect of him, although pernicious, was more benign. She was actually rather timid around him, found him frightening and a nuisance, but opted to withdraw and become more passive rather than to be physically abusive or sadistic with him.

A second distinguishing feature was their fairly rapid attachment to me and consistent follow through in therapy. Without these two processes in place, i.e., Betty's benign, albeit neglectful, relationship with Bobby, and their willingness to take part in therapy, any techniques that I might have used would have failed. When I queried Betty toward the end of therapy about what had kept her coming, she stated that she knew Bobby needed a friend and that I seemed to like him, and she wanted to support that as much as she could. Always ready to seize any opportunity to support her parenting, I told her that that was a "very mom-like" thing to do for Bobby.

When queried further, she stated that she was very frightened of Bobby and of her own developing alcoholism and had made a decision right before they first came to see me that she needed help. She also stated that as a librarian she appreciated anybody who read good literature and, unbeknownst to me, had kept track of the titles of fiction and poetry on my desk. She wryly stated at the same interview, which occurred at approximately 25 months into the therapy, that she thought I read too many murder mysteries. It also helped greatly that Betty and I worked for the same institution, and ease of access to my office was a plus for both of them.

The techniques that I did use can be divided into four categories: facilitating a relationship between Bobby and Betty, uncovering Bobby's previous molestation history, facilitating Bobby's social skills, and focusing on developing empathy in both Bobby and Betty for each other and on Bobby's part as a prevention against further victimizing.

With regards to facilitating Bobby and Betty's relationship, I was very consistent in reframing their conflicts as positive, in equating the two of them, drawing parallels between each of their experiences, and reframing Bobby as "the person who helps you get the therapy you needed, Betty." Bobby's intelligence was valued by Betty, and I referred to both as "very bright" quite often, thus fostering identification with the other. Both also had a fair complexion and blonde hair, and I referred to them as "the two Norwegians," which sometimes became "the two Vikings." The token system gave Betty a vehicle to be more positive to Bobby, and although it went through several fits and starts and eventually was abandoned, it brought about a reduction in his aggression and helped Betty feel more potent as a parent. After the system was dropped she did persist in being somewhat emotionally present and physically rewarding with him. Bobby actually suggested in mid-therapy that we put Betty on a token system to reinforce her emotional support of him and her compliance with his token system.

I routinely contracted with Betty and Bobby to engage in mutually positive activities. What is natural to most families was alien to them. They had never attended events, gone on picnics, or taken a vacation together. We progressed through a list, including trips to the zoo, berry-picking, visits to the park, and picnics. They took a two-week vacation together during the last phase of therapy, which included Betty attending a conference for reference librarians and the two of them going to several amusement parks. They were able to count on more regular times together at home as their relationship improved, and evenings for them fairly regularly involved making popcorn, baking cookies, and either playing chess or reading on the same sofa.

Uncovering Bobby's sexual victimization was a critical piece of the therapy but didn't happen until his sexual victimization of other children became obvious to us. Now that he was more depressed and scared, uncovering was an option. Prior to that he was extremely defensive and I kept asking myself whether my pushing him was a function of my own negative countertransference or whether I was truly being therapeutic. It was also important for Bobby to talk about his sexual victimizing of the two neighbor children, and his reluctant admission that he had molested them on more than one occasion was followed by an admission that several months earlier he had fondled another child in the building. This latter disclosure came about because I had become aware, in working with other sexually aggressive boys, that many were compulsive perpetrators. I felt reasonably comfortable in telling Bobby that I didn't believe him when he told me initially that he had only molested the brother-sister pair, and then only one time. Balancing support and coercion is very challenging with these children, but a necessary skill.

His sexual victimizing made our focus on enhancing his social skills even more critical. Although I question the long-term utility of social skills training in most cases, Bobby did learn some self-monitoring and response management techniques. Bobby's interest in chess, his involvement in a chess club, and his developing friendship with another socially awkward peer were also big steps in his life.

Finally, with regards to empathy, as Betty's relationship with Bobby became more positive, he was better able to talk about himself and the impact of his actions on other people. I was able to comment, after the second phase of therapy, that "I don't think I need to look for any more tacks," to which Bobby looked sheepish.

A critical part of the empathy building with Bobby occurred when, off and on over six to seven months, I would have him draw parallels between his own experience as a victim and his perceptions of the experiences of his three victims. I usually find a significantly reduced capacity for empathy in sexually aggressive boys, but Bobby's depression spoke to his capacity to experience shame and guilt, which seemed to be precursors to a healthier understanding and appreciation of people's impact on him and his impact on them.

Although not a specific therapy technique, my regular behavioral assessment of Bobby with the CBC, particularly as positives could be noted, served to continue to motivate this family; in addition, this gave Betty an opportunity to see her son in a new light. This underscores my contention that two purposes can be served with assessment: to determine what needs changing, and to motivate further change.

OUTCOME OF TREATMENT

The Child Behavior Checklist was frequently utilized throughout the course of therapy and the results are summarized in Table 1. As you can see, Bobby's overt behavior problems had a rather variable course. He exhibited significant behavior problems in all areas except somatic complaints at Time 1, which marked the beginning of therapy. As mentioned earlier, I had believed we were making slow but steady progress in the first phase of therapy, and at ten months into therapy Betty completed a Child Behavior Checklist for the second time. This demonstrated that Bobby was significantly elevated on only five of the nine narrow band factors from the CBC.

Somatic complaints was still unevaluated, but the remaining three factors were just outside of significance. I knew from the Time 2 information that our therapy had been only minimally successful, shared that with Betty, and she agreed to continue our work. I make a point of bringing the CBC results into my therapy sessions with families, as a way both to appraise them of progress and also to refocus on specific goals.

Time 3 was only five months after Time 2, and marked the period of extreme disorganization that followed the detection of Bobby's sexually aggressive behavior. Every scale on the CBC was elevated both from a statistical and a clinical point of view. His tremendous internal distress was being exhibited somatically for the first time. Bobby was now exhibiting what I had determined was more typical of him, a conflicting mixture of anxiety/depression on the one hand and angry/antisocial behavior on the other. The work that we did around disclosure of Bobby's earlier sexual abuse experience, coupled with Betty's gradual warming towards her son and more overt support of him, moved Bobby along significantly by Time 4, which was 21 months into therapy and the beginning of the third and final phase.

His elevations at Time 4 indicate persisting problems with social skills and aggression, two of the more intractable behavior problems child clinicians confront. However, Betty was increasingly able to interact in a less neglectful, less coercive, and more positive and engaged manner with Bobby; coupled with this, his social skills training, and the addition of a friend in his life, continued improvement was made, as evidenced by ratings at Time 5, which were returned to me by mail approximately one month after the end of therapy. Betty clearly saw fewer problems in all areas, although Bobby continued to be relatively uncommunicative. The broad brand factors, internalizing and externalizing, parallel the up and down course of our therapy.

Two ratings, each from different teachers, and obtained at Time 1 and Time 4, also indicate significant progress in school. His definite improvement in social skills and reduction of aggression were very positive signs for future adjustment. Betty brought in the results of a group achievement test shortly before therapy ended, and Bobby's scores in all subject areas were the highest he had ever received.

As further evidence of Bobby's improvement, his stories in response to TAT stimulus cards were much more positive and less depressed. He commented to Card 13MF, "I remember I didn't like this one when you first showed it to me last time." His story was then more appropriate. I also readministered the Rorschach approximately one month before termination. The poor judgment, oppositionality, and impulsivity noted earlier, along with the morbid and aggressive content, had largely disappeared. For example, a measure on the Rorschach, Form Quality, pertains to the accuracy of the child's perception of the inkblots. The lower the score, the less accurate the child's perception. Bobby's overall form quality at intake was .36. At termination, his overall form quality was .71. This latter score is considered appropriate for children of his age.

I have continued to receive occasional Christmas cards from Betty in the intervening six years since termination. She and Bobby had some difficulty during adolescence, and he was arrested for shoplifting, resulting in a period of probation and additional individual counseling. However, he was not institutionalized, and the last I heard, he and Betty were still living together and he was making plans to attend the local university. Around the same time that Bobby was picked up for shoplifting, Betty began a romantic involvement with a man, the first clearly appropriate relationship for her in her lifetime. My sense is that this perturbation in the system triggered Bobby's acting out.

OBSTACLES TO TREATMENT

Unlike the majority of families of sexually aggressive children that I have worked with since, relatively few personal or logistical obstacles existed in my work with Betty and Bobby. Transportation was not a significant problem, since Bobby was very facile at using the city bus lines and Betty worked on the same campus where I taught. Her HMO was relatively generous and reimbursed approximately 20% of the sessions in full. Because of my good working relationship with social services, they were effective in directing Betty and Bobby to me.

OTHER SYSTEMS INVOLVED

Although I now believe that social services and family court involvement are usually a must in working with sexually aggressive children, few other systems were involved on a regular basis with this family. At the time Bobby was found to have molested other children, social services and my understanding of sexually aggressive children were such that an ongoing case was not opened on Bobby by the county social services office.

I did have some difficulty persuading the agency that ran the social skills training group to allow Bobby into its program, given his previous history of sexual aggression. However, once enrolled on a trial basis, he fared reasonably well and was allowed to complete the entire course.

My two school consultations represented my other system involvement. The first came at the beginning of therapy, the second at the time of discovery of his sexual aggression. I spoke with both teachers, providing encouragement and perhaps a better appreciation of Bobby. Visiting Bobby's school also allowed me to see him in a different setting and seemed to help our relationship, since Bobby took the visits as a sign of my interest in him.

MISTAKES

In retrospect, I had reasonable evidence to suspect Bobby of sexually aggressive behavior at the time he and his mother first came in. I don't believe he would have disclosed his sexually aggressive ideation, but an indirect exploration may have reduced the likelihood of his acting out. However, I was not used to thinking about children as sexually aggressive at that stage of my experience with sexually abused children.

A primary mistake was not appreciating the importance of a reasonably full disclosure of earlier victimization in order to facilitate success in my treatment of Bobby. The importance of this was certainly driven home when he acted out sexually 14 months into what I felt was good therapy with a family that was more cooperative than the average. Bobby had organized his view of relationships around his unresolved previous victimization, and I did not appreciate how much this not only directed his life but also interfered with true change.

THERAPIST'S REACTIONS TO THE CASE

Despite Betty and Bobby's initially passive compliance with therapy and gradually more active involvement, Bobby was a difficult boy to treat, since he interacted with me in a very aggressive and intrusive manner. His refusal to cooperate with activities I deemed necessary also made him easy to dislike. Although I reminded myself that my negative countertransference to him was simply a reflection of his lack of experiences of intimacy and fear of relationships, in the heat of the moment, when I realized he was walking out the door with a toy or when he picked his nose and wiped it on my desk, I had a hard time maintaining objectivity and therapeutic neutrality. Betty was also difficult to read, on the one hand open in a rather detached manner, but on the other hand a quietly rejecting mother who also activated my dislike.

However, each of them came with a ticket, and that was the opportunity to do some intellectual sparring with each other and myself. Betty did enjoy arguing, which in a curious way served to develop the therapeutic relationship. I came to appreciate Betty's background as a librarian, since she did live her life in a relatively organized and nonchaotic manner, with the exception of her occasional binge drinking. This type of predictability in Bobby's life, even though it was emotionally barren, buffered him, I believe, against even more serious psychopathology.

I frequently wondered whether I should focus more directly on Betty's drinking, and ended up relegating most of her alcohol treatment to her AA involvement. At the time I was working with them, I was consulting to an agency where the therapists were debating on a regular basis whether therapy could be successful until alcoholic individuals were completely abstinent. My decision to work with Betty and Bobby despite the fact that she continued to binge drink off and on through the first year of therapy left me questioning my abilities on numerous occasions.

I learn from each of the children and families I work with. Betty and Bobby taught me that uncovering previous victimization is crucial, that persistence can pay off, and that truly estranged relationships can be improved within a supportive context.

14

Treatment of a Sexually Reactive Girl

TONI CAVANAUGH JOHNSON

Can children who never fully disclose sexual abuse resolve their own victimization experience? Is talking "as if" one had been sexually abused enough to work through a victimization experience from a therapeutic perspective? The seasoned clinician knows that disclosure and resolution are certainly the goals of treatment with abused children, but with a significant subset of children this doesn't happen, despite the therapist's best efforts, and with another subset it must be done creatively.

A primary contributor to a lack of disclosure is the absence of parental support for disclosure. Yet parental support was evident in this case. Although Elaine's remaining in her marriage with Owen spoke to her significant interpersonal difficulties, she was able to separate from him and did appear increasingly supportive of her children.

Dissociation is dismissed by Dr. Johnson as an explanation for Margy's "lack of memory" or inability to talk about her victimization. Rather, her inability is seen as a conscious process related to her intense fear of her father. I believe that unconscious processes may have been operative, particularly dissociation. Dr. Johnson writes that Margy "looked puzzled" when confronted about a contradictory statement. This behavioral description is also suggestive of dissociation. In dissociation, certain memories can be split off from immediate awareness and become compartmentalized as a separate entity in the mind. These entities are difficult to engage therapeutically. Dissociation occurs under conditions of extreme distress, and if the therapists were upset by Owen's threatening behavior with them, it is easy to imagine how intimidating he was with his children on a daily basis, even more so during the abuse. The end result is that

Margy's sense of self did not contain the fact that she had been molested; her molestation was out of conscious awareness. The diagnosis of dissociative disorder should be made cautiously, but in my opinion it may very well have been present in Margy.

With this case, Dr. Johnson balanced quite nicely two pertinent treatment issues. The first is that Margy had molested other children and the second is that she had been molested herself. This dynamic tension between victim/victimizer needs to be handled respectfully. Programs for older offenders usually focus on the victimizing behavior of the offender, working on the offender's victimization only after significant progress has been made with interrupting the offending behavior. It is important to create safety for future victims, but in my experience a thorough discussion of the offender's own molestation is often the most efficacious approach. This necessitates working on both victim and victimizer issues simultaneously. —Editor

THEORETICAL ORIENTATION

I am the Clinical Director of the Support Program for Abuse-Reactive Kids (SPARK) at the Child Sexual Abuse Center at Children's Institute International, a specialized program for children between the ages of three and twelve who act out sexually with other children. The sexual acting out of SPARK children goes far beyond age-appropriate exploration. The SPARK program has groups for parents, for children who are acting out sexually, and for victimized and nonvictimized siblings. The children's groups are divided by age and sex.

One hundred percent of the girls below the age of 11 previously assessed for the SPARK program for sexual acting out behavior had a prior history of sexual abuse. The sexual activity of the children in the SPARK program has complex origins; however, gratification of sexual feelings is not commonly the drive. Rather, their sexual acting out is a reflection of their anger and confusion related to their abuse experience. Frequently, they show little remorse for their actions. Their primary concern is not for their victim(s), but whether they are caught or punished.

A typical treatment course is 18 months and utilizes group therapy as the primary modality with family therapy as an adjunct. Individual psychodynamic as well as family and systems frameworks guide our therapy. Cognitive therapy is the primary theoretical orientation because of the need to help parents and children understand how their beliefs affect their behavior, and alter these beliefs and behaviors as needed. However, our reliance on group therapy reflects our belief that the socialization process for sexually reactive children has clearly gone awry, and group treatment is the most efficacious approach to correct socialization and social skill deficits (Johnson, 1988, 1989a, 1989b).

DESCRIPTION OF THE CASE*

Margy is the 11-year-old daughter of Elaine and Owen White. We eventually learned that both Margy and her older brother, Ronny, age 12, were molested by Owen, along with two neighbor children, John, age eight, and Valerie, five.

Elaine called SPARK initially, reporting that the previous evening Margy had told her that she had been touching children in their private parts for some time. We eventually determined that Margy acted out sexually with 15 children, including neighbors, children in the day-care home run by Jaqui, the mother of John and Valerie, and schoolmates.

Elaine also informed us that Margy had a several-year history of school difficulty and had been evaluated two years earlier. She reported marital problems, but knew of no instances of sexual abuse to her children. She did recall that several years earlier Ronny had said that her husband had touched his penis once. She remembered both children calling her one time at work to say that their father was masturbating on the kitchen floor while looking at a pornographic magazine. In response to these incidents she had screamed at Owen and threatened to leave him and take the children if he did anything like that again. These confrontations had upset both Ronny and Margy.

This initial family history did not account for Margy's extensive sexual acting out. There was no reported history of any type of abuse in the family of any of the members including the grandparents, no disorders of impulse, no alcohol or substance abuse, no major traumas or losses, no history of multiple partners of the parents, and no major behavior disorders in the children other than Margy's sexual behavior. The only problems uncovered were in the relationship between Elaine and Owen and the instances of Owen's questionable sexual behavior with the children. The marital problems did not fit the pattern we had become accustomed to seeing in parents in the SPARK program. The relationship was described as neither violent nor assaultive, nor had there been any periods of foster care placements or discontinuity in the relationship between the parents and the children.

PSYCHOLOGICAL ASSESSMENT

Margy had been evaluated two years earlier in her hometown in Connecticut due to depression, excessive fears of making a mistake, and feeling that no one liked her. She was quiet, withdrawn, and minimally productive in

*Appreciation is expressed to Marie Ashton, Sandra Ballester, Michael Kitlowski, Sandy Krebs, and the other therapists involved with this case. Special appreciation goes to Joanne Ross Feldmeth for her editorial assistance.

school. She did not even try to make friends. The summary results of the psychological testing indicated:

> Margy is overly defended and guarded about emotionally laden situations. She uses denial and concreteness to defend against her needs. . . . Underneath this defensive style is a child who longs for closeness with others, yet holds fantasied, unrealistic views of how others are likely to react. . . . Her reality testing suffers; she does not see the world as others do. She experiences the world as scary and emotionally impoverished and feels despondent about growing up. Her stories are full of dead and dying mothers and fathers and emotional impoverishment. In one story she told of a lady who was talking to a man who then killed her and then killed everybody. . . . Margy feels terrible about herself: her self-esteem is at rock bottom. The world is seen as so ungiving.

The diagnosis given for Margy was dysthymic disorder. Individual therapy was suggested. The recommendation was "intensive psychotherapy to help Margy understand her emotional conflicts, so that her energy can be freed, and so that she can engage the world in more emotionally gratifying ways." The assumption in the test results was that Margy's reality testing was poor because she saw the world differently from most children. The world is not basically uncaring and scary, so Margy's perceptions were wrong. The report mentioned that Margy suffered from stomachaches constantly.

Her most current school report indicated low achievement. While she was not a behavior problem, she stood out due to her lack of spontaneity, her sadness, and her social isolation. Margy did her homework and finished all her assignments in school, but she was slow in completing her work. Her teacher felt Margy's performance, a low C average, should be better, based on her ability.

Her report cards were similar for the previous several years, with the exception of her first grade report card, which reported good grades and cooperation.

Given the relatively recent previous evaluation, no formal reevaluation was completed. However, prior to the initial interview each parent separately filled out the Child Sexual Behavior Checklist, rating 150 possible sexual behaviors in which the child may have engaged (Johnson, 1990). This checklist is discussed with the parents in the initial interview. The parents also completed the Child Behavior Checklist (Achenbach & Edelbrock, 1983), which provides a behavioral summary of the child from the perspective of each parent.

Margy was also evaluated with the Projective Storytelling Cards (Caruso, 1987) during her initial meeting with us and then again during the final phase of therapy. This was done to assess for changes in her current functioning as reflected by the content of her stories in response to picture stimulus cards.

COURSE OF THERAPY

Initial Interview

Interviews for the White family were scheduled the day after the phone call. In the meantime, Elaine was told to keep Margy at home and supervise her play with other children until she could be interviewed. Elaine was asked to bring in a copy of the earlier evaluation and Margy's report cards from the last several years.

The interviews for the SPARK program include all family members. Interviews take three to four hours. The parents are first interviewed by the coordinator and the potential child therapists. Each child is interviewed by the leader of the group to which the child would be assigned if therapy were offered.

The purpose of the initial interview with the parents is to get a multigenerational family history, including a genogram that covers: details of any sexual or physical abuse, neglect or abandonment, traumas to any family members; whether there is any substance and/or alcohol abuse, or any felonies or imprisonments; and the relationship history between all family members, including extended family members.

The parents are interviewed about the nature of the child's sexual acting-out behaviors, including the initial awareness by the parents, how the parents found out, the parents' reaction, the child's reaction to the discovery of her acting out, the nature of the sexual behaviors, where and for how long they had occurred, the use of any force by the child, and the child's current feelings regarding herself in relation to the sexual behaviors.

A detailed history of the identified child covers birth history, relationships with parents, peers, and authority figures; medical problems; school performance; and interactions with siblings and family members.

The entire White family arrived on time. Elaine and the two children sat close to each other on a sofa with Mr. White standing over them. Shortly into the parental interview, Mr. White denied any problems with Margy, and said that, if any existed, she should pray to the Lord for help. Owen's comments appeared to frustrate Elaine, as judged from the expression on her face.

Because it was evident from the brief time spent with Elaine and Owen together that conjoint interviewing would not be fruitful, separate interviews began. Shortly into his interview, Owen reported to the interviewer that he always carried a gun. He opened his jacket and showed it to the interviewer. He claimed it was not loaded but paced the floor with it. When asked, he did return the gun to his jacket.

His behavior during the interview was belligerent and antagonistic. He deferred questions regarding the history of the family and the children to his wife. His belief was that social workers "fucked everything up."

He did admit to touching Ronny, stating, "Yeah, I touched his penis. I showed him how to jack off. I want him to be a man." He stated further, "A man has the right to masturbate in his own house."

Elaine was a marked contrast, appearing very concerned about Margy. She was open and active throughout the interview and very aware and knowledgeable about every aspect of the history of the children in the family. She reiterated her concerns about Owen's previous sexual behaviors as reported to her by Margy and Ronny. She viewed Owen as a "leech" who didn't work, said she believed he was seeing other women, and reported a nonexistent sex life. She had considered divorce numerous times but reported that both children got upset when they heard the parents arguing. She denied that Owen had abused her physically.

We had several goals in our interview with Margy, including: obtaining the details of her sexual behaviors with other children, determining the drive behind the genesis of her sexual acting out, assessing her feelings about her sexual behaviors and the children she had touched, examining the level of impulsivity and/or compulsiveness of her behavior, determining the presence of force, impressing on her the need to stop acting out, and determining her treatment needs.

Margy stated that she had both fondled and orally copulated many children, naming eight but stating that there were more. Both male and female children, including infants in Jaqui's care and Jaqui's children, were identified as victims. She denied any coercion and stated that the behavior had started two or three years earlier. Margy stated that when she touched children, "an angel was on one shoulder and Satan on the other." She believed she was too weak to withstand Satan's powers and reported that "touching kids makes me feel real bad inside," and "I know I must not do it anymore." She was prompted to tell her mother because her stomach hurt so much. During this portion of the interview, Margy spoke with little affect, slumped over in her chair, with her eyes averted. She did not speak spontaneously and answered questions in a very halting manner. (She denied that anyone had touched her, and then giggled when asked if she had been scared into not telling.)

Our interview with Ronny revealed that his father had touched his penis once but "by mistake." He minimized any sexual contact with his sister, stating that they had "humped once" approximately two years earlier.

Prior to meeting with the parents and sharing our findings, the coordinator and the child therapist met and agreed that Margy's timidity, her lack of acknowledgment of any abuse to her, her humiliation about sexual behaviors, and her readiness to assume culpability argued for individual therapy as an initial intervention. Her level of distress and her concern for the children she had touched were uncharacteristic to children in the SPARK program (Johnson, 1989a).

During our completion interview with the parents, Elaine was tearful and desirous of therapy while Owen was reserved in his response and paced threateningly when told about the need to report to child protective services. We requested that the parents not leave Margy alone with any children and encouraged them to assure her that she was not "bad" but that she did have to stop touching other children. Individual therapy was recommended for Margy, along with parent consultation and family sessions including Ronny. Elaine reported that she would contact us and set up an initial appointment.

We did file a child abuse report with CPS regarding Margy's child victims. Initial intervention by either the police or CPS with families who have a child who is molesting other children is important, so that the court can mandate the child and parents to therapy. Even with a mandate to therapy, it is very difficult to get these parents and children to attend therapy regularly.

After Jaqui called, we interviewed both of her children. John was minimally revealing, but Valerie, only five, reported oral sex by Margy and demonstrated with anatomically detailed dolls fondling, digital penetration of both vagina and rectum, and penile contact to her vagina by Owen.

Immediately after this interview, we called the police, who requested that we interview Margy and Ronny again that same day. We did so and Margy mentioned Owen touching her "on the bottom" and viewing pornographic pictures provided by Owen. Ronny reported watching his father masturbate while watching TV on one occasion.

Police officers who specialized in interviewing child sexual victims were unable to respond to our call and street officers, unskilled in interviewing, arrived for police interviews. We spent some time arguing with them to prevent the removal of Margy and Ronny and John and Valerie from their homes. They appeared concerned about Owen's gun, but after telephone consultation with a specialized police unit they agreed to allow John and Valerie to return home with their parents after a medical evaluation. Medical evidence of sexual abuse was not found in any of the four children. Margy and Ronny were placed in separate foster homes by Child Protective Services, despite the therapist's belief that the children needed to be placed together. Both Margy and Ronny had evidenced an enormous level of anxiety since getting to the hospital for the medical evaluation. Margy had vomited four times and cried intermittently, and Ronny had not spoken a word.

Phase 1

After five days in foster placement, Margy was returned to Elaine's custody, appearing at the initial therapy session even more regressed than when she had been seen earlier. (Elaine had insisted that Owen move from the house after the children were placed in foster care.) At the initial therapy interview, Margy and Elaine were seen together and Elaine was quite supportive of Margy, who appeared to be extremely timid and confused.

Margy was again interviewed separately from Elaine during this session but was unable to elaborate on Owen's abuse of her or to implicate Elaine in collaborating with Owen.

Elaine and the two children were again brought together and the end of the session focused on their safety, where and with whom they were going to live, and everyone's feelings about the allegations. Elaine talked to her children about her sadness and feelings of failure as a mother and protector but vowed to keep them safe now that she knew. Elaine was given the phone numbers of several nonoffending mothers from Parents United (Giarretto, 1982). We assumed that they could provide support to this family at the initial crisis of discovery.

During this initial week, various combinations of therapy were arranged for Elaine, Margy, Ronny, Jaqui, and her two children, Valerie and John.

The initial nine months of therapy which comprised this first phase were characterized by Margy's inability to recall any abuse she sustained, her denial of feelings, her pervasive fear of the courts and of again being removed from her mother's care, persisting shame and guilt over sexual acting out, fear of contact with her father, and repeated questioning of how long she had to stay in therapy. Approximately 15 people interviewed Margy during this first phase, including therapists, physicians, social workers, police officers, numerous attorneys, and a court-appointed expert.

A second medical examination by a specialist in the diagnosis of sexual abuse using a colposcope (Heger, 1985) was held. The findings of this exam were consistent with sexual abuse, including evidence of serious trauma to Margy's rectum. Margy had explained to the physician prior to the exam that she had put her own fingers in her vagina and that she was afraid her father would be blamed if they found any evidence of damage.

Margy's ongoing inability to acknowledge victimization presented a significant dilemma to the therapist. In an attempt to access this apparent lack of memory, Margy was interviewed repeatedly about instances where she felt like things happened that she couldn't remember, blank periods in her life, or "spacing out." Elaine was interviewed about Margy's looking as if she were in a trance. None of these avenues of questioning was fruitful.

However, questions remained as to the course and content of therapy. How hard should a therapist push when the child is not disclosing abuse even when there are three children who are describing abuse to her and there is medical evidence of sexual abuse consistent with a description of the other three children's report? Can therapy be beneficial only when the child acknowledges or remembers the abuse? What course of therapy should be taken under these circumstances? Margy was even farther removed than not remembering. She was stating that nothing had happened. Adding to these initial difficulties was the fact that Margy was reluctant to express any feelings, past or present, about any situation other than court.

Four months into therapy, Margy gradually began to alter her response, stating as the adjudication of her and Ronny's case in Dependency Court approached that she believed Jaqui's children when they said they were abused. This came up because she kept asking if John and Valerie were going to court. When the therapist asked why Margy wanted these two children to go to court, she answered by stating that she wanted them to testify about their abuse by her father because she believed what John and Valerie said her father did. This presented several openings, which were tried repeatedly, including raising the question, since John said that he had watched her father sodomize her, did she believe that also? She persisted in replying, "I can't remember."

Many times victims use the phrase "I *can't* remember" with the emphasis on the "can't." The victim "can't" remember because remembering makes it too real, almost like it is happening again (Lister, 1982). The feelings attached to the abuse again overtake the individual. The somatic response to the abuse is sometimes recreated in the retelling, and the experience is again perceived as overwhelming and even abusive. Other times "I *can't* remember" means "I *won't* remember." This may provide victims with a sense of some control about an uncontrollable situation, and it may also be an expression of anger at people who fail to protect her. There may also be a genuine fear that the details of the molestation are so shameful that others will dislike her if she discloses. In addition, some victims may feel that to tell about victimization is only to be reminded that it was "my fault."

We gradually became convinced Margy "couldn't remember" because of Owen's threats. Through John and Valerie we became aware of several threats, including Elaine, Margy, and Valerie having their uteruses cut out and then killed. Owen had also stated that Elaine would hate all the children and never speak to them again and that after he went to jail the family would have to live on the streets. Owen had threatened to cut off John's penis. The information about these threats was not revealed to Margy but simply used to help understand Margy's denial and further motivate the therapist to continue the discovery process. However, numerous invitations to talk about possible threats or to think of threats and figure out if they were coming true were to no avail. In addition, Margy was difficult to engage in projective play, and in this initial phase her average verbalizations totalled barely five minutes per session of therapy. Despite her shyness and timidity, she was extremely responsive and alert to everything the therapist said, sometimes asking for clarification. The sessions in this phase gradually focused more and more on games such as Toss Across or table pool and included drawing, painting, and molding clay.

Examples of "invitations" delivered by the therapist to Margy included numerous reassurances regarding disclosure, assurances that Margy need not speak specifically about the abuse, repeated suggestions to Margy that children feel better when they share a secret, suggestions that Margy might feel it was her fault and that therapist could alter those bad feelings, and suggestions that she might have questions about why the abuse happened to her and why she wasn't protected. To each of these "invitations," Margy would either say nothing or ask, "How long do I have to come here?" or "Do I have to stay until I remember?"

The therapist considered using hypnosis to provide an opportunity for Margy to begin to tell about the abuse but it was decided that Margy's need not to tell outweighed the benefits of disclosure. Her situation seemed far different from a case where an adult is attempting to retrieve memories for events in childhood.

A gradual softening of Margy's stance did occur over this first phase. For example, on occasion when Margy asked about John and Valerie going to court, she stated, "They were touched by the same person I was." When probed about this statement, Margy looked puzzled and said she hadn't said that. It seemed her lack of memory was most likely due not to dissociation, repression, or denial, but to intense fear of her father.

Another important issue was Margy's sexual acting out with other children. She was more willing to discuss this than any other subject and related details and feelings about it. She described that it began several years earlier and that the children had never resisted. She never asked any children not to tell. She would begin by showing her genitals and asking to see the other child's. She would touch the children in the genitals with her hand and sometimes get them to touch her. She described "humping" the babies she would care for in Jaqui's day-care and initiating oral copulation when changing them. She was convinced that she had never hurt any of the children and that they seemed to like it.

Her sexual acting out behavior was ego-dystonic. She was consumed with shame and feelings of being bad and did not want to continue this behavior.

She was aware of her own sexual stimulation and reported that it felt "good in my body, but bad all over" when she touched the children.

Despite Margy's greater openness on this topic, pursuing her sexual acting-out behavior was fraught with hazards. Since she denied abuse, Margy attributed all of the blame for her sexual behaviors to herself; this fueled an already totally debased sense of her own worth. Numerous attempts were made at connecting previous abuse and sexual acting out in an effort to help her understand that sexual abuse might stimulate the desire to act out sexually with other children. However, Margy persisted in explaining her sexual acting-out behavior by saying that she was not strong enough to rebuke Satan and that it was Satan who tempted her to behave in this manner. This enduring influence of her father on Margy's thinking, even at such a distance, underscored his power in her life.

We found that both Margy and Elaine held the same belief about Satan, with God being the prime motivator behind good acts and Satan promoting bad behavior. God was more powerful than Satan, who could be rebuked, but this took strength of character and prayer. We respected this belief system but encouraged Elaine to decrease the emphasis on the power of Satan and increase the emphasis on Margy's ability to control her own behavior. We suggested other ways for Elaine to respond to Margy's "touching problem." She was encouraged to help Margy understand that Margy was not *all* bad when she touched children. Touching other children was a problem, but this problem was only *one* of many parts of Margy. There were many more positive things about Margy than this *one* part on which she needed to work. We used this framework to help rebuild Margy's sense of self-efficacy and self-esteem. Because of Elaine's continuing high level of support for Margy, she was doing much of this already.

The therapist spoke frequently and candidly with Margy about physical urges and desires to touch other children. Margy's mother was asked to keep a very close watch on her. She was kept away from children unless there was an adult present. Margy was warned not to put herself in situations where there might be children to touch. In the event that Margy found herself with children and wanting to touch them, she was instructed to immediately leave the dangerous situation, if possible (in school she could not leave). She practiced diverting her attention by changing what was going on, thinking about other things, moving around, doing thought-stopping. Margy practiced relaxation exercises and self-guided imagery as a means of diverting her attention, decreasing her sexual urges, and thereby taking control of her behavior. She used self-statements to reinforce her positive coping (Kendall & Braswell, 1985, Meyers & Craighead, 1984).

Margy was also encouraged to talk to her mother and the therapist about her feelings. She was very open with her mother about these feelings and did go to her in the first months. Elaine would listen and then help divert her attention. When Margy would feel in control of the feelings, Elaine would reinforce Margy's ability to take control and not act out. After Margy seemed to have the sexual behavior under control, the therapist checked with Margy every other session about any thoughts, feelings, or physical urges to touch children.

This component of therapy was much less complex and difficult with Margy than with many other children who act out sexually. She was ashamed, wanted to stop, and was aware that it was not good for the children she touched. The major drive behind Margy's sexual behavior was a recapitulation of the sexual behaviors that her father had told her to do with Ronny, Valerie, and John. Margy enjoyed the sensation of the sexual stimulation. This, though, was overshadowed by the guilt she felt about the behavior. For Margy to stop the sexual behaviors, she needed a guide and techniques so that she could do what she wanted to do — stop.

Margy had been masturbating many times a day for some time before she had come into therapy. This behavior continued. She was very open with her mother about when she got the "tingly" feelings and wanted to touch herself and her distress about this "bad" behavior. Elaine's way of understanding masturbation and relating it to Margy was that masturbation was bad, the "devil of lust" was coming over her, and that she had to resist this. While the therapist believed that the compulsiveness of the masturbation needed to be eliminated, a complete cessation of all self-stimulation was not imperative. Some release of sexual tension through masturbation can be beneficial to the control of sexual acting out. The therapist explained this reasoning to Elaine but said that she would not express this idea to Margy if Elaine did not agree. Elaine was against masturbation but she did agree to decrease the focus on the devil and badness.

In the therapeutic sessions Margy practiced the use of the same strategies to stop masturbation as she used for sexual acting out behavior. She was encouraged to take pride when she could control her masturbatory behavior. Margy enjoyed this, although thinking positively about herself was an entirely new experience and very difficult at first.

Margy suffered greatly when she got her menstrual period. She would go to the bathroom every 10 minutes when she was at home and wipe herself. She would use up to ten rolls of toilet paper during one menstrual period. Elaine asked Margy to bring this up with her therapist. Margy asked Elaine to do it. The therapist asked both mother and daughter to come into the session to talk about it. Margy talked about not wanting to be a girl. She hated the blood and saw it as dirty and messy. She couldn't get herself clean or get it to stop. There was clearly an element of fear in this for her.

This began a series of sessions on two levels. One level was on female anatomy, menstruation, reproduction, dating and sex, and the good things about being a female. On another level, the therapist wondered if the threat by Owen that he would cut out the uteruses of the females, which the other children had disclosed, had anything to do with Margy's fears and compulsive wiping away of the blood. Not wanting to speak directly about this threat, the therapist said that if Margy were a boy she wouldn't have a uterus and she wouldn't have to worry about menstruating or anything happening to her uterus. When Margy agreed, the therapist thought she saw something in Margy's face and heard something in her voice that indicated that that was the issue. Elaine, Margy, and the therapist then talked about being a woman and what it meant. They talked about the positive aspects. When asked about the negative aspects of being a woman, Margy said "having a uterus." Elaine said she had had to have hers removed and could no longer have children. Margy nearly jumped up in her chair. "You don't have your uterus?" She then looked somewhat shaken and somewhat relieved. It was hard to know what she was thinking.

The therapist tried to help Margy talk, draw, and use clay in the individual sessions to express the meaning for her of the blood and the fear it aroused, but to no avail. She shut down.

Margy and her mother were given several of the sex education books that the therapist used in the sessions with them. They were encouraged to read them through again together. Margy was willing to do this. The therapist wanted Margy to have free access to the correct information and not feel shame about looking through it. Over the next several months Margy and her therapist talked many times about the menstruation problems. These problems gradually disappeared.

During the initial phase of therapy, Elaine met with Margy's therapist weekly, even if very briefly. This allowed the therapist to develop an alliance with Elaine, inquire about Margy's behavior at home and school, and positively reinforce any progress noted during the previous week. These weekly meetings were usually held at the time of the appointment, although additional appointments were occasionally scheduled. Margy was informed about the content of the meetings. Several conjoint meetings were also held between Elaine, Margy, and the therapist, always with Margy's permission.

After there was no further possibility of criminal charges being filed and after the Dependency Court hearings, Margy was invited to join a group as well as continue in individual therapy. Margy declined this opportunity despite our repeated encouragement, choosing to remain only in individual therapy.

Phase 2

The court proceedings created a greater sense of safety, in that visitation could not occur unless Margy and Ronny wanted it. The focus of therapy could now be aimed specifically at feelings related to the abuse. I introduced several lists of feelings that other children had related to me about their sexual abuse experience. Margy was to go through the lists and circle any feelings she thought she "might" have "if she had been sexually abused." She did this carefully and with no hesitation, choosing the following feelings: panicked, curious, shocked, tearful, nervous, suspicious, disappointed, guilty, dumb, important, disgusting, angry, upset, fearful, scared, terrified, worried, silly, sad, hated, hateful, awful, hurt, fearless, afraid, confused, miserable, stupid, grouchy, and ashamed. Margy opted to work on two of these, "disgusting" and "scary".

When Margy began to retreat from talking in an "as if" type of way about disgusting and scary feelings, we agreed that the drawings she made about the feelings could be about *anything* she felt was disgusting or scary, not just sexual abuse. Initially, she stated that she couldn't think of anything that was disgusting and scary, but with gentle persistence Margy drew a picture of a man who had been shot lying dead in a pool of red blood. The gun was disproportionately large to the size of the gunmen's body. She took a break from drawing but in another session drew a picture of a starving bum with large red flies swarming all around him. Gradually, the pictures began to emerge more rapidly, e.g., a picture of "po-po with red flies," another of a "car accident with a lot of people involved in it with blood coming down." Her last drawing was entitled, "Freddy Cougar in Nightmare on Elm Street, Part I, II, and III." The picture was of a stick figure with a large hat with very long fingernails with red spots all over his face.

Her pictorial representations of the adjectives disgusting and scary are notable for their destructive and aggressive nature, as reflected in the red blood and red flies.

The red flies were noteworthy because Valerie had extreme anxiety reactions to flies and even reported visual hallucinations of flies. The blood probably reflected Margy's fears around menstruation and also an instance wherein Valerie, in a dissociative episode, had attempted to jump out of a third story window, stating she wanted to "be blood." Margy's drawings were stark in quality and frightening in content and reflected her need for release from these powerful internal fears and conflicts.

The next sessions saw Margy continuing to draw pictures of feelings she had selected from the "feelings list." She regularly would protest that she couldn't imagine how she would feel if she were abused, and so the therapist would suggest that she talk and draw the feelings John and Valerie might feel about being abused. This seemed to allow sufficient emotional distance for her to continue to pursue the exercise. Each session she chose a feeling and drew pictures. Her efforts were very good, allowing the therapist to praise her work. This praise appeared to be positively perceived by Margy.

In one session, she chose the feeling "curious" and drew pictures of two guns. These were labeled "Mr. Owen's black gun" and "Mr. Owen's other black gun." She showed both pictures to her mother and brother, which prompted a family discussion about Owen's guns. Elaine recounted that she routinely fought with Owen to keep the guns hidden and unloaded. Ronny recalled a time a gun discharged by accident and they could not find the bullet. Margy remembered that the bullet had been found in a shoe in the parents' closet. Ronny said that he was never scared about the guns but Elaine and Margy said they were. In therapy sessions, John and Valerie talked about Owen's guns being used as threats to keep them from talking.

The session immediately after the gun pictures seemed to mark a small breakthrough after more than a year of therapy. Margy chose the feeling "tearful" and then drew two pictures. The first was of John and Valerie crying with Owen standing near them smiling and saying, "I got you now." Her second picture was of her father's bedroom, with a large bed on which Ronny, John, and Valerie were lying down. Owen was standing at the top of the bed. Margy was asked if she thought Owen had molested only her brother, John, and Valerie, and not her. She stated, "No, I think he must have touched me, too. There is no reason he wouldn't have done that." After a several-second pause, Margy added, "But I don't remember."

Over the course of several months, Margy chose the feelings of "guilty," "scared," "upset," "fearful," "excited," and "afraid." At the end of this period, Margy was better able to talk about feeling regarding her father, who she was now referring to as Owen. Although she stated that she did not have any feelings about Owen, she spoke in detail about her brother's angry feelings towards him. These feelings were related to numerous broken promises unrelated to the sexual abuse. Several weeks after the movement to a greater verbal focus, Elaine brought in a photocopy of a letter Margy had sent to her father. It included a clipping from a religious newspaper written by Lisa, a daughter molested by her father. The father begs forgiveness of her for his sins. The title to the clipping read, "Dad, if you don't read this, then don't write back, Lisa." It was then signed, "Margy and Ronny, your only kids. Goodbye. READ IT!!!!!!!! It will help you." Margy had agreed to allow Elaine to copy it and give it to her therapist while she was away on a class trip.

Two other significant events occurred during this phase. The first was related to Elaine's work in therapy regarding her molestation by her stepfather. This prompted Elaine to confront her mother and stepfather and enabled her to come to some resolution regarding this. Elaine told her children about her molestation and then came to several sessions. The express purpose of these sessions was to allow Margy to discuss feelings about her mother. Elaine told Margy about her feelings about molestation, why she had not told anyone until now, and how angry she was at her mother for not protecting her. She also described in detail her feelings of being different and her constant guilt.

Although Margy denied having "given clues" to her mother about the abuse, Elaine stated that she felt Margy had given numerous clues and she felt stupid for not picking them up. She reminded Margy of how Margy would cling to her and beg her not to go to school meetings at night, and how both children would insist on going everywhere with her, rather than staying at home alone with Owen. She talked about her guilt feelings directly to Margy, who listened attentively to everything Elaine said but said nothing in response.

The other major external event during this phase involved Jaqui, who initiated a lawsuit against Elaine for the sexual abuse of her children through Elaine's homeowner's insurance. The suit was eventually dismissed because it could not be proved that the sexual abuse was "accidental," but Jaqui then blamed Elaine for having been present during Owen's molestation of her children, John and Valerie. This included confronting Elaine in the presence of her two children and accusing her directly. John and Valerie were interviewed by their therapists and Jaqui was interviewed by Margy's therapist, placing all parties in a rather difficult situation, since both women and their children were continuing to be seen at the institute. The consensus of the therapists was that the children had become confused and that Elaine was not present during the sexual abuse. This neutralized the situation somewhat, but Elaine felt devastated by Jaqui's actions.

The next session, Margy, for the first time ever, initiated the session. She clearly was angry about Jaqui's accusation. She stated that her mother had not been present during the sexual abuse and that she wanted her therapist to know that. The therapist said she knew that, adding that if Margy knew that maybe she was beginning to remember some things. Without hesitation, Margy said she could now remember the time when Owen put the knife handle in Valerie's vagina. She then began to demonstrate it with dolls. She reported that all four children—Ronny, John, Valerie, and herself—had been there. Valerie was held on the bed with handcuffs (a detail which had been stated by all three of the other children), her legs were spread, and she was crying. Owen said that he would hurt her but then put the handle of the knife inside her instead of the blade. Margy spoke of being terrified, not knowing what would happen next. She reported that she just watched and felt scared. Full of emotion, she said, "My mother wasn't there. My mother didn't know." Although a court of law would discount a disclosure such as this, given that Margy had previously been told some of the details, the therapist was convinced that Margy spoke from firsthand experience. Her description of how she felt while she watched Valerie being abused was very real and fear could be not only heard in her voice but felt in the room.

Margy again appeared more open and assured in the next session. She created the same scene with the dolls. It was suggested that she speak to the Owen doll, and with only minor hesitation she began to ask why he had lied to Ronny and her, mentioning specific instances. She asked him why he was so mean. Later she said to her therapist in a low voice, "He should be in jail." When asked why, she replied, "For molesting kids." The therapist then asked "Which kids?" and Margy replied, "All of the kids."

Phase 3

After the emotionally charged sessions of the preceding months, the therapy took a new course. During this period, Margy and the therapist spoke as though they had openly discussed and acknowledged the sexual abuse. Despite the fact that she had yet to talk about her own victimization in anything other than these general terms, Margy appeared to be in the recovery phase of treatment.

Margy's progress was clearly seen in her stories to the Projective Storytelling cards (Caruso, 1987). While generally telling of people hurt and dying and families being separated, she also had the heroine finding her way home or solving some problem that helped make things better. There were happy endings. When these stories were compared to those she had told during her initial psychological evaluation, more hope, strength, and emotional resourcefulness were evident.

During this period Margy's grades improved, she developed a wide range of friends at school, became more interested in her clothes and her appearance, and went to a chaperoned dance with a boy. She was more open, direct, and confident with her therapist and she no longer appeared afraid.

Elaine had some difficulty with Margy's individuation, such as spending the night with friends and "going to the mall." Many conjoint sessions were spent on this topic, and Elaine was encouraged to inquire of other parents in Margy's class and of Margy's teacher about age-appropriate activities.

Margy was still unwilling to be completely open about her thoughts and feelings, as evidenced by her refusal to write down her dreams. However, during the final phase Margy and her therapist read the book *Dear Elizabeth* during several sessions (Lickey & Swan, 1989). This provided another opportunity to talk "as if" Margy had been abused. Parallels between Margy's and Elizabeth's feelings were examined, as were differences.

Reading this book prompted a discussion of problems that might arise as sexually abused girls get older, e.g., trusting men, problems with dating and sexuality, etc. Margy gave permission for the therapist to have a session with Elaine regarding issues that might come up in the future due to her sexual abuse. Margy agreed readily to the session, as if she wanted her mother to have this information and store it for her. She did not deny the intimation by the therapist that she had been abused, but she never openly acknowledged it either.

Termination occurred more quickly than the therapist planned. Although Margy stated clearly that she wanted to stop, she had not completed several important goals (Long, 1986), including acknowledging the sexual abuse and sorting out her attributions related to sexual acting out. In addition, she could not clearly articulate feelings regarding her mother and father, and the therapist believed Margy still maintained a powerful and threatening internalized image of her father (Lister, 1982). The world was far less frightening to Margy, but she still felt like a victim. Group therapy was again offered, but Margy refused. This was understandable given the one year and nine months that had elapsed since her initial disclosure.

The last few sessions were spent reviewing the previous 18 months. The clay figures and pictures made together were again looked at. The final session was again initiated by Margy, only the second time in the span of therapy. Margy wanted to know if the therapist was disappointed because she could not remember the abuse. After the therapist said no, Margy responded, "I'm glad." Margy's positive growth was reviewed, both individually with Margy and then later in the session with Elaine. Margy beamed as the therapist spoke to Elaine. Elaine, Margy, Ronny, and their therapists had pizza and soda together as they prepared to say goodbye. As Margy was walking away, she asked her mother, "Do you have Toni's business card, just in case?" After her mother said yes, Margy smiled and turned away.

Specific Techniques Used in Therapy

Given Margy's initial hesitancy to talk, the therapist relied a great deal on nonverbal techniques. For example, Margy enjoyed playing the therapist's rendition of Gardner's Mutual Storytelling (Gardner, 1975). The therapist would draw a squiggle on a large piece of paper and Margy would then create a picture around the squiggle and tell a story about it. Margy would then draw a squiggle and the therapist would create a parallel story with a different and often more adaptive ending. Feelings, coping strategies, and interpersonal relationships were explored with these stories. Her gradual movement towards a more positive outlook and less anxiety was also evident in her stories.

As mentioned earlier, work with clay and other art materials was also a commonly utilized technique. Probably the most useful approach to Margy, given her reluctance to disclose, was the repeated use of an "as if" approach, where Margy could talk about the abuse "as if" it had happened to her. This was evident in our use of a feelings list and other interactions.

Margy's growth could not have been facilitated as readily if Elaine had not been involved in the therapy. Regular parent meetings were crucial to success, as were the numerous conjoint sessions with Margy and her mother, and occasionally, Margy, her mother, and her brother.

OUTCOME OF TREATMENT

Externally, Margy revealed many signs of positive growth. She had numerous friends, her school performance was excellent, she was on the cheerleading squad, and her relationships with her mother and brother were quite adequate. She reported feeling pleased that she had talked about her sexual acting out and that she had stopped it, and she also expressed no remorse and a great deal of satisfaction that her father no longer lived with them. The therapist was impressed with what seemed to be considerably enhanced ability to take care of herself and get help if she needed it.

Projective personality assessment was repeated and indicated increased internal resources of coping, resilience, and problem solving. She felt proud of herself and had plans for the future.

Margy's failure to clearly acknowledge the abuse and put it in an appropriate perspective is troubling and increases the chances of problems later. On the other hand, giving this timid child control over the timing and the content of her disclosures may have been a critical key in helping her build a sense of personal power and mastery. Her remarkable gains in that area are undeniable. The SPARK staff understood that Margy's 18 months with us was only the start of a long process. She was seen several times a year for the following three years until moving out of state. Fears of Owen persisted but gains were persisting in all other aspects of her life.

OBSTACLES TO TREATMENT

A primary obstacle was Margy's inability to disclose. During the first phase of treatment, Owen's intimidation of the children was reinforced by the fact that they saw him four times in the courthouse related to the adjudication hearing in Dependency Court. Even more frightening, he started to park close to their school playground and stare at them. Elaine had to get a restraining order to bring these terrifying "visits" to an end. Each time the children saw Owen they became more anxious. This affected Margy's school work and her interpersonal relationships. In addition, Margy's reaction to the disruption she felt when she was initially placed in foster care separate from her brother also colored her willingness to trust the system and myself. This event was a dramatic fulfillment of Owen's threat that talking about the abuse would break up the family.

OTHER SYSTEMS INVOLVED

Other systems are routinely involved in our work with sexually reactive children. As mentioned before, Margy was interviewed approximately 15 times by different individuals in the early phase of involvement. Although we were assisted eventually by the special child abuse police team, the initial response by untrained policemen was not helpful. However, our continued involvement with protective services and the court system was crucial to creating greater safety for the children. Owen did not exercise his right to have monitored visits with the children in a protective service worker's office.

Margy and Ronny did attend the Kids in the Court System (KICS) program at the Children's Institute, which was designed to educate children about the court process. The preparation for testimony was helpful to reducing anxiety and assuring them about safety during court hearings.

The children's and mother's therapists met weekly and often more frequently to discuss this case because of the confusing and often dramatic incidents of sexual abuse being revealed by the children. Consultation and mutual support of the therapists were essential.

MISTAKES

There were numerous instances when we doubted our abilities. When Jaqui first accused Elaine of being involved in the molestation of her children, this reactivated our own fears that she had somehow contributed to Margy's abuse and that her involvement was what fueled Margy's continued resistance. It may have been that Jaqui and the children should have been interviewed by individuals separate from the case rather than by the children's therapists, who may have been committed to their own perception of the facts by this time.

Other issues pertain to whether or not the therapist should have pushed harder for Margy to disclose, maybe even using techniques such as hypnosis. Whether or not this was truly a mistake is yet to be determined.

THERAPIST'S REACTION TO THE CASE

My feelings ran the gamut of relief, exasperation, sadness, and disappointment at termination. It was difficult to gauge from Margy's behavior how to guide the therapy and I frequently felt that I was guessing about the proper direction. The likelihood of future problems is high because of the failure to clearly acknowledge the abuse and put it in an appropriate perspective.

Other reactions were fear in relationship to initial interactions with Owen and frequent second-guessing, particularly prompted by Jaqui's accusations related to Elaine. Frustration at the initial response of the police to the children and their subsequent separation in foster care also colored my reaction to these children.

However, I did come to the realization that children vary widely in their processing of abuse. If this was truly a beginning step for Margy, it was a good step.

The frustrations of the case were not confined to Margy's resistance. One of the greatest problems for professionals in child abuse treatment is learning to let go of the many aspects of the case they cannot control. Because of a variety of problems, including Margy's persistent denial, the authorities had decided that criminal charges could not be successfully pressed against Owen. As a result, nothing could be done when the staff discovered that he was living with a woman who had two young children.

15
Treatment of a Mildly Retarded Victim Who Is Becoming an Offender

J. ROBERT WHEELER

Can mildly retarded young sex offenders be treated successfully? Dr. Wheeler does us a service by illustrating a theoretically sound and clinically appropriate treatment of this young man. He speaks openly of the minor successes and the major doubts that exist about the efficacy of the treatment. The reader is left with clear concerns about what is ahead of this young boy and with awareness of the problems with self-control that are often evident in language-disordered and mentally retarded children and adolescents. In addition to Randy's victimization of others, treatment considerations include his own sexual abuse and his lack of consistent and positive attachment to a caregiver. In fact, Randy was molested by his mother, a phenomenon we are seeing more and more often in this field. In addition, she was physically abusive of him and terrorized him repeatedly. At the time of treatment, he was living in a residential treatment setting. This provided necessary structure and support, but spoke clearly to the absence of family members who clearly valued him and who could provide additional support for positive change.

For the most part, Randy gave the illusion of openness and cooperation with treatment. He freely recounts his thoughts and urges and talks about his previous abuse. Yet he seems to be speaking in a disembodied voice—his words and actions aren't influenced by each other. This is a common and persistent block to therapy success. The psychological testing also indicated this to be the case, predicting superficial cooperation in the absence of follow through with interventions, despite the tremendous efforts extended and the use of numerous, well-validated treatment procedures. Dr. Wheeler concludes by stating that limited progress has been made. He is not being trite in his admission to feelings of inadequacy; rather, he is stating something we have all felt. — Editor

AUTHOR'S THEORETICAL ORIENTATION

This chapter describes the treatment of a teenage boy who was physically and sexually abused by his mother as a very young child but was referred for treatment as a young teenager because of an emerging pattern of sexually aggressive behavior. Treatment was guided broadly by the perspectives of a clinician trained as a psychologist, whose orientation is fundamentally informed by cognitive-social learning theory. The effects of sexual abuse were conceptualized "as a combination of classically conditioned responses to traumatic stress and socially learned behavior and cognitive responses to the abuse experience" (Berliner & Wheeler, 1987, p. 415). It was assumed that the initial harmful effects of abuse disrupted and profoundly altered the course of the victim's subsequent development cognitively, affectively, interpersonally, and behaviorally. His maladaptive attempts to master his own victimization resulted in a preoccupation with sexual thoughts and overt sexual aggression. These behaviors, in turn, resulted in his continued confinement in a restrictive residential treatment setting, which produced still further alterations in the course and quality of his social and emotional development.

Consistent with the responses of many victims (Browne & Finkelhor, 1986), Randy was an initially anxious, fearful victim whose behavior was characterized during the period of his most severe victimization by learned helplessness. After being removed from the care of his abusive mother, and as the course of his development unfolded, a number of derivative developmental effects emerged. These included signs and symptoms of traumatic sexualization (Finkelhor & Browne, 1985); fundamental alterations in his cognitive-affective processes, characterized by a range of behaviors, cognitions, and feelings consistent with what van der Kolk (1987) has described as the biphasic process of hyperarousal and numbing characteristics of victims of severe trauma. Randy's hyperarousal or "approach" responses included persistent intrusive recollections, angry outbursts, flashbacks, and attempts to "master" the traumatization through behavioral reenactments and identification with his aggressor. Numbing or "avoidance" responses included avoidance of peers and adults, a pronounced preference for solitary activities, and evidence of dissociation and depersonalization. Also evident were a variety of primitive psychological defenses, including denial and splitting.

DESCRIPTION OF CASE

Randy is a 15-year-old mildly mentally retarded youth who was referred initially for psychological evaluation and subsequently for treatment by his social services caseworker. At the time of referral Randy had been living in a group home for two and one-half years. The referral, initiated at the request of the group home staff, was prompted by several incidents in which Randy engaged in sudden sexual attacks on female children. The referral request was initially to assess and subsequently to treat this youth's developing sexual psychopathology. Although his own victimization was recognized by referral sources, the focus of concern was an emerging pattern of sexually aggressive behavior. In addition to specific acts of sexual aggression, various less obvious behaviors, such as Randy's preoccupation with younger children, apparent attempts to fondle the genitals of pets, and a number of incidents of inappropriate sexual touching of staff in the group home, were of concern. Equally frustrating to group home staff was Randy's inability to develop relationships with other peers or adult staff members, his difficulty in acquiring social skills, and what was described as persistent "spacey" behavior both at school and on the living unit.

Prior to his placement in group care, Randy had completed a six-week inpatient treatment course in a children's psychiatric unit, where he had been referred as a result of his accelerating aggressive, oppositional, and sexually inappropriate behaviors at home. These behaviors included physical and sexual assaults against his two sisters, one and two years younger than Randy; verbal intimidation and threats of bodily harm toward his sisters; oppositional and noncompliant behavior with his stepmother; and expulsion from school for disruptive behavior, which took the form of singing and shouting in class and fights initiated with peers. The known sexual assaults of his sisters included incidents in which he had been found attempting to mount one sister sexually and lying on top of the second one mimicking intercourse. In both cases the girls were naked.

Family history was provided by the father, a laborer. Randy's parents had met when Mr. Wilson was in his early thirties and Mrs. Wilson was in her early twenties. Mr. Wilson's personal history was generally unremarkable, except for periods of alcohol abuse when younger. His ex-wife had been raised on a horse breeding ranch in eastern Washington. Her father was reportedly a stern and physically abusive man with stereotypically chauvinistic views about women. She was reportedly subjected to beatings with a horse's harness for relatively trivial misbehavior. Mr. Wilson knew little about his ex-wife's relationship with her mother but believed that it had been warm and affectionate. According to Mr. Wilson, his ex-wife had denied being the victim of sexual abuse. Despite her denial, however, he acknowledged that he suspected that she may have been abused because of the unusual circumstances of her participation in the horse breeding operation. Mr. Wilson reported that, although she was generally excused from "man's work" around the ranch, her father had required her to assist in inserting the stallion's penis into the mare's vagina during breeding. Mr. Wilson found this activity to be unusual and disturbing.

Randy was the oldest of three children born to his parents. Following a three-year period of repeated separations and reconciliations, his parents separated permanently when Randy was six years old. Following the final separation, Mr. Wilson retained custody of the three children. Mr. Wilson remarried when Randy was seven years old. The second marriage was reported to be stable and harmonious.

The history of Randy's sexual victimization was reconstructed from accounts provided independently by Randy and his father. Apparently, physical and possibly sexual abuse of Randy by his mother began during the first two years of his life. According to observations made but not reported at the time by his paternal grandmother, Randy was noted to "freeze" when his mother glared at him. One of his uncles also reportedly had observed Mrs. Wilson masturbating Randy when he was very young while the two laid together on her bed. His sisters later reported numerous observations of abuse of Randy by their mother. They described how they observed their mother deliberately wade with Randy into deep water at a lake and release him, even though he could not swim. On another occasion she reportedly sent him careening alone in a sled down a steep, snow-covered street. They also corroborated Randy's own reports that he was bound hand and foot and his mouth taped shut with duct tape for extended periods of time.

Randy's own recollections were reported in the form of brief visual flashbacks or intrusive fragmentary recollections over a period of approximately three years, beginning when he was 12. Most have occurred during his current treatment, which has been in progress for a little less than a year. His descriptions of the abuse are often hampered by limited verbal language skills and thought processes that are frequently characterized by mental confusion and circumstantiality. He also suffered considerable abuse when he was preverbal or barely verbal, which may affect his ability to recall and describe events. Despite these limitations, his descriptions of specific events and recollections have remained consistent over extended periods of times and across multiple informants. Randy's obsessive preoccupation with his mother's abusive behavior has been most evident and dramatic. In sharp contrast to the many children who avoid or deny the abuse, Randy often relates any current life circumstances to his mother's bizarre or abusive behavior. There have been times in treatment sessions and in the group home setting where Randy appears so preoccupied with the abuse that he is unable to think about or talk about anything else.

Randy's earliest recollections of abuse involve memories of his sisters being fed juice from a glass while he was fed water from a baby's bottle nipple. He also remembered his mother and him both naked and her requiring him to "chase" her around a room. He remembers having his hands and feet bound and his mouth taped and being left for hours in his room. He remembers his mother performing oral intercourse on him and requiring him on numerous occasions to fondle her breasts or genitals. He has no specific recollection of intercourse but does not rule it out. He has especially vivid memories of two events. In the first, he recalls being in bed with his mother while she performed intercourse with two men whom he did not know but describes as "the Mexicans." He has given contradictory accounts of possible abuse by her paramours. In the second, he recalls his mother menacing him with a knife and threatening "to slit my throat" if he should disclose the abuse. The threat was apparently sufficient to ensure his silence for several years.

PSYCHOLOGICAL ASSESSMENT MATERIAL

The psychological assessment of Randy involved review of previous psychiatric records; review of school psychological evaluations and reports; interviews with him and his father and stepmother, jointly and separately; interviews with group home staff members; and administration of psychological testing. Tests administered included the Millon Adolescent Personality Inventory, the Achenbach Youth Self-Report for ages 11–18, and completion by both group home staff of the Achenbach Child Behavior Checklist for ages 4–16.

During the evaluation Randy described his sexual victimization by his mother with apparent openness and candor, though his recall of times and ages appeared unreliable. At several points during the interviews he spontaneously described intrusive recollections of the abuse and attempts to cope with the victimization by avoidant behaviors. For example, he described that while living with his father and stepmother he would sometimes "space out" while performing his household chores and would experience sudden feelings of fear that his mother would come into the house and abuse him. At another point he described how he sometimes got "strange feelings," which he described as ideas that go shooting like bullets through his head in opposite directions. One feeling was related to his recollection of his mother having threatened to slit his throat if he disclosed her abuse of him. The opposing idea was the feeling that he needed to be alone because, "I don't want to hurt the kids" at the group home. As he described the latter feeling he became visibly distressed and agitated and stated that he sometimes became terrified that his mother, whom he invariably identified by her first name, was still inside his head. His father and stepmother independently corroborated other flashback behaviors.

Randy also disclosed during the evaluation much more extensive sexual abuse of his two sisters than he had previously admitted. He described, for example, engaging one of his sisters in a "game" similar to the one his mother had "played" with him, in which he would manipulate or coerce her into removing her clothes, and then would chase her around the room. The "game" progressed to the point that, over time, the children engaged in digital-vaginal, penile-vaginal, anal and oral intercourse. Randy admitted that, as his sexual contact became more invasive, his sisters would become increasingly resistant. He would respond with frank verbal threats and physical intimidation to obtain compliance.

Results from the Millon indicated that Randy reported multiple neurotic symptoms and was emotionally labile. Alternating moods of hypomanic behavior and lethargy and fatigue were predicted. Although normative data on the Millon are unclear with respect to its validity for use with intellectually impaired adolescents, predictions derived from Randy's test responses converged with significant clinical observations. The instrument accurately predicted a tendency on his part to anticipate conflicts with adults and to act in accordance with his expectation, thus ensuring frequent conflicts and disputes. Impulsive acting-out, depression and excessive fantasizing were all correctly predicted. These test impressions were generally consistent with the observations of his group home counselor, reported on the Child Behavior Checklist. On this instrument, Randy obtained significantly elevated scores on internalizing (uncommunicative, obsessive-compulsive), mixed (hostile-withdrawal), and externalizing (aggressive, hyperactive) scales. The Youth Self Report was only partially completed by Randy and therefore the results were not scored or interpreted. At the conclusion of the evaluation Randy was given diagnoses of post-traumatic stress disorder, oppositional defiant disorder, and mild mental retardation.

Psychological assessment data were broadly useful in planning general treatment strategies, especially initially. The Millon test results indicated that, although he was likely to present himself as superficially cooperative and eager to please, Randy would have difficulty in complying with treatment interventions. Behavioral regressions, passive resistance, and solicitation of attention without follow through in complying with treatment regimens were also predicted. As a consequence of these predictions, an attempt was made to keep behavioral assignments and expectations to a minimum. In retrospect, the pacing of assignments probably was still too rapid for this youth's level of functioning. Failure to comply with tasks was met with mild confrontations and consequences coordinated and implemented by group home staff. Every effort was made (not always successfully) by the therapist to avoid becoming exasperated by passive-resistant, argumentative, and avoidant behaviors. Resistant, argumentative, and avoidant behaviors were tolerated by the therapist in moderate doses, and Randy's regular expressions of frustration were met with expressions of support and sympathy, but when necessary firm limits were established and treatment proceeded. Over the course of treatment the benefit of this strategy in reducing oppositional behavior was one of the most obvious effects of treatment. Depressive symptoms appeared mostly to be situationally specific and usually responded to support and minor environmental interventions. Finally, the therapist (and group home) remained vigilant throughout treatment to fantasies and autistic thinking. Fantasy material was a major therapeutic target for modification.

The data from the Achenbach Child Behavior Checklist were somewhat less directly applicable in treatment, except insofar as they corroborated and provided behavioral specification of other test data. The limitations of the Achenbach data were due to their objective, behaviorally specific quality. While this information was helpful in comparing observations in outpatient therapy to those of group home staff, they were less directly useful during in-office sessions because so much of therapy was focused on cognitive-affective functioning, which is inherently more inferential than checklist observations.

COURSE OF THERAPY

Because of the nature of the initial treatment request and the implications of his sexually aggressive behavior in severely limiting the likelihood of his placement in a non-institutional setting, the ultimate goal of treatment was to reduce the risk that Randy would continue or accelerate his sexually aggressive behavior. Treatment of his victimization, while clearly an appropriate goal in its own right, was conceptualized as a necessary but not sufficient component of an overall treatment plan. The initial period of therapy consisted essentially of an extended assessment of Randy's cognitive capacities and enabled establishment of a working rapport. Initial treatment objectives were to facilitate processing of his own victimization and to desensitize him to discussion of his own sexual misconduct.

The treatment process subsequently has evolved through what can be fairly described as a series of stages demarcated by very fluid boundaries. The modality is individual therapy supplemented by homework assignments and frequent consultation with group home staff and occasional consultations with Randy's father and stepmother. Treatment has been complicated considerably by this youth's intellectual limitations, significant evidence of dissociative thinking, and frequently confused, disorganized, and tangential thought processes. Consideration was given to the possibility that psychotic or prepsychotic thought processes were complicating factors. Psychoactive medications were considered and ruled out both during his psychiatric hospitalization and during a psychiatric consultation during treatment. Randy's thought processes have "tightened" considerably over the course of treatment, apparently in response to a combination of feedback, occasional confrontation, and instruction in simple thinking paradigms modeled after problem-solving interventions for impulsive children.

During the initial stage, the focus of treatment was on establishment of rapport and coping with Randy's tendencies to engage in lengthy and often apparently irrelevant digressions and to contradict himself frequently, and on assessment of his ability to appraise social situations and conform his behavior to the requirements of different circumstances. Unsuccessful and probably premature attempts were also made to engage Randy in monitoring his sexual fantasies. Treatment objectives were to desensitize him to discussion of sexuality and sexual aggression and to facilitate cognitive-affective processing of his own victimization. During this time Randy frequently would attempt to divert the conversation exclusively to discussion of his routine daily activities, ask the therapist to go for walks, request to skip the next treatment session, or inquire about the therapist's personal interests or avocations. If allowed to talk uninterruptedly, he would skip from tangent to tangent and become increasingly disorganized and confused.

In some respects and in retrospect, Randy's resistance to monitoring his sexual fantasies was not that dissimilar to the behavior of cognitively more capable adolescent offenders. It appeared that, despite his mild intellectual impairment, Randy was thoroughly sensitized to the social taboos against open acknowledgment and discussion of sexuality in general and deviant sexual fantasies in particular. In retrospect, it seemed that he needed more time to learn that his therapist could be trusted with his fantasies and more assistance in sharpening his thinking and communication skills before they could be readily articulated. The obsessive nature of some of these fantasies probably also mitigated against their disclosure by virtue of this youth's recognition that his fantasy life in general was quite different from that of his peers and quite unacceptable to most persons.

By trial and error the therapist learned that, by gentle but repeated confrontation and redirection of the content of conversation, Randy could be assisted in sharpening the focus of his thinking and in communicating his thoughts and feelings more coherently. Although he initially found these gentle interruptions frustrating and would at times become quite irritated, over time Randy began to take pride in being able to recite the mnemonic, "Think about the question before speaking and then decide what you want to say." As he was able to communicate his thoughts and feelings more effectively, his physical tension and distractibility decreased markedly, though distractibility is still often evident.

During the initial stage of treatment the content centered alternately on discussion of his sexual misconduct with his sisters in particular and on the abuse he experienced by his mother. Randy often became preoccupied with thoughts of his own abuse and preferred to talk about this at length. This appeared to be a consequence of a desire to avoid discussion of his overt acts of sexual misbehavior and denial of his sexually aggressive impulses, as well as his very obvious need to process the trauma of his own abuse. There was also very definitely a self-stimulating aspect to these verbalizations. His affect as he described his abuse reflected mixtures of fear and anger, and he would become physically agitated and at times quite distressed as he described images of the abuse. He would occasionally break into heaving sobs and ask the therapist if he understood what the abuse was like. Often he had great difficulty communicating coherently and his thoughts were frequently confused and jumbled. His descriptions were often dream-like, reported as images without apparent context, predominantly visual in character, with limited detail and with no clear sequence of action or events. He was especially obsessed with memories of being menaced by his mother with a knife, being in bed with "the Mexicans," and being bound and gagged with tape. These reflections were so fragmentary and fleeting that it is difficult to capture them in narrative.

For example, during one of the earliest sessions, the reasons for his being removed from his parents and placed in a group home were being discussed. He had just stated that he masturbated in the bathroom occasionally (which he would alternately deny and admit) and was asked what he thought about when he masturbated. He replied that he thought about his girls and "my real mom." With a mixture of fearfulness and irritation, he then stated, "the Mexicans are going to bed with [mother]. I have a strange feeling. I want to be by myself. I'm not having a problem. I want to be left alone. [Mother] wanted to slit my throat and held a knife at me." And then, fearfully, "I feel like she's inside me."

Randy acknowledged the incidents where he had been caught during or immediately after commission of the sexually aggressive acts that had directly prompted his referral, but almost uniformly denied any sexual motivations or feelings whatsoever. Even when attempts were made to "normalize" and provide reassurance about sexual feelings, he denied experiencing them. He also denied engaging in any of the subtler predatory or incipient behaviors that the staff of the group home had observed and felt certain were stalking of potential victims, which included adult staff members, very young children, and animals. As the content of sessions became more coherent and alternated between processing of his own victimization and discussion of his sexual aggression, some consistent themes of affective and sexual responding gradually emerged and Randy slowly began to acknowledge his sexual impulses.

His acknowledgment of his impulses initially occurred in vague recollections that when angered (which occurred frequently at school and at the group home) he would sometimes have the same feelings he had when abused by his mother; but he could not describe further or elaborate on these feelings. In later sessions he would relate being in a "crabby" mood to his feelings of being mistreated by his mother and would describe specific acts of abuse by her in greater detail. Eventually he explained with considerable clarity that his sexual assaults of his sisters were nearly identical in enactment to one of the characteristic ways his mother abused him. He would "persuade" his sisters to undress and then engage them in a game of "chase" around the home. Although the game started as fun and involved giggling and teasing, it progressed to frank and frightening sexual assaults. He reported much more detailed information about his abuse of them, including admitting having raped both of them and having made extensive use of physical and verbal force to obtain their submission. He also provided more open and candid accounts of the sexual assaults of two preteen girls that had prompted his referral.

The culmination of this phase of treatment occurred in a remarkable session when his grabbing of the breasts of these preteen girls was being discussed. Randy, without prompting by the therapist, related these events to his abuse by his mother. He explained how he would become jealous of the attention paid by his mother to his younger sisters; he remembered that they would be held and nursed by his mother or fed juice out of a bottle, whereas he would be allowed to drink only water out of a baby bottle with a nipple. He stated that what he really wanted was for his mother to hold him against her breast but she refused. Instead, she would have him strip naked and would have him chase her naked around the house, but would not allow him to catch her. Eventually he would become frustrated and begin crying. According to Randy, it was from these experiences that his desire to touch female breasts originated. He also began to report that these feelings were often associated with feelings of anger and general arousal.

After several months, the content and process of therapy gradually shifted and short-term treatment objectives were reconceptualized. The revised objectives were in part responses to practical exigencies and in part revisions based on the initial stage of therapy and the long term goal. The most important external factor impinging on treatment was consideration by caseworkers and group home staff of attempting to place Randy in a therapeutic foster home. The short-term objectives during this stage of treatment were to assist Randy in coping with his anxiety and associated deterioration in behavior apparently resulting from anticipation of a change in placement; to assist him in recognizing (or admitting) and responding more appropriately to his sexual impulses; to continue processing his own abuse experiences with the more explicit focus of linking them to his own impulses to offend; and to initiate interventions to address directly his deviant impulses.

The content of sessions during this stage of treatment was primarily an elaboration of themes established during the initial stage. There were much more detailed descriptions by Randy of and discussions about his mother's sexual and physical abuse of him, his sexual assaults of his sisters, and his sexual impulses. New content focused primarily on discussion of his thoughts and feelings about foster care and the initiation by the therapist of some discussions about the wrongfulness of sexually aggressive behavior.

Randy's descriptions of his mother's abuse of him gradually included more contextual and action-related detail. The connections between her behavior and his own impulses became more tightly linked. The following is a close paraphrase of Randy describing how his mother's abuse affected him.

> Her actions turned me into a person who might do that to others. It's made me wander off and think. It's changed me so I want to go outside and walk away and think. [Randy is asked to describe his thoughts when he goes outside and walks.] My thoughts are hard to get along with. All the things she did made life hard because I got in trouble. [What has he thought about doing?] Touching people on the penis and putting tape on their mouth. So I can feel how it would be one more time. So I can think about it again, so I can talk about it again. So I can get a complete feeling of what it was like.

His descriptions were increasingly like his telling a story about an exceedingly aversive experience and less like the disjointed visual images that characterized earlier descriptions. He also appeared to grow more comfortable in trusting that his accounts would not be challenged or doubted and that he would be allowed freedom to describe his experiences at length. Randy's accounts of his assaults of his sisters were characterized by more candor. He described, for example, how he would deliberately entice one or both of them into a game. In contrast to his earlier accounts, he acknowledged that his sisters were frequently reluctant participants and that he had to persuade them to play and then to undress. He acknowledged for the first time that he would corner one of the girls and physically overpower her until she submitted to his sexual assault. For the first time he also acknowledged that he was aware of signs and symptoms of their intense distress and resistance. They would attempt to end the game as soon as they recognized the direction it was taking, would cry when he pressured them for sex, and would attempt to fight him off physically when he raped them.

Randy provided extensive new information about his sexual impulses. He admitted having previously lied to the therapist when he denied masturbating, having stalked potential victims at night in the group home, and experiencing ongoing impulses to molest young children. Randy acknowledged that unless externally controlled he would continue to molest young children. Some specific disclosures included accounts of masturbating to fantasies of engaging in sex with specific young children he had known or encountered, fantasies about sneaking up behind peer-aged females and grabbing them on the breasts or crotch, and a specific age preference for children under the age of three. Randy also admitted that most often the content of his masturbatory fantasies involved themes of engaging in sex with his mother or sisters. This provided information necessary for reconditioning this youth's masturbatory practices later in therapy. Masturbatory reconditioning was not introduced at this point, however, because of Randy's unreliability in complying with treatment assignments and in reporting about his behavior.

Therapist interventions varied as a function of the content of the session. When Randy was describing his victimization experiences, the therapist responded with emotional support and encouragement and with clarifying statements. When the assaults of his sister were described, the therapist probed and clarified Randy's perceptions about the wrongfulness of his behavior and introduced low level generalizations to expand Randy's comprehension of wrongfulness. These generalizations were primarily to confirm, reinforce, and expand information previously acquired in the group home. The group home staff's directive that intimate "touching is not OK" was broadened conceptually to include appreciation of the sense of personal violation and associated feelings of fear and anger that were associated with unwanted touching on one's breasts, genitals, or buttocks. Additional information about arousing cognitions and sexual responses was also elicited, though Randy tended to resist and deflect this type of inquiry. Randy was frequently confronted firmly when denying having deviant sexual impulses or engaging in stalking of potential victims.

One such instance occurred when Randy asked to hold the infant baby of a volunteer couple who took him on frequent outings. Randy understood very well that holding of infants was prohibited. When confronted over this violation he repeatedly assured his therapist that he had not intended to molest the child. He rationalized that because he had contemplated whether or not to ask to hold the baby before actually requesting permission (a reference to many sessions focused on "think first, then decide what to do") and had decided that he would not actually molest the child, violation of the prohibition was acceptable. The confrontation of this obvious rationalization was repeated and deflected several times. Randy finally reported that, although he did not believe he would have molested the infant, he was definitely feeling sexually aroused.

The conclusion of this stage of therapy was somewhat arbitrarily traced to four consecutive sessions (numbers 25–28). During these sessions Randy for the first time began explicitly correlating his assaultive fantasies with his mother's behavior toward him, acknowledged frankly predatory impulses, began to express anger rather than exclusively fear at the abuse he had experienced by his mother, and spontaneously expressed appreciation and relief at having been allowed "to get my feelings out" about his mother.

During the first of these four sessions Randy provided his first account of his cognitions during one of the assaults that had precipitated his referral. He had grabbed the breasts of a girl sitting next to him on a school bus. Randy stated that he had molested her because he wanted her to feel the way he had when his mother molested him. He provided the following confused but poignant account of his thinking, which is closely paraphrased from his actual words. He said that he had wanted to put the feelings into words but was afraid that if he did so he would begin to cry, so he had to do rather than say what had happened to him. He wanted the girl to feel the way he had felt and wanted her to know what it felt like so that she would be prepared in the future if another boy should attempt to do to her what his mother had to him. While this sounds like rationalizations often verbalized by offenders, in Randy's case it was more likely a means of establishing some mastery over his own traumatization and control over himself. Nonetheless, such coping responses may well be the foundation of rationalizations as the experience of victimization evolves into offending. Randy then stated that he had felt very angry when he thought about his mother.

During the second of these four sessions Randy described how he had awakened one night at the group home and sneaked to the room of a young girl. He stated that as he looked in her door an intrusive recollection of his mother "plopped into" his head, and he felt that he could "get even" with his mother by assaulting this girl. He could not explain what he meant by this statement. At one point he began crying as he admitted that his own temptations to molest were fearful and at times quite overwhelming. His fear of these temptations appeared associated with his growing recognition and appreciation that additional sexual assaults would result in prosecution. Randy for the first time related specific fantasies about committing sexual assaults in specific locations, including a local shopping mall frequented by young mothers with children in strollers, swimming pools, and parks. He also acknowledged that he was very aroused by several young children he had seen while in the waiting room at a mental health center where he was first evaluated.

What appeared to be a tentative step toward resolution of his own abuse occurred during the third of the four sessions, in which he stated that he felt that he did not need to talk as much about his mother but felt relief at having been allowed to do so. He referred to her as a "ghost" who still haunted him, but not so frequently. He commented that all the things she had done to him were leaving him "bit by bit." In a somewhat confused and rambling fashion he explained that he sometimes wished that his mother, with whom he had had no contact for years, would appear at a session and apologize to him for having been so abusive. He fantasized about slapping her, about telling her that he had wanted her to love him but she had not, and about wanting to see her jailed for abusing him. However, he quickly followed these reflections with a comment about how he would be too frightened of his mother to allow such a visit in reality. He made a comment that he would not even want to go to her funeral.

Short-term treatment objectives were again revised as therapy moved into its third stage. The primary change in objectives during this time involved an increased emphasis on targeted interventions designed to modify Randy's sexually aggressive fantasies and behavior, and attempts to assist Randy in recognizing the relationship between his own victimization and his desires to victimize others, with a particular emphasis on attempting to elicit feelings of empathy. Cognitive rehearsals, modified covert sensitization, and simplified relapse prevention strategies were also introduced. The content of sessions included discussion in much greater detail of specific incidents when Randy had attempted to molest another child, masturbation fantasies and behavior, and processing of Randy's verbalizations about his desires to terrorize his victims. Randy continued to talk about his own victimization but did so less frequently, and occasionally would spontaneously state that he felt less of a need to do so.

For the first time Randy provided detailed descriptions of elaborate fantasies of committing sexual assaults. He had fantasies involving the rape of a peer-aged female, a nine-year-old girl, and an infant of either sex. What was most remarkable was how this mildly retarded youth had developed entirely plausible scenarios for assaulting each of these victims. For example, the fantasy about the teenager involved Randy's returning her to her home after they saw a movie together. He would then wait until she had gone to bed and sneak in the window with a weapon, require her to strip while he trained a gun on her, and then rape her. With the nine-year old, he fantasized engaging her in a board game and then assaulting her after her parents had left the two alone. In the fantasy about the infant he would ask the parents of the child to let him hold it and would then leave their immediate presence and assault it. On two subsequent occasions, Randy engaged in behaviors disturbingly similar to this particular fantasy, when inadvertently permitted by a volunteer family to hold their infant. The clearly emerging theme in the content of these discussions was the pleasure Randy anticipated from the terror of his victims.

Randy made the following new disclosures. He admitted several specific incidents in which he had attempted to molest children. He admitted attempting to approach young children swimming in a lake, positioning himself next to a young mother on a bus with the intention of asking her to allow him to hold her infant, and having specific sexual fantasies about a new young male resident at the group home. With the exception of the incident on the bus, each of the others was prevented by the alert actions of group home staff members. Randy also admitted that when brought to his therapist's office building he would masturbate in a toilet stall to fantasies of engaging in sex with his mother.

During one session Randy's impulses to molest children were being discussed. He had acknowledged and discussed his recognition that the behavior was wrong, harmful to others, and would result in negative consequences. But still he felt compelled to continue. Why?

> To get the feeling that [mother] felt. Kinda good. It would feel good touching them and hurting them the first time. But getting caught by the cops would feel bad. It would feel good in the penis. And it would feel good to see them scared. It'd make me feel good to see them scared. It would make me laugh and them cry. It would make me say, "Oh, what's next?"

On another occasion he described the pleasure he derived from hurting small animals and for the first time told how he had watched his mother beat their dogs with a nail-studded board. He talked confusingly about his desires to "squeeze" small animals (e.g., a pet rabbit). He explained that he would enjoy hurting the animal when he was injuring it but believed that he would feel badly afterward. Randy at times appeared quite distressed when he would describe these feelings, recognize their implications, and realize the risk he presented. During one session he broke down crying, saying he was afraid that he would "hurt someone really, really bad."

Targeted interventions were introduced to address these issues. Because of Randy's intellectual limitations, cognitive confusion, and distractibility, the interventions were modified and simplified from those typically employed with adolescent offenders. Initially, a modified covert sensitization exercise was introduced and repeated over several months. After being assisted through "relaxation patter" in becoming relaxed, Randy was taught to imagine a series of rape approach behaviors based on one of his fantasies. During the approach he would be interrupted by either his father or the program director of his group home, who would call police. He would then be taken to jail, which was described in appropriate but very graphic and aversive terms. Randy eventually was able to rehearse the entire sequence aloud without prompting or intervention by the therapist. He was then prompted to rehearse it covertly during office sessions.

After several months of covert sensitization, a three-step cognitive rehearsal procedure was introduced. Randy was taught to recognize "high risk" situations, to consider the alternative consequences of committing versus not committing the assault, and to enact the appropriate decision (generally to exit the situation or to seek contact with a responsible adult in his environment). Various specific strategies to facilitate and reinforce the "correct" decision were taught and rehearsed. The covert sensitization and cognitive rehearsals were repeated at each session for several months and less frequently in subsequent months. During this course of treatment, preventive strategies were also discussed. These focused in simplified terms on identification and early recognition of high risk situations and simple environmental control strategies.

Repeated but unsuccessful efforts have been made to get Randy to monitor his masturbation fantasies, with the intention of assisting him in focusing on more "appropriate" sexual themes during masturbation. Randy has continued throughout treatment to be resistant to discussion of his masturbation practices, alternately admitting and denying deviant fantasies, and he has never been able (or willing) to monitor these fantasies in any systematic fashion. Thus, the therapist has little confidence in his reports of masturbatory fantasies. Randy has expressed great reluctance to employ sexual fantasies involving peer females out of an apparent lingering belief that all masturbation is "bad," despite the efforts of both his therapist and group home staff to alleviate guilt feelings and channel his fantasies in appropriate directions.

During this stage of treatment discussions of Randy's own victimization have been more lucid and here-and-now oriented. Randy has expressed the desire to confront his mother, tell her how angry he is with her, and see her jailed. He also would like "to take out her inside part so she cannot have babies." He wonders how he would react if he actually confronted her and worries greatly that she would deny having committed the abuse he has described. He admits that the idea of seeing her is still very frightening to him. In his most detailed elaboration of this theme he described wanting his therapist to meet with her and then have him join the session. He would then describe to her "all the things that were wrong" that she did to him. He would then ask her why she did those things to him, why she went to bed with the Mexicans, and why she made his Dad find a new wife. Then he would want to ask her if she loved him. He wishes she would admit her offenses, apologize to him, and tell him that she loves him.

Treatment of Randy continues. The ultimate goal of reducing his risk of re-offending remains unmeasured. Process oriented outcomes are measured primarily through his verbalizations and observations by staff members at the group home. Randy has made significant progress in working through his own victimization. He can talk and think about his own abuse experiences more lucidly. He reports that he dissociates less frequently at school and at the group home and is better able to concentrate on tasks at hand. He is less fearful and his affective responses to his victimization are characterized mostly by anger. He has begun to work through his anger through imaginary confrontations with his mother, which have an element of reality to them and are socially and legally appropriate. However, by his own admission he continues to engage in dissociative thinking about his abuse. His ambivalent feelings about his mother continue to confuse him. And he continues to fantasize about engaging in sexual activities with his mother.

Randy is able to identify and describe his deviant impulses. He is more candid in discussing them. He openly acknowledges that he is sexually aroused by young children, that he masturbates to fantasies of engaging in sex with inappropriate partners, and that he experiences temptations to commit sexual assaults. He appears genuinely to be distressed by his recognition that he derives pleasure from hurting others. He has begun to appreciate the connection between the pain that he experienced from abuse and the pain that others would feel if he re-offended. He gets stuck cognitively, however, in reconciling his apparent genuine desire not to hurt others and his appreciation of the fact that he would derive pleasure from the act, if not the result, of hurting.

Randy is able to recognize and identify situations in which he is at risk of re-offending. He appears to be genuinely and appropriately fearful of the consequences to him of re-offending. Cognitively, he can enact effective risk avoidance strategies. However, absent effective adult supervision, he continues to engage in behaviors that appear to constitute stalking or approach of potential victims. He exercises poor judgment in high risk situations. For example, recall the incident when he asked to hold a baby despite recognizing that doing so was expressly prohibited. He rationalized his behavior by stating that he had thought about whether or not he was going to abuse the infant, had decided that he was not, and therefore decided to disregard the rule against holding infants. The glimmer of progress in this incident was that Randy had moved from a stance of complete denial of relevant issues and behaviors to one of rationalizing high risk behaviors.

TREATMENT TECHNIQUES

The basic technique employed in Randy's treatment was talking therapy. Randy's verbal behavior was initially unfocused and digressive. Over time his verbalizations were gradually shaped to focus on abuse themes and sexual fantasies and conduct, consistent with the goal of desensitizing him to discussion of this subject matter. As Randy's thinking became increasingly relevant, therapeutic feedback focused on assisting him in identifying and comprehending his affective responses to his own physical and sexual victimization and on relating his own victimization to his current sexual impulses.

Subsequently, targeted interventions were introduced with the goal of modifying sexually aggressive fantasies and conduct. These included cognitive rehearsals of appropriate escape and coping responses when exposed to "high risk" sexual situations, modified covert sensitization, and simplified relapse prevention strategies. Attempts to implement masturbatory reconditioning were unsuccessful because of this youth's unreliability in reporting honestly about his own behavior and his resistance to completing homework assignments.

OUTCOME OF TREATMENT

Randy probably has made relatively limited progress toward the ultimate goal of reducing the risk he presents of sexually offending. Although most of the time he denies using deviant themes and images when he masturbates, in all likelihood he continues to masturbate to deviant fantasies. He does admit continued occasional fantasies of engaging in sex with his mother. He reports that he is successful in resisting masturbatory fantasies of his sisters, though this obviously cannot be verified. Overall, he is more consistently acknowledging persistent "temptations" to molest very young children, which is desirable clinically and a significant step forward, but regrettably also an accurate assessment of the risk he presents. In short, without continued environmental controls in the form of adult supervision, Randy continues to present a high risk of sexually offending.

OBSTACLES TO TREATMENT

Because of the cooperation of the staff at the group home and Randy's father and stepmother, treatment with Randy has presented relatively few logistical, system-related, or environmental obstacles. The primary obstacles to treatment progress have been the seriousness of this youth's traumatization, his mild mental retardation, and his inability or unwillingness to comply with treatment homework assignments, especially related to monitoring of his masturbation practices and sexual fantasies. Management of the first two obstacles has essentially been accomplished by slowing the pace of treatment and simplifying the interventions to accommodate Randy's level of functioning. Monitoring his masturbation and sexual fantasies has been deferred and possibly will have to be abandoned unless better cooperation can be elicited from Randy.

OTHER SYSTEMS INVOLVED

As noted throughout the chapter, coordination of services with the group home where Randy was a resident has been an important component of treatment. He obviously is not a youth safe to live at this time in a less restrictive setting. Because of the long-term risk he presents to his sisters and the unwillingness of his parents to expose them to the risk of additional assaults, Randy will not return to their care. This issue had been largely resolved prior to his referral for treatment. Consequently, his parents' involvement in treatment has primarily been to provide support to Randy, to continue their relationship with him while he is in group care through regular visitation, and to assist the therapist by providing additional background information as requested. The state social services system has also been involved in supporting his treatment financially as well as in attempting to develop a "permanent" plan to assist this youth, at least until he is 18 years old and possibly longer. To date, the criminal justice system has not been involved.

MISTAKES

Attempting to calibrate therapeutic interventions to Randy's level of functioning and capacity to participate effectively in the interventions has been a process of trial and error that has resulted in some missteps. The therapist erred in attempting to introduce self-monitoring procedures too early in treatment. Not only did Randy fail to cooperate with these efforts but they probably reinforced Randy's tendency to withhold relevant information about his sexual deviance from his therapist. That is, the expectation that he would monitor his sexual impulses was tantamount to expecting that this youth would fully and freely acknowledge his deviance. Given his sensitivity to the implications of punishment and his lack of trust in the therapist early on, this expectation probably reinforced rather than reduced his inhibitions against self-disclosure.

Similarly, knowing how and when to pressure Randy to organize his thought processes more coherently was most challenging and fraught with error. At times the therapist despaired that he would ever be capable of focusing his attention coherently and following a thought to its conclusion. In later months, the therapist worried that he tolerated too much cognitive slippage early on and could have expedited treatment by exerting more control over the therapeutic process.

THERAPIST REACTIONS TO THE CASE

My reactions to this case have fallen into three broad categories. First, I have often felt that effective treatment of this youth would take "forever" because of the enormity of his disturbances. I was simultaneously frustrated by the knowledge that his treatment would necessarily be time-limited because of the exigencies of funding for services. I have tried to reassure myself periodically with the admonition that Randy's cognitive limitations primarily affected the pace but not necessarily the outcome of treatment.

Second, many times I have been confronted with and embarrassed by my own feelings of impatience and exasperation with a youth who, despite many endearing qualities, can be quite persistently oppositional and argumentative. Thankfully, Randy has been nearly endlessly patient and good-humored with me at such times. He has, for example, recognized my exasperation and commented sympathetically that I must be having a bad day. Or occasionally he would recognize his own argumentativeness, catch himself, and offer a genuine apology for arguing over a triviality.

I have found it especially difficult to remain patient in the face of violations of strict rules regarding potentially high risk behaviors, both because of the implications of the safety of others and because of a genuine fondness for Randy and fear that he would be incarcerated for an impulsive offense. I find myself at times wanting to shake him by the collar and ask, "Don't you realize what will happen to you?"

Finally, trite though it sounds, I have often felt quite inadequate to cope with the complexity of Randy and his behavior. Too often my own rationality has simply not been up to the task of understanding the complex forces that resulted in a youth who could simultaneously be so friendly, affectionate and forgiving of others, and yet so openly and guilelessly impelled to engage in such reprehensible behavior.

References

Abraham, K. (1927). The narcissistic evaluation of excretory processes in dreams and neurosis. *Selected papers on psychoanalysis*. London: Hogarth.

Achenbach, T., & Edelbrock, C. (1983). *Manual for the Child Behavior Checklist and revised child behavior profile*. Burlington: University of Vermont Department of Psychiatry.

Alexander, P. C. (1985). A systems theory conceptualization of incest. *Family Process, 24*, 79-88.

American Professional Society on the Abuse of Children (APSAC). (1990). *The Advisor, 3* (4).

American Psychiatric Association. (1987). *Diagnostic and Statistical Manual of Mental Disorders* (3rd ed., rev.). Washington, DC: American Psychiatric Association.

Amsterdam, B. K., & Levitt, M. (1980). Consciousness of self and painful self-consciousness. *Psychoanalytic Study of the Child, 35*, 67-83.

Antonelli, L. (1988). Satan's victim: One woman's ordeal. *Style Weekly*, 38-43.

Authier, K. (1983). Incest and sexual violence. *Family Therapy Collections, 2*, 101-128.

Axline, V. M. (1947). *Play Therapy*. New York: Ballantine Books.

Bagley, C., & Ramsey, R. (1986). Sexual abuse in childhood: Psychosocial outcomes and implications for social work practice. *Journal of Social Work and Human Sexuality*, 4, 33-47.

Believe the Children Newsletter (1987). 4, Manhattan Beach, CA.

Bentovim, A., Elton, A., Hildebrand, J., Tranter, M., & Vizard, E. (1988). *Sexual abuse in the family*. Bristol: John Wright.

Bentovim, A., & Jacobs, B. (1988). Children's needs and family therapy: The case of abuse. In: E. Street & W. Dryden (Eds.). *Family therapy in Britain*. Buckingham, England: Open University Press.

Bentovim, A., & Kinston, W. (1991). Focal family therapy: Joining systems theory with psychodynamic understanding. In: A. Gurman & D. Kniskern (Eds.), *Handbook of Family Therapy* (2nd. ed.). New York: Brunner/Mazel.

Berliner, L., & Wheeler, J. R. (1987). Treating the effects of sexual abuse on children. *Journal of Interpersonal Violence, 2* (4), 415-434.

Bogdan, J. L. (1984). Family organization as an ecology of ideas: An alternative of the reification of family systems. *Family Process, 23*, 375–399.

Bowlby, J. (1973). *Attachment and loss: Separation* (Vol. 2). New York: Basic Books.

Briere, J. (1989). *Therapy for adults molested as children: Beyond survival*. New York: Springer.

Briere, J., & Runtz, M. (1987). Post sexual abuse trauma: Data and implications for clinical practice. *Journal of Interpersonal Violence, 2*, 367–379.

Browne, A., & Finkelhor, D. (1986). Impact of child sexual abuse: A review of the literature. *Psychological Bulletin, 99*, 16–77.

Burlingham, D. (1946). Twins: Observations of environmental influences on their development. *Psychoanalytic study of the Child, 2*: 61–73.

Burlingham, D. (1949). The relationship of twins to each other. *Psychoanalytic Study of the Child, 3/4*: 57–72.

Byng-Hall, J. (1989). *Replicative and corrective scripts*. Presentation to the Institute for Family Therapy, London.

Camras, L. A., Ribordy, S., Hill, J., Martino, S., Spaccarelli, S., & Stefani, R. (1988). Recognition and posing of emotional expressions by abused children and their mothers. *Child Development, 24*, 776–781.

Carroll, J. J., & Steward, M. S. (1984). The role of cognitive development in children's understanding of their own feelings. *Child Development, 55*, 1486–1492.

Caruso, K. (1987). *Projective storytelling cards*. Redding, CA: Casebeer Art Productions, Northwest Psychological Publishers.

Cohen, J., & Mannarino, A. (1988). Psychological symptoms in sexually abused girls. *Journal of Child Abuse and Neglect, 12*, 571–578.

Conte, J., & Schuerman, J. (1987). Factors associated with increased impact of child sexual abuse. *Journal of Child Abuse and Neglect, 11*, 201–212.

Cotroneo, M. (1986). Families and abuse: A contextual approach. In M. A. Karpel (Ed.), *Family resources* (pp. 413–437). New York: Guilford.

Damon, L., & Waterman, J. (1986). Parallel group treatment of children and their mothers. In K. McFarlane & J. Waterman (Eds.), *Sexual abuse of young children* (pp. 244–298). New York: Guilford.

De Young, M. (1984). Counterphobic behavior in multiply molested children. *Child Welfare, 63*, 4: 333–339.

Di Leo, J. H. (1973). *Children's drawings as diagnostic aids*. New York: Brunner/Mazel.

Einbender, A. J., & Friedrich, W. N. (1989). Psychological functioning and behavior of sexually abused girls. *Journal of Consulting and Clinical Psychology, 57*, 155–157.

Ekman, P., & Friesen, W. F. (1975). *Unmasking the face: A guide to recognizing emotions from facial cues*. Englewood Cliffs, NJ: Prentice-Hall.

Everson, M., Hunter, W., Runyon, D., Edelsohn, O., & Coulter, M. (1989). Maternal support following disclosure of incest. *American Journal of Orthopsychiatry, 59*, 197–207.

Fagan, J., & McMahon, P. P. (1984). Incipient multiple personality in children: Four cases. *Journal of Nervous and Mental Disorders, 172*, 26–36.

Faller, K. C. (1988). *Child sexual abuse*. New York: Columbia University Press.

Finkel, M. A. (1988). The medical evaluation of child sexual abuse. In D. Schetky & A. Green (Eds.), *Child sexual abuse. A handbook for health care and legal professionals*. New York: Brunner/Mazel.

Finkelhor, D. (1979). *Sexually victimized children*. New York: Free Press.

Finkelhor, D., & Browne, A. (1985). The traumatic impact of child sexual abuse: A conceptualization. *American Journal of Orthopsychiatry, 55*, 530–541.

Foon, D., & Knight B. (1985). *Am I the only one?* Vancouver, B.C.: D. W. Friesen & Sons Ltd.

Fraiberg, S. H. (1959). *The magic years*. New York: Charles Scribner's Sons.

Freeman, L. (1984). *It's my body*. Seattle: Parenting Press, Inc.

Freud, S. (1900). The interpretation of dreams. In J. Strachey (Ed. and Trans.), *The standard edition of the complete psychological works of Sigmund Freud* (Vols. 4 & 5). New York: Norton.

Freud, S. (1930 [1929]). Civilization and its discontents. In J. Strachey (Ed. and Trans.), *The standard edition of the complete psychological works of Sigmund Freud* (Vol. 21, pp. 59–145). New York: Norton.

Friedrich, W. N. (1990). *Psychotherapy of sexually abused children and their families*. New York: Norton.

Friedrich, W., Beilke, R., & Urquiza, A. (1987). Children from sexually abusive families: A behavioral comparison. *Journal of Interpersonal Violence, 2*, 391–402.

Friedrich, W. N., Einbender, A. J., & Luecke, W. J. (1983). Cognitive and behavioral characteristics of physically abused children. *Journal of Consulting and Clinical Psychology, 51*, 313–314.

Friedrich, W. N., Grambsch, P., Damon, L., Hewitt, S., Koverola, C., Lang, R., & Wolfe, V. (in press). The Child Sexual Behavior Inventory: Normative and clinical comparisons. *Journal of Consulting and Clinical Psychology*.

Friedrich, W. N., & Luecke, W. J. (1988). Young school-age sexually aggressive children. *Professional Psychology Research and Practice, 19*, 155–164.

Friedrich, W., Urquiza, A., & Beilke, R. (1986). Behavior problems in young sexually abused children. *Journal of Pediatric Psychology, 11*, 47–57.

Furniss, T. (1983). Mutual influence and interlocking professional family process in the treatment of child sexual abuse—incest. *Child Abuse and Neglect, 7*, 207–223.

Gardner, R. (1975). *Psychotherapeutic approaches to the resistant child*. New York: Aronson.

Gelinas, D. (1983). The persisting negative effects of incest. *Psychiatry, 46*, 312–332.

Gelinas, D. (1986). Unexpected resources in treating incest families. In M. A. Karpel (Ed.), *Family resources* (pp. 327–358). New York: Guilford.

Giarretto, H. (1982). *Integrated treatment of child sexual abuse: A treatment and training manual*. Palo Alto, CA: Science and Behavior Books.

Ginsberg, B. (1989). Training parents as therapeutic agents with foster/adoptive children using the filial approach. In C. Schaefer & J. Briesmeister (Eds.), *Handbook of parent training* (pp. 442–478). New York: Wiley.

Gnepp, J. (1983). Children's social sensitivity: Inferring emotions from conflicting cues. *Developmental Psychology, 19*: 805–814.

Gold, E. (1984). Long-term effects of sexual victimization in childhood: An attributional approach. *Journal of Consulting and Clinical Psychology, 54*, 471–475.

Goldman, R., & Goldman, J. (1988). *Show me yours!: Understanding children's sexuality*. New York: Penguin Books.

Gomes-Schwartz, B., Horowitz, J. M., & Cardarelli, A. P. (1990). *Child sexual abuse: The initial effects*. Newbury Park, CA: Sage.

Goodwin, J. (1985). Post-traumatic symptoms in incest. In R. Pynoos & S. Eth (Eds.), *Post-traumatic stress disorder in children* (pp. 157–186). Washington, DC: American Psychiatric Press.

Greenspan, S.I. (1979). *Intelligence and adaptation*. New York: International Universities Press.

Gurney, L. (1983). Introduction to filial therapy: Training parents as therapists. In P. Keller & L. Ritt (Eds.), *Innovations in clinical practice: A source book* (Vol. 2, pp. 26–39). Sarasota, FL: Professional Resource Exchange.

Harris, D. B. (1963). *Children's drawings as measures of intellectual maturity*. New York: Harcourt, Brace, & World.

Harter, S. (1983). Cognitive-developmental considerations in the conduct of play therapy. In C. E. Schaefer & K. J. O'Connor (Eds.), *Handbook of play therapy*. New York: Wiley.

Hartmann, H. (1939). *Ego psychology and the problem of adaptation*. New York: International Universities Press.

Heger, A. (1985). *Response: Child sexual abuse, a medical view*. New York: Guilford.

Henry, J. (1971). *Pathway to madness*. New York: Random House.

Herman, J. (1981). *Father-daughter incest*. Cambridge, MA: Harvard University Press.

Hewitt, S., & Friedrich, W. N. (1990). Impact of sexual abuse on preschoolers. Initial and longer-term reactions. Paper presented at the Annual APSAC Conference, Atlanta, GA. April 27.

Irwin, E. C. (1985). Puppets in therapy: An assessment procedure. *American Journal of Psychotherapy, 39*, 389–399.

Jacobvitz, D., & Sroufe, L. A. (1987). The early caregiver-child relationship and attention-deficit disorder with hyperactivity in kindergarten: A prospective study. *Child Development, 58*, 1488–1495.

James, B. (1989). *Treating traumatized children*. Lexington, MA: Lexington Books.

Janoff-Bulman, R. (1986). The aftermath of victimization: Rebuilding shattered assumptions. In C. Figley (Ed.), *Trauma and its wake: Study and treatment of post-traumatic stress disorder* (pp. 15–36). New York: Brunner/Mazel.

Johnson T. C. (1988). Child perpetrators: Children who molest other children: Preliminary findings. *Child Abuse and Neglect, 12*, 219–229.

Johnson, T. C. (1989a). Children who molest: A treatment program. *Journal of Interpersonal Violence, 4*, 185–203.

Johnson, T. C. (1989b). Female child perpetrators: Children who molest other children. *Child Abuse and Neglect, 13*, 185–203.

Johnson, T. C. (1990). *Child Sexual Behavior Checklist*. Unpublished.

Kahn, M. D. (1986). The sibling system: Bonds of intensity, loyalty, and endurance. In M. A. Karpel (Ed.), *Family resources* (pp. 235–258). New York: Guilford.

Kahn, M. D., & Lewis, K. G. (Eds.) (1988). *Siblings in therapy*. New York: Norton.

Karpel, M. A. (1986). Testing, promoting, and preserving family resources: Beyond pathology and power. In M. A. Karpel (Ed.), *Family resources* (pp. 175–232). New York: Guilford.

Kegan, R. (1982). *The evolving self: Problem and process in human development*. Cambridge, MA: Harvard University Press.

Kendall, P., & Braswell, L. (1985). *Cognitive-behavioral therapy for impulsive children*. New York: Guilford.

Klein, M. (1930). The importance of symbol formation in the development of the ego. *International Journal of Psychoanalysis, 11*, 24–39.

Klein, M. (1932). *The psychoanalysis of children*. London: Hogarth.

Kluft, R. B. (Ed.). (1985). *Childhood antecedents of multiple personality*. Washington, DC: American Psychiatric Press.

Koppitz, E. M. (1968). *Psychological evaluation of children's human figure drawings*. New York: Grune & Stratton.

Krieger, M. J., Rosenfeld, A. A., Gordon, A., Bennett, M. I. (1980). Problems occurring in the psychotherapy of children with histories of incest. *American Journal of Psychotherapy, 34*, 81–88.

Krieger, M. J., & Robbins, J. (1985). The adolescent incest victim and the judicial system. *American Journal of Orthopsychiatry, 55*, 419–425.

Larson, N. R., & Maddock, J. W. (1985). Structural and functional variables in incest family systems: Implications for assessment and treatment. In T. Trepper & M. J. Barrett (Eds.), *The assessment and treatment of intrafamilial sexual abuse*. New York: Haworth.

Lickey, J., & Swan, H. (1989). *Dear Elizabeth*. Mt. Dora, FL: Kidsrights.

Lister, E. (1982). Forced silence. *American Journal of Psychiatry, 139*: 872–875.

Long, S. (1986). Guidelines for treating young children. In K. MacFarlane & J. Waterman et al. *Sexual abuse of young children* (pp. 220–243). New York: Guilford.

Marron, K. (1989). *Ritual abuse: Canada's most infamous trial on child abuse*. Toronto: McClelland-Bantam.

McLeer, S., Deblinger, E., Atkins, M., Foa, E., & Ralphe, D. (1988). Post-traumatic stress disorder in sexually abused children. *Journal of American Academy of Child and Adolescent Psychiatry, 27*, 650–654.

Meiselman, K. C. (1978). *Incest*. San Francisco: Jossey-Bass.

Meyers, A., & Craighead, W. (1984). *Cognitive behavior therapy with children*. New York: Plenum.

Minuchin, S. (1974). *Families and family therapy*. Cambridge, MA: Harvard University Press.

Minuchin, S. (1984). *Family kaleidoscope*. Cambridge, MA: Harvard University Press.

Palazzoli, M. S., Cirillo, S., Selvini, M., & Sorrentino, A. M. (1989). *Family games*. New York: Norton.

Piaget, J. (1967). *Six psychological studies*. New York: Vintage.

Rutter, M. (1980). Protective factors in children's response to stress and disadvantage. In M. Kent & J. Rolf (Eds.), *Primary prevention of psychopathology. III. Promoting social competence in children* (pp. 49–74). Hanover, NH: University Press of New England.

Saunders, B. & McClure, S. (1987, September). *Marital and family system functioning among incest families: Clinical and case management implications*. Paper presented at annual meeting of National Association of Social Workers, New Orleans.

Saunders, B., Villeponteaux, L.A., Lipovsky, J., Kilpatrick, D., & Veronen, L. (under review). *Child sexual assault as a risk factor for mental disorders among women: A community survey*.

Schilder, P. (1935). *The image and appearance of the human body*. London: Kegan Paul.

Selman, R. L., & Schultz, L. H. (1990). *Making a friend in youth: Developmental theory and pair therapy*. Chicago: University of Chicago Press.

Sexual Assault Center (1986). *Impact Checklist*. Seattle, WA: Harborview Medical Center.

Shengold, L. L. (1979). Child abuse and deprivation: Soul murder. *Journal of American Psychoanalytic Association, 26*(3) 533–59.

Silver, R., Boon, C., & Stones, M. (1983). Searching for meaning in misfortune: Making sense of incest. *Journal of Social Issues, 39*(2), 81–102.

Sirles, E. (1987). *Structural interventions for work with divorcing child sexual abuse cases*. Paper presented at the annual conference of the American Association for Marriage and Family Therapy, Chicago, IL.

Smith, M., & Pazder, L. (1980). *Michelle remembers*. London: Congdon and Lattes.

Spencer, J. (1989). *Suffer the child*. New York: Pocket Books.

Stein, J., Golding, J., Siegel, J., Burnham, M., & Sorenson, S. (1988). Long-term psychological sequelae of child sexual abuse: The Los Angeles Epidemiology Catchment Area Study. In G. E. Wyatt & G. J. Powell (Eds.), *Lasting effects of child sexual abuse* (pp. 135–154). Beverly Hills, CA: Sage.

Steinglass, P., Bennett, L. A., Wolin, S. J., & Reiss, D. (1987). *The alcoholic family*. New York: Basic Books.

Steward, M. S. (1987). Affective and cognitive effect of illness on children's body image. *Psychiatric Medicine, 5*: 107–113.

Steward, M. S. (in preparation). The impact of health history, locus of control, and hyperactivity on children's drawings of the outside and inside of the body.

Steward, M. S., Furuya, T., Steward, D. S., & Ikeda, A. (1982). Japanese and American children's drawings of the outside and inside of their bodies. *Journal of Cross-Cultural Psychology, 13*, 87–104.

Steward, M. S., Farquhar, L. C., Dicharry, D. C., Glick, D. R., & Martin, P. W. (1986). Group therapy: A treatment of choice for young victims of child abuse. *International Journal of Child Psychotherapy, 36*, 261–277.

Sullivan, H. S. (1953). *The interpersonal theory of psychiatry*. New York: Norton.

Taylor, S. E. (1983). Adjustment to life threatening events: A theory of cognitive adaptation. *American Psychologist, 38*, 1161–1173.

Terr, L. C. (1990). *Too scared to cry: Psychic trauma in childhood*. New York: Harper & Row.

Tierney, K. H., & Corwin, D. L. (1983), Exploring intrafamilial child sexual abuse: A systems approach. In Finkelhor, D., Gelles, R. J. Hotaling, G. T., & Strauss, M. S. (Eds.), *The dark side of families*. Beverly Hills, CA: Sage.

Trepper, T. S., & Barrett, M. J. (1986). Vulnerability to incest: A framework for assessment. In T. S. Trepper & M. J. Barrett (Eds.), *Treating incest: A multiple systems perspective* (pp. 13–25). New York: Haworth.

Van der Kolk, B. A. (1987). *Psychological trauma*. Washington, DC: American Psychiatric Press.

Wheeler, J. R., & Berliner, L. (1989). Treating the effects of sexual abuse on children. In G. E. Wyatt & G. J. Powell (Eds.), *Lasting effects of child sexual abuse*. Newbury Park, CA: Sage.

Winnicott, D. W. (1972). Basis of self in body. *International Journal of Child Psychotherapy, 1*, 7–16.

Winnicott, D. W. (1986). The child in the family group. In C. Winnicott, R. Shepherd, & M. David (Eds.), *Home Is Where We Start From*. New York: Norton.

Winnicott, D. W. (1987). *Babies and mothers*. Reading, MA: Addison-Wesley.

Wolfe, R., Gentile, C., & Wolfe, D. (1989). The impact of sexual abuse on children: A post-traumatic stress disorder formulation. *Behavior Therapy, 20*, 215–228.

Wooden, K. Child Lures, Inc. (personal communication).

Wooden, K. (1981). *The children of Jonestown*. New York: McGraw-Hill.

Index